After Mount Laurel:

The New Suburban Zoning

After Mount Laurel:

The New Suburban Zoning

Edited by Jerome G. Rose
and Robert E. Rothman

TRANSACTION BOOKS
New Brunswick, New Jersey

Library of Congress Cataloging in Publication Data
Main entry under title:

After Mount Laurel: the new suburban zoning.

1. Zoning law—United States—Addresses, essays, lectures. 2. Discrimination in housing—Law and legislation—United States—Addresses, essays, lectures. I. Rose, Jerome G.   II. Rothman, Robert E.
KF5698.A5A33   346'.73'045   77-1468 ISBN 0-88285-040-7

Grateful acknowledgment is made to the following for permission to quote material in copyright:

Journal of the American Institute of Planners, for Jerome G. Rose, "The Courts and the Balanced Community: Recent Trends in New Jersey Zoning Law." Reprinted by permission of the *Journal of the American Institute of Planners,* 39:4 (1973).
Vermont Law Review, for Norman Williams, Jr., "On from *Mount Laurel*: Guidelines on the 'Regional General Welfare' " 1 (1976).
New Jersey Law Journal, for Carl S. Bisgaier, "Some Notes on Implementing *Mount Laurel*—An Admittedly Biased View," 99 (August 19, 1976).
Real Estate Law Journal, for Jerome G. Rose, "The Mandatory Percentage of Moderately Priced Dwelling Ordinance (MPMPD) is the Latest Technique of Inclusionary Zoning," 3 (1974). Copyright by Warren, Gorham, & Lamont, Inc.
Urban Law Annual, for Jerome G. Rose, "*Oakwood at Madison:* A Tactical Retreat by the New Jersey Supreme Court to Preserve the *Mount Laurel* Principle," 13 (1977).
Rutgers—Camden Law Journal, for Jerome G. Rose, "Exclusionary Zoning and Managed Growth: Some Unresolved Issues," 6 (1975).
The Potomac Institute, Inc., 1501 Eighteenth Street, N.W., Washington, D.C. 20036, for excerpts from *In-Zoning: A Guide for Policy-Makers on Inclusionary Land Use Programs,* by Herbert M. Franklin, David Falk, and Arthur J. Levin (1974: The Potomac Institute): pp. 51-69, "Inclusionary Programs and the Larger Public Interest." (*In-Zoning* was undertaken under a grant from the National Science Foundation.)

Jerome G. Rose and Melvin R. Levin, for "What Is A 'Developing Municipality' Within the Meaning of the *Mount Laurel* Decision?" *Real Estate Law Journal* 4 (1976).

Jerome G. Rose, for "Is There A Fair Share Housing Allocation Plan That Is Acceptable to Suburban Municipalities?" *Urban Law Annual* 12 (1976); "The *Mount Laurel* Decision: Is It Based on Wishful Thinking?" *Real Estate Law Journal* 4 (1975); "The Trickle Before the Deluge From *Mount Laurel*," *Real Estate Law Journal* 5 (1976); "A New Test for Exclusionary Zoning: Does It 'Preclude the Opportunity' for 'Least Cost' Housing?" *Real Estate Law Journal* 6 (1977); "After the Recent New Jersey Supreme Court Decisions: What Is the Status of Suburban Zoning?" *New Jersey Municipalities* (May 1977).

Contents

Acknowledgments

We are indebted to a number of people whose assistance made this book possible. Our greatest debt is to the members of the Mount Laurel Impact Committee, those Rutgers–Newark Law School students who worked so hard to arrange the symposium out of which many of these papers came. Those individuals included Rosalie C. Scheckel, Ben Erlitz, Stephen R. Seidel, Michael Lasky, Myra Wrubel, Barbara Greer, Randall Kraker, David Griffiths, and Charles Pasar. We of course also thank the contributors to this volume for their excellent discussions of *Mount Laurel* and its impact.

We are grateful also to Peter Simmons, Dean of Rutgers Law School–Newark, and to George Sternlieb, Director of the Rutgers Center for Urban Policy Research, both of whom encouraged us to undertake this work and who provided us with the facilities of the Law School and the Center.

Finally, we are indebted to the individuals who produced the book itself: Joseph P. Zimmerman for editing the manuscript; Barry O. Jones, the Center's Director of Publications, for designing the book and guiding it through the publications process; and Isabel Vock for proofreading the galleys.

J.G.R.
R.E.R.

About the Contributors

CARL BISGAIER is Deputy Director, Division of Public Interest Advocacy, Department of the Public Advocate.

WILLIAM L. BRACH is a partner in Brach, Eichler, Rosenberg and Silver, Esqs.

PETER A. BUCHSBAUM is the Assistant Deputy Public Advocate, New Jersey Department of the Public Advocate.

SPIROS CARAMALIS is a staff member of the Legislative Services Agency, State of New Jersey.

RICHARD T. COPPOLA is a member of the firm of Alvin E. Gershen Associates.

NICHOLAS CONOVER ENGLISH is an attorney at law, and a partner in the firm of McCarter & English.

DAVID FALK is with the Washington, D.C. law firm of Lane and Edson, P.C.

HERBERT FRANKLIN is with the Washington, D.C. law firm of Lane and Edson, P.C., and is consultant director of the metropolitan housing program of The Potomac Institute.

ALVIN E. GERSHEN is a member of the firm of Alvin E. Gershen Associates.

MARTIN L. GREENBERG is an attorney at law, and New Jersey State Senator for the 28th district. He is the Chairman of the New Jersey Senate County and Municipal Government Committee.

Contributors

THE HONORABLE FREDERICK W. HALL is an associate Justice of the New Jersey Supreme Court (retired).

ARTHUR J. LEVIN is Executive Vice-President of The Potomac Institute.

MELVIN R. LEVIN is Professor of Urban Planning, Livingston College, Rutgers University.

CARL LINDBLOOM is a licensed professional planner in New Jersey.

ALAN MALLACH is president of Alan Mallach/Associates, a housing consultant firm in Trenton, New Jersey.

HARVEY MOSKOWITZ is a licensed professional planner in New Jersey.

ARNOLD K. MYTELKA is an attorney at law and a partner in the New Jersey firm of Clapp & Eisenberg.

JEROME G. ROSE is Professor of Urban Planning, Livingston College, Rutgers University.

GEORGE STERNLIEB is Director of the Center for Urban Policy Research, Rutgers University.

NORMAN WILLIAMS, JR. is Professor of Law, Vermont Law School, and Visiting Professor of Law, University of Arizona.

Introduction

Peter Simmons

Make no mistake about it—from the vantage point of the teacher of land use planning law, we are living in an academic golden age. Not only are our courses and seminars subscribed to overflow, but opinion molders and decision makers, both in the market place and the statehouse, seek our counsel and advice. After years of service as little more than an ignominious footnote to the study of constitutional law, or an appendix to courses in municipal corporations and real estate transactions, we have achieved curricular credibility. While fame may be fleeting, and the masses fickle, we are determined to enjoy our prominence while it lasts, doing what we can to justify and sustain the moment.

Today the opportunity to demonstrate social utility occurs to land use planners and their lawyer consorts on two seemingly diverse fronts: (1) to assist those locked in deadly combat with the purveyors of pornography to circumvent the protections of the First Amendment, and (2) to facilitate the quest "for a decent home in a suitable living environment for every American family. . . ." For every local official rhapsodic over the newly discovered potential for containing, if not eradicating, smut shops and massage parlors through the use of erogenous zones, there is a despondent counterpart racked by fear and resentment that his community is destined to become a haven for low-income refugees from our inner city Black and Latin enclaves. While the employment of land use technology to delimit licentiousness may be a contemporary aberration, planning law has always had considerable social consequences; what is *new*, in spite of long standing warnings from Norman Williams and other commentators, is the general public awareness of its impact. It may be ironic—but it should not be surprising—that land use planning, for all of its reformist or radical connotations, has played basically a conservative role in the development of American residential communities. For every *Mount Laurel* breakthrough there have been countervailing decisions in the pattern of *Belle Terre* and *Eastlake*.

The moral which I draw from these developments is more obvious than profound: although land use planning law has achieved a new prominence as an academic discipline and as a focus for public attention, it is an instrumentality capable of being employed in furtherance of a variety of human ends, some noble and others depraved. With respect to the central issues facing our society—racism and economic inequality—planning techniques can facilitate the implementation of values but they do not determine the nature of those values. In the context of *Mount Laurel* it is clear that planning mechanisms neither build housing nor determine whether we shall exist as one community or two. Land use controls long have been used to promote racial and economic segregation and through such decisions as *Mount Laurel* some impediments to achieving an integrated society can be removed. However it would be a mistake to overestimate the significance of zoning reform in the quest for a just society; at best the reform of zoning law permits us to take better advantage of the opportunities of the market place as a mechanism for social progress, and this has proven to be a force of uncertain pace and direction. In short, absent substantial public intervention in the production and distribution of housing, the achievements of *Mount Laurel* will remain largely symbolic.

While I have suggested that changes in planning law reflect rather than determine fundamental social values, nevertheless the *Mount Laurel* decision has provided concerned professionals with significant opportunities for important public service. The hallmark of the decision is quite clear: the court has mandated changes both in our system of distributing certain costs of government—the burden of including low-and moderate-income families within the tax base must be distributed more broadly throughout the state—and in our system of resource allocation—the locational benefit of undeveloped suburban land is a resource which must be made available to the poor as well as to the wealthy. Both of these changes are to be carried out in accordance with an egalitarian standard of general welfare. How the moral imperative of the decision is to be translated into planning practices remains to be determined, and this is the challenge faced by the contributors to this volume. The essays which follow offer ample evidence of the complexity of the task ahead and valuable insights and suggestions for taking the necessary first steps.

A special word of appreciation is due Robert Rothman and his associates on the Mount Laurel Impact Committee. While a second year student at the law school Mr. Rothman conceived of the idea of the Symposium out of which many of these papers came, and with the aid of his fellow committee members the program was planned and the project carried to completion. The initiative and responsibility of Mr. Rothman and his associates exemplifies that dedication to social justice, long a tradition of the Rutgers Law School.

I
Prelude
to
Mount Laurel

An Orientation
to Mount Laurel

Frederick W. Hall

In opening this series of discussions on the *Mount Laurel* case and its impact, it's very impressive to me that a law school will take that decision and probe it in depth. I assume most of you are not presently students in the land use regulation field, but that you are interested in the social and other implications and impact of that decision. My part in this series is to talk about the relationship of *Mount Laurel* and prior New Jersey law in the field, leading, I suppose, to some appraisal of the case from the historical legal perspective. In other words, to provide a bit about how we got where we are today and some basic orientation for your future programs, which will work out its impact. Certainly others are much more qualified to discuss it from that standpoint than I am.

We're dealing with one facet of land use regulation—the regulatory device of zoning. To put it into legal focus, this is part of the police power, one of the inherent powers of government. Chief Justice Weintraub used to say that the state government had only three inherent powers: the police power, the power to tax, and eminent domain.

3

In the 1926 *Euclid* case, the United States Supreme Court said that zoning to regulate the use and construction of buildings by districts was not a violation of the federal constitution. The United States Supreme Court has stayed away from that field ever since, rather amazingly, except in one or two cases. One this year [1975] called *Belle Terre*,[2] has been described as a fairyland, but I don't think it affects this topic.

Zoning, of course, is only about fifty years old in New Jersey. It took a constitutional amendment in 1927 to permit it, because before that time the courts of this state had said that it violated constitutional prohibitions against undue interference with private rights and property, particularly land, and that it was beyond the police power. The state constitutional amendment (as amended in the 1947 Constitution) reads:

> The Legislature may enact general laws under which municipalities, other than counties, may adopt zoning ordinances limiting and restricting to specified districts and regulating therein, building and structures according to their construction, and the nature and extent of their use, and the nature and extent of the uses of land, and the exercise of such authority shall be deemed to be within the police power of the State. Such laws shall be subject to repeal or alteration by the Legislature.[3]

This is a constitutional declaration that zoning is an element of land use regulation within the police power of government. Today we might well think that a constitutional amendment is unnecessary, for the power exists without it.

The amendment did not itself authorize municipalities to enact land use regulations. Rather it authorized the legislature to so authorize municipalities. The zoning enabling act,[4] adopted pursuant to this authorization, was adopted in 1928 and has remained practically unchanged until its recent revision.[5] The now-standard statute is directed essentially toward the physical and economic aspects of zoning, not social characteristics or social impact. It talks about lessening congestion in the streets and providing adequate light and things of that nature as proper objects of zoning. It also includes the general provision that zoning ordinances shall promote health, morals, or the general welfare.

This is the usual police power language, whether the words are in the statute or not, and we said so in *Mount Laurel*. Every police power ordinance must promote and not hinder the general welfare. Because the statute is so general, its construction and implementation have necessarily been assumed by the courts. Similar statutes were enacted by every state, and the same course of judicial implementation has followed. Of course, that law has been almost entirely state court law and properly so—there is increasing recognition that land use regulation belongs in state, rather than federal, courts because state courts are better acquainted with the land use controversies being fought out daily at the trial level, and they are in a much better position to deal with them than the federal courts.

Now let us consider the New Jersey decisions leading up to *Mount Laurel*. Except for New York, New Jersey has more court decisions on zoning and land use regulation than any other state—over 1,000 reported decisions. Professor Norman Williams has made an exhaustive study of all state zoning cases for his recently published treatise.[6] Some of his conclusions follow. The attitude and approach of courts toward zoning cases has varied from state to state and has also varied within a state from time to time. For example, in New Jersey, as indicated above, the 1928 constitutional amendment was enacted to overcome the consistent judicial rejection of zoning regulations. Except for a brief period from 1927 to 1930, New Jersey courts remained somewhat hostile to zoning for almost two decades. But since the creation of the new court system in 1948, the judicial approach to zoning has been the exact opposite, until recently. In what I like to think of as the modern law of zoning, the cases have almost universally upheld every municipal land use regulation that was put forward, at the expense of the developer, the land owner, or the objecting neighbor. New Jersey came to be classified as a pro-zoning regulation state. There were a couple of cases that seemed to have gotten lost in the shuffle during that period, but to me were quite important. One of them was *Duffcon Concrete Products, Inc. v. Borough of Cresskill*.[7] That case held that Cresskill, in Bergen County, could keep out all industrial use beçause other places in the region were suitable for that kind of use; thus Cresskill could be a completely residential community. Then *Borough of Cresskill v. Borough of Dumont*,[8] the so-called Chinese Wall case, held that Cresskill, in changing its ordinance, had to consider the effect on people in the adjacent municipality of Dumont. As is common in much of New Jersey, particularly in the northeastern part, you can't tell when you are out of one municipality and into another one. Those two cases stood out as early examples of a court, in reviewing a municipality's zoning regulation, considering something broader than the particular municipality.

But two cases that became leading cases in the country upheld the restrictions of local zoning. One was *Lionshead Lake, Inc. v. Wayne*.[9] There the court upheld rather low minimum floor areas for housing throughout the municipality without regard to the number of occupants in the house or any other considerations. That case was the subject of much scholarly writing.[10] The other case was *Fischer v. Township of Bedminster*,[11] which involved a five-acre minimum lot size restriction in the County of Somerset. It was sustained because Chief Justice Vanderbilt said that the municipality hadn't changed since the late 1700's, and had exactly the same number of people, and so forth and so on, and therefore such a restriction was perfectly reasonable. As an aside, that ordinance has recently been changed and the five-acre limitation has largely been broken down by a trial court.

Another case I should mention at this point is *Pierro v. Baxendale*.[12] Holding that a municipality could prohibit motels while permitting boarding houses, the court, in rather striking language, revealed its approach and attitude at the time. The court indicated its satisfaction with the thought that conscientious municipal officials had finally been sufficiently empowered to adopt zoning measures designed to preserve the "wholesome and attractive characteristics of their communities and the values of taxpayers' property."[13] There is similar language in Mr. Justice Douglas's opinion in *Belle Terre*. The *Lionshead Lake* concurring opinion considered the minimum floor-area requirement an "important legislative action" which represented the governing body's best judgment as to what zoning restrictions were required to promote the health, morals, and general welfare of the community as a whole. In the view of the concurring judge, "decent respect for its problems and sincerity required that its action remain unimpaired in the absence of clear showing that it was arbitrary, unreasonable or beyond the authority of the general Zoning Act."[14] By 1955, however, the New Jersey Supreme Court began to worry about the effects of its decisions, so we find this paragraph in *Pierro*:

> We are aware of the extensive academic discussion following the decisions in the *Lionshead* and *Bedminster* cases, . . . and the suggestion that the very broad principles which they embody may intensify dangers of economic segregation which even the more traditional modes of zoning entail . . . . In the light of existing population and land conditions within our State these [municipal zoning] powers may fairly be exercised without in anywise endangering the needs or reasonable expectations of any segments of our people. If and when conditions change, alterations in zoning restrictions and pertinent legislative and judicial attitudes need not be long delayed.[15]

Then we come to *Vickers v. Township Committee of Gloucester Township*.[16] This involved a large developing municipality in Camden County which prohibited all mobile home use anywhere within its borders. The court went to great lengths to explain that it was leaving the ordinance undisturbed because the municipal governing body had decided this prohibition was in this community's best interests and because of the presumed validity of municipal action. As a member of that court, I wrote a dissent which attracted considerable attention. Perhaps the court was really saying that mobile homes are not particularly attractive and a municipality that felt that way could bar them; some other kind of housing might have led to a different result. But I don't think that makes any difference at all, and I said so in the dissent. What I tried to say in that dissent was that a court should be concerned with defining the outer limits of the zoning power and with deciding how much consideration a court must give to a municipal determination by way of ordinance.

There had been an earlier case—*Moyant v. Paramus* [17]—in which I broke a little ground in a majority opinion on the problem of the validity of an ordinance. That case concerned a very common kind of ordinance—a solicitor's ordinance—but the most extreme I had ever seen. In order to sell from house to house, or solicit sales, the solicitor had to get a license with a photograph, a local doctor's certificate of good health dated within three weeks of the license application, a police record or certification of the absence of one, and a posted bond of $1,000. Even when all this had been done, the chief of police could still deny the application. Well, that was a little too much, so I said there that the presumption of validity is only a presumption and may be overcome or rebutted not only by clear extrinsic evidence, but also by a showing on its face or in the light of facts of which judicial notice can be taken, of transgression of constitutional limitation or the bounds of reason.

So that was the basis for what I said in *Vickers* on the subject. I'll read that because it conveys the thought better than a paraphrase:

> While it has long been conventional for courts to test the validity of local legislation by the criterion of whether a fairly debatable issue is presented, and if so to sustain it, it makes all the difference in the world how a court deals with that criterion. Proper judicial review to me can be nothing less than objective, realistic considerations of the setting—the evils or conditions sought to be remedied, a full and comparative appraisal of the public interest involved and the private rights affected, both from the local and broader aspects, and a thorough weighing of all factors, with government entitled to win if the scales are at least balanced or even a little less so. Of course, such a process involves judgment and the measurement can never be mathematically exact, but that is what judges are for—to evaluate and protect all interests, including those of individuals and minorities, regardless of personal likes or views of wisdom, and not merely to rubber-stamp governmental action in a kind of judicial laissez-faire. The majority approach attaches exclusive significance to the view of the governing body that, in its summary opinion, the "welfare" of the municipality would be advanced. On this criterion it is hard to conceive of any local action which would not come within the "debatable" class. [18]

What happened was that the majority of the court in the zoning field had used a principle which had been of great value in civil rights legislation and legislation of that type—the so-called liberal approach if you want to use labels—that the legislation protecting civil rights was good because the legislature said it was good. But the application of this approach to local zoning legislation had exactly the opposite effect, pointed out in *Vickers*, of keeping out of the community all those people who didn't want to live in the kind of housing that the municipality wanted constructed for one reason or another. *Vickers* was a five-to-two opinion (Justice Schettino voted with me), and for several years after that, for some reason, the supreme court got very few zoning cases. Maybe everybody was discouraged by the court's opinion about challenging local regulation. But various things began to happen. You know what Mr. Dooley said about the United States Supreme Court following the election returns. I think what he meant was that appellate courts must and do take account of what's going on in the world around them—what conditions exist, how conditions have changed, and whether old rules or principles still fit. That's part of the nature of the judicial process.

And in this land use regulation field, some things began to happen. First I'll mention the legal things and then I'll mention some of the factual things that led to *Mount Laurel*. Some cases began to say that, when dealing with facilities of broad public benefit, "the general welfare" is not confined to the particular municipality but extends beyond local boundaries. The first one was *Roman Catholic Diocese of Newark v. Ho-Ho-Kus Borough*.[19] Ho-Ho-Kus, in response to a fuss about the building of a regional Catholic High School in a residential zone, passed an ordinance which had the effect of prohibiting the use. The court came almost to the point of saying a municipality must take into account the educational welfare of the area beyond its own boundaries. The next was *Kunzler v. Hoffman*[20] brought by a neighbor challenging the granting of a variance to a private mental hospital. While the hospital was going to be located in one of the rural districts in Morris County, it was going to serve a wide section of the state. The court there said that it was quite proper for the municipality to consider the region's needs for that kind of a facility.

Then came *DeSimone v. Greater Englewood Housing Corp. No. 1*,[21] which was assigned to me to write. That case, which involved the question of low- and moderate-income housing, was not a difficult one, and I think it perhaps has been cited to stand for more than it actually does. What happened there was this. A church organization in Englewood formed a non profit corporation to erect a subsidized, low-income housing project. Englewood is a wealthy community, in large part residential. One ward, the fourth ward, is literally on the other side of the railroad tracks and is a black ward. Englewood is one of the few towns in

Bergen County with a significant black population, and the housing in that ward was generally poor. The land the church group proposed to use was in a residential zone which was exclusively white. They applied for and were granted a variance by the municipality, so when the case got to the trial court it was in the form of a challenge by neighbors to municipal action. In other words, it involved a positive act by a municipality rather than a rejection. It was sustained in the trial court and we sustained it above. I wrote a sentence in the opinion which said that the variance could not well have been refused. What I meant was that when you have got that kind of a facility, it must be given favorable consideration if it fits in. The particular site in *DeSimone* was well located and under the negative variance criteria of NJSA 40:55-39 (d) the variance would not damage the rest of the community. Although it was introducing multifamily housing to a single-family housing neighborhood, the area was so physically protected that it could be done without upsetting a viable neighborhood. We thought people were really protesting because they didn't want black people living outside of the fourth ward. The case was decided, of course, in favor of the project. I have never heard whether the project was erected, although I hope it was. (That's one problem with being an appellate judge—you seldom find out what happens to a case you've decided.)

Then *Robinson v. Cahill* [22] was decided. While this case had nothing to do with land use regulation, the holding was based on the philosophy that the state constitutional requirement for thorough and efficient education could not be paid for by our tax scheme, which is based primarily on the ratables available within the separate municipalities. Of course how that case is going to end up is not yet known, but all that led to *Mount Laurel*.

Also, things had changed factually. A great many segments of New Jersey, particularly in the northern metropolitan New York and the southern Camden-Philadelphia area, had been going through a period of rapidly changing living conditions. Business and industry for one reason or another had moved out of the central cities and people had moved from the central cities to new houses in the suburbs. As cities were being worn out, the housing worsened and the people having to occupy that housing were at a disadvantage. Meanwhile, the suburban municipality was indulging in fiscal zoning; that is, to keep taxes low it was encouraging good ratables—industrial and commercial uses—and discouraging school children. (As you know, local taxes are the primary source of funds for municipal and school services.) To discourage the presence of school children, these developing municipalities were imposing all kinds of restrictions—limiting new construction to single-family housing on large lots, with large minimum floor area—while trying to attract industry. But this left the central cities and their residents in a terribly bad state, because the poor of all kinds were largely congregated in the cities. Thoughtful people and the courts came to realize that social dangers and detrimental housing patterns had developed. Also, both the federal and state governments were developing a greater responsibility to their less affluent and fortunate members.

In addition, state court members began to realize that New Jersey's system of land use regulation by municipalities was not working. Municipal government had become entirely too parochial. Indeed this wasn't confined to New Jersey, as you will learn from a fascinating book, *The Zoning Game*, by Richard Babcock, published in 1966.[23] Babcock, one of the great land use lawyers in the country, got a Ford Foundation grant in the early 1960's to find out how local land use regulation was actually working. After visiting practically every state in the union and even England and Canada, he concluded that it wasn't working well at all. All these things came to the front when we considered the *Mount Laurel* case.

Now I would like to discuss what I believe the case means and does.

It is not my place to defend *Mount Laurel* and you will certainly be hearing criticism and suggestions about it in your future meetings. You must remember that when an appellate court is deciding a case, it can decide only the case before it—and not by way of dictum, every other case in the field that might possibly come up. (Although once in a while we put in something we think may be helpful.) A court can't deal with everything in one opinion, whereas the legislature can. In *Mount Laurel*, we had before us a developing municipality, so that is what the case talks about. The case did not say that it does not apply to central cities, or that it does not apply to suburbs, or that it does not apply to rural areas with a need for low- and moderate-income housing. It dealt with developing municipalities where parochialism, with its wall of exclusion erected by local legislative edict, had become prominent.

The court dealt with the case from the standpoint of state constitutional law. Now, New Jersey's constitution has neither a due process nor an equal protection clause. But its Article One, Paragraph One reads this way: "All persons are by nature free and independent, and have certain natural and unalienable rights, among which are those of enjoying and defending life and liberty, of acquiring, possessing, and protecting property, and of pursuing and obtaining safety and happiness." Does that language sound familiar? It is patterned after the Declaration of Independence. It has been construed by our courts over a period of time to be our due process and equal protection clauses with the same effect as if we had the federal constitutional language.

The municipality of Mount Laurel was a veritable gold mine of things wrongly done, so we could talk about a great many exclusionary devices. We found these to be basic violations of this state constitutional provision because housing, one of the basic needs of life, was entitled to constitutional protection. This is what I said in that connection: a municipality, by its land use regulations, must presumptively make realistically available an appropriate variety and choice of housing which must affirmatively include an opportunity for low- and moderate-income people who so desire to live there, at least to the extent of the municipality's fair share of the present and prospective regional need therefor, unless the particular municipality can demonstrate peculiar circumstances which dictate it should not be required to do so. In other words, it introduced the regional fair share doctrine. But the main point of what I was saying— and perhaps didn't say clearly enough—was that a municipality, through land use regulations, must make suitable land for that type of housing affirmatively available and must undertake its fair share of that for the region, unless there has been regional zoning on the subject. The housing itself would be built by either some agency of government or by private sources—not by the municipality, for that isn't a municipality's business. I was trying to promote the desirability of regional zoning, which to me is not forbidden by our constitution, but requires legislation; I was suggesting that such legislation might come, but it hasn't happened yet. Procedurally, the case shifted the burden of proof: when it is shown on the face that the municipality has not met this constitutionally required affirmative obligation, it must establish why that requirement should not be imposed upon it. Zoning can no longer be used to restrict housing simply to protect the tax base or the environment, unless there is a real environmental problem that must be met and can be met only that way. Thus the approach attacked the fiscal zoning problem.

The case stops short of a strong affirmative remedy. The remedy was a negative one in that it told a municipality that its ordinance was no good in part, and that it had a certain period of time in which to do better. We used this remedy because under our present land use regulation scheme, the municipality is the repository of power. It should have the first crack at changing the ordinance. But we encouraged the plaintiffs to return to court if the municipality didn't do what the court expected.

I might mention in conclusion some things the opinion does *not* do. This is a housing opinion, a rights opinion, put practically on a moral basis. The exclusion of housing for the poor and others who don't want or can't buy big houses on large lots and so forth is immoral, and it's not hard to find that it is also unconstitutional. But don't expect the opinion to solve all problems because it won't. It's just a beginning, as I look at it. It's a little bit like *Brown v. Board of Education* in the school desegregation field—a start to do something about the housing of the poor. But it's not a planning decision addressing the needs of the cities. We've got to revitalize our central cities somehow, because no matter what you do by way of court edict or legislation, there are many who want to live in the city and are going to live in the city, because that's where they want to be, or that's where the housing is, or that's where the jobs may be. This opinion doesn't help that directly, although it's very much on the mind of everybody who thinks about it.

It also does not deal with the red hot issue of timed growth or managed growth. How far can a municipality go in managing its growth? You may have noticed a recent Ninth Circuit Court of Appeal's decision in the *Petaluma* case.[24] The trial court had knocked out a growth-limitation provision in an ordinance, but the court of appeals reversed. Now if you think of Petaluma alone, it doesn't sound so bad, but if every municipality in the greater San Francisco area did the same thing, where would you be? In a similar case, the New York Court of Appeals sustained timed growth in the town of Ramapo.[25] I did mention in the opinion that growth provisions to be upheld will have to provide for low- and moderate-income housing very early in the timetable.

I leave you with this chronology of New Jersey zoning law and a little bit of insight to the *Mount Laurel* opinion. I know that it is food for a lot of thought for people much more able than I am to create ways to correct the social evils that must be corrected if we are to exist as a true democratic society. That was the court's approach to this case and I don't think it is going to tolerate much evasion.

NOTES

1. *Village of Euclid v. Ambler Reality Co.*, 272 U.S. 365 (1926).
2. *Village of Belle Terre v. Borais*, 416 U.S. 1 (1974).
3. N.J. MUNICIPAL ZONING ENABLING ACT, N.J.S.A. 40:55-30 et seq.
5. N.J. MUNICIPAL LAND USE LAW, Chapt. 291, Laws of N.J. 1975.
6. Williams, *American Planning Law: Land Use and the Police Power,* (1974).
7. 2 N.J. 509 (1949).
8. 15 N.J. 238 (1954).
9. 10 N.J. 165 (1952).
10. See: e.g. Haar, "Zoning for Minimum Standards: The Wayne Township Case," 66 Harv. L. Rev. 1051 (1953).
11. 11 N.J. 194 (1952).

12. 20 N.J. 17 (1955).
13. 20 N.J. at 29.
14. 10 N.J. at 179.
15. 20 N.J. at 29.
16. 37 N.J. 232 (1962), *cert. den.* 371 U.S. 233 (1963).
17. 30 N.J. 528 (1959).
18. 37 N.J. at 260.
19. 42 N.J. 556 (1964), and 47 N.J. 211 (1966).
20. 48 N.J. 277 (1966).
21. 56 N.J. 428 (1970).
22. 62 N.J. 473 (1973), *cert. den.* 414 U.S. 976 (1973).
23. Babcock, *The Zoning Game,* 1966.
24. *Construction Industry Assoc. of Sonomo County v. Petaluma,* 44 L.W. 2093 (1975).
25. *Golden v. Ramapo,* 30 N.Y. 2d 359, 285 N.E. 2d 291 (1972).

The Courts
and the
Balanced Community

Jerome G. Rose

Numerous judicial decisions in New Jersey have held that "the essence of zoning is to provide a balanced and well-ordered scheme of activity." [1] In 1971, in the *Madison Township* case [2] a Superior Court held that the entire zoning ordinance of the municipality was invalid on the grounds that "it failed to promote reasonably a balanced community in accordance with the general welfare." [3] Thus, a "balanced community" seems to have become a standard of the validity of zoning regulation that, like motherhood, receives public support even though many engage in private practices to avoid it.

The "balanced community" standard of zoning validity has been accepted quietly and without controversy. There is a subliminal appeal to things that are "balanced." Psychologically, "balanced" means healthy and upright; just as "unbalanced" means unhealthy and maladjusted. Legally, "balance" means equity and fairness on the Scales of Justice. Politically, a "balanced community" indicates that there is something for everyone—a basic tenet for political survival. With such appealing connotations there is little wonder that planners and lawyers have been attracted to the

14

proposition that a balanced community is not only a goal of zoning regulation but is in fact a standard by which its validity may be determined.

The primary shortcoming of "balanced community" as a societal goal and legal standard is that it has many different meanings under different circumstances. For example, "balanced community" may be defined to include socioeconomic balance, fiscal balance, ecological balance, regional balance, and temporal balance. This paper will examine each one of these definitions and then will examine the role of the courts in enforcing this standard.

Socioeconomic Balance

Does the standard of a "balanced community" require each municipality to contain any given proportion of the low-income and racial minority residents of the state? To what extent does this standard determine the validity of the zoning ordinances?

Zoning ordinances have been used to prevent members of racial minorities and low-income families from moving from the central cities to suburban areas. The effect of such exclusionary zoning laws is to concentrate the poor and racial minorities in the cities and to restrict the use of the suburbs to middle- and upper-class residents. As a result, cities are required to undertake the higher social-welfare costs of the poor and thereby bear a greater proportion of the costs that, in all fairness, should be more equitably distributed within the state. In addition to the dangers inherent in geographic polarization by race and class, the socioeconomic imbalance created by exclusionary zoning tends to deny to the excluded groups the opportunity for better housing, better schools, greater employment opportunities, and better municipal services. Such exclusion may be regarded as contrary to the ideals of democracy and has been held to be contrary to the principles of the United States Constitution.

In the early days of zoning, the United States Supreme Court invalidated a municipal ordinance that zoned the city into racial districts and restricted the use and occupancy in each district to members of the prescribed race.[4] More recently the court has said that "legal restrictions which curtail the civil rights of a single group are immediately suspect. That is not to say that all such restrictions are unconstitutional. It is to say that courts must subject them to the most rigid scrutiny."[5]

Although there are many similarities between community imbalance based upon race and imbalance based upon class or wealth, the courts have nevertheless tended to treat racial discrimination differently from discrimination against the poor. A number of reasons have been proposed[6] to explain this difference in judicial treatment: (1) race is an inherited characteristic, beyond the ability of a person to change; (2) poverty, unlike race, is more a matter of degree than of kind; (3) current morality permits acceptance of distinctions based on wealth more readily than distinctions based on race.

In spite of the differences between racial and economic imbalance, it seems very clear, as the Supreme Court has observed, that evidence is available to show that discrimination against low-income groups is, to a large extent, discrimination against racial minorities, thereby requiring the ordinance to be "scrutinized with great care." [7] It is also true that some zoning ordinances operate to exclude many middle-income class families from the suburbs as well, but as the court said on another occasion, "the reality is that the law's impact falls hardest on the minority." [8] Thus an examination of the validity of laws excluding the poor is equally pertinent to the issue of racial balance as it is to the issue of economic balance within a community. [9]

INTERSTATE EXCLUSION

When a state attempts to exclude the poor from its jurisdiction, the United States Constitution may be invoked to invalidate such exclusion. In *Edwards v. California*, [10] the Supreme Court held that the right to move from state to state is a constitutionally protected right under the commerce clause of the Constitution. Justice Douglas agreed with the decision of the majority but, in a concurring opinion, asserted that interstate travel is protected by the Constitution because it is one of the privileges and immunities of United States citizenship." [11] More recently, in *Shapiro v. Thompson*, [12] the Supreme Court invalidated the laws of several states that imposed a one-year residency requirement upon applicants for welfare assistance. This time the court held that such restrictions violated the equal protection clause of the Fourteenth Amendment. In an opinion written by Mr. Justice Brennan, the court said:

> The purpose of deterring the immigration of indigents cannot serve as justification for the classification created by the one-year waiting period, since that purpose is constitutionally impermissible . . . More fundamentally, a state may no more try to fence out those indigents who seek higher welfare benefits than it may try to fence out indigents generally. [13]

INTRASTATE EXCLUSION

For the past two decades, zoning laws have been used extensively in New Jersey as a device by which some municipalities have sought to exclude the poor from other municipalities within the state. In a series of decisions, in a period from 1952 to 1963, the New Jersey Supreme Court has upheld such zoning devices to exclude the poor as minimum floor-space requirements,[14] minimum lot-size requirements,[15] prohibition of construction of multifamily units,[16] prohibition of mobile homes on individual lots,[17] and prohibition of mobile-home parks anywhere in the township.[18]

In the past few years, the courts seem to have moved away from this early line of decisions and a judicial principle seems to be evolving from recent New Jersey decisions that zoning law may not be used to exclude people on the basis of wealth or socioeconomic status.

In 1970, in *DeSimone* v. *Greater Englewood Housing Corp., No. 1*,[19] the New Jersey Supreme Court held, in an opinion written by Justice Hall, that "public or semi-public housing accommodations to provide safe, sanitary and decent housing, to relieve and replace sub-standard living conditions or to furnish housing for minority or underprivileged segments of the population outside of ghetto areas is a 'special reason' adequate to meet that requirement of N.J.S.A. 40:55-39 (d) and to ground a use variance." Justice Hall's statement apparently is designed to offer the *alternative* that public or semipublic housing for *either minorities or the underprivileged segment of the population* would suffice to meet the "special reason" requirement of the cited use variance provision.

In 1971, two Superior Court decisions enlarged upon this evolving concept. In the *Madison Township* case,[20] the court held invalid a township zoning ordinance that sought to restrict multifamily construction to about five hundred to seven hundred additional units, none of which could contain three or more bedrooms and which divided most of the remaining vacant land to zones requiring one and two acre minimum lots with minimum floor space of 1,500 square feet and 1,600 square feet respectively. In a decision written by Judge Furman, the court held the ordinance invalid because it *"fails to promote reasonably a balance community in accordance with the general welfare."* The court cited with approval a statement in a recent Pennsylvania decision:

> The question posed is whether the township can stand in the way of the natural forces which send out growing population into hitherto undeveloped areas in search of a comfortable place to live. We have concluded not. A zoning ordinance which primary purpose is to prevent the entrance of newcomers in order to avoid future burdens, economic or otherwise, upon the administration of public services and facilities cannot be held valid.[21]

Later in 1971, the Superior Court held invalid a Glassboro zoning ordinance requiring that new apartments contain at least 70 percent of the units with no more than one bedroom, no more than 25 percent with two bedrooms and no more than 5 percent with three bedrooms and also requiring such expensive amenities as a swimming pool or tennis court, central air conditioning, and automatic garbage disposal.[22] The court determined that the ordinance was designed to restrict the population to adults and to exclude children because of the municipal cost of education. In responding to that finding, the court said:

> There is a right to be free from discrimination based on economic status. There is also a right to live as a family, and not be subject to a limitation on the number of members of that family in order to reside any place. Such legal barriers would offend the equal protection mandates of the Constitution.[23]

Then, in 1972, the Superior Court held, in unequivocal terms, that a Mount Laurel zoning ordinance that prohibited multifamily dwellings, except on a farm for farmers, is invalid for the reason that such ordinance discriminates against the poor and deprives them of adequate housing and the opportunity to secure subsidized housing.[24] In a decision written by Judge Martino, the court said that it would be an improper use of the zoning power "to build a wall against the poor income people." [25]

Thus, in the past two years, the New Jersey courts appear to have formulated a principle that a well balanced community requires some undetermined amount of social balance and that zoning laws may not be used to exclude people of low income from the jurisdiction.

Fiscal Balance

Does the obligation of elected municipal officials to provide essential municipal services (within the limits of available revenue) permit the use of the zoning power to maintain its fiscal balance?

The limited sources of municipal revenue and the increasing costs of municipal services provide an annual challenge to officials to find ways to achieve the fiscal balance required by law and political survival. In their effort to maintain fiscal balance, municipal officials tend to stimulate industrial and commercial rather than residential development. The zoning power is used to exclude housing in order to limit the need for school construction and other costs made necessary by increased population.[26] The term, "fiscal zoning" is applied to zoning laws enacted for this purpose.

One of the most frequently posed questions of zoning law today is whether fiscal zoning is valid. An analysis of the New Jersey decisions reveals that the answer to this question depends upon whether the court determines that the zoning power is used: (1) to increase ratables and revenue, or (2) to decrease residential development and municipal costs.

FISCAL ZONING TO INCREASE REVENUE

In the past few years, a number of New Jersey decisions have distinguished exclusionary fiscal zoning from the revenue-raising zoning cases cited above and have held that fiscal zoning to exclude residential development is invalid. In the *Madison Township* case,[30] it was conceded that the underlying objective of the zoning law in question was fiscal zoning, designed to avoid school construction and other costs resulting from increased population.[31] The Superior Court agreed that the use of zoning power to alleviate "the tax burden and harmful school congestion" was valid if done "reasonably and in furtherance of a comprehensive plan."[32] However, the court held that the use of the zoning power to stabilize the tax rate by the exclusion of new low and moderate income housing was an invalid exercise of the police power.

In the *Glassboro* case,[33] where the zoning law restricted the number of bedrooms in a garden apartment complex, the court rejected the argument that judicial sanction may be given to municipal efforts to avoid an increase in the tax burden.[34] Even though the testimony persuaded the court that the municipal cost of education of children in the proposed project exceeded the tax revenue to be derived therefrom, nevertheless the court held that the municipality could not validly use its zoning power to restrict its population to adults and to the exclusion of children. The court said:

> The effort to establish a well balanced community does not contemplate the limitation of the number in a family by regulating the type of housing. The attempt to equate the cost of education to the number of children allowed in a project or a community has no relation to zoning. The governmental cost must be an official concern but not to an extent that it determines who shall live in the municipality.[35]

A year later (1972), in the *Mount Laurel* case[36] involving a zoning ordinance prohibiting multifamily dwellings, Judge Martino reaffirmed the distinction between exclusionary fiscal zoning and revenue raising fiscal zoning when he said:

> Local legislative bodies know better than to state that more low-income producing structures will mean a high tax rate. This is what the courts have abhorred as fiscal zoning . . . What local governing body would raise an objection to bringing a factory into a neighborhood because it would increase the population of the economically poor? While it may be an argument that it would affect property values, and while it is

proper to zone in certain instances against factories, it is improper to build a wall against the poor-income people.[37]

Thus the rule seems to have been established that fiscal zoning for revenue increases may be valid but that fiscal zoning to minimize municipal expenses by excluding people is invalid. However, this principle may be more easily stated than applied. The challenge of the courts during the next few years will be in distinguishing between valid zoning amendments from residential to light industrial[38] and invalid "insincere" industrial zoning designed to exclude residential development.

FISCAL BALANCE AND EQUITABLE DISTRIBUTION OF MUNICIPAL SERVICE

An analysis of fiscal balance would be incomplete without an examination of the effects of the relationship of tax ratables upon the distribution of essential municipal services. A number of recent decisions have limited the constitutional obligation of municipal governments to provide equality in the distribution of municipal services.

At the end of the summer of 1971, in *Serrano* v. *Priest*,[39] the California Supreme Court held the California system of school financing invalid on the grounds that it violated the equal protection clause of the Fourteenth Amendment of the United States Constitution. In California, as in most other states, revenue to support the public schools is derived from property taxes within the school districts. Districts with substantial tax ratables are therefore able to spend larger sums per pupil and still maintain a lower tax rate than districts with a lower ratio of ratables per pupil. The *Serrano* decision held that the equal protection clause is violated when the level of spending for education depends on the wealth of the school districts.

Within a short time after the *Serrano* decision the system of school finance was held invalid in Texas by *Rodriguez* v. *San Antonio Independent School District*,[40] in New Jersey by *Robinson* v. *Cahill*,[41] and in a number of other states.[42] The *Serrano* decision, and those that follow it, are based upon the following reasoning:

1. The system of school financing discriminates on the basis of wealth[43] which is a "suspect classification" when it relates to a "fundamental interest";
2. Education is a "fundamental interest" because of its relation to individual success and the needs of a democratic society;
3. A law based upon a "suspect classification" and relating to a "fundamental interest" can be justified only if the state can show that it has "a compelling interest which justifies the law [and] that the distinctions drawn by the law are *necessary* to further its purpose."[44]

4. The present system of school finance is not necessary to accomplish any "compelling state interest."

After invalidating the system of school finance on the above reasoning, the California Supreme Court remanded the *Serrano* case to the trial court for additional evidence. In the meantime, the *Rodriguez* case was appealed to the United States Supreme Court. On March 21, 1973, the Supreme Court, in a 5 to 4 decision [45] rejected the *Serrano* reasoning adopted by the lower court in *Rodriguez* and held that the Texas system of school finance did not violate the equal protection clause because:

1. The school finance system was not based upon a "suspect classification" because of "the absence of any evidence that the financing system discriminates against any definable category of 'poor' people."
2. Education is not a "fundamental right" within the meaning of the equal protection clause of the Federal Constitution.
3. Where the law is not based upon a "suspect classification" and does not involve a "fundamental interest," its validity does not depend upon a "compelling interest" but requires only that there be "some rational relationship to a legitimate state purpose." The court then found that such a rational relationship does exist between the system of school finance and a legitimate state purpose.

It seems clear that the court's decision was influenced by the realization that acceptance of the *Serrano* principle would have a great impact [46] upon the ability of local governments to maintain fiscal balance if they were required to provide equal distribution of municipal services. In reflecting upon this problem, the court said:

Moreover, if local taxation for local expenditure is an unconstitutional method of providing for education then it may be an equally impermissible means of providing other necessary services customarily financed largely from local property taxes, including local police and fire protection, public health and hospitals and public utility facilities of various kinds. We perceive no justification for such a severe denigration of local property taxation and control as would follow from appellees' contentions. It has simply never been within the constitutional prerogative of this court to nullify statewide measures for financing public services merely because the burdens or benefits thereof fall unevenly depending upon the relative wealth of the political subdivisions in which citizens live. [47]

Within two weeks after the *Rodriguez* decision, the New Jersey Supreme Court expressed its own concern for the implications of the *Serrano* principle upon municipal fiscal balance. In *Robinson* v. *Cahill*, [48] the court held that the New Jersey system of school finance does not violate the equal protection clause of the state constitution but does violate the state constitutional provision requiring a "thorough and efficient system of free public schools."[49] Thus the court affirmed the invalidity of the system of educational financing. However, by basing its decision on this narrower ground the court was able to limit the application of its ruling to the financing of education and without leading to a requirement of equalization of all municipal services.

Thus for a brief period during the interval from the summer of 1971 to the spring of 1973 it appeared as though the courts would establish a principle by which the equal distribution of municipal services might be included within the meaning of the federal and/or state equal protection clause. However, the United States Supreme Court and the New Jersey Supreme Court have both declined to so hold because of the potential "convulsive implications" of such a doctrine upon municipal home rule and because of the difficulties involved in the judicial administration of such a principle.

Ecological Balance

Does the standard of a "balanced community" require each municipality to balance the ecological consequences of development against the socioeconomic consequences of nondevelopment?

In recent years, the courts have begun to recognize that ecological and environmental factors are entitled to greater weight in creating the "balanced community" required for zoning validity. This realization has been long in coming. In American history, land *development* has been the essence of land-use policy. From the Northwest Ordinance of 1787, to the Homestead Act of 1862, to the large scale FHA mortgage insurance programs in aid of home ownership in the 1950s, the objective of national land-use policy has been the *development* of land. Our property tax system accentuates this policy by assessing the value of vacant land for tax purposes at its "highest and best use" for *development*. Thus, in the absence of some form of tax relief,[50] farmers, to avoid payment of high property taxes based on development value, are pressured into selling their land for development. Only recently has the goal of "urban development" been translated into the pejorative, "urban sprawl."[51] Only recently has consideration of the ecological consequences of development been weighed against the forces of profit incentive, proprietary rights, municipal prerogative, and social need.[52] When conflict arises between advocates of environmental protection and advocates of social need, i.e., low income housing, the encounter of these forces frequently produces manifestations of acute ideological schizophrenia.

When this conflict reaches the courts it usually takes the form of an attack upon the validity of flood plain zoning or agricultural zoning. There are sufficient differences between the two to treat each separately.

FLOOD PLAIN ZONING

Flood plain zoning imposes restrictions on the use of lands that are useful in reducing flood levels by absorbing water from rains and run off. To the extent that such land is covered with structures or paved surfaces flooding and flood damage may be increased because the run off is accelerated instead of being absorbed into the ground. Flood plain zoning also restricts the use of wet lands for the purpose of preserving its sponge-like capacity to create a natural detention basin for flood waters in time of heavy rainfall.

The validity of such a zoning ordinance in New Jersey was considered in *Morris County Land Improvement Co.* v. *Parsippany-Troy Hills Township*.[53] In a decision written by Justice Hall, the New Jersey Supreme Court held zoning ordinances restricting the use of land for flood water-detention purposes to be invalid because it constituted a taking of land for public purposes without just compensation. Although the court conceded that the determination of whether any zoning ordinance is a valid regulation or an invalid taking is always a matter of degree but that "there is no question that the line has been crossed when the purpose and practical effect of the regulation is to appropriate private property for a flood water basin or open space."[54] The court stated that public *acquisition* rather than *regulation* was required and pointed to the authority granted to governmental agencies to purchase or condemn property needed for flood control.[55]

Until recently, the *Parsippany-Troy Hills* case represented the prevailing judicial attitude in most states toward environmental zoning.[56] However, in 1972 the courts of a number of states have begun to recognize circumstances in which ecological considerations might outweigh the owner's right to develop his land. The courts in Massachusetts[57] and Wisconsin[58] have upheld the validity of laws that prohibit the draining, filling, and dredging of wetlands even though the owner is thereby prevented from developing his land. In New York, the Appellate Division upheld an ordinance that rezoned land from multiple family dwellings to single family residences because of the town's ecological need for new systems of water supply and sewage disposal. The court held that the long-range ecological considerations outweighed the owner's proprietary rights.[59]

In New Jersey, one of the unanswered questions of flood plain zoning is the effect of the *Parsippany-Troy Hills* decision upon the recently enacted

Flood Plains legislation.[60] This new law provides two forms of control: it directs the State Department of Environmental Protection to regulate development of land in floodways, and it directs municipalities to regulate development of land in *flood fringe areas* within one year or submit to state regulations. *The Parsippany-Troy Hills* decision invalidated the zoning ordinance on constitutional grounds, i.e., that the ordinance resulted in an unconstitutional taking of private property without just compensation. It is likely that eventually the New Jersey Supreme Court will be asked to rule upon the validity of this new legislation. It will be interesting to see what changes, if any, have taken place in the past decade, in the judicial attitude toward ecological considerations in the constitutional balance of interests.[61]

AGRICULTURAL ZONING

The second category of cases in which the proponents of environmental protection are pitted against the proponents of proprietary rights are the cases involving agricultural zoning.[62] This type of zoning ordinance restricts the use of land to agricultural uses for the purpose of limiting the cost of municipal services, protecting the scenic quality of open space, preserving ecological balance, and postponing the intrusion of problems associated with increased population. Agricultural zoning is distinguishable from flood plain zoning in that land zoned for agricultural use retains economic value without which the regulation would be confiscatory and invalid.[63]

The New Jersey courts have not been called upon to determine whether the limited use of land for agricultural purposes is a reasonable use of the land, and therefore have not ruled on the charge that the restriction constitutes an unreasonable economic burden and is therefore confiscatory and void. The legal problem is somewhat complicated in New Jersey by the fact that a New Jersey farmer may escape the burden of real property taxation resulting from assessment based upon development value. The Farmland Assessment Act[64] permits a farmer to have his land assessed at agricultural rather than potential development value. The farmer who continues to use his land for farming can hardly claim that he is deprived of its reasonable use. The speculator-purchaser of farmland who avails himself of the tax benefits of the Farmland Assessment Act may be estopped from arguing unreasonable economic burden because of his affirmation of agricultural use required by the act. In spite of the arguments for validity of agricultural zoning made possible by the Farmland Assessment Act, it is very likely that the New Jersey courts will not uphold agricultural zoning where a high development value of the land imposes an unreasonable and disproportionate burden on the landowner in order to achieve a public purpose.

Once it is clearly established that agricultural zoning is not a valid means of preserving open space in the path of urban development, responsible government officials will become reconciled to the necessity of public acquisition of such land with the payment of just compensation. The New Jersey Green Acres Land Acquisition Act of 1961 [65] is a step in the right direction. However, it is unlikely that sufficient public funds could be made available to acquire all the land required to fulfill the open space needs of the state. It is very likely that the purchase of less than the full fee simple, i.e., the development right, will be necessary to maximize the impact of the government acquisition program. Even better than that, it may be possible to preserve open space without any cost to government and with compensation to owners of preserved open space land by requiring owners of developable land to purchase the development rights of owners of "preserved land." Legislation to establish such a system has been proposed in Maryland and is being prepared in New Jersey. [66]

Regional Balance

Does the standard of a balanced community in accordance with the general welfare require a municipality to consider the needs and welfare of all of the people of the region or of the state? [67]

In a few states, the zoning enabling legislation imposes an *express* obligation upon municipalities to consider regional needs. [68] In a number of states, including New Jersey, the courts appear to be developing the principle that even in the absence of specific legislative instructions, nevertheless there is an *implied* obligation of municipalities to consider regional needs when enacting zoning ordinances. [69]

The argument for an implied requirement to consider regional needs is based upon the most prestigious of zoning precedents. In the landmark case of *Village of Euclid* v. *Ambler Realty Co.*, [70] the United States Supreme Court upheld a municipal zoning law designed to prevent the encroachment of central city industry into a suburban community. While recognizing the power of the local government to exclude industrial use within its boundaries, the court declared that in the future there might be "cases where the general public interest would so far outweigh the interest of the municipality that the municipality would not be allowed to stand in the way." [71]

In the nearly fifty years that have elapsed since the *Euclid* case, the prophecy contained therein has come to pass: aggregations of urban population have created problems of water supply, solid waste disposal, air and water pollution, transportation, education, and land-use control that transcend municipal boundaries. Courts, particularly in New Jersey, have begun to recognize circumstances where the general public interest (i.e., regional or state interest) so far outweighs the interest of the municipality that local zoning laws will not be allowed to stand in the way.

In 1949, the New Jersey Supreme Court expressed an awareness of the problem when in *Duffcon Concrete Products* v. *Cresskill* [72] it said:

> What may be the most appropriate use of any particular property depends not only on all the conditions, physical, economic and social, prevailing within the municipality and its needs, present and reasonably prospective, but also on the nature of the *entire region* in which the municipality is located and the use to which the land in *that region* has been or may be put most advantageously. The effective development of a *region* should not and cannot be made to depend upon the adventitious location of municipal boundaries, often prescribed decades or even centuries ago, and based in many instances on considerations of geography, of commerce, or of politics that are no longer significant with respect to zoning. [emphasis added]

Nine years later, the New Jersey Supreme Court once again expressed its self-conscious awareness of the problem when it upheld a zoning ordinance excluding apartments from the municipality but tempered the decision by arguing that there was not showing of regional needs. [73] The court said:

> It is quite another proposition to say that a municipality of 960 acres must accept uses it believes to be injurious, in order to satisfy the requirements of a county. There, of course, is no suggestion that a county is so developed that Hasbrouck Heights is the last hope for a solution, and hence we do not have the question whether under the existing statute the judiciary could resolve a crisis of that kind. [74]

Then in 1971, in the *Madison Township* [75] case, the Superior Court declared the township zoning ordinance invalid on the grounds that it failed to promote reasonably a balanced community in accordance with the *general welfare of the entire region.* [76] The following year the Superior Court invalidated the Mount Laurel Township zoning ordinance where there was a finding that "it was the intention of the township committee to take care of the people of Mt. Laurel Township but not make any area of Mt. Laurel a home for the county." [77] The court cited with approval the statement from *Duffcon* that the municipality must consider regional needs in determining the appropriate use of land within the municipality.

Taken together, these decisions indicate that even in the absence of express statutory instructions to consider regional needs, the New Jersey courts may impose a judicial requirement that municipal zoning laws be consistent with regional needs.

Temporal Balance

Does the standard of a "balanced community" recognize and sanction the uneven and intermittent stages in which municipal development proceeds in time?

Balance within a community is not static; it is always in a dynamic and changing state. The forces of social, economic, political, and physical change constantly interact upon each other along a continuum of time. Today's community balance may become tomorrow's imbalance. Today's placid and fallow fields may become a center of tomorrow's teeming activity. All components of community structure do not grow and develop with equal and uniform progress. Houses, streets, utilities, water supply, schools, and recreational facilities do not emerge abruptly as a monolithic community infrastructure in the required proportions of a balanced community.

The urban planning process is designed to provide plans and programs for rational and interrelated community growth. Zoning laws are enacted to allocate land to meet the projected community needs on which the plans are based. Until recently, zoning laws have not been devised to coordinate the *sequence* of development to maintain a community balance *during the process* of development over a period of time.

In 1972, the New York Court of Appeals was called upon to determine the validity of a zoning ordinance that permitted residential development to proceed only in accordance with such a plan for sequential development and timed growth.[78] The zoning ordinance of the Town of Ramapo, in Rockland County, New York, was designed to achieve the following policy of zoning and planning:

1. To economize on the costs of municipal facilities and services to carefully phase residential development with efficient provision of public improvements;
2. To establish and maintain municipal control over the eventual character of development;
3. To establish and maintain a desirable degree of *balance* among the various uses of land; [emphasis added]
4. To establish and maintain essential quality of community services and facilities.[79]

The zoning ordinance was based upon a comprehensive master plan for future growth and upon a Capital Budget providing for the location and sequence of capital improvements for a period of eighteen years.

Residential development is permitted only after obtaining a special permit, the issuance of which is conditioned upon the availability of five categories of facilities and services:

1. public sanitary sewers or approved substitutes
2. drainage facilities
3. improved public parks or recreation facilities, including schools
4. state, county, or town roads
5. firehouses

Special permits for development would be issued only when the services and facilities were available. A point system was created to assign values to each such facility and a permit would be issued only when fifteen development points were applicable to the proposed development. A prospective developer could advance the date of development by agreeing to provide those improvements which would bring the proposed plat within the number of development points required by the ordinance. Thus, residential development becomes a function of the availability of municipal improvements and may proceed in accordance with the overall program of orderly growth incorporated into the eighteen-year Capital Plan.

The New York court upheld the system even though development of the land could be prevented for a period of up to eighteen years. The court conceded that an ordinance that *permanently* restricted the use of property so that it could not be used for any reasonable purpose would constitute an unconstitutional taking of the property. However, the court characterized the restriction of use for up to eighteen years as a *temporary* restriction and concluded that the property could be put to a reasonable use within a reasonable time.

The question whether the New Jersey courts would uphold an eighteen-year restriction of land use would be answered by *Lomarch* v. *Mayor of Englewood*.[80] In *Lomarch,* the court held that an Official Map Act providing for a "freeze" on development of land for a one-year period would be an unconstitutional deprivation of property unless the owner was compensated for the "option" price of the "temporary taking." Based upon this decision, there is little reason to assume that the New Jersey court would accept the reasoning in the *Ramapo* case that an eighteen-year postponement of use is only a "temporary restriction" rather than a permanent deprivation; nor would the New Jersey court accept *Ramapo's* reasoning that the restriction is "substantial but not absolute."

Nevertheless, there is appeal to the argument that rational and comprehensive planning contemplates a process of development over a period of time and that it is reasonable to assume that the development will take place sequentially rather than all at once. Some land will be developed before others and some land will not be "ripe" for development until community services and facilities are available. Therefore it does not seem unreasonable to permit zoning law to regulate that development to take place in an orderly way.

The Court As A Balancing Agent

When a court determines that a municipality has failed to comply with the requirements of, or has exceeded the authority granted under, the zoning enabling legislation, it will find such exercise of power to be *ultra vires* and invalid. If the court finds that a municipal zoning ordinance imposes an unreasonable burden upon a person or unreasonably discriminates against him, the ordinance will be declared a violation of due process clause or equal protection clause of the Fourteenth Amendment. In all cases, the role of the court is negative. Its decision invalidates the ordinance but does not provide the affirmative measures necessary to create the desired "balance" in the community. This form of decision is in accordance with the traditional role of the judiciary in our governmental system.

Under the traditional view, it is the function of the legislature to formulate public policy and to enact laws to carry out this policy. The courts may not intervene in this process unless and until a real issue arises involving the application of those laws. As applied to an imagined "scale of community balance" the traditional role of the court would be only to remove those zoning laws that upset the balance. The courts may not add a new program or develop an affirmative plan to restore equilibrium.

This traditional role of the courts seems to be changing. Courts have begun to take a more active role in seeking community balance by requiring affirmative municipal action to redress the alleged legal wrong. Numerous federal courts have assumed this role in the past few years. In 1972, a New Jersey Superior Court adopted this role in prescribing its remedy.

The *Gautreaux* case [81] has attracted national attention because of the seven year battle involving the Federal Court and the Chicago City Council. The court ordered the Chicago Housing Authority to adopt a policy of site selection for public housing that would place public housing in white communities in an effort to achieve racial integration. The court directed the Chicago Housing Authority to build integrated public housing on sites in accordance with a detailed and comprehensive program and timetable. This order was affirmed by the Court of Appeals. The Supreme Court denied certiorari. The Housing Authority was unable to comply with this order because the Chicago City Council refused to approve the sites for integrated public housing in white areas. In April 1972, the court ordered the Housing Authority to disregard the City Council requirements and to acquire the property for housing in the designated white section of town.

In another public housing case,[82] a federal district court ordered county officials to join with the municipal authorities in finding sites for public housing outside the central city. In its decision, the court said, "For better or worse, both by legislative act and judicial decision, this nation is committed to a policy of *balanced* and dispersed public housing" [emphasis added]. On appeal, the decision and remedy were upheld by the Court of Appeals for the Fifth Circuit.[83] In another decision,[84] municipal officials were ordered to submit a plan that would equalize municipal services within the jurisdiction. In an earlier case,[85] the court ordered municipal officials to devise a plan to accommodate the needs of low income families including public housing and "requiring the exercise of the fiscal and eminent domain powers of the city if such be necessary and reasonably feasible under the law to accomplish the objective." The city officials were ordered to report back to court every three months to show progress in complying with the court order.

With this background and judicial precedent, the New Jersey Superior Court in 1972 in the *Mount Laurel* case[86] ordered affirmative municipal action to eliminate the economic discrimination perpetrated by the municipal zoning ordinance. The court ordered the municipality to do four things: (a) undertake a study to determine the extent of the housing needs of the community; (b) determine the number of low and moderate income housing units necessary to meet those needs; (c) develop a plan of implementation to accomplish that goal; and (d) report and describe any factors that interfere with the implementation of the plan.

Thus the courts seem to have undertaken the delicate and difficult task of maintaining community balance that the legislatures have been reluctant to accept. This is an unfortunate development because the nature of the problem is one that is best resolved by the kinds of political negotiation and compromise upon which a democratic legislative process is based. The legislative process has defaulted on this critical issue and as Governor Cahill predicted,[87] if the legislature fails to meet its responsibility, there will be no alternative but for the courts to step in and fill the void.

Implications For Planners

The role of the professional planner in the judicial process would be greatly enhanced if the courts determine that the validity of a zoning ordinance depends upon its propensity to promote a balanced community. Such a decision would constitute judicial affirmation of the philosophy of the planning profession that the quality of life may be improved by planning in a rational manner for the allocation of available resources for the satisfaction of community needs. Such a decision would affirm the judicial recognition of the pertinence and probity of planning studies and of the planning process by which those studies may be used to measure the impact [88] of zoning proposals upon community balance.

It should be recognized, however, that the various definitions discussed above may not in fact be illustrations of the various means of "community balance." Rather, they may be nothing more than a listing of community constraints [89] that are traditionally and routinely studied by planners in the process of devising a land-use plan; i.e., socioeconomic balance refers to the demographic and sociological studies; fiscal balance refers to economic base studies; ecological balance refers to environmental impact studies; regional balance refers to studies of intergovernmental relationships, the significance of which planners have long recognized; temporal balance refers to sequential development that is the essence of the planner's tool of systematic programming.

Judicial acceptance of the balanced community standard of zoning validity would also tend to strengthen the bond between the planning and legal professions. Such a decision would reinforce the existing practice of relying upon the expert testimony of professional planners to determine whether the allocation and designation of land use is reasonable. When the validity of a zoning ordinance is challenged on the grounds that it does not promote a balanced community a team of lawyers and planners would be required to prepare and present the case for each side of the controversy.

The lawyer-planner team would be able to provide the kinds of evidence upon which a court could determine whether a given zoning ordinance does or does not promote a balanced community. In addition, the lawyer-planner team would be able to assist the court in providing a remedy that goes beyond a mere declaration of invalidity of the ordinance. It is precisely this issue that has given the courts the greatest concern. [90] If the courts determine that zoning ordinances must promote a balanced community, then they must be prepared to participate in the process by which that balance is defined and in fashioning a remedy by which that balance may be achieved. In both of these endeavors, planners will have an opportunity to join in the process by which planning principles may be translated into land-use law.

NOTES

1. *J. D. Construction Corp.* v. *Board of Adjustment of Freehold*, 119 N.J. Super. 140, at 147 (1972); *Kozesnik* v. *Montgomery Township*, 24 N.J. 154, at 169 (1957): *Berdan* v. *City of Paterson*, 1 N.J. 199, at 204 (1948).
2. *Oakwood at Madison, Inc.* v. *Township of Madison*, 117 N.J. Super. 11 (1971). At the time of preparation of this article (March 1973), the New Jersey Supreme Court had heard oral arguments on appeal of the *Madison Township* and *Mt. Laurel* cases, *infra*, note 24, but no decision had been rendered.
3. *Id.*, at 21.
4. *Buchanan* v. *Warley*, 245 U.S. 60 (1917). Although legal scholars have debated this point, this decision was based upon the reasoning that the zoning ordinance constituted an unreasonable deprivation of the property of the white seller rather than a deprivation of a black purchaser's equal protection of the laws.
5. *Korematsu* v. *United States*, 323 U.S. 214 (1944).
6. *See*: Note, "Exclusionary Zoning," 84 *Harv. L.R.* 1645, 1657 (1971).
7. *Bolling* v. *Sharpe*, 347 U.S. 497, 499 (1954).
8. *Hunter* v. *Reickson*, 393 U.S. 385, 391 (1969).
9. "careful examination on our part is especially warranted where lines are drawn on the basis of wealth or race, two factors which would independently render a classification highly suspect and thereby demand a more exacting judicial inquiry." *McDonald* v. *Board of Election Commissioners*, 394 U.S. 802, 807 (1969).
10. 314 U.S. 160 (1941).
11. *Id.* at 177-186.
12. 394 U.S. 619 (1969).
13. *Id.* at 631.
14. *Lionshead Lake Inc.* v. *Wayne Tp.*, 10 N.J. 1965 (1952), app. dism. 344 U.S. 919 (1953).
15. *Fisher* v. *Bedminster Tp.*, 11 N.J. 194 (1952).
16. *Fanale* v. *Hasbrouck Heights*, 26 N.J. 320 (1958).
17. *Napierkowski* v. *Gloucester Tp.*, 29 N.J. 481 (1959).
18. *Vickers* v. *Gloucester Tp. Committee*, 37 N.J. 232 (1962), *cert. den.* 371 U.S. 233 (1963).
19. 56 N.J. 428 (1970).
20. *Oakwood at Madison, Inc.* v. *Township of Madison, supra*, note 2.
21. *National Land and Investment Co.* v. *Kohn*, 419 Pa. 504, 215 A. 2d 597 (1965).
22. *Molino* v. *Mayor and Council of Borough of Glassboro*, 116 N.J. 195 (1971).
23. *Id.* at 204.
24. *Southern Burlington Co. NAACP* v. *Tp. of Mt. Laurel*, 119 N.J. 164 (1972).
25. *Id.* at 176.
26. *Gruber* v. *Mayor and Township Comm. of Raritan Tp.*, 39 N.J. 1, 9 (1962).
27. 28 N.J. 529, 535 (1959).
28. 47 N.J. Super. 306 (Law Div. 1957).
29. *Id.* at 328.
30. *Supra*, note 2.
31. *Id.* at 18.
32. *Id.* at 18.

33. *Supra*, note 22.
34. *Id.* at 203.
35. *Id.* at 203.
36. *Supra*, note 24.
37. *Id.* at 176.
38. *Gruber* v. *Mayor and Township Comm. of Raritan Tp.*, *supra*, note 26.
39. *Serrano* v. *Priest*, 5 Cal. 3d 584, 96 Cal. Rptr. 601, 487 P.2d 1241 (1971.
40. *Rodriguez* v. *San Antonio Independent School District*, 337 F. Supp. 280 (W.D. Tex. 1971).
41. *Robinson* v. *Cahill*, 118 N.J. Super. 223, 287 A.2d 187 (1972).
42. e.g., Minnesota: *Van Dusartz* v. *Hatfield*, 334 F. Supp. 870 (D. Minn. 1971); Wyoming: *Sweetwater County Planning Comm.* v. *Hinkle*, 491 P.2d 1234 (Wyo. 1971).
43. Discrimination in municipal services based on *race* is highly suspect and is subject to exacting judicial scrutiny. *Hawkins* v. *Town of Shaw*, 437 F. 2d 1286 (1971). *See*: Anderson, "Toward the Equalization of Municipal Services: Variations on a Theme by *Hawkins.*" 50 *Journal of Urban Law* 177 (1972).
44. *Westbrook* v. *Mihaly*, 2 Cal. 3d 765, 87 Cal. Rptr. 839, 471 P.2d 487 (1970).
45. *San Antonio Independent School District* v. *Rodriguez*, ___ U.S. ___, (41 U.S.L.W. 4407, March 21, 1973).
46. *See* D. Hagman "Property Tax Reform: Speculations on the Impact of the *Serrano* Equilization Principle," 1 *Real Estate Law Journal* 115 (1972). *See also* W. Bateman and P. Brown, "Some Reflections on *Serrano* v. *Priest*", 49 *Journal of Urban Law* 701 (1972).
47. *supra*, note 45 at 4423.
48. *Robinson* v. *Cahill*, ___ N.J. ___, ___ A.2d ___ (Supreme Court, A-58, April 3, 1973).
49. N.J. CONST. Art, VIII, Sect. IV, para 1.
50. *See infra*, note 64 and discussion pertaining thereto.
51. *See* Note, "The Scope of State and Local Action in Environmental Land Use Regulation," 13 *Boston Col. Inc. & Com. L.R.* 782 (1972).
52. On January 13, 1973, New Jersey Governor William Cahill suggested that we strike a balance between economic growth and sound environmental planning. In talking about the New Jersey coastal region he said:
The area is under intense and constant development pressure which threatens to destroy its precious environmental assets. The pressure must be *balanced* against environmental demands. This *balance* cannot be achieved piecemeal, but must be accomplished on a region-wide basis. [emphasis added] *New Jersey Environmental Times* 5 no. 3 (Jan. 1973): 1, 4.
53. 40 N.J. 539 (1963).
54. *Id.* at 555.
55. e.g. N.J.S.A. 58:16A.1 et seq. and N.J.S.A. 40:69-4-1 *et seq. See also* New Jersey Green Acres Land Acquisition Act of 1961, N.J.S.A. 13:8A.1, *et seq.* for similar authority for open space, parks, playground, and conservation purposes.
56. e.g., *Vartelas* v. *Water Resources Comm'n.*, 146 Conn. 650, 153 A.2d 822 (1959).
57. *Turnpike Realty Co.* v. *Town of Dedham*, 72 Mass. 1303, 284 N.E. 2d 891 (1972).
58. *Just* v. *Marinette County*, 201 N.W. 2d 761 (Wis. 1972).

59. *Nattin Realty Inc.* v. *Ludewig,* 67 Misc. 2d 828 (Sup. Ct. 1971), aff'd 40 A.D. 2d 535 (1) (2d Dep't. 1972).
60. Stat. N.J. Acts Ch. 185 Public Laws of 1972, App'd. Dec. 14, 1972.
61. Although the decision was not based on this issue, Judge Furman felt obliged to recognize the relevance of ecological considerations in the *Madison Township* case. In the last substantive paragraph of the opinion in that case the court said:
   Only engineering data and expert opinion and, it may be, ecological data and expert opinion could justify the ordinance under attack. These were lacking both in the legislative process and at the trial. The record fails to substantiate that safe-guarding against flood and surface drainage problems and protection of the Englishtown aquifer would be reasonably advanced by the sweeping zoning revision into low population density districts along the four water courses and elsewhere or the exclusionary limitations on multi-family apartment units.
   It would seem that from this day forward no zoning litigation will be complete without the presentation of ecological experts by both sides.
62. *See:* Note, "Protection of Environmental Quality in Nonmetropolitan Regions by Limiting Development," 57 *Iowa L.R.* 126, 143 (1971).
63. *Katobimar Realty Co.* v. *Webster,* 20 N.J. 114, 122, 118 A. 2d 824, 828 (1955); *Morris County Land Improvement Co.* v. *Parsippany-Troy Hills Tp.* 40 N.J. 539 (1963).
64. N.J.S.A. 54:4-23.1.
65. N.J.S.A. 13:8A-1 *et seq.*
66. *See:* Rose, "Development Rights Legislation May Change the Name of the Real Estate Investment Game" 1 *Real Estate Law Journal* 276 (Winter 1973).
67. For a general discussion of this issue see Walsh, "Are Local Zoning Bodies Required by the Constitutions to Consider Regional Needs"? 3 *Conn. L.R.* 244 (1971).
68. e.g., Colo. Rev. Stat. Sec. 106-2-14 (1963); 9 Del. Code Ann. Sec. 2603 (a) (1953).
69. In addition to the New Jersey decisions discussed herein, recent Pennsylvania decisions have required municipalities to consider regional needs. e.g., *In re Kit-Mar Builders,* 439 Pa. 466, 268 A.2d 765 (1970); *In re Girsh,* 437 Pa. 237, 263 A.2d 395 (1970). For other citations see Walsh, *supra* note 67 at 247-250.
70. 272 U.S. 365 (1926).
71. *Id.* at 390. See Weinberg, "Regional Land Use Control: Prerequisite for Rational Planning," 46 *N.Y.U.L.R.* 786 (1971).
72. 1 N.J. 509, 513 (1949).
73. *Fanale v. Borough of Hasbrouck Heights,* 26 N.N. 320, 139 A.2d 749 (1958).
74. *Id.* at 328, 139 A.2d at 753-754.
75. *Supra,* note 2.
76. *Id.* at 20-21.
77. *Supra,* note 24 at 169.
78. *Golden* v. *Ramapo,* 30 N.Y. 2d 359, 334 N.Y.S. 2d 138 (1972).
79. Town of Ramapo Zoning Ordinance, Section 46-13.1, A.
80. 51 N.J. 108, 237 A.2d 881 (1968).
81. *Gautreaux* v. *Chicago Housing Authority,* 296 F. Supp. 907, 304 F.Supp. 736 (N.D. Ill. 1969), aff'd. as to program of relief, 436 F.2d 306 (7th Cir. 1970), *cert. denied,* 402 U.S. 992 (1971).
82. *Crow* v. Brown, 332 F.Supp.382 (N.D.Ga. 1971).

83. *Id. aff'd per curiam,* 457 F.2d 788 (5th Cir. 1972).
84. *Hawkins* v. *Town of Shaw,* 437 F.2d 1286 (5th Cir. 1971).
85. *Southern Alameda Spanish Speaking Organization* (SASSO) v. *City of Union City, California,* 424 F.2d 291 (9th Cir. 1970).
86. *Supra,* note 24.
87. *New Horizons in Housing: A Special Message to the Legislature,* William T. Cahill, Governor of New Jersey, P. 5 (Mar. 27, 1972).
88. "Impact Zoning: The Newest and Best Answer to Housing's Number 1 Problem," *House and Home,* August, 1972; For a critique of this article, see Frank Beal and Frank S. So, "Editorial; The New Improved 1973 Zoning Model is Now at Your Dealer's Showroom," *Planning, The ASPO Magazine* 260 (Nov. 1972).
89. F. Stuart Chapin, Jr., *Urban Land Use Planning,* 107 *et. seq.* (1965).
90. In the oral arguments of the appeal of the *Madison Township* case, *supra,* note 2, and the *Mt. Laurel* case, *supra,* note 24, on March 5, 1973, the New Jersey Supreme Court indicated, by its questions to counsel, a greater interest in the alternate forms of judicial remedies available to it than in the arguments on the merits of the case.

II
Analysis
of the
Decision

A Review of the Mount Laurel Decision

Frederick W. Hall

Any discussion in New Jersey in late 1975 of current perspectives on land use zoning, which is the topic of this portion of your program, cannot help but be concerned with the *Mount Laurel* case, decided by the Supreme Court on March 24th [1975]. Those in charge have asked me, as the author of the opinion for a unanimous court, to review it from the point of view of attempting to assist you municipal officials and your attorneys in understanding its implications and in applying it as called for in your various municipalities. Although the request is unusual, I have agreed to do so for the reason stated, within certain limitations.

What I have to say has, of course, not been submitted to or approved by the court. As most of you know, I am no longer a member of it, having retired some months ago. The thoughts to be expressed do represent, however, the plain meaning and implications of the decision as I believe every member of the court understood them at the time the opinion was filed. I have no reason to believe that they are not still held just as firmly. Of course, I do not mean to predict the views of the court on questions which may arise beyond the context just mentioned and any such views I may express must be considered personal. Further, in view of the peculiar position I occupy, I feel that all that I can appropriately say is contained in this paper and that I should not enlarge upon it by entertaining questions.

Before dealing with the specific holdings and implications of *Mount Laurel*, mention should be made, particularly for the benefit of the lay members of the audience, of the scope and purpose of an opinion of an appellate court. Its purpose is to express in writing the decision of the court in the particular case before it and the reasons for the decision, in light of the proofs, other facts of which the court may properly take note, and applicable law. The point to be emphasized is that the court is deciding a specific case grounded in certain facts, and is not attempting to solve all the possible cases that could arise in the field involved. Legislation can provide in advance, and frequently does, for all aspects and details of a field; judicial opinions cannot. But they can by their approach and language indicate the general spirit in which the court views the issue and the overall problem and may set forth some guidelines to aid future action in related aspects of the subject. This is especially true when the case is an important public one, such as *Mount Laurel*, and the opinion followed that general line.

A few words about the background of the decision, a good part of which was placed in evidence or referred to by counsel and is to be found in the factual portion of the opinion. One element is the well known fact that New Jersey, with its two very densely populated metropolitan areas, has, even in times of prosperity, long had a serious housing shortage, especially affecting the less affluent members of our society. The legislature has so declared time and again, governors' messages have reiterated it and called for action in the strongest terms and state agency studies have consistently established and publicized it. But little positive correction has taken place. Large segments of our population are compelled to live in substandard and dilapidated housing by reason of their economic condition. This situation is not confined to our central cities nor to the so-called minority members of the population. It exists in all types of municipalities and with respect, for example, to young couples, elderly people, and families with numbers of children who just cannot afford or are not accommodated by the kinds of better housing which most outlying municipalities permit to be built.

The second important element in the background of the decision is the explosive population, commercial, and industrial growth in the last twenty-five years outside the central cities and the built-up suburbs and the course of municipal land use regulation which accompanied it. The details are familiar and need not be repeated in full. The consequence has been phenomenal expansion of the so-called outer-ring residential municipalities, at the expense of crumbling cities and older suburbs, with residential growth limited by zoning ordinances in practically every such municipality to large houses on large lots, and in some cases, to apartments so confined in size that they cannot be occupied by families with school children. Indeed, high municipal walls have been erected and defended in the name of the local property tax rate. Despite clear warnings from governors and others against this parochial perversion of land use regulation and strong indication by the court in earlier cases that municipalities cannot hide behind boundary walls without regard for the world outside or without providing for decent housing for those of low and moderate income, the pattern has continued. While the first case directly raising these basic questions involved Mount Laurel, dozens of other municipalities had acted in the same way and are affected by the decision.

So I come to the principal holdings and implications of the decision. The basic principles are elementary and the spirit of the opinion is plain. Land use regulations, to meet the state constitutional requirements of substantive due process and equal protection of the laws, must promote, and not be contrary to, the general welfare. What does or does not promote the general welfare, and so whether particular municipal or state legislation is constitutional, is a question for the judicial branch of government to decide. The matter of whose general welfare is to be served and not violated by the inclusion or omission of zoning ordinance provisions depends upon the general importance of the subject matter and whether regulation has a substantial impact beyond the borders of the particular municipality. If so, the welfare of the state's citizens beyond those borders cannot be disregarded and must be recognized and served.

In the matter of housing we are concerned with one of the most basic human needs, and proper provision for adequate housing of all categories of people is an absolute essential in promotion of the general welfare required in all local land use regulation, absent zoning on a regional basis, of which more later. So the court held that the presumptive obligation arises for each developing municipality affirmatively to plan and provide, by its land use regulations, the reasonable *opportunity* for an *appropriate variety and choice of housing,* including low and moderate income housing by way of multi-family dwellings, townhouses, mobile homes, small houses on small lots and the like, to meet the needs, desires and resources of all classes of people who may desire to live within its boundaries. Negatively, it may not adopt regulations or policies which thwart or preclude that opportunity. When a municipality has not so acted, the heavy burden shifts to it to establish a valid basis for its action or non-action. To phrase the holding in another way, the court was saying that the exclusion of people wishing to live in the community because they could not afford the only housing permitted by the zoning ordinance was just as wrong as excluding them from residence because of their race, religion or national origin. Such fundamentals clearly must over-ride any so-called "home rule" or local fiscal considerations.

This zoning for the living welfare of people is the essential spirit of the opinion and it must be in the light of that spirit that its implications and its application to other situations are to be derived and tested. I fear that already there has been too much narrow nitpicking and card matching by municipal officials, attorneys, planners, and even some lower court judges, seeking to distinguish the case or its application, when regard for this essential spirit might have dictated a different answer to the particular question. For example, we spoke of the holding applying to "developing municipalities"—large, sprawling, and with much vacant land remaining—because that was the case in Mount Laurel. But we did *not* say that the same principle would *not* apply to smaller or other types of municipalities with available land, not to parts of now rural townships as growth and demand reach them, nor to generally built-up suburbs and central cities, although different circumstances might involve different considerations and different remedies.

The opinion went on to specifically strike down certain types of regulations utilized to carry out the policy of excluding all but expensive housing. The opinion held requirements throughout a developing municipality of only single-family dwellings on large lots to be improper; minimum house size to be artificial and unjustifiable; bedroom restrictions in multi-family dwellings, where allowed, to be arbitrary; and removal of land from residential use by excessive allocation for industrial and commercial purposes to be unreasonable. It also spoke of the necessity for inclusion of low- and moderate-income housing in planned unit developments unless opportunity therefor has already been realistically provided elsewhere in the municipality. And it very pointedly said that when a municipality zones land for industry and commerce, which are, of course, primarily designed for local tax benefit purposes, it must also zone to permit adequate housing within the means of the employees of such uses. This includes porters as well as presidents, and stenographers as well as scientists.

One of the significant holdings of the decision is that the zoning power may not be used to exclude the less expensive forms of housing—those more likely to increase municipal government and school costs—for the sake of the local property tax rate. This may well call for some change in the tax structure to something more equitable than the present uneven system, a change which can only come from another branch of government having that policy responsibility. The implications of this whole problem are thoroughly explored in Chapter 9 of a report of the state Economic Policy Council very recently released, which I commend to your attention. Municipalities immediately affected by *Mount Laurel* may well find it most advisable to take the lead in urging changes in this area.

Also pointed out in the opinion is the fact that true ecological and environmental factors may lessen the extent of a given municipality's obligation under the decision, or dictate the location of certain types of housing in one location rather than another, or call for clustering or some comparable technique to preserve important ecological considerations. There would appear to be no reason why courts, in this connection, should not consider county or regional environmental plans—provided they are proved to be sound and reasonable and not simply devices to avoid all growth—and direct where and to what degree the more dense residential uses are to go. Caution ought to be exercised in enacting so-called environmental impact ordinances, of which there has been a recent flurry. Some seem to me to be so all encompassing, so devoid of standards and so harassing to land-owners as to amount to transparent methods to preclude growth entirely.

This leads to mention of an argument made by some against the *Mount Laurel* rationale which should not pass unnoticed. I refer to the contention that a municipality should be able to decide its own physical and population make-up and ought to be let alone when it does so. This view necessarily means that a majority of its citizens should be able to dictate to those within as well as all those without what kind of people can live in the municipality and in what kind of dwellings. The answer, of course, is that such a thesis has no place when we are dealing with a matter of constitutional dimensions—decent housing within the financial reach of those who wish to live in the community. Any so-called majority—I have a great deal of trouble concerning when and by whom the gate in the wall can be slammed shut—cannot override the fundamental rights of others. It has been the function of courts for centuries to protect against just that sort of thing. All interests can be accommodated with some sensible planning and a good will approach.

In conclusion, allow me to mention the matter of the remedy directed by the *Mount Laurel* opinion. The suit was not brought by a landowner or developer who sought to have his particular property zoned for low and moderate income housing—a result the decision does not compel. The location of such zones or the handling of their location by the special exception procedure is for the municipality to decide, assuming its choice is realistic and reasonable. Rather this was a suit by poor people who wanted to live in the township and the result was a declaration of invalidity of the zoning ordinance to the extent of the failure to provide the municipality's *regional fair share* of low- and moderate-income housing, which deficiency it was properly given the first opportunity to correct. The concepts of the "region" and "fair share" have been much bandied about since. They present no real problem in *Mount Laurel* and are the main subjects involved in the *Madison* case pending before the court, so I should not comment other than to say I doubt they are as difficult to translate into reasonable application in a particular case as has been made out in some quarters. A little common sense, hard thinking and good faith ought to produce a result a court would accept.

But I do wish to comment on another aspect of the remedy. The imposition of the obligation on each municipality to afford the opportunity for its fair share of the demand in its region for low- and moderate-income housing rests on the basis that as yet there is no general way to bring about appropriate zoning for every municipality in a region, although many uses may belong more properly in one municipality than in another. The opinion suggested that regional zoning authority was a logical and desirable legislative step, regional planning now being permissible and in some cases compulsory. It would seem that such a step would also require inter-municipal tax sharing if the property tax structure remains as at present. Such a device is in use in other states and in fact is no stranger to New Jersey. The special Hackensack Meadowlands district has, by legislation, both regional zoning and inter-municipal tax sharing, which have been upheld by the Supreme Court.

The decision in *Mount Laurel* is not, as some have suggested, mere "wishful thinking" by the court. The court does not live in a vacuum and it was fully realized that the decision would not immediately and in itself produce low and moderate income housing in outlying municipalities but was only a first step. It was apparent nothing along this line would be accomplished until the court established the legal nature and extent of the municipal obligation to provide this *opportunity* through appropriate land use regulations. The court has fully appreciated that the bulk of lower income housing will still remain in the cities and other suburbs, which cannot be abandoned, but must be rehabilitated and revitalized, with all inhabitants having the chance for suitable employment and to become imbued with an active spirit of civic and personal responsibility. The task is a huge and vital one and cannot be accomplished by a court alone. The municipalities affected by *Mount Laurel* and its implications owe the duty to act in the spirit of the opinion, by making appropriate provision in their ordinances and by fully cooperating with subsequent housing efforts. I sense that the court will not tolerate evasion or avoidance and will move forward to direct further steps in the process as found necessary.

Although the court has a rather full arsenal of weapons to combat recalcitrance, I earnestly trust they will not have to be used. I close by quoting a paragraph from the opinion:

There is no reason why developing municipalities like Mount Laurel, required by this opinion to afford the opportunity for all types of housing to meet the needs of various categories of people, may not become and remain attractive, viable communities providing good living and adequate services for all their residents in the kind of atmosphere which a democracy and free institutions demand. They can have industrial sections, commercial sections and sections for every kind of housing from low cost and multi-family to lots of more than an acre with very expensive homes. Proper planning and governmental cooperation can prevent over-intensive and too sudden development, insure against future suburban sprawl and slums and assure the preservation of open space and local beauty. We do not intend that developing municipalities shall be overwhelmed by voracious land speculators and developers if they use the powers which they have intelligently and in the broad public interest. Under our holdings today, they can be better communities for all than they previously have been.

What Is a "Developing Municipality"?

Jerome G. Rose
and Melvin R. Levin*

The question whether a municipality is a "developing municipality" is a new threshold issue created by the decision in *Southern Burlington County NAACP v. Mount Laurel.*[1] Here, the New Jersey Supreme Court held the Mount Laurel zoning ordinance invalid because that municipality failed to provide for its share of the housing needs of the region of which it was a part.[2] This newly established standard for the validity of zoning ordinances does not apply to all municipalities, but only to "developing municipalities, like Mount Laurel."[3] Consequently, when a zoning ordinance is challenged, it is now necessary for a court in New Jersey to test its validity by the traditional standards generally applied before the *Mount Laurel* decision *and, in addition,* if the municipality is a "developing municipality," by new standards formulated by that decision.

* The authors express their appreciation for the assistance of Douglas K. Wolfson, a student at Rutgers Law School, in the preparation of this article.

Criteria of Zoning Validity Established
Before *Mount Laurel*

The zoning ordinances of *all* municipalities must comply with a number of commonly accepted standards of validity:

STATUTORY AUTHORITY

A valid municipal zoning ordinance must be within the police power authority delegated by the state legislature and must be designed to achieve the objectives set forth in the enabling legislation.[4] In New Jersey, such power is delegated to municipalities in New Jersey Statute Sections 40:55-50 et seq. Section 40:55-32 provides:

> Such regulations shall be in accordance with a comprehensive plan and designed for one or more of the following purposes: to lessen congestion in the streets; secure safety from fire, flood, panic and other dangers; *promote health, morals* or *the general welfare;* provide adequate light and air; prevent the overcrowding of land or buildings; avoid undue concentration of population. Such regulations shall be made with reasonable consideration, among other things, to the character of the district and its peculiar suitability for particular uses, and with a view of conserving the value of property and encouraging the most appropriate use of land throughout such municipality. [Emphasis added.]

The legislative statement of purposes makes it clear that the essence of the zoning power delegated to municipalities is the mandate to exclude and to restrict.[5] Under the statutory authority granted by the legislature, a municipality may exclude commercial and industrial uses in residential districts;[6] restrict the height and bulk of buildings;[7] restrict the density of population;[8] and employ all of these prohibitions to prevent the overcrowding of land and undue concentration of population and to conserve the value of property with due consideration to the suitability of particular uses to the character of the character of the community.[9] However, all such restrictions must be justified by the purpose of "promoting the general welfare."[10]

SUBSTANTIVE DUE PROCESS

All municipal powers authorized by the legislature are nevertheless limited by federal and state constitutional provisions, the most pervasive of which is the due process clause. This constitutional provision subjects all police power regulations to the test of *reasonableness*.[11] Thus, even though a ·given zoning ordinance may be within the scope of legislative authority, it must nevertheless be calculated to achieve the authorized purposes without undue harshness: The owner of property may not be deprived of all of the use of his property; he/she must be permitted some *reasonable* use of his/her property to satisfy the requirements of the due process clause.[12]

EQUAL PROTECTION OF THE LAWS

A valid municipal zoning ordinance must comply with the equal protection clause requirement that there be a rational basis for imposing greater or lesser restrictions upon different parcels of land.[13] If any classification of land or persons is subjected to a hostile discrimination or is given an unfair advantage, the equal protection clause will be invoked.[14] If the classification involves a "suspect classification" or a "fundamental interest," the law will be subjected to "strict judicial scrutiny" and will be upheld only if there is a "compelling interest" of the government involved.[15] If there is no "suspect classification" or "fundamental interest" involved, then the usual presumption of validity will prevail and a court will uphold the classification as long as there is "some rational relationship to a legitimate state purpose."[16] A classification based upon race is suspect; but wealth is not.[17] The right to a fair trial is a fundamental right;[18] but the right to adequate shelter is not.[19] Thus, a zoning law that tends to deprive poor people of an opportunity to find or seek adequate shelter in a given community has been determined not to violate the equal protection clause.[20]

In New Jersey before the *Mount Laurel* decision and presently in most other states where the *Mount Laurel* principles have not been adopted, zoning ordinances resulting in higher costs of housing construction, thereby tending to exclude residents of lower income, have been upheld when tested against the traditional standards of zoning validity.[21]

Zoning Criteria Created by the *Mount Laurel* Decision

In the *Mount Laurel* decision, the New Jersey Supreme Court created additional criteria for testing the validity of zoning ordinances of developing municipalities in New Jersey. Those additional standards of validity are:

1. The zoning ordinance must provide for the municipality's "fair share" of the housing needs of the region.[22]
2. The housing needs to be met must include *prospective*, as well as present, housing needs of the region.[23]

3. If a municipality zones for industry and commerce for local tax benefit purposes, it must zone to permit adequate housing within the
   means of the employees involved in those uses.[24]
4. Provisions must be made for multifamily housing, small dwellings on
   very small lots, and areas where high density is permitted.[25]
5. There may be no bedroom or similar restrictions on multifamily
   housing, no artificial and unjustifiable minimum lot or building size
   requirements, and no fiscal zoning.[26]

The court found these new criteria to be required by an interpretation
of the concept of "promotion of the general welfare."[27] The court determined that "adequate housing of all categories of people is certainly an
absolute essential in promotion of the general welfare."[28] It is interesting
and important to note that the requirement of "promotion of the general
welfare" considered by the court is not the requirement of the zoning
enabling legislation.[29] Instead of relying upon this clearly expressed
statutory requirement, the court based its decision upon "the basic state
constitutional requirements of substantive due process and equal protection of the laws."[30] [Emphasis added.] Unhappily, there is no express
provision for due process or equal protection of the laws in the New Jersey Constitution.[31] Thus, a judicial declaration that they are nevertheless
inherent in the provisions of Article I, paragraph 1 of the Constitution[32]
was required.

The *Mount Laurel* case would become a landmark decision if it did
nothing more than to create a new state constitutional requirement that
adequate housing is an essential ingredient of general welfare. The decision takes on even greater significance because of its holding, in a state
notorious for its staunch protection of home-rule prerogatives, that "general welfare" must be interpreted to include the *entire region* of which it
is a part. The court said: "[T]he general welfare which developing
municipalities like Mount Laurel must consider extends *beyond their
boundaries* and cannot be parochially confined to the claimed good of the
particular municipality."[33] [Emphasis added.]

Limited Application of the New Zoning Criteria

The judicial promulgation of a municipal obligation to provide for regional needs beyond municipal boundaries raises fundamental questions
about the proper role of the judiciary in matters involving legislative policy decisions. It is very likely that the New Jersey Supreme Court considered this problem when it decided that the newly created criteria for
zoning validity should not apply to all municipalities. As the Appellate
Division observed, "[T]hroughout the decision, the Supreme Court was
careful to limit application of the doctrines announced therein to the so-

called 'developing communities.' The fact that Justice Pashman found it necessary to issue a concurring opinion disagreeing with this restriction served to underscore the intentional and conscious decision of the Supreme Court to adhere to basic limitation (sic) expressly referred to throughout the carefully explored analysis of the problem presented."[34]

The New Jersey Supreme Court described expressly, and in some detail, the characteristics classifying a municipality as a "developing municipality," subject to the additional zoning requirements of the *Mount Laurel* decision:

> As already intimated, the issue here is not confined to Mount Laurel. The same question arises with respect to any number of other municipalities of sizable land area outside the central cities and older built-up suburbs of our North and South Jersey metropolitan areas (and surrounding some of the smaller cities outside those areas as well) which, like Mount Laurel, have substantially shed rural characteristics and have undergone great population increase since World War II, or are now in the process of doing so, but still are not completely developed and remain in the path of inevitable future residential, commercial and industrial demand and growth. Most such municipalities, *with but relatively insignificant variation in details*, present generally comparable physical situations, courses of municipal policies, practices, enactments and results and human, governmental and legal problems arising therefrom. It is in the context of communities now of this type or which become so in the future, rather than with central cities or older built-up suburbs or areas still rural and likely to continue to be for some time yet, that we deal with the question raised. [Emphasis added.][35]

Did the court intend to restrict the application of the decision to a limited number of municipalities with "relatively insignificant variation in details"? This remains to be determined by the multitude of decisions that will undoubtedly follow. But there is some doubt about this interpretation. Note that the last sentence of the above-quoted paragraph appears to establish three categories of municipalities:

1. Developing municipalities like Mount Laurel
2. Developed municipalities, such as central cities or older built-up suburbs
3. Areas still rural and likely to continue to be for some time yet

There appears to be an implication that only the first category of municipalities is covered by the decision and that the second and third categories are exempt. But the position of those communities that are not exactly like Mount Laurel but nevertheless do not fit squarely into the second and third categories is ambiguous. It would appear that the more difficult cases are going to involve a fourth category: municipalities that differ from Mount Laurel with more than relatively insignificant variation in details but are neither older, built-up areas nor rural communities. To determine whether a given municipality is a "developing municipality" or whether it fits into one of the other three categories, it will be necessary to examine certain of its characteristics and compare them with Mount Laurel.

Characteristics of a Developing Municipality

SIZABLE LAND AREA

A developing municipality is one that has "sizable land area."[36] Thus, it will be necessary to determine whether the land area of the municipality in issue is, in fact, "sizable." The determination of what is sizable is a comparative judgment that should be made only after an analysis of the land area of the 567 municipalities in the state. The land area of municipalities ranges from tiny Shrewsbury Township with only .09 square miles to Hamilton Township with over 113 square miles. The median size of municipalities is 4.3 square miles. The average (arithmetical mean) size is 13.2 square miles.

The New Jersey Supreme Court has determined that Mount Laurel's 22 square miles is sizable.[37] In *Segal Construction Company v. Borough of Wenonah*,[38] the Appellate Division held that the Borough of Wenonah, with only one square mile, does not have a "sizable land area."[39] In *Wilann Associates v. Borough of Rockleigh*,[40] the Appellate Division held that the Borough of Rockleigh, with 1.0 square mile, was not a developing municipality within the meaning of the *Mount Laurel* decision.[41] In *Pascack Association, Ltd. v. Township of Washington*,[42] the Appellate Division noted that the *Mount Laurel* decision is limited to "developing municipalities" with sizable land area and determined it was inapplicable to the Township of Washington (Bergen County) with its 2.87 square miles, which it characterized as a "small, almost completely developed municipality."[43]

Thus, it now seems clear that a municipality with 22 square miles or more is "sizable"; one with 2.87 square miles or less is not "sizable." It would not be unreasonable to argue that a municipality with land area substantially under the average of 13.2 square miles and certainly one with less than the median of 4.3 square miles is not sizable. As the land area of a municipality approaches the arithmetical mean in size, it becomes susceptible to a characterization of having "sizable land area."

LOCATION OUTSIDE CENTRAL CITY AND OLDER BUILT-UP SUBURBS

A developing municipality is one that is outside the central city and older built-up suburbs.[44] There are a number of possible reasons why the supreme court adopted this characteristic as a standard. In the first place, it seems clear that the court intended to exempt the central city and older built-up suburbs from additional responsibilities to provide for the housing needs of the region. Thus, the new standard of zoning validity applies only to the newer and more recently developed or developing municipalities. This result is consistent with the underlying purpose of the decision: to open up the suburbs to migration by low- and moderate-income families currently trapped within the central cities and older suburbs. Additional housing facilities within the central cities would help meet the housing needs of the region but would not help to achieve the court's other purpose of fostering economic and racial integration within the state.

Another possible reason for the court's adoption of this standard might be its intention to define "outside" the central city to mean "adjoining" or "in close proximity to" the central city. This interpretation would be consistent with the other criteria that tend to include municipalities located within concentric rings of growth around and having a symbiotic relationship with, older areas. This interpretation would, at the same time, exclude municipalities that are at a substantial distance away from the central cities and are less dependent upon the resources and consequently less responsible for the needs of the central city. The difficult question, not answered in the decision, is the standard for determining whether a given municipality is "in close proximity to" or at a substantial distance away from the central cities. The court directed attention to the fact that Mount Laurel is approximately 10 miles from Philadelphia and Camden.[45] This distance would therefore be included within the meaning of "outside" the central city. How far this distance may be extended is unclear.

LOSS OF RURAL CHARACTERISTICS

The criteria for determining when a given municipality has "shed its rural characteristics" is somewhat subjective. Nevertheless, it is possible to conclude that a formerly rural community has changed when there is a significant change in population density and use of land. In a recent report by the Regional Plan Association, it was observed that at about 100 persons per square mile, the rural feeling begins to change to urban.[46] A population of approximately 2,090 to 4,000 persons per square mile is a typical density for a suburban area.[47]

The standards for comparison of the proportions of various land uses for a rural area are less precise. A typical rural community has predominately agricultural or undeveloped land use with a minimal commercial use and little or no industrial use. A municipality begins to shed its rural characteristics when it zones substantial amounts of its area for commercial and industrial uses and a significant proportion of that land is in fact used for those purposes. The growth of the Township of Mount Laurel illustrates this process. In 1950, Mount Laurel was primarily rural and agricultural and had no sizable commercial or industrial development. Its population of 2,817 people in 22 square miles gave it a population density of under 130 people per square mile. By 1970, its population density had grown to over 500 people per square mile.

During this same period, 29.2 percent of the land in the jurisdiction (4,121 acres) was zoned for industrial uses and about 100 acres were, in fact, used for industrial purposes.[48] The rest of the land so zoned (approximately 4,000 acres) remained undeveloped. There was testimony at the trial that if the land zoned for industrial use were, in fact, utilized for industrial purposes about 43,500 industrial jobs would be created.[49] The court noted that it is a typical municipal practice to zone much more land for industrial purposes than is warranted by reasonable projections of need for such purposes.[50] However, once zoned for industrial use the land would tend to be withheld from residential development.

Thus, the proportion of the total amount of municipal land zoned for industrial use and the actual number of acres so used are significant for a number of reasons:

1. Both factors provide evidence of the extent to which the municipality has begun to "shed its rural characteristics." A rural community will have little, if any, land zoned or actually used for industrial purposes.
2. The designation of a large amount of area for industrial purposes raises a suspicion that the municipality is under pressure for residential development and is trying to avoid its regional obligations by zoning an unrealistically large amount of its land for industrial purposes. This is the kind of municipality the court had in mind when it created the category of "developing municipalities like Mount Laurel."
3. To the extent that industrial jobs are in fact created, a need arises to house the employees who work within the municipality.
4. To the extent that industrial ratables are created, the municipality receives a benefit in the form of revenue that is available to help pay for the municipal services required by additional housing facilities.

The amount of land zoned for retail business purposes is a similar, albeit less significant, index of the extent to which a community has shed its rural characteristics. In Mount Laurel approximately 1.2 percent of the land was zoned for such use.[51] Although the percentage of total land area is small, most of that amount, approximately 169 acres, was, in fact, used for retail purposes in a handful of neighborhood commercial districts and along the turnpike interchange.[52] Mount Laurel does not have a major shopping center or concentrated retail commercial area, i.e., "downtown." The retail business uses are distributed among a number of neighborhood shopping areas. This characteristic is more typical of a sub-urban than a rural community where the population density is usually insufficient to support more than one local village shopping area.

GREAT POPULATION INCREASES SINCE WORLD WAR II

A developing municipality will have had great increases in population in the three decades since 1940. The court noted the following increases in the population of Mount Laurel in the period from 1940 to 1970:

    1940—Population of 2,200
    1950—Population of 2,817
    1960—Population of 5,249
    1970—Population of 11,221

It directed attention to the fact that the population of Mount Laurel al-most doubled in the decade between 1950 and 1960 and doubled again in the next ten years.[53]

Although there was no explicit discussion in the court's opinion of the significance of an analysis of population figures during a thirty-year period, it is very likely that these statistics were intended to provide a basis for distinguishing three categories of municipalities:

Developing municipalities. The population thirty years ago will have been relatively small. During this period, the proportionate increases will have been significant and the incremental trend will continue up to the time of analysis, providing evidence for a projection of continuing growth and development of the municipality.

Predeveloping municipalities. The population thirty years ago will have been relatively small. During this period, there will have been relatively insignificant increases in population indicating that the municipality re-mains relatively small and undeveloped, and has a population growth that is not significant enough to use as a basis for projecting future population increases.

Postdeveloping municipalities. The population during the thirty-year period may or may not indicate significant growth but recent population counts indicate a slowing or a termination of the previous growth. This category could include both those municipalities that had substantial population thirty years ago that have not grown very much since that time and also those communities that have grown substantially during the thirty-year period but have since reached a peak and are no longer in a period of growth or development.

It seems clear that the New Jersey Supreme Court considers changes in population during the past thirty years to be a significant factor in determining whether a given municipality is a "developing municipality."[54] The population growth figures of many municipalities will undoubtedly be similar to those of Mount Laurel up to the 1970 census. But we can expect litigation regarding the period *after* 1970 and particularly after 1973, when there was a significant decrease in housing starts in the nation in general and a dramatic decrease in new housing construction in the suburbs in particular. This data is subject to conflicting interpretation: On one hand, it may be argued that the dramatic decrease in population growth is evidence that the municipality has reached its saturation point and that therefore it is no longer "developing." But it may also be argued that the decreased rate of growth is itself evidence of the exclusionary zoning practices that the *Mount Laurel* decision is intended to eliminate, and that if those exclusionary zoning obstacles were removed, the municipality would continue to develop.[55] When faced with these opposing arguments, a court would be wise to avoid becoming entangled in the maze of contradictory expert testimony that can be produced, based upon alternative theories of population projection methods,[56] to support either theory. If population statistics do not indicate a clear and unambiguous trend, the other factors here discussed should be used to determine whether a municipality is "developing" within the meaning of the *Mount Laurel* decision.

INCOMPLETE DEVELOPMENT

A "developing municipality" is one that is not completely developed. In *Mount Laurel*, 65 percent of the township was still vacant land or in agricultural use.[57] On the other hand, in the *Demarest* case[58] where only 2.5 percent of the land area of the municipality (33.6 acres) was undeveloped, the Appellate Division held that it was not a "developing municipality" within the meaning of the *Mount Laurel* decision.[59] In the *Washington Township* case, the Appellate Division held that where only 3 percent of the township (approximately 106 acres) was "readily and quickly available for development," the *Mount Laurel* decision was inapplicable.[60] In the *Cinnaminson* case, the trial court found that the municipality is "substantially developed" although 17.8 percent of the land (after subtracting flood prone land) is undeveloped.[61]

In determining whether a municipality is "completely developed," it will be necessary to examine both the *amount* of land undeveloped and the *nature* of that land.[62] The amount of undeveloped land is significant in terms of both its relative size, i.e., its proportion of all of the land in the municipality (and possibly in the region) and its actual size, i.e., the number of acres involved. Judicial decisions have held that where the proportion of undeveloped land approaches 65 percent, the municipality is "not completely developed."[63] Where the proportion is closer to 3 percent, the municipality is "completely developed."[64] The difficult cases will involve proportions between those figures. The proportion of remaining undeveloped land is significant because where the municipality is almost completely developed, the imposition of high-density development on a remaining small proportion of land could result in disproportionate population increases in a relatively brief period of time.[65] Also, the actual number of acres of undeveloped land may be significant. A court might select a given density per acre and use the chosen figure to compute the number of dwelling units that might be built on the undeveloped land to ameliorate the housing need of the region.[66]

However, the quantity of undeveloped land taken alone could provide a misleading index of whether the municipality has reached its limits of development. The Appellate Division, in the *Washington Township* case,[67] astutely identified this issue when it characterized the nature of the land to be considered as "readily and quickly available for development."[68] This observation recognizes the common practice of builders and developers to utilize the most desirable land first and to leave the most difficult, troublesome, and expensive land in the municipality for last. This practice is especially significant, since the higher costs of developing the land left for last frequently prompt the developer to seek permission to develop at higher densities to generate sufficient income to recoup these costs. In some cases, a higher density may not be inappropriate for that land. In other cases, the very reasons why the land was left for last also make it entirely inappropriate for high-density development. It is thus necessary to examine the nature of the undeveloped land to determine why it was not readily available for development.

There are a number of reasons why some land remains undeveloped after most of the other land in the municipality has been developed:

Land assembly problems. The small size of individual parcels, multiplicity of ownership, limited feasibility of grouping because of distance or terrain, holdout or unreasonable sellers, and similar problems frequently make it impractical or costly to assemble sufficient land to interest a developer or builder of size. This land usually becomes available in bits and pieces and lends itself to individual, custom-built development at a later date.

Agricultural use. In many municipalities, a varying proportion of vacant land may be devoted to the production for sale of agricultural products. The *Mount Laurel* decision failed to distinguish between land seriously committed to agricultural use and land on which agricultural activities are a temporary holding operation pending eventual development. The court characterized 65 percent of Mount Laurel Township as "still vacant or in agricultural use." [69]

This judicial failure to differentiate between vacant and agricultural land assumes that land used for agricultural purposes is always readily available for housing and other development. Although this assumption may be realistic in many municipalities, it is contrary to the public policy established in a state constitutional amendment, [70] the Farmland Assessment Act of 1964 [71] and numerous other state programs designed to protect and preserve agricultural activites within the state. [72] Whether a given parcel of agricultural land is or is not readily available for development is a question of fact upon which evidence should be introduced at the trial.

Large private estates. A significant amount of land in a municipality may be included in one or more large privately owned estates. Frequently, such estates include one or more houses and a disproportionate amount of adjoining land is an amount in excess of the direct needs of the structures. As the municipality develops, economic and other forces increase the likelihood that all or a part of the land in the estate will become available for development. Obviously, the extent of the financial pressures, the willingness and ability of the owner to preserve the estate, and other factors will vary in each case, and the availability of the land for development will become a question of fact at a trial.

Public parks, playgrounds, and institutions. It could be argued that parks and other public land should not be included in the category of vacant or undeveloped land. This is particularly true in many cases where deed or other legal restrictions preclude development. However, the existence of a large expanse of undeveloped land in a municipality, frequently highlighted by colored maps and aerial photographs, requires examination and explanation. Evidence, if available, of governmental intention to discontinue existing uses would be relevant.

Country clubs, camps, colleges, and other quasi-public activities. Land owned by golf clubs, private institutions, religious and fraternal organizations, and other quasi-public entities is frequently withheld from development for indeterminate periods of time. Whether any such parcel is readily available for development is a question of fact.

Proximity to water, sewer, and other utilities. In areas where wells and septic tanks are not feasible, development may depend upon the availability of water, sewer, and other utilities. It is not unusual to find an area in a municipality that remains undeveloped for a period while awaiting the construction of these improvements. Whether or not such land is readily available for development will depend upon evidence relating to the timing of projected capital improvements and the feasibility of development without such improvements.

Soil, topography, and drainage. Steep slope, poor drainage, or diabase or other hardrock subsoil condition are among the most common ecological reasons for leaving land undeveloped. The reluctance to develop is usually not motivated by a concern for ecological degradation, but rather by the high cost of overcoming the environmental constraints. The cost of filling wetlands or other poorly drained areas, the cost of excavating hardrock subsoils, or the cost of overcoming the construction, drainage, and access problems of steep slopes makes such land relatively unmarketable in the absence of some special economic incentive. Such an advantage may become available in the form of cluster zoning provisions that permit relatively unsuitable land to be included in the calculation of site size for higher-density development in anothe part of the construction site.[73] Such an advantage may become available in the form of higher-density development permitted by zoning amendment or variance. In either case, it is questionable whether such land should be considered to be readily available for development for the purposes of determining whether a municipality is "not completely developed" within the meaning of the *Mount Laurel* decision.

LOCATION IN THE PATH OF INEVITABLE FUTURE GROWTH

A developing municipality is one that is in the path of inevitable future residential, commercial, and industrial demand and growth. The court described Mount Laurel as situated in "a most strategic location from the standpoint of transport of goods and people by truck and private car . . . "[74] The court pointed out the proximity of Mount Laurel to the New Jersey Turnpike, Interstate 295, Routes 73, 38, and 70, and U.S. 130.[75] It directed attention to the fact that industrial districts comprise most of the land on both sides of the Turnpike and Routes I-295, 73, and 38.[76] This industrial zone includes over 4,000 acres or over 29 percent of all the land in the township.[77]

These facts tend to demonstrate a municipal awareness and acceptance of its destiny of inevitable industrial growth, from which there will emanate a demand for and growth of commercial and residential uses. It is at this point that the court cites the testimony that if the industrial districts were fully developed, approximately 43,500 additional jobs would be created.[78] The implication of this projection is that the municipality would have a need for, and an obligation to provide, sufficient housing to meet this demand.[79]

It was on the basis of this kind of reasoning that the Township of Holmdel was ordered to amend its zoning ordinance to provide for reasonable areas where 2,100 units of low- and middle-income housing could be built.[80] The trial judge based this decision on the testimony of the plaintiff's planning expert that Holmdel has 7 percent of the jobs in the county and that there is a need for 30,000 moderate- and low-priced housing units in the county.[81]

However, this analysis cuts both ways. The same reasoning provided part of the basis for the Appellate Division holding that the Township of Washington is not a developing municipality because Washington Township has no industry and little commerce whereas other communities in the region have both.[82] The other reasons for this conclusion were that Washington Township is almost completely developed and that the proposed multifamily development would increase the Township's population by a proportion that was more than its fair share of the housing need of the region.[83]

LOCAL GOVERNMENT A "MUNICIPALITY" IN THE SAME SENSE AS MOUNT LAUREL

There are no unincorporated areas in the state of New Jersey. All of the area within the state is allocated to 567 municipalities. Many of these local governments are municipalities in law but are *not* independent, self-sustaining local governments in fact. Some municipalities may be more accurately described as neighborhoods of adjoining communities of which they are a part. Such neighborhood local governments may be recognized by their lack of a shopping area; minimal expenditures for municipal services; reliance upon other municipalities for water, sewer, education, fire, police, or other facilities or services; and relative lack of industrial ratables and employment opportunities. It is not unusual for such neighborhood local governments to join with other municipalities in an arrangement by which duplication and overcapacity may be avoided by each providing "regional" facilities to be used by other governments in the area.

This characteristic is significant because such a local government, unlike the more independent and self-sustaining Mount Laurel, may not have the ability to fulfill the obligations imposed upon "developing municipalities" by the state supreme court.

The wide disparity in the range of municipal services within the state may be illustrated by comparing the municipal expenditures and revenue of Mount Laurel with those of the Borough of Rockleigh. The total expenditures for municipal functions (excluding public education) in 1973 for Mount Laurel was $1,383,333.42,[84] compared with only $86,611.00 for Rockleigh.[85] Included in these totals, Mount Laurel spent $448,171 for public safety, including fire, police, civil defense, and environmental inspection and control, while Rockleigh spent only $14,200; Mount Laurel spent $444,139 for public works, including streets, drainage, sewers, garbage disposal, etc., while Rockleigh spent only $36,351. To pay for these services Mount Laurel realized a total revenue (from all sources) of $6,537,157, while Rockleigh's total revenue was only $251,330.[86] These statistics tend to illustrate the fact that some municipalities have insufficient municipal services, facilities, and resources to assume the obligations of a "developing municipality." The Appellate Division expressed this thought in the *Rockleigh* decision[87] when it said that where the municipality is small, substantially developed with only rudimentary utility and transportation facilities and none for public education, "constitutional considerations do not require the creation or enlarging of existing public services to accommodate the relatively small number of persons who could be housed in judicially mandated multifamily units on the few remaining acres available for that kind of development. . . . "[88]

Unanswered Questions

The *Mount Laurel* decision imposes significant legal consequences upon a determination that a given municipality is a "developing municipality."[89] For this reason, the court set forth, in as much detail as appropriate for a judicial instrument, those characteristics that define "developing municipality." However, the form and style of a judicial opinion does not lend itself to the task of detailed, extensive, and precise definition that is common in legislative instruments. As a result, there are a number of ambiguities and unresolved issues raised by the judicial definition of "developing municipality."

What Is a "Sizable Land Area"?

The 567 municipalities in New Jersey range in size from .09 square miles to 113 square miles. Mount Laurel is 22 square miles. How much smaller than 22 square miles may a municipality be and still be characterized as having a "sizable land area"? A legislative definition that would prescribe the minimum and maximum range is needed to preclude the necessity for a series of judicial determinations of this issue.

Is the Distance from a Central City Relevant? If So, How Far Away May It Be?

A "developing municipality" is "outside" a central city.[90] Is the use of the word "outside" intended to indicate a *proximity to* the central city, or is it intended only to *exclude* central cities from the obligations of developing municipalities?[91]

How Old or Built-up Does a Suburb Have To Be To Be Excluded from the Definition?

Older suburban municipalities vary in age from barely old to very old and from barely built-up to very built-up. At what point does a relatively older built-up municipality escape the requirements of the *Mount Laurel* decision?

At What Point in Its Development Has a Municipality Shed Its Rural Characteristics?

Is population density the primary characteristic to be used? Is 100 persons per square mile the definitive criterion? Is a municipality with 200 persons per square mile no longer rural? What proportion of industrial and/or commercial land uses are possible without losing rural characteristics? Is partial residential development necessarily inconsistent with a rural character?

What Constitutes Great Population Increases Since World War II?

How much less than a doubling of population in the decade of the 1950s and again in the decade of the 1960s will qualify as a "great population increase"? To what extent is it significant that the base population is appreciably higher or lower than the population in Mount Laurel in the comparative decades? Is it possible to have a great population increase based upon actual numbers of people, rather than proportionate increases? What evidence is necessary to prove the allegation that a municipality has become substantially or fully developed and is beyond the stage of "developing"?[92]

Under What Circumstances Is a Municipality Not Completely Developed?

How much less than 65 percent of the land may be vacant or in agricultural use before the municipality is considered to be completely developed? Suppose the percentage of undeveloped land is not large, but the actual amount of undeveloped acreage is substantial? Suppose 70 percent of the land is undeveloped but most of that is made up of wetlands, floodplains, and steep slopes? Suppose the major portion of the vacant land is comprised of a number of successful farming operations or a large estate of a prominent wealthy family? To what extent will factors relating to the ready availability for development be considered?

WHAT FACTORS WILL BE USED TO DETERMINE THE INEVITABLE FUTURE RESIDENTIAL, COMMERCIAL, AND INDUSTRIAL DEMAND AND GROWTH?

Is all land within the boundaries of the Bos-Wash growth corridor inevitably subject to future demand and growth? If nearby surrounding areas have already experienced intensive industrial and commercial growth does this fact preclude or confirm the inevitability of similar growth in undeveloped areas? To what extent does a high percentage of land zoned for industrial or commercial uses confirm, or a low percentage of land zoned for this purpose deny, the inevitability of future demand and growth? Is this factor to be used as a device to assign housing obligations to municipalities with substantial ratables?

TO WHAT EXTENT SHOULD PLANNING ISSUES RELATING TO THE REASONABLENESS OF THE ZONING RESTRICTIONS AFFECT THE DETERMINATION OF "DEVELOPING MUNICIPALITY"?

Is the impact of the proposed development upon the ability of the municipality to provide essential services and facilities relevant to the question of whether the municipality is a "developing municipality"?[93] Is it possible for a jurisdiction to be a "developing municipality" within the judicial definition but nevertheless be inappropriate for intensive multifamily development from a planning or public policy perspective? Should the decision be influenced by possible harmful consequences of the proposed development upon local or regional traffic, downstream flooding from storm runoff, insufficient water, sewer, educational, or other municipal facilities?[94] Is there any room for consideration of *optimum* municipal size, as well as a potential for additional growth and development? Is there any judicial obligation to preserve and protect any proportion of the attractive, stable, albeit homogeneous, communities in the state?

Conclusion

It seems clear that *Mount Laurel* will become a landmark decision because of the judicially created requirement that a valid zoning ordinance must provide for regional housing needs. Most planners would probably support this judically imposed planning constraint.

However, this is only one side of the equation. What is needed to balance this decision is an equally forceful judicial expression of the importance of another planning constraint, i.e., the *suitability* of each municipality to accommodate the required housing units. Only after the New Jersey Supreme Court responds to this other half of its challenge will it become possible to translate the insight and idealism of the *Mount Laurel* decision into feasible programs of balanced community growth. The recent order by the court for reargument in *Oakwood at Madison v. Township of Madison* [95] to consider a list of eighteen questions posed by the court, indicates a possibility that the New Jersey Supreme Court may address this other half of the problem in the *Oakwood at Madison* decision.

NOTES

1. 67 N.J. 151, 336 A.2d 713 (1975).
2. *See:* 67 N.J. at 189, 336 A.2d at 733-734 n. 22, where the court reiterated its contention that dealing with zoning problems on the basis of territorial limits of a municipality was unrealistic. Cf. *Duffcon Concrete Prod., Inc. v. Cresskill,* 1 N.J. 509, 64 A.2d 347 (1949).

   For a discussion of some of the problems created by the concept of region, see Rose, "Exclusionary Zoning and Managed Growth; Some Unresolved Issues," 6 Rutgers Camden L.J. 689 (1975).
3. This limitation in the application of the *Mt. Laurel* criteria is demonstrated by the fact that Justice Hall used the phrases "developing municipality like Mount Laurel," "such municipalities," and the like, a total of fifteen times. See 67 N.J. at 160, 173, 174, 179, 180, 185, 186, 187, 188, 190, 191, 336 A.2d at 717, 724, 727, 728, 731, 733.

   See also the concurring opinion of Justice Pashman, who expressed the view that the principles enumerated in the majority opinion should not be limited to the particular facts of the *Mt. Laurel* case. 67 N.J. at 194, 336 A.2d at 735. Justice Pashman, in voicing his dissatisfaction with the restrictive approach taken by the majority, stated:

   > The majority has chosen not to . . . consider the degree to which the principles applicable to developing municipalities are also applicable to rural ones and to largely developed ones . . . Exclusionary zoning is a problem of such magnitude and depth as to require that the Court extend these principles to all municipalities in the State. . . .

   Id. at 208, 336 A.2d at 743.
4. *See:* e.g., *Roselle v. Wright,* 21 N.J. 400, 409, 410, 122 A.2d 506, 510, 511 (1956) (exclusion of storage garages from a business zone held not to come within the enabling statute); see also *Katobimar Realty Co. v. Webster,* 20 N.J. 114, 122, 123, 118 A.2d 824, 828 (1955): Schmidt v. Newark, Bd. of Adj., 9 N.J. 405, 88 A.2d 607 (1952).

5. *See:* N.J. Stat. Ann. § 40:55-30 (1948), general purposes and powers, which sets forth the extent and scope of the municipality's power to regulate, restrict, and exclude.
6. *See:* e.g., *Duffcon Concrete Prod., Inc. v. Cresskill,* note 2 *supra*; cf. Jenpet Realty Co. v. J.B. Ardlin Inc., 112 N.J. Super. 79, 270 A.2d 413 (App. Div. 1970), prohibition of residential use in an industrial district held valid.
7. *See:* e.g., *Harrison R. Van Duyne, Inc. v. Senior,* 105 N.J.L. 257, 143 A. 437 (Sup. Ct. 1928); cf. Brookdale Homes v. Johnson. 123 N.J.L. 602, 10 A.2d 477, *aff'd* 126 N.J.L. 516, 19 A.2d 868 (Sup. Ct. 1940), where the court limited the power to restrict building heights so as to not arbitrarily deprive a person of the use of his property. See also N.J. Stat. Ann. § 40:55-30 (1948), which specifically enumerates:
    > The authority conferred . . . shall include the right to regulate and restrict the height, number of stories, and sizes of buildings . . .
8. *See:* e.g., *Fischer v. Bedminster,* 11 N.J. 165, 89 A.2d 378 (1952), where the court upheld a 5-acre minimum zoning requirement; cl. *Kirsch Holding Co. v. Manasquan,* 59 N.J. 241, 281 A.2d 513 (1971); *J.D. Constr. Corp. v. Freehold Bd. of Adj.,* 119 N.J. Super. 140, 290 A.2d 452 (L. Div. 1972); *Molino v. Mayor & Council of Glassboro.* 116 N.J. Super. 195, 281 A.2d 401 (L. Div. 1971).
9. *See:* e.g., *Lionshead Lake v. Wayne,* 10 N.J. 165, 89 A.2d 693 (1952), where the court upheld minimum building sites, thus controlling the density of the community, preserving property values, and promoting the general welfare.
10. *See: Euclid v. Ambler Realty,* 272 U.S. 365 (1926), where the Supreme Court stated that zoning regulations "find their justification in some aspect of the police power, asserted for the public welfare." See also Schmidt v. Newark Bd. of Adj., note 4 *supra*; *Collins v. Margate City Bd. of Adj.,* 3 N.J. 200, 69 A.2d 708 (1949).
    Cf. *Belle Terre v. Boraas,* 416 U.S. 1 (1974), where the Supreme Court (Douglas, J.) said:
    > The police power is not confined to the elimination of filth, stench, and unhealthy places. It is ample to lay out zones where family values, youth values, and the blessings of quiet seclusion, and clean air make the area a sanctuary for people.
11. *See:* e.g., *Kirsch Holding Co. v. Manasquan,* note 8 *supra*, at 251, 281 A.2d 513, 518 (1971), which indicated that an otherwise valid zoning ordinance cannot stand if it is unreasonable, arbitrary, or capricious.
12. *See: Cobble Close Farm v. Middletown Bd. of Adj.,* 10 N.J. 442, 92 A.2d 4 (1952), where the court held that requiring a particular owner to confine the use of his buildings in one particular zone to those uses permitted by the zoning ordinance was not unreasonable or arbitrary, where the buildings could reasonably be devoted to permissible uses.
    But see *AMG Associates v. Springfield,* 65 N.J. 101, 319 A.2d 705 (1974), where the court stated that zoning property into idleness by restraint against all reasonable use was invalid as confiscatory and amounted to a taking without just compensation.
13. *See:* e.g., *Schmidt v. Newark Bd. of Adj.,* note 4 *supra*; *Rhonda Realty Corp. v. Lawton et al.,* 414 Ill. 313, 111 N.E.2d 310 (1953).
14. *See: Schmidt v. Newark Bd. of Adj.,* note 4 *supra*, where the court addressed the issue of equal treatment. The court explained:
    > The statute provides for general, uniform, and comprehensive use zoning.

The local legislative body is restrained accordingly, apart from the constitutional guarantees against arbitrary interference with the basic right of private property. It is fundamental in the constitutional and statutory zoning process that all property similarly situated be treated alike. *Id.* at 421, 88 A.2d at 615.

See also *Rhonda Realty Corp. v. Lawton et al.*, note 13 *supra*.

15. *See:* e.g., *Hunter v. Erickson*, 393 U.S. 385 (1969), in which the Court stated that where a suspect classification was involved (in this case, race), the burden of justification was "far heavier" than other classifications.

16. *See:* e.g., *Hyland v. Mayor & Township Comm. of Morris*, 130 N.J. Super. 471, 327 A.2d 675 (App. Div. 1974), *aff'd* 66 N.J. 31, 327 A.2d 657 (1974): *Kirsch Holding Co. v. Manasquan*, note 8 *supra*.

It should be noted that the heavy burden of showing that there is no rational relationship to a legitimate governmental interest rests upon the individual challenging the ordinance. *Bogart v. Washington*, 25 N.J. 57, 135 A.2d 1 (1957). Cf. *Belle Terre v. Boraas*, note 10 *supra*, which held that restrictions on the number of unrelated or unmarried persons living together was a legitimate interest of the municipality.

17. *See:* e.g., *Loving v. Virginia*, 388 U.S. 1 (1967). Compare *Hunter v. Erickson*, note 15 *supra* (racial classifications are constitutionally "suspect" and therefore subject to the "most rigid scrutiny") with *Rodriguez v. San Antonio Ind. School Dist.*, 411 U.S. 1 (1973) (wealth held not to be a suspect classification in the area of school funding).

In *Rodriguez*, the court explained its conclusion as follows:

[W]e perceive no justification for such a severe denegretion of local property taxation and control as would follow from appellees' contentions. It has simply never been within the constitutional prerogative of this court to nullify statewide measures for financing public services *merely because the burdens or benefits thereof fall unevenly depending upon the relative wealth of the political subdivisions in which citizens live.* [Emphasis added.] *Id.* at 54.

But see *Serrano v. Priest*, 5 Cal. 3d 584, 487 P.2d 1241, 96 Cal. Rptr. 601 (1971); *Robinson v. Cahill*, 62 N.J. 473, 303 A.2d 273 (1973).

18. A state may not, for example, accord full appellate review of criminal convictions to some, while effectively denying it to others. *See,* e.g., *Draper v. Washington*, 372 U.S. 487 (1963); *Douglas v. California*, 372 U.S. 353 (1963); *Griffin v. Illinois*, 351 U.S. 12 (1956).

19. *See;* e.g., *James v. Valtierra*, 402 U.S. 137 (1971), where California's referendum approval requirement of low-rent public housing projects was held constitutionally sound. The implication of such a holding is that the right to adequate shelter (as long as the shelter can be denied by a vote of the people of the state) cannot be a fundamental right. *Lindsey v. Normet*, 405 U.S. 56 (1972).

20. The court in *Lindsey v. Normet*, *id.*, considered a constitutional challenge by tenants of housing which had been condemned as unfit for human habitation against the Oregon forcible entry and detainer statute, which provided summary eviction procedures upon nonpayment of rent and did not allow a defense of uninhabitability.

In rejecting the plaintiff's equal protection argument, the Court stated:

[W]e do not denegrate the importance of decent, safe, and sanitary housing. But the Constitution does not provide judicial remedies for every social and economic ill. We are unable to perceive in that document any constitutional guarantee of access to dwellings of a particular quality . . . Absent constitutional mandate, the assurance of adequate housing and the definition of landlord-tenant relationships are legislative, not judicial, functions. *Id.* at 74.

21. *See: e.g., Fanele v. Hasbrouck Hts.*, 26 N.J. 320, 139 A.2d 749 (1958); *Pierro v. Baxendale*, 20 N.J. 17, 118 A.2d 401 (1955); *Lionshead Lake v. Wayne*, 10 N.J. 165, 89 A.2d 693 (1952); *Fischer v. Bedminster*, 11 N.J. 194, 93 A.2d 378 (1952); *Flora Realty & Inv. Co. v. LaDue*, 362 Mo. 1025, 246 S.W.2d 771 (1952) (minimum lot size upheld); *DeMars v. Bolton Zoning Comm'n*, 19 Conn. Super. 24, 109 A.2d 876 (C.P. 1954); *Thompson v. Carrollton*, 211 S.W.2d 970 (Tex. Civ. App. 1948).

See also *Gautier v. Jupiter Is.*, 142 So. 2d 321 (Fla. App. 1962), where the court affirmed a judgment that dismissed a complaint of property owners who had attacked a zoning ordinance as arbitrary and unreasonable. The court pointed out that if the land was used as an apartment house or hotel, it would only be a matter of time until a series of alterations would result in a disintegration of the whole zoning plan. And see *Molmar Associates v. Board of County Comm'rs*, 260 Md. 292, 272 A.2d 6 (1971), where the court sustained the validity of a county zoning ordinance imposing a maximum percentage limitation upon the number of bedroom units allowable within the multifamily apartment buildings.

See generally Williams, 2 *American Planning Law: Land Use and the Police Power* § § 59-67 (1975). For a collection of selected cases from various jurisdictions, see Annot., 48 A.L.R.3d 1210 (1973).

22. 67 N.J. at 188-189, 336 A.2d at 732-733. Cf. Listokin, "Fair-Share Housing Distribution: Will It Open the Suburbs to Apartment Development?" 2 Real Estate L.J. 739 (1974), in which the author discusses the concept of fair-share housing and sets out a list of governmental institutional bodies which have either implemented or proposed fair-share plans. *Id.* at 740-741.

23. 67 N.J. at 188, 336 A.2d at 732.

24. *Id.* at 187, 336 A.2d at 732.

25. *Id.*

26. *Id.*

27. 67 N.J. at 188-189, 336 A.2d at 727.

28. *Id.*

29. N.J. Stat. Ann. § 40:55-32 Compare the court's analysis with the concurring opinion of Justice Mountain, in which he indicated that in reaching the same conclusion as the majority, he would base his decision on the interpretation of "general welfare" as it appears in the zoning enabling legislation rather than the state constitution. 67 N.J. at 193, 336 A.2d at 735.

30. 67 N.J. at 174, 336 A.2d at 725.

31. The New Jersey Constitution provides:

> All persons are by their nature free and independent, and have certain natural and unalienable rights, among which are those of enjoying and defending life and liberty, of acquiring, possessing, and protecting property, and of pursuing and obtaining safety and happiness. N.J. Const. art. I § 1.

32. For an examination and discussion of why the protections afforded by the state constitution were invoked as the basis for the decision in *Mt. Laurel*, see

Rose, "The Mount Laurel Decision: Is It Based on Wishful Thinking?" 4 Real Estate N.J.61 (1975).

33. 67 N.J. at 179, 336 A.2d at 727-728. In so interpreting "general welfare," the court cited approvingly its prior holding in *Kunzler v. Hoffman*, 48 N.J. 277, 225 A.2d 321 (1966), which pointed out that general welfare "comprehends the benefits not merely within the municipal boundaries but also those to the regions of the state relevant to the public interest to be served." *Id.* at 288, 225 A.2d at 327.

34. *Pascack Association Ltd.* v. *Washington*, Dkt. No. A-3740-72 (App. Div., June 25, 1975). The Appellate Division went on to find that Washington Township was not a developing municipality within the meaning of the *Mt. Laurel* decision, thereby reversing the lower court determination that Washington Township had to provide a "balanced community." Unofficial slip opinion at 17.

35. 67 N.J. at 160, 336 A.2d at 717.

36. *Id.* at 160, 336 A.2d at 717.

37. *Southern Burlington County NAACP v. Mount Laurel*, note 1 *supra*.

38. 134 N.J. Super. 421, 341 A.2d 667 (App. Div. 1975).

39. *Id.* at 423, 341 A.2d at 668.

40. Dkt. No.A-3224-72 (App. Div., May 29, 1975).

41. *Id.*, unofficial slip opinion at 2.

42. Dkt. No. A-3790-72 (App. Div., June 25, 1975).

43. *Id.*, unofficial slip opinion at 17-18.

44. 67 N.J. at 160, 336 A.2d at 717.

45. *Id.* at 161, 336 A.2d at 718.

46. *See*: "Regional Plan Association Report," N.Y. Times, June 16, 1975, p. 17.

47. *Id.*

48. 67 N.J. at 162-163, 336 A.2d at 719.

49. *Id.* at 163, 336 A.2d at 718. Note that the court here has placed an affirmative duty to provide for housing in such a situation. The court stated:
    Certainly when a municipality zones for industry and commerce for local tax benefit purposes, it without question must zone to permit adequate housing within the means of the employees involved in such uses.
    Id. at 187, 336 A.2d at 732.

50. *Id.* at 163, 336 A.2d at 718. The court said in part:
    [A]s happens in the case of so many municipalities, much more land has been zoned than the reasonable potential for industrial movement or expansion warrants.

51. 67 N.J. at 163, 336 A.2d at 719.

52. *Id.* at 163, 336 A.2d at 719.

53. *Id.* at 161, 336 A.2d at 718.

54. For a detailed analysis of Mount Laurel's population rise and the problems arising therefrom, see 67 N.J. at 161-164, 336 A.2d at 718-719.

55. Cf. *Segal Constr. Co. v. Wenonah Zoning Bd. of Adj.*, 134 N.J. Super. 421, 341 A.2d 667 (App. Div. 1975), where the court compared the growth characteristics of the Borough of Wenonah to the relevant Mount Laurel figures. After determining that the population from 1960-1970 had increased only 13 percent, the claim of exclusionary zoning was rejected by the court. The court found that "the record does not support any conclusion that Wenonah has endeavored by its zoning to exclude the more modestly circumstanced." 134 N.J. Super, at 423, 341 A.2d at 668.

56. *See:* Greenberg, Krueckeberg, & Mautner, *Long-Range Population Projections for Minor Civil Divisions: Computer Programs and User's Manual* at 2 (1973); see generally, Krueckeberg & Silvers, *Urban Planning Analysis: Methods and Models* 259-287 (1974).
57. 67 N.J. at 162, 336 A.2d at 718.
58. *Fobe Associates* v. *Demarest*, Dkt. No. A-1965-73 (App. Div., July 2, 1975).
59. *Id.*, unofficial slip opinion at 4.
60. *Pascack Association, Ltd.* v. *Washington*, note 34 *supra*, unofficial slip opinion at 10.
61. *Camden Nat'l Realty* v. *Cinnaminson*, Dkt. No. L-37016-73 (L. Div. Burlington Co., July 8, 1975).
62. *See: e.g., Segal Constr. Co.* v. *Wenonah Zoning Bd. of Adj.*, note 55 *supra* where the court indicated that because of the small amount of land that remained available, Wenonah could not be characterized as developing within the meaning of the *Mt. Laurel* decision. *Id.* at 423, 341 A.2d at 668.
63. *See: Southern Burlington County NAACP* v. *Mt. Laurel.* note 1 *supra*.
64. *Fobe Associates* v. *Demarest*, note 58 *supra*.
65. *See: e.g., Pascack Association Ltd.* v. *Washington*, note 34 *supra*; cf. *Segal Constr. Co.* v. *Wenonah Zoning Bd. of Adj.*, note 55 *supra*.
66. *See: e.g., Pascack Ass'n, Ltd.* v *Washington*, 131 N.J. Super. 195, 329 A.2d 89 (L. Div. 1971).
67. *Pascack Association, Ltd.* v. *Washington.* note 34 *supra*.
68. *Id.*, unofficial slip opinion at 10.
69. 67 N.J. at 162, 336 A.2d at 718.
70. N.J. Const. art. VIII, § 1. The relevant section provides:
    (b) The legislature shall enact laws to provide that the value of land, not less than 5 acres in area, which is determined by the assessing officer of the taxing jurisdiction to be actively devoted to agricultural or horticultural use, and to have been so devoted for at least the 2 successive years immediately preceding the tax year in issue, shall, for local tax purposes on application of the owner, be that value for which such land has for agricultural or horticultural use.
71. N.J. Stat. Ann. § § 54:4-23.1 et seq. (1964). See also *Terhune* v. *Franklin*, 107 N.J. Super. 218, 258 A.2d 18 (App. Div. 1969), where the court said in relevant part:
    The basic legislative intent to be gathered from the statute, is that all lands devoted to agricultural or horticultural purposes, as defined therein, are to be subject to assessment at the new, lower standard.
    Id. at 221, 258 A.2d at 20.
72. E.g., *see Report of the Blueprint Commission on the Future of New Jersey Agriculture* (1973).
73. See generally Williams, note 21 *supra*, at 218-224.
74. 67 N.J. at 162, 336 A.2d at 718.
75. *Id.*
76. *Id.*
77. *Id.* at 162, 336 A.2d at 719.
78. *Id.* at 163, 336 A.2d at 719.
79. *Id.* at 187, 336 A.2d at 732. See also passage cited at note 49 *supra*.
80. *Middle Union Associates* v. *Holmdel*, Dkt. No. L-1149-72 (L. Div., May 15, 1975).
81. Id., unofficial slip opinion at 17.

82. *See Pascack Association, Ltd.* v. *Washington,* note 34 *supra,* where the court indicated:
    > Unlike other Pascack Valley communities, Washington Township's commercial zone is extremely limited and was clearly designed to serve only the local needs of its residents. . . .
    > It is in this context that we hold that the Township's zoning ordinance . . . is not invalid in failing to zone plaintiffs' tract for multifamily construction.

    Id., unofficial slip opinion at 19.
83. *Id.,* unofficial slip opinion at 19.
84. *See: 36th Annual Report of the Division of Local Government Services, 1973: Statements of Financial Condition of Counties and Municipalities* at 407.
85. *Id.* at 508.
86. Compare the expenditure data, *id.* at 407, 508.
87. Wilann Associates v. Rockleigh, note 40 *supra.*
88. *Id.,* unofficial slip opinion at 3-4.
89. See: e.g., 67 N.J. at 174, 336 A.2d at 724, where the court mandated that every such municipality *must,* by its land use regulations, presumptively make realistically possible an appropriate variety and choice of housing. . . . [I]t cannot foreclose the opportunity of the classes of people mentioned for low and moderate income housing and in its regulations must *affirmatively* afford that opportunity. . . . [Emphasis added.]
    See also 67 N.J. at 187, 336 A.2d at 732, where the court in a more detailed fashion declared that a developing municipality
    > . . . must permit multifamily housing, without bedroom or similar restrictions, as well as small dwellings on very small lots, low cost housing of other types and, in general, high density zoning, without artificial and unjustifiable minimum requirements as to lot size, building size and the like, to meet the full panoply of these needs. Certainly when a municipality zones for industry and commerce for local tax benefit purposes, it *without question must zone* to permit adequate housing within the means of the employees involved in such uses. [Emphasis added.]
90. See: 67 N.J. at 160, 336 A.2d at 717. In *Mount Laurel,* the court indicated the criteria for determining whether or not a given community is "developing." This passage, which is destined to be often cited in the *Mount Laurel* aftermath, provides the guidelines and factors which will be relevant to the eventual determination of whether the municipality in question will fall within the sweep of the mandates of the *Mount Laurel* decision.
91. At least one Appellate Division case has already confronted the issue of interpreting the meaning of the phrase "outside the central cities." In *Fobe Associates* v. *Demarest Mayor, Council, Bd. of Adj.,* note 58 *supra,* the court found the Borough of Demarest not to be a "developing municipality" within the meaning of *Mount Laurel.*
    The court said in relevant part:
    > Indeed the court [referring to the New Jersey Supreme Court in the *Mount Laurel* decision] limits its mandate to provide "the opportunity for an appropriate variety and choice of housing for all categories of people who may desire to live there," to developing municipalities (67 N.J. at page 187). *Excluded* are "the central cities and older built-up suburbs. . . . (67 N.J. at 160)." [Emphasis added.]

    Id., unofficial slip opinion at 4-5.

92. Compare, e.g., *Fobe Associates* v. *Demarest*, note 58 *supra*, with *Wilann Associates* v. *Rockleigh*, note 40 *supra*.
    In the former, the court relied on the fact that the community of Demarest was very small, with less than 3 percent of the land in the municipality available for development, and therefore was fully developed.
    In the latter, the court stated:
    > Rockleigh must be characterized as a tiny, substantially developed community of settled and long-standing character with only rudimentary utility and transportation facilities, and none for public education.

    Id., unofficial slip opinion at 3.
    In addition, in determining that Rockleigh was beyond the stage of developing, the court cited the facts of *Hankins* v. *Rockleigh*, 55 N.J. Super. 132, 133, 150 A.2d 63, 64 (App. Div. 1959), in order to show that "only nine houses have been built since 1959," which indicates that Rockleigh was not likely to develop further.
93. See: e.g., *Wilann Associates* v. *Rockleigh*, note 40 *supra*, where the court did, in fact, consider the ramifications of the proposed development on the municipality's ability to provide essential services.
    In so doing, the court alluded to the following factors:
    > Rockleigh boasts no public sewer system and soil conditions prevalent in the Borough require large acreage lots in order to properly break up and treat sewerage. There are no public schools in the Borough and the current road network in the Borough consists of four two-lane thoroughfares built on narrow rights of way. The residents of the Borough are not served by any form of mass transportation linking the community with major population and commercial centers.

    Id., unofficial slip opinion at 3.
94. *Id.*, see also note 40 *supra*.
95. *Oakwood at Madison, Inc.* v. *Madison*, 117 N.J. Super. 11, 283 A.2d 353 (L. Div. 1971), *on remand* 128 N.J. Super. 438, 320 A.2d 223 (L. Div. 1974), cert. granted 62 N.J. 185, 299 A.2d 720 (1972).

The Irrelevance of the
"Developing Municipality" Concept

Peter A. Buchsbaum

The Spring 1976 issue of the Real Estate Law Journal contained a lengthy article by Professors Jerome G. Rose and Melvin R. Levin on the meaning of the term "developing municipality" as used in *Southern Burlington County NAACP* v. *Tp. of Mount Laurel.*[1] The authors gave this term such great attention since, they asserted, exemption from the burdens of *Mount Laurel* would accrue to municipalities which fell into the "developed" pigeonhole.[2] The detailed analysis of the kinds of facts which would lead to one classification or another thus followed from the assumption that substantially different standards of review would be applied to zoning ordinances from "developing" as contrasted with "developed" communities.

This pivotal assumption is, by the case law, unsupported. The record of reported precedents[3] as opposed to the unreported cases improperly relied upon by Professors Rose and Levin. Although two reported lower court cases have applied the exemption, the basic legality of the "developing community" exemption is under attack in two cases currently pending before the Supreme Court.[4] The important issue concerns the very propriety of such an exemption and not its legal parameters. Legal commentary which treats the exemption as established law and merely attempts to flesh out its details must be regarded as premature. We should not be busy describing criteria that may not and ought not exist.

This observation is particularly necessary because the rationale for a "developing" municipality exemption from *Mount Laurel* is nonexistent. This is not dealt with at all by Rose and Levin. Both *Mount Laurel* and earlier decisions of the New Jersey Supreme Court make it abundantly clear that obstruction of housing opportunity will not be countenanced anywhere in New Jersey. The lower courts have thus made a basic mistake in regarding the "developing municipality" terminology in *Mount Laurel* as a license for economic discrimination.

Careful perusal of the *Mount Laurel* opinion itself rebuts the reading given to it by the Appellate Division and endorsed by Professors Rose and Levin.[5] There are two alternative readings which may be given to understand the inclusion of the developing municipality concept in the *Mount Laurel* holding. The court could simply have intended to leave determining responsibilities of developed communities to another day and a case which squarely presented this issue. On the other hand, the court could have intended a negative pregnant, that is, endorsement and preservation of the status quo in built-up communities. To borrow a phrase from another area of land law, the Court's phraseology could have been intended as mere words of description rather than words of limitation. To choose the proper alternative, resort should be had, as it was conspicuously not in *Wenonah* and *Closter*, to other sections of the *Mount Laurel* opinion and to other court opinions.

The *Mount Laurel* opinion essentially rests on three related principles. First, it confers on low- and moderate-income persons a state constitutional right to be presumptively protected from unreasonable land use ordinances which cause economic barriers to residency within a community.[6] Second, it shifts the burden of proof and requires municipalities to prove that their land use practices do not discourage and, indeed, affirmatively encourage, the construction of housing for low- and moderate-income persons.[7] Third, it adopts fair share of regional low- and moderate-income housing need as a measure of the extent of the municipal constitutional affirmative duty.[8] For the purpose of this discussion, the question thus becomes whether these three concepts inherently implicate all municipalities or whether they can really be limited to just one class of municipality.

The constitutional right to protection against barriers to housing derives from the "findings of an extreme, long term need in this state for decent low and moderate income housing" and the resulting "basic importance of housing and local regulations restricting its availability to substantial segments of the population."[9] These words, which create a constitutional right to equal opportunity, cannot sensibly be restricted along geographical lines. If shelter is of fundamental importance in Mount Laurel it cannot be of less importance in Washington, Demarest or Wenonah. If a housing crisis impacts Mount Laurel, it surely does not stop at the borders of nearby but more developed communities. And if the Court is telling the poor that they have a right to be free from economic discrimination in one community, it cannot in good conscience, be telling them that they may be excluded elsewhere. Thus, the first key ingredient of *Mount Laurel*, its constitutional element, cannot be squared with the geographically narrow interpretation supported by the Appellate Division and the Rose-Levin article.

The second thrust of the opinion, its imposition of negative and affirmative obligations on communities, also has an inherently broader sweep.[10] To be sure, judicial curtailment of large lot zoning, for example, may not be particularly significant in communities with little vacant land. Yet built-up communities usually have some land available for use or re-use and the ability of our less advantaged citizens to gain access to this land can be inhibited by multifamily exclusions or restrictions. This is in fact the case in the *Washington Township* appeal. Further, all communities can undertake affirmative steps suggested by *Mount Laurel* to provide decent low- and moderate-income housing in their developed areas. It is ironic that the very class of communities which is proposed for exemption from *Mount Laurel* is the class which has most frequently taken these affirmative steps, such as establishment of a housing authority,[11] passage of a resolution of need for New Jersey Housing Finance Agency assistance,[12] or participation in the several programs established under the federal Housing and Community Development Act of 1974.[13] Clearly, therefore, developed communities which are impacted by the housing crisis and could provide shelter to low and moderate income citizens are capable of responding to the needs of such citizens even though the response may differ somewhat from those "developing" communities. For this reason, the negative and affirmative obligations imposed by *Mount Laurel* are as applicable to built-up communities as to those with substantial vacant land.

The third basic *Mount Laurel* concept—fair share of regional needs as the measure of minimal duty—is also inherently inconsistent with any geographical restriction on the scope of that opinion. The Appellate Division holdings in *Wenonah* and *Closter* must be regarded as a finding that the fair share of those communities is zero, that since these communities cannot contribute much, they need contribute nothing. This result is simply inconsistent with the language of *Mount Laurel*, with the common understanding of the concept of "fair share," and with common sense.

The brief description of fair share in *Mount Laurel* contains a number of factors in a fair share calculation which would impose some measurable obligation on developed communities.[14] These factors include the needs of present, or former, residents of substandard housing and present or potential in-commuting employees. Existing fair share plans such as those for Burlington, Camden, Gloucester, and Mercer counties all contain some allocation for the central cities in these counties as well as for the developing suburbs. To be sure, the approach taken to meeting fair share may be different in different types of communities, but this circumstance does not result in an exemption for built-up areas.[15]

The common sense of the situation follows the language cited above and the patterns that have been developed in actual fair share plans. As a matter of equity, can developed municipalities fairly be required to shoulder a burden for whose creation they are partially but not solely responsible? Take for example the case of Bergen County. According to its own estimates contained in its application for funds under the Housing and Community Development Act of 1974, it has an obligation to house over 11,000 families of employees who are currently working in, or expected to work in, the county, but do not now live there. This employment based figure represents one measure of need which is similar to one of the factors suggested for fair share under *Mount Laurel*. It thus may be regarded as a partial, but legitimate quantification of need under *Mount Laurel*. Juxtaposed against this 11,000 plus figure is the municipal concession during oral argument in the Supreme Court in *Demarest* and *Washington* that only one or two municipalities in Bergen County could be classified as developing within the strict confines of *Mount Laurel*. If this concession is accurate—and the spate of decisions from Bergen County exempting municipalities appears to bear out its accuracy—then the entire burden of satisfying Bergen County's fair share of low- and moderate-income housing need will be imposed on only one or two municipalities. Such a result is both unjust and absurd. It is unjust because these one or two municipalities do not, by themselves, create the housing shortage in Bergen County. It is absurd because, together, the other sixty-nine, mostly small, municipalities in Bergen County have far more resources to deal with the housing shortage than do the supposedly non-exempt ones. These sixty-nine communities cumulatively contain a significant supply of land which is closer to major services and employment centers than those in the reportedly non-exempt communities. They have developed an infrastructure of sewers, schools, roads, etc., which makes their land more available for high density development, than sites in outlying suburbs might be. The Appellate Division has emphasized the unfairness of imposing large new burdens on relatively small residential communities. It has never even asked the question as to the fairness of imposing new infrastructure burdens solely on developing communities, or whether it is more efficient to use existing infrastructures which might only need limited expansion, rather than requiring developing municipalities to construct completely new infrastructures. To put the matter more concretely, what sense is there in requiring *Mount Laurel* to construct new sewers for the benefit of an apartment project when Washington Township already has the sewers available?

This discussion of fair share, like the discussions of equal opportunity and municipal obligation, leads to one conclusion: the use of the term "developing municipality" in *Mount Laurel* must be regarded as a prudent determination to deal with the kind of community the Court had before it and to delay until a later time an explicit statement as to the obligations of other kinds of communities. The developing municipality phraseology cannot be read as justification for allowing certain built-up areas to maintain exclusionary practices and to provide an exemption from the obligation imposed explicitly on *Mount Laurel* and like towns to be "better communities for all than they presently have been." [16] The powerful concept of equality as rooted in *Mount Laurel* cannot be so fragile as to be halted at the edge of a single-family residential suburb.

These conclusions find support not only in the *Mount Laurel* precedent but in earlier cases of the Supreme Court to which resort may be had in order to place this landmark precedent in context. In particular, *DeSimone* v. *Greater Englewood Housing No. 1*, which sustained a variance for a subsidized project in the City of Englewood, contained an assertion that a denial of the variance could not have been sustained because of the need for housing in Englewood.[17] Thus, this highly developed city would not have been allowed by the Court to make a land use decision which ignored housing needs. It had an obligation to act to promote housing opportunity.

The case of *Sente* v. *Clifton*, which was dismissed as moot, also signals judicial unsympathy for land use barriers created by built-up communities.[18] At issue in that case was a minimum living space requirement which allegedly restricted the ability of the poor to occupy apartments in Clifton.

Clearly foreshadowing the *Mount Laurel* opinion, the Court advised that "regulations of this kind drastically affect the availability of housing", particularly, according to the record, the opportunity to find housing in Clifton.[19] Since the consequences of this ordinance could be so great in the "fundamental area of housing perhaps the municipality should be called upon to justify this particular enactment." [20]

The municipal burden of justification suggested by the Court, of course, mirrors the shift of burden of proof which was the core of the *Mount Laurel* technique for evaluating allegedly restrictive zoning ordinances.[21] The fact that Clifton is a "developed" municipality did not constrain the Court. The implication is that restrictive ordinances in substantially developed communities must be given the same judicial scrutiny as restrictive ordinances in communities which have a great deal of vacant developable land. The language in *Sente* can therefore be seen as reflecting the view that arbitrary barriers to housing opportunities must be viewed with greater judicial skepticism no matter where they are found.

Neither of these two cases have been discussed in any of the opinions or published commentary which has followed *Mount Laurel*. Yet these opinions demonstrate that small communities should not be fighting to define themselves out of *Mount Laurel*. All municipalities in the state will have to take cognizance of *Mount Laurel* and change their land use practices in compliance with that decision.

Suggested Standards

I would conclude this article with some brief commentary on the standards which should be applied to built-up communities. A few basic criteria can now be implied.

The touchstone of municipal obligation for a municipality with little vacant land will probably be a requirement that they do what they can "without grossly disturbing existing neighborhoods."[22] Such an obligation could include rezoning of particular parcels where appropriate, as suggested by Justice Pashman's concurrence in *Mount Laurel*, and the opinion of the Court in *DeSimone*. It might also include a blanket prohibition of certain kinds of restricted practices which had not been definitively outlawed prior to *Mount Laurel*. For example, bedroom restrictions in apartment complexes were treated by the Court as being "so clearly contrary to the general welfare" that it seems difficult to imagine the court sustaining such restrictions anywhere in the state.[23] Other occupancy restrictions like minimal living space requirements involved in *Sente v. Clifton Supra*, could meet a similar fate.[24]

Blanket prohibitions on non-occupancy restrictive practices might also be quite extensive. In granting dismissal to eleven Middlesex County municipalities which were sued as part of a county-wide zoning suit, Judge Furman set forth a number of restrictions which would have to be removed from their ordinances and which he presumably felt to be exclusionary regardless of whether the municipalities were technically "developing".[25] The zoning changes which municipalities agreed to include, in addition to removing bedroom criteria, included "deletion of special exception procedures for multi-family housing and provision for it as allowable use; reduction of excessive parking space requirements in multi-family housing; reduction of excessive minimum floor area requirements in multi-family or single-family housing or both; reduction of excessive minimum lot sizes for multi-family or single-family housing or both; increase of maximum density of multi-family housing to fifteen units per acre; increase of maximum height of multi-family housing to 2-½ stories or higher; deletion of a multi-family housing ceiling of 15 percent of total housing units within a municipality; rezoning from industry to multi-family residential and from single-family to multi-family residential." [26] The Supreme Court might well hold these provisions to be unreasonable as restricting a municipality's ability to do what it can.

Thus, while the established communities might not have to undertake rezoning of massive numbers of acres, as may be the case with communities with much open land, they will probably be required to take the basic steps enumerated above so that they bear their burden in meeting the housing crisis which afflicts so many of New Jersey citizens. As a result, New Jersey municipalities are ill-advised to pursue Professors Rose's and Levin's bright promise of exemption. Rather, they should, as indicated by *Mount Laurel,* seek advice as to appropriate measures which evidence a good faith effort to curtail economic barriers to housing opportunity. Pertinent legal commentary directed to such good faith compliance with the inevitable is the more useful and productive present task of legal scholars.

NOTES

1. 67 N.J. 151 (1975). *Cf.* 4 Real Estate L.J. 359 (1976).
2. Id. at 367-368.
3. Administrative Office of the Courts, *Manual on Style: Judicial Opinions* and *Standards for Publication: Judicial Opinion* (Approved by N.J. Supreme Court May 2, 1974) both flatly state that unreported opinions are not to be relied on as a precedent. *Manual on Style* at 3; *Standards for Publication* at 3. Therefore the reliance on numerous unreported cases as precedents governing the significance and extent of the "developing municipality" exemption is misplaced since no Court could rely on these cases.
4. *Pascack Assn. v. Tp. of Washington,* certif. granted, 69 N.J. (1975), and *Fobe Associates v. Mayor and Council of Demarest,* certif. granted, 69 N.J. 74 (1975). Compare *Segal Construction Co. v. Borough of Wenonah,* 134 N.J. Super. 421 (App. Div. 1975); *Nigito v. Borough of Closter,* ___ N.J. ___ (App. Div. 1976) (approved for publication 6 / 10 / 76).
5. 4 Real Estate L.J. at 359-360. In a subsequent article, "The Trickle Before the Deluge from Mount Laurel", 5 Real Estate L.J. 69, 72 (1975), Prof. Rose briefly acknowledges some question as to the underlying validity of the exemption, but the thrust of this article, like the earlier one, concerns the contours of the exemption and assumes its logic and viability.

6. 67 N.J. at 175.
7. 67 N.J. at 179-180.
8. 67 N.J. at 190.
9. 67 N.J. at 179.
10. 67 N.J. at 179-180.
11. *See:* 67 N.J. at 192.
12. N.J.S.A. 40:55J.
13. P.L. 93-383, 42 U.S.C.A. 5301, *et seq.*
14. 67 N.J. at 190.
15. The Camden County Plan, for example, requires only rehabilitation and re-placement in Camden City, while imposing an obligation for new construction of additional housing units in such communities as Cherry Hill.
16. 61 N.J. at 191.
17. 56 N.J. 428 (1970). *cf.* 56 N.J. at 443.
18. 66 N.J. 204 (1974).
19. 66 N.J. at 208.
20. *Id.*
21. 67 N.J. at 180-181.
22. 67 N.J. at 218. (Pashman, J., concurring).
23. 67 N.J. at 183.
24. See: *Kirsch Holding Co. v. Borough of Manasquan,* 59 N.J. 241 (1971).
25. *Urban League of Greater New Brunswick v. Mayor and Council of the Borough of Carteret.* N.J. Super (Ch. Div. 1976) (approved for publication May 9, 1976).
26. Slip opinion at 11-12.

On from *Mount Laurel:*
Guidelines on the
"Regional General Welfare"

Norman Williams, Jr. *

The mid-1970's is a time of major transition in American planning law. This transition can be briefly described as a movement away from that judicial deference to municipal autonomy and home rule which was the predominant note in the case law in most of the leading states during the 1950's and 1960's.[1]

As usual in this area of the law, the initiative for major change has come from the courts, rather than from the legislatures. The change in attitude is apparent in three different lines of cases. The most important

* This article is based on a paper prepared in 1975 by the author as a consultant to the Advisory Commission on Housing and Urban Growth of the American Bar Association. The Advisory Commission, whose Report was issued in 1976, is funded as Project N. III. PD-12 by the U.S. Department of Housing and Urban Development. The material, submitted for the consideration of the Advisory Commission, contains the opinions and views of the author, and do not necessarily reflect those of the Advisory Commission or of the U.S. Department of Housing and Urban Development.

(and most dramatic) of these has of course been in the rapid expansion of anti-exclusionary case law.[2] The same underlying skeptical attitude as to what local governments are doing also has been apparent recently in two other areas: an almost complete turn-about in the case law dealing with the now increasingly recognized importance of the comprehensive plan as the basis for zoning; and a tightening of the criteria for granting variances.

There has been a long anti-exclusionary tradition in American law, for the courts recognized from the start that land use controls had a potential for such purposes. In the early leading case on zoning,[3] the Supreme Court held that a Cleveland suburb was not legally required to accommodate an alleged regional trend of industrial development, and could determine its own policy in this respect; but the Court added an explicit warning:

> It is not meant by this, however, to exclude the possibility of cases where the general public interest would so far outweigh the interest of the municipality that the municipality would not be allowed to stand in the way.[4]

Moreover, the early case law was more explicit in warning against the misuse of zoning controls to prevent inexpensive housing. In the earliest leading cases upholding single-family districts, the argument was made that such districts would be inherently exclusionary; but the courts thought otherwise, on the ground that at that time new single-family housing was available at moderate cost.[5] Again, in the early Massachusetts and New York cases upholding acreage zoning, the opinions recognized that such requirements might be exclusionary, and stated that this would be invalid.[6]

This long-standing anti-exclusionary attitude faded for a while, during the period of extreme judicial deference to municipal autonomy, but it has returned in strength in the 1970's.

Mount Laurel

Mount Laurel[7] provides, at long last, a well thought out argument which holds invalid both the general principle of exclusionary zoning and an entire pattern of exclusionary devices. The rationale of the opinion is based upon the notions of "regional general welfare" and "fair share," and these in turn are derived from broad language[8] in the New Jersey State Constitution, rather than being based upon a statutory or a federal constitutional ground.

The *Mount Laurel* decision is the culmination[9] of a major trend in the 1970's. While nearly a dozen other states have given a clear indication of an anti-exclusionary attitude in various types of cases, mostly in dictum, *Mount Laurel* is thus the most important zoning opinion since *Euclid*.[10] It is reasonable to assume that similar lawsuits and holdings will be forthcoming in other states, and so a detailed analysis of the *Mount Laurel* opinion is in order.

Under the decision, the "general welfare" is not only a broad additional ground which is available to justify zoning and other land use regulations as against challenges brought by developers; it is also the basis for an affirmative requirement to which local governments are required to conform—that is, that land use regulations must be shown to operate to promote, and not be contrary to, the general welfare. Furthermore, adequate provision for housing is explicitly found to be an important element of the "general welfare."

More specifically, making "realistically possible an appropriate variety and choice of housing"[11] normally includes making provision for a variety of housing types—presumably including a range of density levels, building types, and (quite emphatically) costs, or at least low- and moderate-cost housing. In effect, housing has been promoted to the status of a preferred use.[12]

Moreover, the need for housing, as part of the general welfare, is defined as the regional need,[13] and not merely the need within that particular municipality. Each [developing] municipality has the responsibility of helping meet the regional need, by providing an opportunity for such housing through local land use regulations.

As a logical consequence of this view, the opinion specifically grants standing to challenge local restrictions to certain nonresidents of a municipality who might wish to live there, but are in effect prevented from doing so.

Finally, the decision is explicit on another critical point. If a municipality accepts some intensive and/or low-cost housing, this does not necessarily mean that it must open its doors to unlimited amounts of such housing: each municipality's responsibility is limited to its "fair share" of the regional need.

Turning to the town's affirmative defenses, the *Mount Laurel* opinion dealt with the two obvious arguments, fiscal and ecological. Regarding the first, the court reaffirmed the New Jersey doctrine that it was appropriate—as against suits brought by neighbors—for a municipality to seek out and encourage "good" tax ratables. However, the opinion was equally explicit in ruling out fiscal considerations as a justifiable basis for excluding "bad" ratables, such as low- and moderate-cost housing.

On the ecological issue, the court held that such considerations could provide an appropriate defense against proposed more intensive housing in a specific location—that is, in suits brought by developers. However, the court was obviously conscious of the fact that many municipalities might attempt to use such arguments too broadly, and so took a quite restrictive view of the role of ecological justifications, holding that this argument would be effective only where the ecological problems are "substantial and very real."[14]

The net result of the above was to establish equal access to housing as being of fundamental constitutional importance at the state level. This "right" was somewhat limited by the notion of equitable distribution of housing between municipalities (fair share), so that this right of access to housing is not a "personal" right in any given plaintiff to move wherever he might choose.

As a result, developing municipalities in New Jersey are on notice that they no longer have the power to totally exclude all intensive or less expensive housing; they must accept their fair share of regional needs. Moreover, they do not have the final say on what is their "fair share." However, they do have the assurance that there is a limit: that is to say, permitting one low-income project does not necessarily set a precedent requiring them to accept an indefinite number of similar units. This assurance is essential if cooperation is to be expected from a substantial number of towns. Moreover, the towns retain a substantial degree of locational control, since as long as an adequate amount of appropriate land is zoned or otherwise made available to permit more intensive housing in some way (specifically including by special permit), a town could, for example, guide the location of such housing away from ecologically sensitive sites, or from locations where the resulting traffic would create special danger. Therefore, at least in the first instance, towns have the power to decide where such housing should go. If they do not exercise this,[15] they should expect to be subject to litigation and judicially imposed remedies.

Finally, every developing municipality must make possible, via its land use regulations, a mixture of building types, denisty levels, and income groups. As long as this is done, it would seem that a town is then free, if it so chooses, to zone other areas for low-density development. Furthermore, the opinion strongly implies (without actually deciding) that a town may also regulate its own rate of growth, so long as provision is made for low- and moderate-income housing at an early date in such a scheme.

The questions which remain unsettled after this opinion are manifold. Some of the more important of these are as follows:

1. The opinion does not make clear how affirmative a duty is involved in connection with low- and moderate-income housing opportunities, or the provision of such units.

2. There is no mention of the problem of the extent of the duty in connection with more expensive (and intensive) housing.
3. The opinion is in terms specifically limited to developing municipalities with substantial development pressure and substantial vacant land. No attempt is made to lay down the appropriate principles either for rural municipalities without development pressure, or for substantially built-up towns.

Under the *Mount Laurel* case, therefore, in the absence of significant planning reasons justifying otherwise, every developing municipality must provide the opportunity for a heterogeneous mixture of housing types. There is a strong presumption, but not a completely irrebutable one, that this opportunity must be provided; if a town wishes to argue to the contrary, the reasons which would point to a different conclusion must be substantial ones. (The same types of reasons of course are relevant in regard to a decision on what is a "fair share.")

The Legal Background

Mount Laurel is not an isolated phenomenon, but the logical culmination of a major trend in current law. Anti-exclusionary case law has expanded suddenly in the 1970's, but without any clearly-defined rationale or theoretical basis until *Mount Laurel*. Several different rationales have been tried out in the rather substantial volume of such litigation.

The prevailing rationale in *Mount Laurel*—that zoning must be shown to promote the regional general welfare—is almost (but not quite) original in that decision, and so there is not much to be said in tracing the history of this doctrine. It is of course familiar law that the "general welfare" is an appropriate basis for action under the police power, and this has served as additional support for restrictions on the use of land, as against claims made by developers, as for example often in the case of aesthetic restrictions. It was in the *Madison* case,[16] also in New Jersey, that this doctrine was first invoked as a restriction on the powers of local governments on behalf of those excluded by zoning restrictions; the New Jersey Supreme Court decided to adopt this as the basis for the definitive opinion in *Mount Laurel*.

Most of the other cases have been argued primarily on equal protection grounds, following the lead of the cases on racial segregation by governmental action; the courts have handled this in various ways. Two important federal decisions have explicitly adopted a rationale which is at least closely allied to equal protection.[17] Under this approach, a town is under no duty to use the power to regulate land use; but if it does, it must use it on behalf of all groups in the population.[18]

A second and basically different rationale has evolved in a series of decisions from Pennsylvania. In these decisions, specific zoning devices have been held invalid per se, but without much concern for providing an effective remedy.[19] The resulting rationale is purely mechanical, and there is no indication whatever of any special concern for low- and moderate-cost housing; in keeping with the current attitude in Pennsylvania zoning law generally, these decisions are strongly developer-minded.

A more recent line of federal cases has taken still another and different line. As the flood of anti-exclusionary litigation has increased, an increasing number of rather doubtful cases have been brought involving rather difficult side issues, serious counter-arguments, or rather unusual remedies; it is not surprising that plaintiffs have begun to lose in such cases. In such decisions, following the lead of the Supreme Court,[20] the courts have tended to reject equal protection arguments in the exclusionary context, on the ground that housing is not a "fundamental interest," so that there is no reason to scrutinize such complaints with special care.[21]

To complete the picture, it must be noted that in the state courts, which are far more familiar with zoning law and practice, the anti-exclusionary attitude has continued to spread. In addition to the states mentioned above, recent decisions have made this clear in several other states, particularly in the northeast.[22]

The Potentially Broad Scope of "Regional General Welfare"

The "regional general welfare" was not the only possible rationale for *Mount Laurel*. (The opinion might have been placed more explicitly on equal protection grounds).[23] The reasons for the choice of this rationale are quite understandable, but the fact remains that it opens up a far larger field of potential questions as to the appropriate scope of the judicial function. Once the decision is made that a zoning ordinance must promote the "regional general welfare," the courts thereby undertake to decide a substantial number of matters of policy which are normally considered to be legislative in nature: the appropriateness of various patterns of distribution of both people and their activities, and also basic questions in growth policy.

What *Mount Laurel* decides is that the predominant recent pattern in both zoning and development—permitting only large single-family houses on large lots on almost all residential vacant land[24]—does not tend to promote the regional general welfare. The opinion goes one step further and states that, in order to promote the "regional general welfare," the strong (though conceivably rebuttable) presumption is that at least the developing municipalities must provide the opportunity, through their land use regulations, for a mix of density levels, building types and incomes.

However, the opinion does indicate that an alternative procedure might be acceptable: since no doubt there are some municipalities where such a mix would not make good planning sense, or at least where the proportions could be varied widely, a rational allocation of housing needs through a regional planning process could conceivably produce a better result than that provided through litigation. (Such an allocation would naturally have to proceed upon criteria which are acceptable to the courts.) This suggestion is of course an open invitation to the legislature, and to local and regional governments, to go to work on legislation, institutions, and processes along these lines.

Additional Questions Opened Up by Mount Laurel

The *Mount Laurel* case suggests a large number of major questions of public policy on metropolitan dynamics, i.e., on the distribution of people and activities. Obviously it would be desirable to have these settled by legislation, in part directly, and in part by delegation to qualified administrative agencies acting under legislative direction. However, if no such legislation is forthcoming, at least some of the questions will need to be decided by the courts in the course of carrying out their responsibility to provide appropriate remedies where injury to a defined legal right is shown or is likely to result. In this type of situation, the judicial function overlaps with the legislative.

Some of the more important of these questions are as follows:

1. How a region is to be defined for the purpose of determining regional need(s).
2. How to define the extent of the regional need for various types of housing.
3. The criteria for distribution of the regional need for housing, as among the various municipalities within the region.

It is in connection with the third type of question that many of the most difficult and important policy issues arise. In addressing these problems, the courts—in default of legislative action—will necessarily be adopting major policies on (or affecting) the distribution of people and activities throughout the region. This is already apparent from *Mount Laurel*. Some of the policies implicit in that opinion, and henceforth to be enforced (if necessary) by the courts, involve the opportunity for access to decent housing within various cost ranges. In adopting such a policy, the courts can point, as the court did in *Mount Laurel*, to the intent and language of a number of statutes which have set forth housing and land use policies along these lines.

However, *Mount Laurel* represents the adoption, as a constitutional principle, of a quite different policy on the distribution of regional functions—a policy which has no such statutory base: the right of persons to live somewhere near where they work. This principle is necessarily involved in the statement that, if a municipality decides to accept a substantial amount of employment, that decision carries with it the duty to provide the opportunity for appropriate housing.

As the discussion below demonstrates, in order to provide an effective remedy in implementing the decision to bring an end to exclusionary zoning—and particularly in order to do so under a rationale based on regional general welfare—the courts will need to spend a great deal of time on basic questions which normally would be considered legislative in nature.[25]

Definition of a Region

The first and most obvious question, in moving forward from *Mount Laurel*, is how the courts are going to define a region in the absence of definitive legislative or administrative action. On this question, the conceivable possibilities extend over a wide range: from an entire metropolitan New York-New Jersey metropolitan area at one extreme, to a group of a few towns at the other. There can be no question whatever that such a decision—on what is "the region"—will have a major impact on subsequent decisions as to how much and where housing needs might be met. Naturally, exclusionary towns will argue in favor of minimizing the size of a region and, above all, in favor of excluding from the definition of their region any central city with a substantial low-income and minority population. The housing civil rights public interest groups will argue in favor of expanding the region, in order to bring together the central city and those municipalities which have substantial vacant land and development potential.

There is, of course, a great deal of literature on what is meant by a "region." The essential point here is that most of the conventional definitions[26] no longer work well in the metropolitan areas of the 1970's.

The widely deplored (but usually quite undefined) phenomenon of "suburban sprawl" has brought about a scatteration of settlements across the open countryside, beyond or near the "suburban fringe" (which latter is no longer a clear-cut concept in many areas). Moreover, the amount of cross-commuting, usually by private car, between adjacent counties or groups of counties has created new and more complex problems.

Despite such problems as those mentioned above, the delineation of a region (large or small) usually does not present insuperable difficulties; the area of continuous settlement usually coincides roughly with the area within which substantial numbers of people commute to work in the old centre, though there are exceptions.[27] The more difficult problems arise in connection with delineating sub-regions within larger metropolitan regions such as New York, Chicago and Los Angeles. Agreement on a standard set of sub-regions within such areas would of course be convenient for everyone; yet some experience with this problem suggests that different sub-regions may well be appropriate in connection with the analysis of different types of problems.

In effect, the actual sub-region as defined may depend upon the problem.[28] For example, for water quality purposes the sub-region will naturally be a watershed. For purposes of determining housing needs, the region will be the local area of intensive cross-commuting: the "commutershed," usually ranging from one to three counties, together with some allowance for out-migration from one or more "central cities" which may be more distant.

The problem of defining a region varies widely as among different situations. The essential point is that not all situations are equally difficult; assuming that the *Mount Laurel* type of problem will occur on a nationwide basis, some definitions will be relatively simple. The obvious case is of a small to medium-size city, surrounded by vacant land, and located within a single county. In that situation, the "region" is self-defining. If a similar city were located near or at a county boundary, with suburbs in both counties, a small additional complication is added; if it were located at a state boundary, the situation would become considerably more complex. Finally, at the other extreme in the case of a large metropolitan area, such as the New York-New Jersey area, the metropolitan region is made up of a series of sub-regions. The entire region is clearly split in three by the Hudson and the East Rivers; on the New Jersey side of the Hudson River there are some instances of rather clear sub-regions,[29] and in other instances the definition is extraordinarily difficult. (As bad luck would have it, *Mount Laurel* arose in Burlington County, which, along with Passaic County, is one of the two counties in New Jersey which are clearly impossible as potential sub-regions. Burlington County includes a substantial strip of the booming Delaware Valley industrial belt, a large area of the Pinelands, and a bit of the Shore.[30]

In such a large metropolitan area, the question of defining sub-regions will undoubtedly raise difficult issues in some situations, and relatively easy ones in others. In general, the guiding principle should be that, in a suit brought against one municipality (or a few), the region normally should include any nearby central city which has a substantial lower-income population.

A particular housing sub-region thus will often cross county lines—including most of one county and half of the next one, for example. Yet, when it comes to thinking about implementation, it may be wise to adjust the eventual estimates of need back to a county basis, at least in those areas where counties are fairly effective units of government,[31] and except in some instances where the county is an impossible unit.

In cases of doubt, it should be remembered that regions have been established for various purposes by official government action(s), and these may be adaptable for use in court. The most obvious case involves the SMSAs adopted by the U.S. Bureau of the Census.[32] An even more convincing case may be made in these situations where, by governmental action and indeed sometimes by interstate compact, regions which have been defined for certain purposes—such as a regional transportation planning body—may (as it has in the New York and Philadelphia regions) have evolved into a general-purpose regional planning commission not attached to any level of government.[33]

How to Define Housing Need

The criteria for defining the need for housing in a region and/or a local area are relatively clear-cut. The need for low- and moderate-cost housing normally would include the following:

1. All those persons living in substandard housing.
2. All those, in excess of normal occupancy limits, who are living in overcrowded housing.
3. All those living in accommodations where they are forced to pay more than a stated percentage (as 20-25 percent) of their income for rent.
4. For a region, the expected future need for dwelling units, based upon an analysis of future employment (particularly low-wage employment), demographic trends, etc.
5. A percentage of future non-residents, including particularly those who may be working in future low-wage employment in the general area.
6. For a town, those who have been recently forced to move elsewhere because of the absence of suitable housing[34] at prices which they could afford.
7. Usually, for a town, a proportion of the public employees of the particular town in question, and a percentage (perhaps one-half) of all those current non-residents who are in fact working in town.

The Mechanism for Determining Need

Making estimates of present and future housing need is a well-established professional specialty, with significant experience having been accumulated in various contexts.[35] The guiding principle is of course that, in order to make realistic estimates, it is necessary to start with a larger unit, and to proceed from that to smaller units. Specifically, this means that the first estimate should be made for the entire metropolitan region as a whole. If that region is large enough to include sub-regions, the estimate would then be allocated down to the various sub-regions (normally to counties, or to some unit about that size). The allocation procedure then proceeds from the counties to the municipalities.

There is no great difficulty in doing this, although (as indicated above) major policy questions are involved, particularly at the latter step. It was urged before the court in *Mount Laurel* that, following the opinion below, the decree should require the preparation of such a plan by joint action of plaintiffs and defendants, with whatever professional help would be appropriate. The appellate court declined to do so, thus modifying the lower court decree in this respect. Instead, it expressed its faith that Mount Laurel would move on its own to implement the new judicial policy. This is an understandable decision, particularly since the New Jersey legislature has not yet complied with the decree to come up with a new method for financing public schools, as ordered by the New Jersey Supreme Court in *Robinson v. Cahill*.[36]

As indicated in the opinion, there is no great difficulty in gaining access to the required professional expertise for this purpose. Often both regional and county planning boards are in existence, and many of them have done a great deal of work on this problem. Moreover, a court could appoint a special master to work with local officials for this purpose under judicial supervision.

If (as seems likely) at least some towns will continue to stall and resist, the courts may have to take a more active role. The opinion clearly envisaged such a possibility, inviting the plaintiffs to come back if local legislative or administrative relief is not forthcoming.

The Criteria for Allocating Housing—"Fair Share"

A substantial number of county and regional planning agencies in the United States have been (and are) working on the allocation of total housing needs—and particularly for low- and moderate-income housing—as among municipalities within their particular area. Consequently, there has been some experience in choosing the criteria to control such distribution.[37]

As indicated above, the selection of such criteria present major policy decisions as to the future of various sorts of towns. The criteria actually utilized often have included the following:

1. The existing need in the town (see above).
2. The amount of employment in the municipality,[38] and the number of non-residents working there.
3. The size of future employment, and in particular the extent of vacant land zoned to encourage such employment.
4. The availability of public services for new development. Obviously, a town with substantial unused school capacity[39] would be a better place for low- and moderate-cost housing than one where all the schools are already overcrowded. Likewise, a town with available vacant land which is already sewered has obvious advantages over a town where sewer construction would be prohibitively expensive. The availability of public transportation would be another important criterion.
5. The availability of vacant land, zoned for residence and suitable for construction of intensive inexpensive housing—that is, land which is relatively flat and dry, which is not prime agricultural land, and which has no special problems deriving from ecological sensitivity.
6. A town's relative wealth—that is, its ability to support additional inexpensive housing. The towns with good vacant land are often the wealthiest ones.
7. A policy of equalizing the distribution of income groups—that is, of encouraging additional inexpensive housing until the amount of such housing reaches the average for the metropolitan area as a whole,[40] and, perhaps, not beyond that (One possible criterion here, mentioned in Justice Pashman's concurring opinion in *Mount Laurel*, is the question of a "tipping point" . . . assuming that such a concept has reality, as for example in the schools.)
8. In some instances, involving outer low-density towns with little employment and not much development pressure, it may be appropriate to take into account varying types of possible contributions to regional needs—either some low- and moderate-cost housing, or alternatively a major (and tax-exempt) regional recreational facility, as a large public park.[41]
9. In those counties where the ratios between employment and population are fairly consistent in most or all towns, that county ratio may be useful in projecting future housing need. Another possible analytic tool worth investigating is the average length of travel to work, varying as among different income categories.
10. If there are officially adopted regional (or state), county, and even local plans which specify or bear upon the local need for housing, they are of course important elements to consider and may, if reasonable, even be found to be controlling.[42]

A specific problem arises on how to deal with the wealthy rural towns, which are often found just beyond the suburban fringe. Since the criteria for allocating housing need from the sub-region to the municipality usually place heavy emphasis on existing and future employment, such towns may resist the growth of employment—and thus the benefits of "good ratables." In such a situation, a locally generated need for low- and moderate-cost housing will be present, but only in token quantities (as for example to provide for the local businessmen's children who wish to stay in town.) The question is to what extent such towns should have to take a substantial part of the regionally-generated need, for people working elsewhere. Since these tend to be prestige towns, it is reasonable to expect that, if so, the housing will in fact be produced in such areas, though at a higher cost level.

In essence, there are only three choices available, each with some real, but different, disadvantages:

1. To require such towns to zone for substantial amounts of intensive housing. In that case a substantial number of people will have to drive a considerable distance between the places of employment and their residences, which is not necessarily a desirable pattern.
2. To let these towns more or less alone, with the requirement limited to a few units for the locally generated need. Naturally this is likely to be resented in other areas.
3. To impose upon such towns a duty to accept not only employment, but some low-wage employment, in which case it would be appropriate also to require inexpensive housing to go along with it.

Low- and Moderate-Cost Housing

An important question, which is bound to be widely discussed, is to what extent the *Mount Laurel* opinion imposes on developing towns some sort of affirmative duty to take further action to encourage low- and moderate-cost housing—that is, whether the towns' legal duty goes beyond repealing zoning and other restrictions which would preclude such housing.

Obviously, some towns are likely to zone substantial tracts of land for more intensive housing and then sit tight, hoping that no developers will turn up who want to build inexpensive housing (and possibly making this somewhat unpleasant for anyone who does), but taking no additional action. This situation is certain to occur, and the question is what will happen next.

It is now being argued that the *Mount Laurel* decision may be a nullity, since no large-scale government programs are available which would provide the necessary subsidies to permit the creation of low- and moderate-cost housing, and since the courts cannot require the towns to spend their own money for this purpose.

If the courts are actually determined to implement the *Mount Laurel* decision, strictly within accepted concepts of the judicial function, there are ways in which this can be done without costing a single town one cent. One obvious possibility would be to hold the entire zoning ordinance invalid for failure to provide for the needed housing. This was considered and rejected in the *Mount Laurel* opinion, where the lower court's decision to do just that was explicitly reversed. However, in the Northeast Corridor, mobile homes are selling for approximately half the price of a new single-family detached house, and indeed frequently for considerably less. In this situation, in an appropriate lawsuit, a court would be justified in giving the town a choice of two alternatives, either: (a) to find some other way to subsidize some inexpensive conventional housing, or (b) to zone a substantial tract for mobile homes.[43]

Moreover, even though the elaborate housing subsidy programs of the late 1960's were in effect repealed by unilateral Presidential act, it is not true that there are no subsidies at all: at least some token money is available. Some federal subsidies are contemplated under Section 8 of the Housing Act of 1974 in ways that are not entirely clear. In addition, some states, such as New Jersey, have housing finance agencies which can provide some help along these lines. The extent of such aid varies, of course, among the other states.

In addition, other ways are available by which towns can make possible some low- and moderate-cost housing, if they really wish to do so. For the same reasons, therefore, a court is in a position to exert some pressure in this direction, if it wants to. If a substantial development is proposed, it is possible for a developer to provide at least some moderate-cost units, by skewing the rents so as in effect to subsidize these from the more expensive housing. Moreover, inexpensive housing is (in nearly all cases) necessarily more intensive housing, and so a windfall (an increase in land values) is likely to be involved. It may be possible to arrange matters so that the windfall goes not to the pre-existing landowner but to the actual developer, and then can be used in part to provide a subsidy for the less expensive housing.[44] Under such a system, the first step would be to amend the zoning regulations so that some land would be available for development in either of two ways: at low density (1-2 acres) or much more intensively (say five to the acre, gross density)—but the latter density would be available only if a stated percentage of the total dwelling units were in low- and moderate-cost housing.

To put the same point differently, the question is how to make it possible for the developer to buy the land at a price reflecting the previously permitted density. So defined, the problem thus is how to shift bargaining power away from the preexisting landowner and towards the developer. The usual way to think about doing this is by some type of "floating zone," which is intended to encourage competition among land owners to sell to a developer by increasing greatly the number of tracts potentially eligible for higher density development, and thereby keeping down the price of land. The problem with this is two-fold. It may be totally ineffective, i.e., it may or may not work, depending on varying conditions in the local housing market. Moreover, this would abdicate public locational control, and so in effect threaten everyone.

Other methods of accomplishing the same purpose are of course possible, though not much discussed. Under one possible arrangement, a few tracts (the most appropriate ones) are designated on a master plan as appropriate for more intensive housing, with the proviso that if no action ensues within (say) two years, other tracts may be made available, or conceivably the permission may be withdrawn from those first designated. In this situation it is possible to predict with some confidence that, near the end of the two-year period, bargaining power will begin to shift. Such an arrangement would not only be more effective for the stated purpose, but would retain the public locational control.

The Judicial Role in Metropolitan Policy-Making

Once the courts have decided to intervene seriously against exclusionary zoning, the necessary result is that they will be passing upon and deciding major questions of public policy—questions of a sort which are normally considered appropriate for legislative decision, or for administrative decision under legislative guidelines. The *Mount Laurel* court already has done so in several respects and this necessity will recur in future litigation, particularly in connection with the criteria for allocation of regional housing need to particular municipalities.

In some instances the courts thus are actually adopting specific regional development policies as principles of constitutional law; in others, their decisions will have a major impact on other such policies. Among the more important examples of this are the following:

1. There is now a broadly stated, and not precisely defined, right to expect housing of reasonable quality, and at reasonable cost, to be made realistically possible in developing municipalities. Obviously this does not represent an innovation in policy; most states already have adopted such a policy broadly and explicitly in housing legislation and the larger states have done so repeatedly, particularly in legislative findings and statements of purpose.
2. Moreover, such housing must have access to good residential land, suitable for intensive development. Clearly it will not do to map locations for such housing only in undesirable areas, such as indus-

trial or ribbon commercial, or at locations involving special construction difficulties and thus extra-high construction costs. This is implicit throughout *Mount Laurel* and clearly stated in New Jersey
case law involving analogous situations, as for example schools.[45]
Again, this policy can be derived easily from the enabling legislation
for both planning and zoning ("orderly development," "most appropriate use of land," etc.).

3. The majority opinion explicitly adopted a policy, on the constitutional level, in favor of dispersal of low income residents to the
outer parts of metropolitan areas, where most of the new jobs are
located and where there are better public services and, generally, a
more attractive environment.

4. As an accompaniment to the above, the decision explicitly adopted a
policy that people have a right to live near their place of work, if
they want to. This passage is phrased in terms of living within the
same town (i.e., if a town accepts the benefits of new employment,
it must provide for the appropriate housing), but it clearly has implications for other nearby towns for several reasons. In some instances there will not be enough land appropriate for development
in one town to take care of the resulting housing, or the most convenient locations for such housing may be in the next town. In all
these situations the spillover goes into the distribution of regional
need. The question is of course, how near? A great deal turns upon
the answer to this question. Not everyone will want to live in the
same town where he works, and the difference between 15 minutes
and 30 minutes driving time often makes a large difference in the
estimate of the housing need. The two policies discussed immediately above are in a completely different situation from the first
two, for it cannot really be argued that the legislature has already
adopted them, explicitly or even implicitly.[46] They are necessary
elements in the implementation of a declared constitutional right,
and as such fall into the area of overlap between the appropriate
areas for legislative policy-making and for judicial definition of constitutional policy.

5. Implicit in the above is a movement towards equalizing the burden
resulting from new development, particularly under the current tax
set-up. If the *Mount Laurel* policy is implemented, the result will
be a move towards bringing more low income population to the
richer towns, which are by definition better able to provide public
services for such population.

6. The opinion explicitly provides that towns may use their land use
powers to protect ecologically sensitive areas, although this is restricted to only a few really ecologically important areas within each
town.[47]

In other instances, the policies adopted in *Mount Laurel* (on a constitutional basis) will have a major impact upon other major public policies,
which involve basic questions regarding metropolitan structure and
dynamics. The first and most important of the latter involve the question

of the location of employment, which is perhaps the most basic of all questions on regional structure.

In this respect the impact of the decision (and particularly the policy on dispersal of housing) may point in both directions. If more housing is available for lower-income employees in outer areas, this may encourage the dispersal of those categories of employment which include a low-wage component. On the other hand, if such a decision is combined in some states with a basic change in school financing, the result will be to reduce (or to minimize) the importance of ratables; this would tend to reduce the incentive to encourage employment in the outer areas.

All this may in some respects run counter to current thinking on metropolitan structure, which has been focussing along rather different lines. For example, in the New York-New Jersey region much thought is being given to encouraging a concentration of employment in larger centers located throughout the region; both the Tri-State Regional Planning Commission and the private Regional Plan Association have adopted plans along these lines. The impact of *Mount Laurel* upon these policies is not yet clear.

Second, in a closely related matter, it is the pattern of concentration (or dispersal) of employment which will determine the economic feasibility of public transportation systems in the outer parts of the region. Decisions such as *Mount Laurel* therefore may have a substantial impact upon that problem.

Third, with regard to another public problem, the desegregation of schools, the impact of *Mount Laurel* will be clearly favorable. Under recent trends, suburban schools have been increasingly de facto segregated as middle-income-white; central city schools have been moving in the opposite direction, primarily as a result of residential segregation. (In this situation the highly controversial present practice of bussing in order to promote racial integration is not a very effective attempt to promote such integration, by adopting the only device available for that purpose.) To the extent that *Mount Laurel* will contribute to alleviating this situation, it will be to the good.

Finally, the impact on the central cities must be considered. Much of the rhetorical discussion about exclusionary zoning has been focused on the most overt problem: the low-income blacks locked into the central city slums. *Mount Laurel* does, of course, point in the right direction to provide some relief for this problem. However, it seems probable that the eventual practical results will be to provide more open housing opportunities in the suburbs for middle and moderate income groups, including of course some blacks but consisting primarily of members of various white ethnic groups. To the extent that more of these people will now be able to leave the cities, this may have a considerable effect upon the population structure of those cities, and upon leadership patterns there.

The Need for Legislative Direction

In default of legislation, then, the courts will be handling major policy questions for which most judges have no special expertise, and which are normally considered legislative in nature. The situation obviously cries aloud for legislative intervention in order to deal with some of these. Moreover, since the impact of *Mount Laurel* has been to remove (or at least to make invalid) a large part of the existing system, the situation now is ripe for reconsideration and revamping of that system. To do so will require a high quality of vision and professional skill, plus a large dose of political courage.

If such a re-vamping is undertaken, with special concern for these problems emerging from *Mount Laurel*, the following considerations should be paramount:

1. The most obvious immediate need is to create the necessary machinery to determine overall housing need, and to allocate this to different municipalities. In the absence of such machinery, we must anticipate chaos: to the extent that there is any action at all, each town (or group of towns) will be trying to make a rather low estimate of the extent of its own responsibility, on the basis of different (and probably conflicting) regions, and using different criteria to determine and to allocate such need. Since the latter represent major decisions on policy, they are particularly appropriate for legislative determination, or perhaps rather for detailed spelling-out by a professionally staffed administrative agency acting under broad (but clear) legislative guidelines.

2. The dominant fiscal pressure on land use decisions must be removed, or else one must be prepared to accept the fact that these pressures will remain dominant. Land uses vary widely in their fiscal implications for the municipality in terms of tax revenue brought in and services required. As long as these differences remain important to the municipalities, there is no reason to expect that local officials will ignore such considerations. Several possible courses of action are available here: (a) In order to remove the fiscal influences completely, it would be necessary to abolish the local real property tax, and replace it with other tax revenues—perhaps a combination of an income tax and a lower state-wide property tax, with funds allocated to towns by some formula based upon need. (b) A lesser, and more likely, version of this would be to do the same for the financing of education, the largest single local expense. Neither of these is likely to be politically popular, and there are other lesser measures which could do smaller parts of the job. (c) For example, the state could pay for the extra educational expenses resulting from subsidized housing, thus removing the financial penalty for accept-

ing such housing, on the theory that since the benefits are state-wide, it is reasonable for the state to bear the burden. (This would have an analogy in the federal payments to "impacted" school dis-tricts.) (d) Another possible lesser measure is to provide for regional sharing of the benefits of good "ratables," along the lines of the recent legislation in Minnesota.[48]

3. The government has still another powerful weapon to influence land use, and is continually exercising this—the planning and construc-tion of major public works, particularly highways, highway inter-changes, and major sewers. As with the tax system, when this factor comes into play, the zoning system tends to operate not as an active force, but rather as a register of decisions made elsewhere and for other reasons. If planning is to be at all effective in the realm of housing, these various governmental powers affecting land use must be consolidated, or at least coordinated more closely.

4. Various statutes and other governmental actions have given a special status to various categories of ecologically sensitive land. A legisla-tive declaration of policy is needed to deal with the potential—but probably unnecessary—conflict between ecological considerations and housing needs.

5. The above considerations have already defined in large part the ap-propriate roles for state or regional level planning and land use con-trols. A major part of that role is to indicate in advance the appro-priate locations for the two extremes in density—that is, those areas which, primarily for ecological reasons, should be left open or at most receive very low density development, and those areas which, primarily because of their location to human artifacts on the land, are appropriate for concentrations of more intensive activity.[49]

NOTES

1. On the other hand, the courts are apparently prepared to accept an expansion of the public powers, state and local (and regional), to deal with environmen-tal protection.

2. The anti-exclusionary case law is particularly timely, since the late 1970's and the 1980's will be a period when the most pressing need in the housing mar-ket will be for relatively small dwelling units, for young married couples and the elderly—and that is in effect the opposite of what is permitted under prevailing land use requirements in most areas.

3. *Village of Euclid v. Ambler Realty Co.*, 272 U.S. 365 (1926).

4. *Id.* at 390.

5. *Brett v. Bldg. Comm'r of Brookline*, 250 Mass. 73, 145 N.E. 269 (1924); *Mil-ler v. Bd. of Pub. Works of Los Angeles*, 195 Cal. 477, 234 P. 381 (1925), *appeal dismissed*, 273 U.S. 781 (1926); and *see* State *ex rel. Twin City Bldg. and Inv. Co. v. Houghton*, 144 Minn. 1, 174 N.W. 885 (1919), *rev'd on re-hearing*, 145 Minn. 13, 176 N.W. 159 (1920). *See generally* N. Williams, *American Land Planning Law*, § 50.02-50.09. (1974).

6. *Simon v. Town of Needham*, 311 Mass. 560, 42 N.E.2d 516 (1942); *Gignoux v. Village of Kings Point*, 199 Misc. 485, 99 N.Y.S.2d 280 (Sup.Ct., Nassau Co., 1950).

7. *S. Burlington County NAACP v. Township of Mount Laurel*, 67 N.J. 151, 336 A.2d 713 (1975), *appeal dismissed and cert. denied*. 423 U.S. 808 (1975).
8. Deriving originally from the Declaration of Independence.
9. It is wholly fitting that this reversal should have come in New Jersey for two reasons. First, the New Jersey Supreme Court has been fortunate in having as one of its members a most distinguished judge in this field of law, Justice Frederick Hall. Justice Hall has been primarily responsible for turning the American judiciary around on this critical issue. Second, the rationale to uphold exclusionary zoning was developed in that state, and therefore needs to be destroyed there. This rationale, developed in the 1950's and early 1960's, was intended to (and did) encourage municipalities to practice exclusionary zoning and depended upon the following propositions:
   1. The statutory and constitutional power to zone for the "general welfare" is intended to provide municipalities with broad powers to control land use for various purposes, and should be interpreted as referring to the welfare of each municipality as a separate unit.
   2. The vague phrases deriving from the end of §3 of the Standard Zoning Enabling Act (conservation of property values, taking into consideration the character of the district and its peculiar suitability for particular uses, and encouraging the most appropriate use of land) represent additional grants of municipal power, and serve to justify exclusionary zoning.
   3. There is something called "balanced zoning," which in practice turns out to mean no more multiple dwellings, and
   4. "Fiscal zoning" to improve a municipality's position on tax ratables is an appropriate goal for police-power action.
   The rationale has been used to uphold a broad variety of restrictive devices, as follows:
   1. On the exclusion of multiple dwellings from a community: *see Guaclides v. Borough of Englewood Cliffs*, 11 N.J. Super. 405, 78 A.2d 435 (App. Div. 1951); and *Fanale v. Borough of Hasbrouck Heights*, 26 N.J. 320, 139 A.2d 749 (1958);
   2. On the exclusion of mobile homes: See *Napierkowski v. Township Comm. of Gloucester*, 29 N.J. 481, 150 A.2d 481 (1959), and *Vickers v. Township of Gloucester*, 37 N.J. 232, 181 A.2d 129 (1962), *appeal dismissed*, 371 U.S. 233 (1963):
   3. On minimum building size regulations: *see Lionshead Lake, Inc. v. Wayne Township*, 8 N.J. Super. 468, 73 A.2d 287 (L. Div. 1950), *rev'd*, 9 N.J. Super. 83, 74 A.2d 609 (App. Div. 1950), and 13 N.J. Super. 490, 80 A.2d 650 (L. Div. 1951), *rev'd*, 10 N.J. 165, 89 A.2d 693 (1952), *appeal dismissed*, 344 U.S. 919 (1953); and
   4. On minimum lot size; *see Fischer v. Township of Bedminster*, 11 N.J. 194, 93 A.2d 378 (1952), (five acres).
10. *Village of Euclid v. Ambler Realty Co.*, 272 U.S. 365 (1926).
11. *S. Burlington County NAACP v. Township of Mount Laurel*, 67 N.J. 151, 173, 336 A.2d 713, 724 (1975), *appeal dismissed and cert. denied*, 423 U.S. 808 (1975).
12. As indicated below, the notion of a preferred use under *Mount Laurel* is quite different from the notion in (for example) a series of recent Michigan cases, where the idea was eventually disapproved. Since the Michigan courts normally are rather developer-minded, the notion of a "preferred use" was there

interpreted to imply that a developer could choose his own site, and that the town then had very little power to dispute that location. *See Kropf v. City of Sterling Heights*, 391 Mich. 139, 215 N.W.2d 179 (1974), *overruling Bristow v. City of Woodhaven*, 35 Mich. App. 205, 192 N.W. 2d 322 (1972), and *Simmons v. City of Royal Oak*, 38 Mich. App. 496, 196 N.W.2d 811 (1972).

13. This holding follows a strong trend in New Jersey case law over recent decades. As early as 1949, in *Duffcon Concrete Products, Inc. v. Borough of Cresskill*, 1 N.J. 509, 64 A.2d 347 (1949), the court held that there was no need for a small town on the Palisades to zone for industrial development, because it was appropriate to take into account regional considerations, including the existence of better industrial land not far away. Moreover, in a more recent (and little-noticed) decision, *Kunzler v. Hoffman*, 48 N.J. 277, 225 A.2d 321 (1966), the court took a step farther, which in effect undermined the established rationale for exclusionary zoning discussed in Note 9 *supra*. In that case, a town in outer Morris County approved a "d" variance for a mental hospital, and this approval was challenged by neighbors on grounds that such a facility would cater to the general welfare of a larger region, and not to the welfare of that particular municipality. The court upheld the variance, and praised the municipal authorities for taking a broader view of general welfare.

  See also: Borough of Cresskill v. Borough of Dumont, 15 N.J. 238, 104 A.2d 441 (1954); *Kozesnik v. Township of Montgomery*, 24 N.J. 154, 131 A.2d 1 (1957); *Roman Catholic Diocese of Newark v. Borough of Ho-Ho-Kus*, 42 N.J. 556, 202 A.2d 161 (1964), and 47 N.J. 211, 220 A.2d 97 (1966).

14. *S. Burlington County NAACP v. Township of Mount Laurel*, 67 N.J. 151, 187, 336 A.2d 713, 731 (1975), *appeal dismissed and cert. denied*, 423 U.S. 808 (1975).

15. Or if they do so unreasonably, as by zoning only a quarry for more intensive housing.

16. *Oakwood at Madison, Inc. v. Township of Madison*, 117 N.J. Super. 11. 283 A.2d 353 (L. Div. 1971), and *see also* 128 N.J. Super. 438, 320 A.2d 223 (L. Div. 1974).

17. *Southern Alameda Spanish-Speaking Organization v. City of Union City, Cal.*, 424 F.2d 291, 295-96 (9th Cir. 1970); *Kennedy Park Homes Assn., Inc. v. City of Lackawanna*, 318 F. Supp. 669, 696-97, (W.D.N.Y., 1970), *aff'd on somewhat different grounds*, 436 F.2d 108 (2d Circ. 1970), *cert. denied*, 401 U.S. 1010 (1971).

18. For more recent Federal cases with a similar attitude, *see Joseph Skilken and Co. v. City of Toledo*, 380 F. Supp. 228 (N.D. Ohio 1974); *United Farm Workers of Florida Housing Project v. City of Delray Beach*, CA72-1270 (S.D. Fla. 1972), *rev'd*, 493 F.2d 799 (5th Cir. 1974).

19. *National Land and Inv. Co. v. Kohn*, 419 Pa. 504, 215 A.2d 597 (1965) (4-acre zoning); *Appeal of Kit-Mar Builders, Inc.*, 439 Pa. 466, 268 A.2d 765 (1970) (2-acre zoning); *Appeal of Girsh*, 437 Pa. 237, 263 A.2d 395 (1970) (no multiple dwellings). For a comparison of the two rationales, in their actual effect, *see* Williams, Doughty and Potter, *The Strategy on Exclusionary Zoning: Towards What Rationale and What Remedy?*, 1972 LAND USE CONTROLS ANNUAL 177,201.

20. The cases which have come before the Supreme Court have not brought out the serious questions involved in the exclusionary pattern, and so the Court has clearly been reluctant to enter this field. As a result, in a series of cases, all of which involved difficult side issues, the Court has been moving towards

the doctrine that housing (unlike the right to vote) is not a "fundamental interest," and thus that a challenge on equal protection grounds can be met merely by a showing of some rational basis for the restriction in question. See *James v. Valtierra,* 402 U.S. 137 (1971) (referendum on public housing); *Lindsey v. Normet,* 405 U.S. 56 (1972) (landlord's right to evict): *Village of Belle Terre v. Boraas,* 416 U.S. 1 (1974) (number of students who can live together as a family); *Warth v. Seldin,* 422 U.S. 490 (1975) (standing of non-residents to sue).

21. *Acevedo v. Nassau County,* 369 F. Supp. 1384 (E.D.N.Y. 1974), *aff'd,* 500 F.2d 1078 (2d Cir. 1974); *Mahaley v. Cuyahoga Metropolitan Housing Authority,* 355 F. Supp. 1245, 1257 (N.D. Ohio 1973); *Warth v. Seldin,* 495 F.2d. 1187 (2d Cir. 1974), *aff'd,* 422 U.S. 490 (1975); *Ybarra v. Town of Los Altos Hills,* 370 F. Supp. 742 (N.D. Cal. 1973).

22. *Golden v. Planning Bd. of Town of Ramapo,* 30 N.Y.2d 359, 334 N.Y.S. 2d 138, 285 N.E.2d 291 (1972); *Barnard v. Zoning Bd. of Appeals of Town of Yarmouth,* 313 A.2d 741 (Me. 1974); *Town of Gloucester v. Olivo's Mobile Home Court, Inc.,* 111 R.1 120, 300 A.2d 465 (1973); *and compare: Zelvin v. Zoning Bd. of Appeals of Town of Windsor,* 30 Conn. Sup. 157, 306 A.2d 151 (1973), and *Bd. of Appeals of Concord v. Housing Appeals Comm.* 294 N.E.2d 393 (Mass. 1973). Moreover, the major midwestern states have been moving in the same direction. On Mighigan, *see* above; on Illinois, *see Oak Forest Mobile Home Park, Inc., v. City of Oak Forest,* 27 Ill. App. 2d 303, 326 N.E.2d 473 (1975); on Ohio, *see Forest City Enterprises v. City of Eastlake,* 41 Ohio St.2d 187, 324 N.E.2d 740 (1975); on California, *see Town of Los Altos Hills v. Adobe Creek Properties, Inc.,* 32 Cal. App. 3d 488, 108 Cal. Rptr. 271 (1973). About a dozen states, including almost all the important states in zoning law, except Maryland and Texas, have thus now spoken on the issue. (1975).

23. Presumably the choice of a "general welfare" rationale was part of the effort to keep away from the United States Supreme Court, which is the normal arbiter of equal protection matters. Another possibility was a "right to travel" rationale; but the court wisely avoided this, since such a right is necessarily personal, and it would have been difficult to combine this with a rationale setting some limits to the amount of housing each town would have to take.

24. The pattern is spelled out in Williams and Norman, *Exclusionary Land Use Controls: The Case of Northeastern New Jersey,* 22 SYRACUSE LAW REVIEW 475, 480 (1971) and 4 LAND USE CONTROLS QUARTERLY 7 (1970). *See also,* NEW JERSEY DEP'T OF COMMUNITY AFFAIRS, LAND USE REGULATION, THE RESIDENTIAL LAND SUPPLY, (1972).

25. While this whole matter obviously raises serious questions, there is no reason for either surprise or over-concern; for, in two major fields of constitutional law, the courts have been handling this sort of problem for nearly 20 years—in connection with both the desegregation of schools and the reapportionment of legislative bodies.

The parallel between problems of desegregation and reapportionment, and the problem of the termination of exclusionary land use controls, is a close one. A strong case can be made that, in dealing with the end of exclusionary zoning, the courts should proceed immediately under the procedures established in those two earlier sets of precedents. (The lower court in *Mount Laurel* was convinced by this argument; the appellate court was not.)

Moreover, to do so in this type of situation will not provide a precedent for doing so in all sorts of other situations. In a few particularly important and special situations, judicial action can appropriately include both (a) fashioning a remedy and (b) retaining jurisdiction to supervise its implementation. The criteria which will define and delimit these situations may be described as follows:

The first and essential element of the situation is that the legislature is paralyzed and unable to act—because an arrangement which violates basic rights of a substantial minority is eminently satisfactory to a large majority.

Second, in these situations the implementation of the newly-declared right requires some rather elaborate action by governmental agencies other than the court. Such implementation will often require complex reorganization of administrative (or even legislative) arrangements, where the importance of the declared right must be consistently balanced against other considerations—or against intransigent resistance, masked as other legitimate considerations. In such a situation, those who are in charge of the machinery by which the right would normally be implemented are in reality adversary parties; for by implementing the right they would be losing what they regard as substantial personal advantages for themselves and their constituents—jobs for legislators facing reapportionment, zoning protection for segregationists, and tax base enhancement in these zoning situations. It is therefore to be expected that many of them will react by resisting implementation—and the potential means of evasion are plentiful. To put the point bluntly, it is not realistic to depend on the good faith reaction of such people in carrying out implementation of the right.

Third, both the type and the amount of action required in implementation of the right may vary widely between different geographical situations. The point is obvious in connection with desegregation and reapportionment; in connection with zoning, a town with rapidly growing employment and large areas of vacant land zoned for industry is in a completely different situation from a remote rural township where there is almost no employment at all.

Finally, in some instances, what looks like a simple and obvious remedy may in fact accomplish nothing at all. For example, if the attention is focused upon the principle of lot size, a decree that merely authorizes smaller lot sizes is likely to result merely in increased profits for the developer, rather than lower costs for the consumers of the housing. It is also likely to make it more difficult to preserve environmentally valuable and ecologically fragile open space, and can encourage the other disadvantageous effects of sprawl.

26. Traditionally, the definition of a region has focused on one, or both, of two criteria: (1) an area of continuous settlement which a) is surrounded by vacant land or farms and forest, and b) has substantial amounts of travel to work involved between the outer parts and the center, or around the outer areas; or (2) a watershed.

27. Princeton Junction, New Jersey, is an obvious example; outward expansion from the New York and Philadelphia metropolitan areas has not quite yet met there, and on a travel-time map from central Manhattan it appears as about the equivalent of lower Brooklyn. In fact, people commute from there to three metropolitan areas—New York, Philadelphia, and Trenton.

28. Incidentally, while a region almost always has a center, and occasionally may have more than one, a sub-region often does not.

29. Sometimes including Rockland County, and perhaps even Orange County in New York; but, they both also have strong links to Westchester County, across the Hudson.
30. In *Mount Laurel*, the court adopted as the region the area within 20 miles of downtown Camden. This area—the Northern part of Burlington, Camden, and Gloucester Counties—corresponds rather well to that part of the Delaware Valley industrial belt centering on Camden, (and so, close to Philadelphia), which is now under strong development pressure outward from those two cities. In effect, this is the situation of the region around a medium-sized city mentioned above, located at a state boundary and therefore with substantial pressure from the central city across the river (Philadelphia)—but nonetheless fairly easily definable.
31. For example, New Jersey has statutory authorization for county housing authorities.
32. These do have their shortcomings. For example, only in New England do their boundaries deviate from county lines; as a result, both the Mohave Desert and the wilderness area of northern Minnesota are located within SMSA's.
33. No attempt is made there to explore all the permutations and combinations which the courts will run across in attempting to define regions. The mobility of the American population is constantly creating new problems in this regard. For example, a current study of the luxury housing market in Miami Beach has turned up the curious fact that, in considering the demand for such condominiums there, the alternative often considered is not something in Florida, but the cost of an apartment on Park Avenue in New York. Sternlieb, A Study of Rent Control in the Greater Miami Beach Luxury Housing Market, 1975 (published in report form by Rutgers Center for Urban Policy Research, New Brunswick, N.J.).
34. *S. Burlington County NAACP v. Township of Mount Laurel*, 67 N.J. 151, 159, 336 A.2d 713, 717 (1975), *appeal dismissed and cert. denied*, 423 U.S. 808 (1975).
35. The preparation of such plans is now a HUD requirement in connection with the recipients of all grants under both the 701 program and the new Housing Act of 1974. See 39 Fed. Reg. 43382-84 § §600.70 and 600.72.
36. 62 N.J. 473, 303 A.2d 273 (1973), and 63 N.J. 196, 306 A.2d 65 (1973).
37. The experience, as of a couple of years ago, has been summarized in BROOKS, LOW-INCOME HOUSING, THE PLANNERS' RESPONSE, an A.S.P.O. publication in 1972. For more recent experience, *see*, eg. DELAWARE VALLEY REGIONAL PLANNING COMMISSION, REGIONAL HOUSING ALLOCATION PLAN, 1970-2000 (adopted July 25, 1973), and its implementation at the county level in BUCKS COUNTY PLANNING COMMISSION, BUCKS COUNTY HOUSING PLAN (September 1974); Tri-State Regional Planning Commission, DWELLINGS AND NEIGHBORHOODS, THE HOUSING ELEMENT OF REGIONAL PLANNING (September 1974), and the following Tri-State technical staff reports: HOW TO THAW THE ZONING FREEZE IN THE SUBURBS (June 1971) and A RECONNAISSANCE OF SELECTED HOUSING ALLOCATION PLANS (February 1973).
38. In the better studies a further breakdown is made as to present (and future) low-wage employment.
39. Now that the impact of the lower birth rate in the 1970's is being felt in the elementary schools, this is a real possibility, even in some growing areas.
40. The question of how to treat the size of the existing low and moderate income population has been handled in different ways in these allocation schemes. In

some, the existence of such a population is regarded as presupposing a need for additional housing within their means; in another, the existence of a large group of this type is held to imply the undesirability of encouraging its growth.

41. Assuming that this is not restricted to local residents.

42. *See particularly : Allen-Dean Corp. v. Township of Bedminster, Somerset County* Superior Court (L. Div.) No. L 36896-70 P.W. and L28061-71 P.W., announced February 24, 1975, an important decision which turns around New Jersey law on the comprehensive plan doctrine, on the basis of more recent statutes.

43. If such a decision becomes frequent, it is not inconceivable that this will lead to increased popularity for housing subsidies. A state-wide building code to ensure good mobile home construction would be appropriate here.

44. This matter has been explored intensively in a report to the Princeton Regional Planning Board in Princeton, New Jersey, by Anthony Downs and his staff at Real Estate Research Corporation, which will be published soon.

45. *Roman Catholic Diocese of Newark v. Borough of Ho-Ho-Kus,* 42 N.J. 556, 202 A.2d 161 (1964).

46. One perhaps might argue the contrary on the level of legislative intent, if one considers the scheme of land use controls realistically as including all governmental actions which have a major impact on land use. The combined impact of the present official land use control system, plus the reliance of local real property taxation (and so on "good ratables") to finance major public services, is to provide financial rewards to the exclusionary suburbs and financial penalties for those which take a more socially-minded view on housing. In a word, this is a system for subsidizing anti-social conduct.

47. It seems probable that in most instances there is no need for a conflict between securing land for low- and moderate-cost housing and protecting land in ecologically sensitive areas. Figures on the subject are scarce, but they do exist for New Jersey. Williams and Norman, *supra* note 24. For example, in the state's prime growth area in Middlesex County, there are (or there were in 1970) some 56,000 acres of vacant land which are dry, flat, and zoned for residence. The County Planning Board has estimated the need for low and moderate cost housing at about 23,000 dwelling units—i.e., at 10 to the acre (with an allowance for streets and public facilities); the need is perhaps 3,000 acres. In such instances, there obviously is sufficient room for both.

48. 24 MINN. STAT. 473 (f).01 *et. seq.* (extra session) 1971.

49. This comes close to the system involved in the Hawaiian statewide zoning.

Fair Share and Regional Need

Harvey S. Moskowitz and Carl Lindbloom

The Mt. Laurel decision[1] called upon New Jersey's developing municipalities to "make realistically possible an appropriate variety and choice of housing . . . and . . . affirmatively afford the opportunity (for low and moderate income housing), at least to the extent of the municipality's fair share of the present and prospective regional need . . . "[2]

In theory at least, the mandate of the Court is clear. Developing municipalities must adopt land use regulations which allow for all types of housing and must, in a positive manner, provide for a fair share of their regional housing need for low- and moderate-income housing.

But there is a large gap between theory and practice. Indeed, the Supreme Court itself fully recognized the difficulties involved in the practical application of the decision. Six months after *Mount Laurel*, the Court sent a letter to all counsel involved in the *Oakwood at Madison v. Township of Madison* case, another exclusionary zoning appeal.[3] The letter contained what has become known as the "18 questions," all of which deal with the very practical considerations of how to best implement the admirable objectives of Mt. Laurel.

Whether *Mount Laurel* will lead to increased housing opportunities for low- and moderate-income families still remains to be seen. The depressed state of the home building industry and the absence of meaningful federal or state programs has slowed new housing construction considerably. [4] Even where municipalities have zoned land for multi-family construction or where zoning variances have been granted, developers have been reluctant to act. The high cost of construction loans, new consumer protection laws giving renters additional rights, rent leveling, and talk of tax changes altering the present tax shelter advantages for investors have all contributed to the overall situation.

But even recognizing the problems, the mandate of the Court is clear—municipalities must proceed in laying the groundwork to improve low and moderate income housing opportunities. It would appear, therefore, that a logical first step in planning for housing is to determine need based on the Mt. Laurel guidelines. The purpose of this paper is to outline how municipalities can determine the housing region in which they are located and their fair-share of the present and future low- and moderate-income housing of the region.

Defining the Region

The *Mount Laurel* decision did not define what the Court meant by a "region" although it did say that "confinement to or within a certain county appears not to be realistic, but restriction within the boundaries of the state seems practical and advisable." [5]

In certain situations, however, the county is an appropriate region. In the *Urban League* of Greater New Brunswick case [6] Judge David Furman did accept Middlesex County as the region. He noted:

> "Regions are fuzzy at the borders. Middlesex County is a Standard Metropolitan Statistical Area . . . an area . . . specified as an integrated economic and social unit with a large population nucleus. Twenty of the 25 municipalities joined in a Community Development Block Grant application . . . A county master plan and a wealth of applicable statistics are available through the County Planning Board.
>
> Someone employed in any municipality of the county may seek housing in any other municipality, and someone residing in any municipality may seek employment in any other municipality. Residence within walking distance of the place of employment, or within the same municipality, is no longer a desideratum. Nor is the availability of public transportation a major factor. The county is crisscrossed by arterial highways, including the New Jersey Turnpike and the Garden State Parkway. Mobility by automobile is the rule. A large proportion even of low income wage earners within the county own automobiles and many of those travel regularly 20 miles or more to their places of

employment. The entire county is within the sweep of suburbia. Its designation as a region for the purpose of this litigation, within larger metropolitan regions, is sustained."[7]

The use of regions as a planning tool is not new. There are water regions (often called basins), sewer regions, physical, political, or retail market regions, to name a few. The definition of a region largely depends, interestingly enough, on the availability of statistical evidence relating to the primary subject of investigation. A drainage basin is determined by the geographic limits of the topography and the natural flow of water. This calls for knowing the elevation of the land. Retail markets regions, vital in determining shopping center locations, are determined by analyzing readily available statistical evidence on shoppers' habits.

The determination of a housing region is somewhat more complex. The Federal Housing Administration defines a housing region as the area within which dwellings are in competition. But they go on to point out its similarity with the labor market area. [8]

The *Mount Laurel* decision touched on this point, calling for communities which zone for industry and commerce to provide for adequate housing within the means of the employees involved in those uses. Indeed, relevant studies conducted over a period of time in widely spaced geographic areas appear to establish that jobs and employment may be the principal determinant in residence location.[9] With this as the critical criterion, one valid method for determining the housing region is to determine the location of jobs of the residents of the community: Where do the people who live in town work?

Fortunately, these statistics are available from the U.S. Census. But in some cases, particularly where a municipality may border another state or county, the census breakdown may be too broadly defined to be of any value. In this type of situation, the region can be delineated by establishing a theoretical travel line of between thirty to forty-five minutes beyond the municipality's borders using the predominant mode of transportation during peak travel hours.

A thirty minute journey to work appears to be the maximum that most people will travel from home to job.[10] In New Jersey, however, it is the authors' view that forty-five minutes may not be an unreasonable upper limit.

It must be emphasized that there are situations where commuting patterns may not be appropriate or offer much assistance in determining the housing region. Developing communities where a very high percentage of the work force is employed in one plant or industrial location outside the municipality are probably in this category.

Municipalities with a large number of industries within their boundaries employing the majority of residents and pulling in many from outside would also require a different method of regional delineation.

What method to use would depend on the particular circumstances.
County planning boards may have considered sub-regions within their
jurisdiction and these may be appropriate for purposes of the delineation.
Other regional determinants such as retail markets or river basins may
offer some assistance in special cases.

Finally, although completely arbitrary, the Court in *Mount Laurel* simply settled on a twenty mile radius as the housing region.

Housing Need

Once the region has been established it is then possible to determine
the existing need and project future demand. The *existing* housing need
for low and moderate income units is a local rather than a regional determination. It is an "in place" calculation based on how much of the municipality's present housing stock is either deteriorated or dilapidated and
how many of the present residents pay more than the commonly accepted
yardstick of twenty-five percent of their annual income for housing.[11] Fortunately, the present need for each of New Jersey's 567
municipalities has been calculated by the State Department of Community Affairs.[12] One need only to look up a particular municipality to determine this total *existing* need.

Existing need may also be computed in other ways. For example, if a
developing municipality has managed to attract considerable industry, its
present need, in addition to the replacement of physically deficient units
and providing for residents paying over 25 percent of their income for
housing, should include housing for the workers in these plants. Indeed,
the essence of *Mount Laurel* was that jobs and housing are closely related.

It would not be difficult to determine the deficiency in the present
housing supply *within* the municipality in terms of the number of jobs at
various salary or wage levels. A variation of this formula was used by the
authors in a case involving Holmdel Township, Monmouth County.[13]
Holmdel's present need, as estimated by the state, was just under 100
units. But Holmdel had managed to attract 7,300 jobs, or seven percent
of the total in Monmouth County.[14] Testimony in the case pointed out
that the average sales price of all houses in Holmdel was over $70,000
and the building inspector testified that the raw cost of housing (without
land) was approximately $50,000.

Given this situation, the *present* need for low- and moderate-income
housing was estimated to be considerably above the State estimate. With

an estimated County low and moderate income housing need of 30,000 units, Holmdel's share of this need was estimated as the same proportion as its share of the county employment base or seven percent. This figure of 2,100 low- and moderate-income housing units was accepted by the Court as the Township's *present* need.

In summary, judgement on the part of the planner is needed when an outside agency (such as the State or county) estimates the existing need. Intimate knowledge of local conditions may call for either an upward or downward revision.

Future low- and moderate income housing need will depend on regional projections of employment for the region. Each job generates about 0.7 households since about 30 percent of all households have more than one job holder.[15] Thus, 100,000 new jobs will require 70,000 dwelling units. Job projections for municipalities, counties and regions are available from a variety of sources such as the Regional Plan Assocation, Tri-State Planning Commission, Port of N.Y. & N.J. as well as county planning boards. One excellent source is the 1973 Rutgers study, *Modeling State Growth, New Jersey, 1980.*

Another method is to aggregate all vacant industrial land in the region and use the common yardstick of ten to twenty employees per acre to arrive at a total employment range. By comparing the municipality's future employment projection to the total future regional employment and multiplying this figure by 0.7, a fair share future housing need can be determined.

An example may make the process clearer. Montgomery Township in Somerset County was the plaintiff in a recent exclusionary zoning case. As part of the defense in the case, a fair-share analysis was prepared based on the following criteria:

1. Need projections should be based on existing available data and simplified analyses.
2. The 1970 U.S. Census provides a readily available, inexpensive and uncontestable data base applicable to all jurisdictions.
3. Housing need is directly related to jobs.
4. Short term (5-10 years) projections are most appropriate for zoning use.
5. Housing regions should be based largely on commuting patterns.

The first step was in defining the region. Using 1970 Census data, it was found that approximately forty-four percent of all work trips of Montgomery residents were within Somerset county and thirty-six percent were to neighboring Mercer county. The remaining twenty percent were scattered to other counties, New York and Pennsylvania. The housing region was thus defined as Somerset and Mercer counties.

Determining the future (1985) job projections for the region was the next step and this was determined by using data prepared by Regional Plan Association.[16] They projected that both counties would have just over 81,000 jobs by the target year. Multiplying by 0.7 (the ratio of jobs to dwelling units) the region's future housing need was estimated at approximately 56,000 dwelling units.

Montgomery's fair share of this need was then determined by comparing the ratio of available non-residential land in the Township compared to the total of such land within the region. The Township had about 2,700 acres so zoned and the region approximately 37,200. The ratio was just over seven percent so that Montgomery's fair share of the region's projected housing need was seven percent of 56,000 units or approximately 3,920 dwelling units.

Some judgement is called for in totaling vacant non-residential or employment generating land. While municipalities have become much more knowledgeable in zoning land for various uses, there still is a tendency to "lump" all remaining or problem land in an industrial category. The planner should delete lands obviously unsuited for industrial development. These include land with steep topography, flood plains, or land with soil problems.

Low- and Moderate-Income Share

In our example, Montgomery's fair share of *total* housing need based on future job projections was 3,920 dwelling units. Obviously, providing this number of units would pose no problem in communities with large land areas. Montgomery, for example, has 32.8 square miles and even at extremely low densities, could easily accommodate the future housing demand.

The problem, of course, is to determine the percentage of future housing that is required for low- and moderate-income families. This can be determined by finding the average sales price of housing in the community and comparing this to the median family income. Assuming that a family can afford a house valued at 2½ times its annual income, the planner can then determine the percentage of families that can afford single-family homes and the percentage that require subsidies or other housing types.

Referring back to the previous example, the average sales price of all single-family houses in Montgomery Township was $40,000.[17] A family would require an annual income of $16,000 (at 2½ times sales price) to afford a $40,000 house.

But in the entire housing region (consisting of Somerset and Mercer counties) only about 30 percent of all families had reached this income level.[18] Thus, 70 percent of all families in the region could not afford to purchase a house in Montgomery Township.

Based on the guidelines set down by *Mount Laurel*, the Township must now make available 70 percent of its future housing need, or 2,745 units, for low- and moderate-income families. We should also add to this figure the existing need, estimated by the State at thirty-three units, for a total of approximately 2,780 low- and moderate-income units.

The Montgomery Township case was decided in favor of the Township, based on their fair-share analysis. But the Court took some exception to one part of the technique which was based on the relationship between available land zoned for employment in the Township to that land area so zoned in the region.

The Court was concerned that a community might be able to eliminate its fair-share by eliminating its vacant employment zones. To eliminate that possibility, a variation of the job potential technique can be used. The variation compares actual *projections of job growth* (as opposed to vacant industrial land) of the municipality to that of its region. For example, if the municipality is expected to capture five percent of the projected job growth of the region during the study period, then it is responsible for five percent of the regional housing need.

This revised technique is complicated somewhat by the need to develop local job growth projections. Such information is usually available in the local master plan, or the municipal planner can prepare projections with his knowledge of the community and area growth potential.

To assist in projecting job growth, past trends in such growth is available on a municipal basis in most states. For example, in New Jersey the Department of Labor & Industry, Division of Employment Security provides, on a municipal basis, annual data on employment covered by State-run employment compensation. Such information can also be used in developing regional job growth projections where existing projections are unreliable, outdated or non-existent.

Kinds of Housing

The present dearth of federal and State housing programs limits to some extent the options that a municipality can exercise in providing for low- and moderate-income housing. Since single-family detached housing is usually too expensive, municipalities must zone sufficient land for apartments, town houses, mobile homes or other types of multi-family housing to accommodate the future fair-share.

Timing

Mount Laurel did not say that all of the land necessary to accommodate the more intensive type of residential development must be rezoned immediately. Indeed, the joining of the issues of housing and jobs, and the methods by which fair-share is determined, strongly suggest that a time frame is needed to achieve balanced housing objectives. It is suggested that the municipality's responsibility is to ensure that the zoning ordinance reflects present housing needs and foreseeable future demands and that the zoning is amended as future job projections become a reality.

The proper vehicle for this distinction may be the comprehensive master plan identifying the areas slated for rezoning to higher density residential use and the circumstances when the rezoning should be accomplished. It also suggests the need for a continuing planning process as opposed to the once a decade master plan and zoning revision which now passes for local planning in New Jersey.

Summary

Determining a municipality's fair-share of regional low- and moderate-income housing needs should pose no problem to local planners. The process may be summarized as follows, keeping in mind that good judgement may suggest alternate methodology in certain situations.

Step	*Source*
1. *Determine region by analyzing where people who live in the municipality work.*	U.S. Census; Tri-State Planning Commission; county planning boards
2. *Determine existing low and moderate income housing needs.*	"An Analysis of Low & Moderate Income Housing Need in New Jersey," Department of Community Affairs, 1975.
3. *Determine future jobs for the region.*	a. "Projections for the New York Urban Regions 31 Counties," 1985-2000, Regional Plan Association, 1973 b. "People & Jobs," The Port Authority of N.Y.-N.J., 1974. c. "Modeling State Growth," New Jersey 1980, Rutgers, 1973. d. County planning boards

4. *Determine number of households resulting from new jobs by multiplying by 0.7.*

5. *Calculate local share of new housing by determining ratio of locally zoned job producing land to the region's similarly zoned land or by projecting local employment and comparing it to the region's projected employment.*

   a. Local Master plans
   b. Local zoning ordinances
   c. State Division of Employment Security

6. *Determine average value of single-family home in municipality and minimum family income necessary to purchase house.*

   Local realtors

7. *Determine percentage of families in region with annual income below that needed to purchase single-family home.*

   U.S. Census

8. *Multiply percentage derived in 7 to local fair share derived in 5 and then add existing low and moderate income need (2).*

9. *Review local zoning code to ensure that sufficient land is zoned to accommodate 8 at reasonable densities.*

The *Mount Laurel* case is significant because it adds housing to an ever increasing list of planning problems that must be solved on a regional basis. There is universal agreement that air and water pollution, waste treatment, transportation and environment are proper regional planning matters.

Even land use controls have recognized regional ramifications. In *Cresskill v. Dumont* (1954) and *Kozesnick v. Montgomery Township* (1957), the courts noted that local ordinances must consider impacts on land beyond municipal boundaries.

The old Municipal Planning Act,[19] required communities to consider land outside their jurisdiction if it relates to the general planning of the municipality.[20] The new Municipal Land Use Law [21] maintains this requirement.[21]

In *Mount Laurel*, the Court added housing as a planning element to be considered on a regional basis. In fact, the Court noted that while a municipality may be uniquely suited for a single housing type, they could only exercise this prerogative if a binding regional housing plan takes up the slack.

To a great extent, New Jersey municipalities and the Legislature have continued to raise the ancient war cry of "home rule" to fight any attempts to apply rational planning to vexing problems. Home rule authority, however, also calls for home rule responsibility. The Court in *Mount Laurel* may have given us our last opportunity to save local initiative. By recognizing regional needs, *Mount Laurel* is a clarion call for rational judgement, which translated means regional planning and action.

NOTES

1. 67 N.J. 151 (1975).
2. Ibid., p. 174.
3. 128 N.J. Super. 438, 445 (Law Div. 1974).
4. In New Jersey, the State Department of Labor & Industry reports new housing construction was down close to 60 percent during the first nine months of 1975 compared to the similar period in 1973.
5. Ibid., pp. 189-190.
6. *The Urban League v. Carteret, et als.,* Superior Court of New Jersey, Chancery Division, Middlesex County, Docket C-4122-73.
7. Ibid., pp. 9 & 10 of opinion.
8. Department of Housing & Urban Development, *F.H.A. Techniques of Housing Market Analysis* (Washington, D.C.: Government Printing Office).
9. For an excellent and complete discussion of these studies see "Exclusionary Zoning, Pitfalls of the Regional Remedy," by Burchell, Listoken and James in James W. Hughes, ed., *New Dimensions in Urban Planning, Growth Controls* (New Brunswick, N.J.: Center for Urban Policy Research, Rutgers University, 1974).
10. Ibid., p. 39.
11. For low- and moderate-income families only. The break between moderate and above may vary depending on whose criteria is used. The State, for example, established $8,500 (approximately) as the breakpoint.
12. "An Analysis of Low & Moderate-Income Housing Need in New Jersey," Department of Community Affairs, Trenton, N.J., 1975.
13. *Middle Union Associates v. Zoning Board of Adjustment of Township of Holmdel* (#L-1149-72 P.W., 5/15/75).
14. Estimated 1975 Holmdel population was 7,500.
15. Based on 1970 Census statistics.
16. *Projections for the New York Urban Regions 31 Counties, 1985-2000,* Regional Plan Association, 1973.
17. The best sources of this information are local realtors who usually can supply lists of local housing sales over a period of time.
18. From U.S. Census data.
19. R.S. 40:55-1.1 to 40:55-1.29.
20. R.S. 40:55-1.11.
21. R.S. 40:55D-1 to 40:55-92.

Is There a Fair Share Housing Allocation Plan That Is Acceptable to Suburban Municipalities?

Jerome G. Rose *

The decision of the Supreme Court of New Jersey in *Southern Burlington County NAACP v. Township of Mount Laurel*[1] has focused the attention of planners and land use lawyers throughout the country on the complex problem of devising a plan by which the housing needs of a region may be allocated to municipalities within that region. This problem is acute in New Jersey where the *Mount Laurel* decision held invalid a municipal zoning ordinance because it failed to provide for the fair share of the housing needs of the region of which the municipality was a part.[2] The problem also exists in many other parts of the country where legislative and administrative bodies have attempted to allocate to suburban communities a fair share of the housing needs of a metropolitan area.[3].

Some municipalities have responded with their own constructive programs to provide for their fair share of regional housing needs.[4] Other

* The author expresses his appreciation for the assistance of Douglas K. Wolfson, a student at Rutgers Law School, in the preparation of this article.

communities have resisted the effort of extra-municipal agencies to intervene in what is perceived to be a local affair of local government. To some municipalities, the imposition of a fair share allocation plan by an outside agency threatens the character, the identity and the integrity of the community.[5]

It is very likely that much of the opposition to fair share allocation plans is caused by the ambiguity and uncertain consequences of applying the formulae that have been devised for the computation of fair share allocations.[6] During the past few years many fair share allocation plans have been formulated.[7] Each is designed to achieve a particular objective and each bases the allocation plan on a different set of standards.[8] The misapplication of an allocation plan to a purpose for which it was not intended can produce results that are not consistent with sound planning principles. In the selection or formulation of a housing allocation plan it is essential to consider the *purpose* for which the plan is intended and the *nature of the governmental process* by which it is to be implemented. In addition, the *criteria* on which the allocation is based should be selected to be consistent with the plan's purpose and administrative process.

The Purpose of the Fair Share Allocation Plan

The usual purpose of a fair share housing allocation plan is to promote a greater choice of housing opportunities and to avoid undue concentration of low and moderate income persons in central cities or older built-up suburbs.[9] Congress has described this objective as one of the express purposes of the housing assistance plan requirement of the Housing and Community Development Act of 1974.[10] The 1974 Act also describes the following as one of the objectives of that legislation:

> the reduction of the isolation of income groups within communities and geographical areas and the promotion of an increase in the diversity and vitality of neighborhoods through the spatial deconcentration of housing opportunities for persons of lower income . . .[11]

The housing allocation plans created in response to the *Mount Laurel* decision should be designed to achieve the same purpose.[12] The New Jersey supreme court made that purpose clear when it stated that every developing municipality "must, by its land use regulations, presumptively make realistically possible an appropriate variety and choice of housing. More specifically, presumptively, it cannot foreclose the opportunity of the classes of people mentioned for low and moderate-income housing and in its regulations must affirmatively afford that opportunity, at least to the extent of the municipality's fair share of the present and prospective regional need therefor."[13] Thus it should be clear that the purpose of a fair share housing allocation plan is to provide an opportunity for low and moderate-income families to escape from the older central cities to the newer developing suburbs.[14] An allocation plan that fails to achieve this objective or, even worse, serves to increase the concentration of low and moderate-income families in central cities or older built-up suburbs, would be inconsistent with the objectives of both the 1974 Act and the *Mount Laurel* decision.

The Nature of the Governmental Process Responsible for Implementing the Fair Share Allocation Plan

The allocation plans created for the Implementation of the Housing Assistance Plans of the 1974 Act as well as allocation plans designed for implementation by an administrative agency can provide for a wide range of opportunities for administrative discretion in their application. Such plans are designed to determine the eligibility of government applicants for federal funding or other benefits and anticipate the opportunity for negotiation and compromise in an on-going administrative process. Housing plans for such a governmental process can be effective even though they are intricate, complex and even ambiguous.

A fair share housing allocation plan designed in response to the *Mount Laurel* decision, to be implemented by a court, must be evaluated by different criteria.[15] Such a plan should be created to help the court determine whether the land use regulations adopted by the duly elected legislative body of a municipality have so clearly denied an appropriate variety and choice of housing that they violate the "general welfare" principles of the state constitution.[16] A fair share housing allocation plan designed for the judicial process cannot assume an on-going administrative process of negotiation, compromise and adjustment between the courts and the municipal governing bodies. The test of the utility of a judicially implemented allocation plan is not whether it can achieve an optimum condition of integration by a continuing and persistent administrative process, but rather whether it provides a range of possibilities of housing choice that can be evaluated by a standard of reasonableness. The state of the art of the planning profession is such that a precise and exact formulation of the optimum range of housing variety in a given community cannot be provided. A court should not be misled by the purported exactitude of the print-out of computer-programmed housing allocation models.

Assorted Criteria for Housing Allocation

A plan for the allocation of a "fair share" of low and moderate-income housing units to municipalities will adopt one or more criteria on the basis of which the allocation will be made. There is no principle of planning, logic or morality that makes any one criterion more correct than any of the others. Each has its advantages, disadvantages and professional proponents. The selection of one standard, rather than another, can result in a very substantial difference in the number of units to be "assigned" to a municipality and upon which the validity of its zoning ordinance will depend.[17]

For the purpose of illustrating the application of each of the following criteria of fair share allocation, let us assume that the "region" has been delineated and that the regional need for housing units for low and moderate income persons has been postulated for a period of time.

ALLOCATION BASED UPON NEED

This principle is designed to allocate housing units for low and moderate income families to those municipalities having the greatest need for such housing. This need may be measured by such factors as vacancy rate, deterioration, overcrowding, and percentage of families paying over 25 percent of their income for shelter. The difficulty with this criteria is that it would allocate the greatest obligation for housing to urban areas where there is the greatest overcrowding and deterioration. Thus, an exclusionary suburban municipality within the region would have a small allocation of housing units while a municipality, more like a central city or older built-up suburb, would be assigned a larger share. Such an allocation would not achieve the objectives of the *Mount Laurel* decision.

To overcome this objection it would be necessary to base the allocation on future rather than existing housing need, on the assumption that most future growth and housing need will be in the suburbs. To accomplish this, it is necessary to predict the housing need of the future for each of the municipalities within the region. There are two commonly accepted techniques for making this prediction: extrapolation and prediction of future employment opportunities. The extrapolation technique is based upon the assumption that the trends indicated by census and similar data will continue in the same direction and rate as previous years. Thus if one of the municipalities had a population increase of 200 persons per year for the past five years it would be predicted that this rate of increase will persist for the next five or ten years and a projection of future population would be made on that assumption.

The next step in this process would be to ignore the same census data relating to the socio-economic composition of the population by income levels and assign a proportionate share of the regional need for housing for low and moderate income families to that municipality. Thus even though an exclusionary suburban community had been increasing in population by 200 persons of upper income per year, the projection of future population would assume a continuation of the same rate of increase but would reject an assumption of the same socio-economic composition. Population prediction by extrapolation is subject to criticism for this reason and because it assumes a continuation of existing population trends. This assumption has not been supported by the facts of the past few years during which the rate of suburban growth in the middle-Atlantic states had declined significantly.[18] It is presently unclear whether the growth rate of suburban communities in the middle-Atlantic states will resume. If such growth does resume, it is uncertain what the rate of that growth will be.

Because of the inherent weakness of the extrapolation technique of population prediction, some housing allocation formulas have adopted the "prediction of future employment opportunities" method of predicting the size and composition of future suburban populations.[19] This method seeks to forecast future population characteristics based upon a prediction of family income that may be derived from anticipated changes in employment opportunities in the region. The future employment opportunities in turn are predicted on the basis of interviews and surveys of representatives of industries that might reasonably be expected to consider the region for future growth and expansion.

Thus, it should be apparent that there are serious methodological weaknesses in the techniques for predicting the size and composition of future population. Consequently the computation of future housing need based upon those predictions is similarly suspect.

ALLOCATION BASED UPON ECONOMIC AND RACIAL INTEGRATION

This criterion is designed to allocate housing units for low- and moderate-income families to those areas having the fewest low-income and racial minority families within their communities. If this standard is to be used, it is important to direct attention to the similarities and differences between economic integration and racial integration. There is no question but that the denial of an opportunity for housing to any person by a municipality on the grounds of race would violate our federal Constitution[20] and federal[21] and state[22] laws. However, the disparity in housing facilities[23] and other material advantages based upon differences in wealth[24] has not usually been held to violate the law. The *Mount Laurel* decision has been the most dramatic recent departure from this otherwise well established principle of constitutional law.[25] The *Mount Laurel* decision does not, however, purport to address the issue of racial discrimination directly.[26] The court made this distinction clear at the beginning of the opinion:

> We will, therefore, consider the case from the wider viewpoint that the effect of Mount Laurel's land use regulation has been to prevent various categories of persons from living in the township because of the limited extent of their income and resources. In this connection, we accept the representation of the municipality's counsel at oral argument that the regulatory scheme was not adopted with any *desire or intent* to exclude prospective residents on the obviously illegal basis of race, origin or believed social incompatibility.[27]

There is little question, however, that the court was well aware of the fact that discrimination against the poor usually falls most heavily upon racial and ethnic minorities.[28] Nevertheless, the *Mount Laurel* decision does not purport to provide a remedy for racial discrimination directly.[29] The decision prescribes a remedy directed specifically to the problem of economic discrimination in the suburbs. A fair share housing allocation plan adopted to comply with the *Mount Laurel* principles should similarly be directed specifically to the problem of economic discrimination in the suburbs.[30]

The use of this standard to formulate a fair share housing allocation plan is comparatively easy. Census data will disclose the income of the residents of each of the municipalities within the designated region. The proportion of low and moderate income residents in each municipality can be calculated and an allocation of low- and moderate-income housing would be made in averse proportion to existing proportions. Thus, a municipality that has very few low- and moderate-income residents would have a large share of low- and moderate-income housing units assigned to it while another municipality that already has a very large proportion of low- and moderate-income residents would receive a small allocation. Such an allocation system would achieve directly the *Mount Laurel* objective of economic integration in the suburbs[31] and would foster indirectly the additional benefit of racial integration. On the other hand, the allocation of any significant number of low- and moderate-income housing units to central cities, older built-up suburbs or to municipalities with existing large amounts of low- and moderate-income housing would subvert the purpose of the *Mount Laurel* decision.[32]

ALLOCATION BASED ON THE PREMISE THAT AN EQUAL SHARE IS A FAIR SHARE

Under the equal share formula each municipality would receive an allocation of an equal share of the regional housing need, regardless of size, population or other significant characteristics. This principle of allocation is based upon the misconceived premise that "equality" can be equated with "fairness." From the perspective of a planner, this principle makes little sense because the planning process should be designed to formulate rational plans and programs that are custom-made to meet the specific needs of and to utilize the available resources of a particular community. An allocation system that ignores real and substantial differences among municipalities must be characterized as "arbitrary and irrational" rather than "fair." [33] In addition, such a system would be oblivious to the underlying purpose of the *Mount Laurel* decision, to avoid undue concentrations of low- and moderate-income persons in central cities and older built-up suburbs. [34]

ALLOCATION BASED ON POPULATION PROPORTIONS

The use of this criterion would allocate a share of the regional need for low- and moderate-income housing units to each of the municipalities within the region based upon the proportion of population of each municipality to the total population of the region. This technique is only one step removed from the oversimplistic principle of "equal share." The population proportion technique is an improvement over the equal share technique because it begins to recognize that there are differences among municipalities within a region and that those differences are relevant in a rational system of allocation of low and moderate income housing units. [35] The improvement is insufficient, however, because only one of the many relevant factors that differentiate municipalities is considered. [36] The allocation of low- and moderate-income housing would be based exclusively upon the total population. This standard is a gross measure of the difference among municipalities when the objective is to avoid undue concentration of low and moderate-income persons in central cities or older built-up suburbs. The use of this standard would contravene the purpose of the *Mount Laurel* decision because it would allocate the greatest share to the most populous central cities and would allocate the smallest share to the most exclusionary suburbs.

ALLOCATION BASED UPON PROPORTION OF EXISTING JOBS

The use of this criterion would allocate a share of the regional need for low- and moderate-income housing to each municipality within the region based upon the relationship of the number of jobs within each municipality to the total number of jobs within the region. This technique is appealing because it begins to address the issue of the suitability of the municipality to accommodate the low- and moderate-income families for whom the housing is allocated. In addition, the information upon which the allocation is made is readily available and is not based upon indefinite or conjectural assumptions. This allocation technique also responds well to a test of fairness because it would impose the greatest obligation on those municipalities that reap the advantage of tax revenues from the industrial enterprises that now provide the jobs and that would provide suburban jobs to city residents.[37] This standard is appealing to planners who seek to conserve human and natural resources by reducing the amount of time and energy required for the daily trip from residence to place of employment and to the judiciary seeking to implement the *Mount Laurel* decision with a comparatively simple and easily administered principle.

The primary disadvantage of this criterion is that its application would result in the allocation of a few low- and moderate-housing units to the most exclusionary residential suburbs with few jobs and would frequently impose the greatest obligation upon those communities that have already assumed the greatest share of such housing. In addition the adoption of this system of allocation would permit "exclusionary-minded" municipalities to avoid further allocations of low- and moderate-cost housing by discouraging industrial and commercial development.[38]

ALLOCATION BASED UPON PROPORTION OF FUTURE JOBS

This technique was designed to retain the advantages of the existing jobs allocation formula and eliminate its disadvantages. It would achieve neither purpose. By allocating a share of the regional need for low and moderate income housing to each municipality based upon the proportion of future rather than existing jobs, the allocation becomes dependent upon indefinite and conjectural assumptions; obligations are imposed without regard to the actual municipal revenue; and there is no assurance that the jobs will ever materialize in fact.[39] The supposed advantage of this technique is that it would permit the allocation of a share of housing to "exclusionary" suburbs that offer only expensive housing and no job opportunities. It would also permit allocation of housing to other suburbs that discourage residential development by zoning large tracts of land for industrial use even though the likelihood of any such industrial use in the foreseeable future is slight.

The weakness of this technique derives from the need to predict the future or to rely upon the prediction made by each municipality con-

tained in the allocation of land zoned for industrial use. Since the allocation of housing would be based upon the relationship between the
number of acres of land in each municipality zoned for industrial and/or
commercial use and the total number of acres zoned for such use in the
designated region, a municipality that has no industry or commerce to
provide jobs for low- and moderate-income persons and has no revenue to
support the costs associated with such housing would nevertheless receive
a substantial housing allocation if the zoning ordinance of the municipality
contains a substantial amount of vacant land zoned for industrial and/or
commercial use. The difficulty with this technique is that the obligations
of a municipality can easily be avoided by reducing or eliminating the
amount of land zoned for industrial and/or commerce use.[40]

ALLOCATION BASED UPON SUITABILITY OF THE MUNICIPALITY
FOR LOW- AND MODERATE-INCOME HOUSING

If a fair-share housing allocation plan must comply with principles of
rational and comprehensive planning then the suitability of the municipality for low- and moderate-income housing should be the criterion upon
which that allocation plan is based.[41] In fact it would require a judgment
bordering upon professional irresponsibility to propose that housing for
low- and moderate-income families should be allocated to an area where
there are few jobs, no public transportation, insufficient educational, medical and social services, inadequate water and sewer facilities and inordi-
nate ecological risks. These and other factors, including the fiscal capacity
of the municipality to provide the requisite services and the allocation of
land within the jurisdiction, are among the many factors considered and
evaluated in the planning process.[42]

The critical issue that must be comprehended by the judiciary and
other intervenors in the planning process is that there is no objective
method of weighing each of the many factors of "suitability." It is precisely for this reason that, after the planning studies are made and professional opinions are offered, the planning process must be continued in a
forum comprised of elected representatives with a democratic and constitutional mandate to make policy decisions.[43] This creates a difficult dilemma for a court seeking to implement the *Mount Laurel* municipality. If an easy-to-apply allocation formula (such as number of jobs) is
adopted, the allocation will be made without regard to the many other
critical principles and practices of the planning process. Such an allocation would be vulnerable to attack as an arrogant disregard of the integrity and purpose of the planning process.[44] On the other hand, if the
allocation formula considers the many factors involved in the "suitability"
of each municipality, then the judgment of the court on these issues

would be vulnerable to attack as an unwarranted intrusion into the legislative process.[45] It is questionable whether a court can avoid this dilemma by appointing a professional planner to formulate the housing allocation plan. Such an appointed expert could bring to the process nothing more than professional competence and seasoned judgment. The professional planner would have no special ability or mandate to make the policy decisions upon which any allocation plan must eventually rest. This observation may disclose the weakest assumption upon which fair share allocation plans and the *Mount Laurel* principle are based.

ALLOCATION BASED UPON THE OBLIGATION OF EVERY MUNICIPALITY TO TAKE CARE OF THE HOUSING NEEDS OF ITS OWN CONSTITUENTS

This method of allocation is designed to meet local, municipal housing needs rather than regional housing needs. Consequently it does not purport to comply with the theory of the *Mount Laurel* decision. Its primary advantage, however, is that it may be capable of achieving the objectives of the *Mount Laurel* decision more readily than allocation formulas designed to achieve more idealistic but politically assailable regional housing needs. The objective of the *Mount Laurel* decision can be achieved only if a variety and choice of housing is made available in most, if not all, of the municipalities within the state.[46] As a practical matter, this means that apartments, townhouses and aggregated, higher-density dwelling unit construction must be permitted under municipal law.[47] If all municipal governing bodies *willingly* permit a limited amount of such construction, there is reason to predict that more housing will be built in this voluntary way than will ever be built as a result of a judicially mandated and politically resisted fair share housing allocation plan.

The purpose of a "take-care-of-our-own" allocation plan is to propose a formula that is more acceptable politically to the constituents of municipalities to whom the state constitution has granted the power of home rule.[48] This plan rests upon the assumption that most fair-minded people recognize a need to provide housing for themselves, when they become elderly, for their children, for the policeman, fireman, teachers and other municipal employees who provide essential government services, and even to those who work within the community or who have recently left because of an inability to find satisfactory housing within their means. All judicially proclaimed ideals to the contrary notwithstanding, local opposition to apartments and less expensive housing becomes manifest only when it is possible for local residents to conjure up the threat of invasion of hordes of outsiders whose numbers and presence may threaten the safety, security and amenities of the community they seek to preserve. There is no need to call forth such images to correct the inequities of restrictive zoning ordinances. There is no need to arouse the fears or to deny the legitimate concerns of suburban residents.[49] There is no need to pit the powers of the courts against the prerogatives of the legislature.

Conclusion

The *Mount Laurel* decision opened a new era in exclusionary zoning litigation by mandating that each developing municipality must provide for its fair share of the regional housing needs. The court did not, however, specify the criteria by which each municipality's fair share is to be determined.

This article has considered eight possible criteria for determining the fair share allocation of every developing municipality. If exclusionary zoning laws constitute the evil sought to be removed by the *Mount Laurel* decision (rather than the national system of distribution of resources that causes great disparities in ability to afford housing) then the appropriate principle to be adopted by the courts would be the one that declares invalid, as unreasonable, any zoning ordinance that fails to reasonably provide for the housing needs of its own constituents. Such a standard would be consistent with the principles of sound planning, the limits of judicial power and the fundamental principle of democracy that the power to make decisions of public policy must rest ultimately upon the consent of those whose lives will be governed thereby.

NOTES

1. 67 N.J. 151, 336 A.2d 713. *cert. denied,* 423 U.S. 808 (1975).
2. *Id.* at 174, 336 A.2d at 724-25.
3. The following governmental and institutional bodies have either implemented or proposed fair-share plans:

    Dade County Metropolitan Planning Board; Delaware River Valley Regional Planning Commission; Fairfax County, Va.; The Greater Hartford Process, Inc.; the State of Massachusetts; Metropolitan Washington Council of Governments; Metropolitan Dade County Planning Department; Metropolitan Council of the Twin Cities Area; Miami Valley Regional Planning Commission; Middlesex County (N.J.) Planning Board; the State of New Jersey; New York State Urban Development Corporation; Sacramento Regional Area Planning Commission; and the San Bernardino County Planning Department. Others developing fair-share mechanisms have included the University of Pennsylvania's Fels Center of Government and the St. Louis Metropolitan Section of the American Institute of Planners.

    Listokin, *Fair-Share Housing Distribution: Will It Open the Suburbs to Apartment Development?*, 2 REAL ESTATE L.J. 739, 740-41 (1974) (footnotes omitted) [hereinafter cited as Listokin].

4. *Id.*
5. The "controlled growth" position may merely be a convenient justification by suburban communities for retaining their exclusive nature. The popularity of such a position poses a direct threat to fair share programs. *See* Finkler, *Non-growth as a Planning Alternative,* ASPO REP. No. 283 (Sept., 1972).
6. For a review of the first year of post-*Mount Laurel* litigations see Rose, *The Trickle Before the Deluge from* Mount Laurel, 5 REAL ESTATE L.J. 69 (1976).
7. For an excellent overview of the existing and implemented fair share plans see Brooks, *Lower-Income Housing: The Planner's Response,* ASPO REP. No. 282 (July-Aug., 1972) [hereinafter cited as Brooks]. *See also* Listokin, *supra* note 3, at 743 (analyzes the variations in the types of housing to be allocated).
8. Perhaps the most frequently mentioned standards used in determining fair share housing allocations are grounded upon considerations of equality, need, distribution, suitability, and the availability of jobs. *See* Brooks, *supra* note 7, at 20; Listokin, *supra* note 3, at 743.
9. *See:* Brooks, *supra* note 7; Listokin, *supra* note 3.
10. 42 U.S.C. § 5304(a)(4) (1970).
11. *Id.* § 5301(c)(6).
12. *See:* note 2 and accompanying text *supra.* The New Jersey supreme court cited approvingly Listokin, *Fair Share Housing Distribution: An Idea Whose Time Has Come?*, in INSTITUTE FOR ENVIRONMENTAL STUDIES, NEW JERSEY TRENDS 353 (1974). 67 N.J. at 190-91, 336 A.2d at 733-34.
13. 67 N.J. at 174, 336 A.2d at 724.
14. This may necessarily be predicated on the availability of land appropriate for residential development. For an investigation of the characterization of a municipality as a "developing municipality" see Rose & Levin, *What is a 'Developing Municipality' within the Meaning of the* Mount Laurel *Decision.* 4 REAL ESTATE L.J. 359 (1976) [hereinafter cited as Rose & Levin].
15. In considering the remedies available in *Mount Laurel,* the court noted:

> We are not at all sure what the trial judge had in mind as ultimate action with reference to the approval of a plan for affirmative public action concerning the satisfaction of indicated housing needs and the entry of a final order requiring implementation thereof. Courts do not build housing nor do municipalities. That function is performed by private builders, various kinds of associations, or, for public housing, by special agencies created for that purpose at various levels of government. The municipal function is initially to provide the opportunity through appropriate land use regulations and we have spelled out what Mount Laurel must do in that regard. It is not appropriate at this time, particularly in view of the advanced view of zoning law as applied to housing laid down by this opinion, to deal with the matter of the further extent of judicial power in the field or to exercise any such power.

67 N.J. at 192. 336 A.2d at 734.
16. The court based its decision on "the basic state constitutional requirements of substantive due process and equal protection of the laws," *id.* at 174, 336 A.2d at 725, rather than the express statutory requirement that zoning regulations promote the general welfare. N.J. STAT. ANN. § 40:55-32 (1967). *See* note 43 *infra.* For an examination and discussion of why the protections afforded by the state constitution were invoked as the basis for the decision in the Mount Laurel case see Rose, *The* Mount Laurel *Decision: Is It Based on Wishful Thinking?*, 4 REAL ESTATE L.J. 61 (1975) [hereinafter cited as Rose].

    See also Urban League v. Mayor & Council of Borough of Carteret, 142 N.J. Super. 11, 359 A.2d 526 (Ch. 1976) (indicating that if a zoning ordinance is in derogation of the general welfare encompassing housing needs, it would be struck down as unconstitutional).

17. If a court determines that a particular municipality has not, in fact, met its fair share, then under the *Mount Laurel* holding, the zoning ordinance will be considered as "presumptively contrary to the general welfare and outside the intended scope of the zoning power." 67 N.J. at 185, 336 A.2d at 730.

    In *Urban League v. Mayor & Council of Borough of Carteret*, the court responded to the argument that a municipality might be exempted from *Mount Laurel* criteria if there existed only minimal vacant acreage: "but a municipality is not exempt from the constitutional standards of reasonableness on its zoning ordinance because it is not 'developing' within *Mt. Laurel*." 142 N.J. Super. at −, 359 A.2d at 533.

18. *See:* U.S. BUREAU OF THE CENSUS, U.S. CENSUS OF POPULATIONS 32-5, 34-5, 40-5 (1970).

19. In *Mount Laurel* the court considered future employment opportunities to be an important factor in terms of housing need. "Certainly, when a municipality zones for industry and commerce for local tax benefit purposes, it without question must zone to permit adequate housing within the means of the employees involved in such uses." 67 N.J. at 187, 336 A.2d at 732. Moreover, in discussing the determination of fair share, and the factors involved therein, the court indicated that "in arriving at such a determination the type of information and estimates . . . concerning the housing needs of persons of low- and moderate-income now or formerely residing in the township in substandard dwellings and those presently employed or reasonably expected to be employed therein, will be pertinent. *Id.* at 190. 336 A.2d at 733. *See also* Urban League v. Mayor v. Council of Borough of Carteret, 142 N.J. Super. 11, 359 A.2d 526 (Ch. 1976).

    By the year 2000, the deficiencies in low- and moderate-income housing for industrial employees within each municipality would be of disastrous proportions under present zoning . . . It is pertinent to note that at the present an estimated 75,000 residents of the country are employed outside the county, as compared to an estimated 55,000 residents elsewhere who are employed within the county.

20. U.S. CONST. amend. V. XIV.

21. *See: e.g.*, 42 U.S.C. § § 3601-5 (1970): *cf. id.* § § 1981, 1983. Note particularly *id.* § 3604 which provides in pertinent part that "It shall be unlawful . . . (2) to refuse to sell or rent . . . or to refuse to negotiate for the sale or rental of, or otherwise make unavailable or deny, a dwelling to any person because of race . . . " and *id.* § 3605, entitled "Discrimination in the financing of Housing," which makes it unlawful to deny a loan or other financial assistance to a person for the purpose of purchasing, constructing, repairing or maintaining a dwelling. *See generally United States v. Bob Lawrence Realty, Inc.*, 474 F.2d 115 (5th Cir.), *cert. denied.* 414 U.S. 826 (1973); Sanborn v. Wagner, 354 F. Supp. 291 (D. Md. 1973); *United States v. Real Estate Dev. Corp.*, 347 F. Supp. 776 (N.D. Miss. 1972); *Williamson v. Hampton Management Co.*, 339 F. Supp. 1146 (N.D. Ill. 1972); United States v. Mintzes, 304 F. Supp. 1305 (D. Md. 1969).

22. *See:* N.J. STAT. ANN. § 10:5-12g-i (Supp. 1976) which proscribes discriminatory practices in the sale or rental of dwellings. The statute is patterned after

the federal Fair Housing Act, and uses substantially the same language. *See* note 21 *supra*.

23. *See: e.g., James v. Valtierra*, 402 U.S. 137 (1971), where California's referendum approval requirement of low-rent public housing projects was held constitutionally sound, implying that the right to adequate shelter (where the shelter can be denied by a vote of the people of the state) is not a fundamental right. *See also Lindsey v. Normet*, 405 U.S. 56 (1972).

The court in *Lindsey* considered a constitutional challenge by tenants of the Oregon forcible entry and detainer statute, which provided summary eviction procedures upon nonpayment of rent and did not allow a defense of uninhabitability. In rejecting plaintiff's equal protection argument, the Court said:

> We do not denegrate the importance of decent, safe, sanitary housing. But the Constitution does not provide judicial remedies for every social and economic ill. We are unable to perceive in that document any constitutional guarantee of access to dwellings of a particular quality . . . Absent constitutional mandate, the assurance of adequate housing and the definition of landlord-tenant relationships are legislative, not judicial, functions.

Id. at 74.

24. *See: San Antonio Independent School Dist. v. Rodriguez*, 411 U.S. 1 (1973) (wealth held not to be a suspect classification in the area of school funding). In *Rodriguez*, the court explained its conclusion as follows:

> We perceive no justification for such a severe denegration of legal property taxation and control as would follow from appellees' contentions. It has simply never been within the constitutional prerogative of this court to nullify statewide measures for financing public services *merely because the burdens or benefits thereof fall unevenly depending upon the relative wealth of the political subdivisions in which citizens live.*

Id. at 54 (emphasis added). *But see Serrano v. Priest*, 5 Cal. 3d 584, 487 P.2d 1241, 96 Cal. Rptr. 601 (1971). *See also Robinson v. Cahill*, 62 N.J. 473, 303 A.2d 273, *cert. denied*, 414 U.S. 976 (1973).

25. It should be noted, however, that the *Mount Laurel* court expressly disavowed any reliance on federal constitutional principles. 67 N.J. at 174, 336 A.2d at 725. *See also* note 16 and accompanying text *supra*.

26. 67 N.J. at 159, 336 A.2d at 717.

27. *Id.* (emphasis added). *See also* Urban League v. Mayor & Council of Borough of Carteret, 142 N.J. Super. 11, −, 359 A.2d 526, 530 (Ch. 1976) where the court similarly dismissed claims of wilfull racial discrimination and proceeded to address the exclusionary aspects of the defendants' zoning ordinances.

28. 67 N.J. at 159, 336 A.2d at 717. *See also Urban League v. Mayor & Council of Borough of Carteret*, 142 N.J. Super. 11, −, 359 A.2d 526, 530 (Ch. 1976) ("the impact of low density zoning is most adverse to blacks and Hispanics, who are disproportionately of low and moderate income").

29. 67 N.J. at 159, 336 A.2d at 717. As an appropriate remedy, the court suggested:

> We have in mind that there is at least a moral obligation in a municipality to establish a local housing agency pursuant to state law to provide housing for its resident poor now living in dilapidated, unhealthy quarters.

Id. at 192, 336 A.2d at 734.

In concurrence Justice Pashman forcefully stated:

The problems we begin to face today are of awesome magnitude and importance, both for New Jersey and for the nation as a whole. It will not do to approach them gingerly; they call out for forceful and decisive judicial action.

. . . The question is whether the suburbs will act to accommodate this growth in an orderly way or will simply and blindly resist.

. . . The shape of the possible disaster can now be foreseen. The inevitable alternative to assumption by suburban communities of an obligation to provide for their fair share of regional housing needs is an increase in the size of slums with all their attendant miseries. The consequences of such economic, social, and racial segregation are too familiar to need recital here . . . Justice must be blind to both race and income.

. . .

. . . Like animal species that overspecialize and breed out diversity and so perish in the course of evolution, communities, too, need racial, cultural, social and economic diversity to cope with our rapidly changing times.

67 N.J. at 220-21, 336 A.2d at 749-50 (Pashman, J., concurring). *See also Urban League v. Mayor & Council of Borough of Carteret*, 142 N.J. Super. 11. _____ . 359 A.2d 526, 530 (Ch. 1976) ("[N]o credible evidence of deliberate or systematic exclusion of minorities was before the court").

30. 67 N.J. at 159, 336 A.2d at 717. *See Urban League v. Mayor & Council of Borough of Carteret*, 142 N.J. Super. 11. –. 359 A.2d 526. 541 (Ch. 1976), where the court determined that the first fair share allocation would be to "correct the present imbalance, that is to bring each defendant municipality up to the county proportion of 15% low- and 19% moderate-income population."

31. 67 N.J. at 159, 336 A.2d at 717.

32. *Id.* at 160, 336 A.2d at 717. For a discussion of how the *Mount Laurel* principles are applicable to a municipality which is located outside the central cities and older built up suburbs see Rose & Levin, *supra* note 14, at 370-71.

33. The court in *Mount Laurel* apparently recognized the need to direct a certain amount of attention to the differences between municipalities, as evidenced by its limitation of the *Mount Laurel* mandate to those municipalities which can appropriately be characterized as "developing." Justice Hall used the phrases "developing municipality like Mount Laurel," "such municipalities," and the like, a total of fifteen times. *See* 67 N.J. at 160, 173, 174, 179, 180, 185, 186, 187, 188, 190, 191. 336 A.2d at 717, 724, 727, 728, 731, 732, 733. *But see id.* at 194, 336 A.2d at 735 (Pashman, J., concurring). Justice Pashman voiced dissatisfaction with the restrictive approach taken by the majority:

The majority has chosen not to . . . consider the degree to which the principles applicable to developing municipalities are also applicable to rural ones and to largely developed ones . . . [E]xclusionary zoning is a problem of such magnitude and depth as to require that the Court extend these principles to all municipalities in the State . . .

Id. at 208, 336 A.2d at 743. *See also Urban League v. Mayor & Council of Borough of Carteret*, 142 N.J. Super. 11, –. 359 A.2d 526, 537-41 (Ch. 1976) (the court painstakingly described the existent condition as to each defendant municipality); Rose & Levin, *supra* note 14, at 369-81.

The *Mount Laurel* court was also aware of possible environmental and ecological problems which might be relevant:

> The present environmental situation in the area is . . . no sufficient excuse in itself for limiting housing therein to single-family dwellings on large lots . . . This is not to say that land use regulations should not take due account of ecological or environmental factors or problems. Quite the contrary. Their importance, at last being recognized, should always be considered.

67 N.J. at 186, 336 A.2d at 731.

34. 67 N.J. at 159, 336 A.2d at 717. *But see Urban League v. Mayor & Council of Borough of Carteret,* 142 N.J. 11. —. 359 A.2d 526. 541-42 (Ch. 1976) where the projected need of housing was allocated to each of the defendant municipalities equally. In support of this determination, the court stated:

> Subtracting 4,030 from the 18,697 low and moderate income housing units needed in the county to 1985, the balance is 14,667 or approximately 1,333 per municipality. There is no basis not to apportion these units equally. Each municipality has vacant suitable land far in excess of its fair share requirement without impairing the established residential character of neighborhoods. Land to be protected for environmental considerations has been subtracted from vacant acreage totals. No special factors, such as relative access to employment, justifies a deviation from an allocation of 1,333 low and moderate housing units, plus the allocation to correct the imbalance, to each of the 11 municipalities.

Id.

35. *See:* note 34 *supra.*

36. For an example of other factors that distinguish municipalities from each other see Rose & Levin, *supra* note 14, at 369-81.

37. This technique is also consistent with *Mount Laurel* principles. 67 N.J. at 187, 336 A.2d at 732: "Certainly when a municipality zones for industry and commerce for local tax benefit purposes, it without question must zone to permit adequate housing within the means of the employees involved in such uses."

38. Such a policy might not be in the best fiscal interests of the particular municipality. The existing policy of land use regulation for a fiscal end derives from New Jersey's tax structure. What occurs in a typical municipality is that:

> sizeable industrial and commercial ratables are eagerly sought and homes and the lots on which they are situated are required to be large enough, through minimum lot sizes and minimum floor areas, to have substantial value in order to produce greater tax revenues to meet school costs. Large families who cannot afford to buy large houses and must live in cheaper rental accommodations are definitely not wanted, so we find drastic bedroom restrictions for, or complete prohibition of, multi-family or other feasible housing for those of lesser income.

67 N.J. at 171, 336 A.2d at 723. The court also pointed out the inadequacies of such a practice:

> One incongruous result is the picture of developing municipalities rendering it impossible for lower paid employees of industries they have eagerly sought and welcomed with open arms (and, in Mount Laurel's case, even some of its own lower paid municipal employees) to live in the community where they work.

Id. at 172, 336 A.2d at 723.

39. If no jobs do in fact materialize, the lower income or unskilled employee may not be able to find work at all. The court in *Mount Laurel* was astutely aware of the potential problems in such a situation:

> In a society which came to depend more and more on expensive individual motor vehicle transportation for all purposes, low income employees very frequently could not afford to reach outlying places of suitable employment and they certainly could not afford the permissible housing near such locations. These people have great difficulty in obtaining work and have been forced to remain in housing which is overcrowded, and has become more and more substandard and less and less tax productive. There has been a consequent critical erosion of the city tax base and inability to provide the amount and quality of those governmental services—education, health, police, fire, housing and the like—so necessary to the very existence of safe and decent city life.

> *Id.* at 172-73, 336 A.2d at 724.

40. It should be noted, however, that the court in *Mount Laurel* may have had precisely this result in mind—*i.e.*, breaking up the usual municipal practice of zoning an excess amount of vacant land for industrial and commercial uses. *See id.* at 163, 336 A.2d at 718. *See also* note 39 *supra*.

41. *See:* Listekin, *supra* note 3, at 746, 754-55. (Massachusetts fair share plan guided by suitability considerations).

42. The fiscal capacity of a municipality is an appropriate factor to be considered in determining whether that municipality is a suitable place for housing, except when fiscal factors are considered for the purpose of excluding certain categories of housing. *See South Burlington County NAACP v. Township of Mount Laurel.* 67 N.J. 151, 185-186, 336 A.2d 713. 731. *cert. denied.* 423 U.S. 808 (1975):

> We have previously held that a developing municipality may properly zone for and seek industrial ratables to create a better balance for the community vis-à-vis educational and governmental costs engendered by residential development, provided that such was " . . . done reasonably as part of and in furtherance of a legitimate comprehensive plan for the zoning of the entire municipality." Gruber v. Mayor & Township Comm. of Raritan Township. 39 N.J. I. 9-11 (1962). We adhere to that view today. But we were not there concerned with, and did not pass upon, the validity of municipal exclusion by zoning of types of housing and kinds of people for the same local financial end. We have no hesitancy in now saying, and do so emphatically, that, considering the basic importance of the opportunity for appropriate housing for all classes of our citizenry, no municipality may exclude or limit categories of housing for that reason or purpose. While we fully recognize the increasingly heavy burden of local taxes for municipal governmental and school costs on homeowners, relief from the consequences of this tax system will have to be furnished by other branches of government. It cannot legitimately be accomplished by restricting types of housing through the zoning process in developing municipalities.

43. *Compare:* 67 N.J. at 194, 336 A.2d at 735 (Mountain, J., concurring) (agreeing with the majority, but basing his conclusion on his interpretation of the term "general welfare" as it appears in N.J. STAT. ANN. § 40:55-32 (1967): "[zoning] regulations shall be in accordance with a comprehensive plan and

designed for one or more of the following purposes: to . . . promote . . . the general welfare . . . "), *with id.* at 151, 336 A.2d 713 (Hall, J., majority opinion). One significant difference between the two opinions rests on the availability of legislative review. Justice Mountain would have permitted the state legislature, as opposed to the judiciary, to effectively change the interpretation of "general welfare" through the legislative process. Justice Hall, on the other hand, would find this result nearly impossible in that the conclusions are grounded on inherent due process and equal protection clauses of the state constitution. *See* Rose, *supra* note 16.

44. The then-effective New Jersey municipal zoning enabling legislation provided:
    Such regulation shall be in accordance with a comprehensive plan and designed for one or more of the following purposes:
    Such regulation shall be made with reasonable consideration, among other things, to the character of the district and its peculiar suitability for particular uses, and with a view of conserving the value of property and encouraging the most appropriate use of land throughout such municipality.
    N.J. STAT. ANN. § 40:55-32 (1967) (repealed effective Aug. 1, 1976). *See Rockhill v. Chesterfield Twp.*, 23 N.J. 117, 128 A.2d 473 (1957) (where the court held that zoning regulations had to be in accordance with a comprehensive plan and designed to serve the public welfare); *see also Udell v. Haas*, 21 N.Y. 2d 43, 288 N.Y.S. 2d 888, 235 N.E.2d 897 (1968).

45. *See:* N.J. CONST. art. 3, par. 1. *See also Maule v. Conduit & Foundation Corp.*, 124 N.J. Super, 488, 307 A.2d 651 (L. Div. 1973); *West Morris Regional Bd. of Educ. v. Sills*, 110 N.J. Super. 234, 265 A.2d 162 (Ch. 1970); *cf. Busik v. Levine*, 63 N.J. 351, 307 A.2d 571 (1973), *appeal dismissed*, 414 U.S. 1106 (1973).

46. *See:* 67 N.J. at 187, 336 A.2d at 731-32:
    As a developing municipality, Mount Laurel must, by its land use regulations, make realistically possible the opportunity for an appropriate variety and choice of housing for all categories of people who may desire to live there, of course including those of low and moderate income.

47. As to this practical effect, the court in *Mount Laurel* noted that a developing municipality like Mount Laurel
    . . . must permit multi-family housing, without bedroom or similar restrictions, as well as small dwellings on very small lots, low cost housing of other types and, in general, high density zoning, without artificial and unjustifiable minimum requirements as to lot size, building size and the like, to meet the full panoply of these needs.
    Id. at 187, 336 A.2d at 732.

48. *See:* N.J. CONST. art. 4, § 6, par. 2:
    2. The Legislature may enact general laws under which municipalities . . . may adopt zoning ordinances limiting and restricting . . . buildings and structures, according to their construction, and the nature and extent of their use, and the nature and extent of the uses of land, and the exercise of such authority shall be deemed within the police power . . .
    Pursuant to this constitutional provision, there is a strong presumption in favor of validity of a zoning ordinance. *See, e.g., Kirsch Holding Co. v. Borough of Manasquan*, 59 N.J. 241, 281 A.2d 513 (1971); *Harvard Enter-*

prises, Inc. v. Board of Adjustment, 56 N.J. 362, 266 A.2d 588 (1970); *Bogart v. Washington Twp.*, 25 N.J. 57, 135 A.2d 1 (1957); *Molino v. Mayor & Council of Glassboro*, 116 N.J. Super, 195, 281 A.2d 401 (L. Div. 1971).

49. In addressing these fears and images the *Mount Laurel* court stated:

> There is no reason why developing municipalities like Mount Laurel, required by this opinion to afford the opportunity for all types of housing to meet the needs of various categories of people, may not become and remain attractive, viable communities providing good living and adequate services for all their residents in the kind of atmosphere which a democracy and free institutions demand. They can have industrial sections, commercial sections and sections for every kind of housing from low cost and multi-family to lots of more than an acre with very expensive homes. Proper planning and governmental cooperation can prevent over-intensive and too sudden development, insure against future suburban sprawl and slums and assure the preservation of open space and local beauty. We do not intend that developing municipalities shall be overwhelmed by voracious land speculators and developers if they use the powers which they have intelligently and in the broad public interest. Under our holdings today, they can be better communities for all than they previously have been.

67 N.J. at 190-91, 336 A.2d at 733-34.

Eighteen Questions for the Parties in the Oakwood-at-Madison Case

New Jersey Supreme Court

In September, 1975, after all oral arguments had been completed in *Oakwood at Madison v. Township of Madison,* the Clerk of the New Jersey Supreme Court sent the following letter to the attorneys in the action posing eighteen questions and requesting supplementary briefs and oral arguments. The attorneys responded to these questions and reappeared before the court for an additional oral presentation.

The questions posed by the court are particularly significant because they point up the serious issue of justiciability raised by the questionable ability of the courts to administer the judicial process set in motion by the *Mount Laurel* decision.

The text of that communication from the Supreme Court is reprinted here.

Re: Oakwood at Madison v. Twp. of Madison
A-80 / 81-75 (A-52 / 53-74)

Gentlemen:

The Supreme Court has ordered reargument in the above case and has tentatively scheduled it for October 20 or 21, 1975. You are each requested to file supplementary briefs (simultaneously) on or before October 7 as to the following points:

1. Is it necessary, for fair share purposes, for the Court to fix a specific "region", or may the municipality zone on the basis of any area which it reasonably may regard as an appropriate region?

2. Is it sufficient that the ordinance permits satisfaction of the housing needs of low and moderate income people as a single category, or is it necessary that separate estimates of the housing needs for low income, as distinguished from moderate income, people, be formulated and the number of necessary housing units in each category be determined?

3. What are to be the determinants of the income qualifications for low income and moderate income categories, respectively, as of any given date?

4. In framing zoning regulations to achieve the opportunity for adequate low and moderate income housing, how does a municipality accommodate the lag in the rate of rise of median income behind the rate of rise in construction and land costs? During such a period, must the municipality continually revise the zoning ordinance to reduce the size and increase the density of permissible housing in order to accommodate such lag? Are the 1970-1975 figures in the record suitable for 1975 and beyond?

5. Can a developing municipality, in the light of the evidence in this case, "affirmatively afford the opportunity" for adequate low and moderate income housing (*Mt. Laurel*, 67 *N.J.* at 174) short of eliminating all minimum bulk, size or density requirements, not mandated by health statutes or regulations, in sufficiently large areas zoned residential?

6. In view of the absence of assurance of any degree of public subsidization of privately built housing, must the zoning regulations be such as to permit a developer, operating privately, to build housing of a character which will both meet normal profit incentives and be affordable by low and moderate income renters and purchasers? Or is a municipality entitled to assume that a given degree of subsidization will be forthcoming?

7. Are "density bonus" provisions in zoning ordinances valid as against existing zoning law or the general police power authority of municipalities (*i.e.* relaxation of requirements as to maximum units per acre or percentage of lot for building, in return for agreement by builder to rent some units at low rental rates)?

8. What other valid zoning devices are available to encourage construction of low and moderate income housing?

9. In order to affirmatively provide low and moderate income housing, may the zoning ordinance set aside residential zones in which, for purposes of single-family unattached houses, *maximum* lot widths, are

fixed (*e.g.* 25 feet, 30 feet, 40 feet); or in which *minimum* density units per acre may be fixed for multi-unit housing? (*e.g.* 15 or 20).

10. In seeking to encourage lower housing costs to accommodate low income purchasers and renters, how does the municipality resolve the dilemma that low income families generally require more bedrooms than upper income families, which in turn increases the cost of construction of housing units?

11. If the Court affirms the determination of the trial court that the ordinance, as amended, still does not affirmatively provide adequately for low and moderate income housing, how specific should the Court be as to the terms of an ordinance which will satisfy *Mt. Laurel*? Do the interests of bringing this litigation to a final determination dictate some degree of specificity in the determination of the Court?

12. In connection with the latter question, would it be serviceable for the Court to appoint a Special Master to consult with the municipality and frame specific zoning guidelines to assist the municipality in meeting the Court's judgment?

13. Referring to the trial court's opinion, 128 *N.J. Super.* at 443, invalidating the AF multi-family zone because "construction of efficiency and one-bedroom units will dominate", how would plaintiff and *amici* modify the ordinance as to the AF zone to render it valid?

14. In considering what is Madison's fair share of low and moderate income housing for an appropriate region, is it not necessary to determine whether the areas which the municipality seeks to exempt from fair share requirements on ecological grounds, are factually entitled to such exemption (a question the trial court found unnecessary to decide)? Should there be a remand for that purpose?

15. Independently of the general question as to the validity or invalidity of the ordinance on the fair share issue, has the corporate plaintiff factually established its entitlement to be relieved of the restrictions of the ordinance as to its own property on grounds of unreasonableness to the point of confiscation? See *Schere v. Township of Freehold*, 119 *N.J. Super.* 433, certif. den. 62 *N.J.* 69.

16. Plaintiff and *amici* are invited to submit an outline of the basic contents of a zoning ordinance, including specific provisions governing residential zones, which in their opinion would satisfy that *Mt. Laurel* case.

17. Discuss the relevance of *Construction Industry Association of Sonoma County v. City of Petaluma* decided August 13, 1975, 9th Circuit Court of Appeals, which has been summarized at 44 Law Week 2093.

18. What effect, if any, should be given to the financial ability of the municipality to meet the fiscal requirements of additional schools, police,

firemen, utilities, etc. in determining its fair share of moderate and low income housing?

III
Implementation
of the
Decision

Notes on Implementation

Carl S. Bisgaier

The *Mount Laurel* decision[1] has resulted in a flurry of legal, planning, sociological and political analyses. More has been written in its wake than actually has been done, but, after all, the decision broke some new ground in an area where few municipalities or agencies of government ever intended, let alone desired, to tread. Now that the Supreme Court has spoken, the question of implementation has been the major concern of those in need of housing and their advocates. Opponents of the decision have begun to regroup, and battle lines are forming over several issues linked to implementation. Those who wished that the decision had never been rendered now have converted that wish into an assertion that it can't be implemented. My purpose here is to dispel that notion and to note certain perspectives on implementation and the questions that, arguably, are still unresolved by the decision.

Having represented (along with Kenneth Meiser and Peter J. O'Connor) the plaintiffs in the *Mount Laurel* case for almost six years, I do start with a fundamental bias. It is this: I believe that every municipality in New Jersey has the responsibility to act affirmatively to accommodate the housing needs of the low and moderate income citizens in this state. Furthermore, I do not believe that there is any great difficulty, either from a planning or legal perspective in implementing the letter and spirit of *Mount Laurel*. Although Princeton Township seems to be one of the few municipalities that have so acted, I believe that there is not a single municipality, if the spirit moved it, that could not immediately implement the decision. So much for disclosing one's bias.

Issues Uncovered

The Supreme Court held, in a nutshell, that every developing municipality has an obligation to provide the opportunity for the satisfaction of its fair share of the regional need for housing of persons of low and moderate income. This "opportunity" must be provided through non-exclusionary (or "inclusionary") land-use controls and other "necessary and advisable" action.

The critics have uncovered the following issues:

1. how does one define "low" and "moderate"?
2. how does one determine "need"?
3. what is an appropriate "region"?
4. how does one calculate "fair share"?
5. what about environmental factors?
6. how does one project future "need" and "fair share"?
7. what does "developing" mean?
8. what is a "non-exclusionary" or "inclusionary" ordinance?
9. what other action is "necessary and advisable"?

Several cases now pending before the Supreme Court may resolve some of these issues. In *Oakwood-at-Madison, Inc. v. Madison Township.,*[2] the Supreme Court is grappling with much of the above, and in *Pascack Ass'n Ltd. v. Mayor and Council of Twp. of Washington,*[3] and *Fobe Assoc. v. The Mayor and Council of the Borough of Demarest,*[4] the "developing municipality" issue may be resolved. I believe that a rule of reasonableness will prevail on virtually every issue; that is, the Court, upon establishing broad guidelines and supporting the trial judge's power to fashion remedies to meet particular cases, will leave it to the trial judge to pass upon the reasonableness of each particular approach.

Reasonableness

In determining reasonableness and in analyzing differing approaches, two factors must be kept in mind. First, concepts such as "fair share," "region," and the like do not lend themselves to precision. They will not be derived from an irrefutable logic. Judgments will be required.

In making those judgments, the second factor is of utmost significance. We must always remember what we are about: providing housing opportunities for people. This concern seems to be lost in much of the academic discussion on these issues. A substantial number of people in this state are now being foreclosed from decent housing opportunities by the past action and present inaction of innumerable municipalities. The Supreme Court has determined that our Constitution does not permit government to act (or fail to act) that way.

The true test of "reasonableness," in this context, is whether the approach that is used works: is it the best approach to the end of providing housing for people in need and does it account for all of these people? The following is a point-by-point analysis of each "problem" delineated above.

DEFINITION OF "LOW" AND "MODERATE" INCOME

A person or family is of low or moderate income if either one of two conditions is met: (a) the person or family earns (or gets) an income that would make them eligible for any of the various state or federal programs that provide housing subsidies, or (b) the person or family cannot now afford housing that is built conventionally, but could afford such housing if it were built under land-use and building restrictions relaxed to a point consistent with the minimum necessary for the protection of health, safety and general welfare.

The second category is necessary since, in fact, there are many, not eligible for subsidy programs who need and want housing but who have been priced out of the conventional housing market at this time only because of excessive land-use and building restrictions; that is, they have been artificially locked out.

DETERMINING "NEED"—A CONVENTIONAL METHODOLOGY

Most people seem to agree that "need" is a function of several factors: (a) persons now living in substandard housing; (b) persons living in over-crowded conditions; (c) persons paying above 25 percent of their income for rent or carrying-charges on homes owned; and (d) persons employed in an area in which they cannot afford housing because of land-use or building restrictions.

Persons living in environmentally unsound areas might also be considered, but that is too unwieldy as a category and may include the greater part of our urban population. Some analysts would include persons living in areas overly concentrated with persons of low and moderate income. Such concentrations have been cited by Congress as the primary cause of the urban problems we are experiencing today. (See 42 U.S.C. 5301(a)(1).) Thus, a poor person, living in a standard house but in an area overly concentrated with low- or moderate-income persons, may be said to be a person in "need."

REGIONS

It is necessary to determine "region" because it is crucial to the concept of "fair share" and reallocation. The goal of a fair-share methodology is to ascertain the need generated by a region, and then to allocate or reallocate the persons in need in the region to the region's component municipalities according to a "fair-share" formula.

The concept of "region" is at the other end of the spectrum from that of the "tight little island." It recognizes that municipalities and their citizens relate to other municipalities and their citizens and that, just as it makes sense to analyze recreation, water and sewer, transportation, and commerce and industry from a regional perspective, it also makes sense to analyze housing from such a perspective. There is a lot of experience in ascertaining regions, for many different purposes: "market areas" or regions are ascertained for labor trends, for commercial marketing of all kinds of products (including housing), and for statistical purposes (e.g., the use by the Census of Standard Metropolitan-Statistical Areas— SMSA's).

The problem here is to develop a satisfactory methodology for ascertaining distinct regions for fair-share allocation purposes. In *Mount Laurel,* the Court chose a twenty-mile radius around the City of Camden. In *Madison,* the trial court essentially looked to the metropolitan Newark-New York City area. In some cases, the equation of region with county may work (such as Cape May or Warren). In all cases, the designation will be imperfect, since almost every municipality relates to a somewhat different region from all others.

The practicalities of the situation demand some simplicity of approach. Thus, the Delaware Valley Regional Planning Commission used all of its nine counties (including Burlington, Camden, Gloucester, and Mercer) as its region for these purposes. The Department of Community Affairs may soon provide a uniform structure for the state by publishing its own regional designations.

One fact is of utmost significance. Whatever area is designated as a region for "fair-share" purposes must not be self-defeating: that is, it must contain within itself the ability to respond to the need it generates. Thus, it would be useless to designate counties such as Hudson or Union as their own region, given the enormity of the need generated in these counties and the lack of land and other resources to deal effectively with that need. Designating Morris County as its own region would be wasteful; it has the land and resources to respond to a much greater need than it generates.

Fair Share Calculations, the New Math, and the Protection of our Environment

Once a region is chosen and the need generated within that region determined, a fair-share housing allocation model must be devised to determine each component municipality's fair share of the regional need; that is, its particular allocation of needed units for low- and moderate-income persons in the region.

Although this may appear an overwhelming task, it has been done already in many areas throughout the country, and we have at least ten years experience in working with these calculations. Various methodologies of differing complexity have been used. The Department of Community Affairs is now developing one of its own. At least five New Jersey counties (Burlington, Camden, Gloucester, Mercer and Middlesex) have already formulated such plans. All methodologies use a weighting of at least three of four criteria: "equalization," "employment," "available vacant developable land," and "relative wealth." Although there are variations of these criteria, they are the basic concepts used.

Equalization is a factor that treats the component municipalities of a region on the basis of their relative numbers of low- and moderate-income populations. The simplest way of using this concept is to determine that each municipality in the region shall have the same percentage of low- and moderate-income populations. The simplest way of using this concept is to determine that each municipality in the region shall have the same percentage of low-, moderate-, middle- and upper-income people. Thus, if the regional percent of "low-income" people is 7 percent, and X municipality has fifty low-income people, and seven percent of its population is seventy-five people, then X municipality has a "deficit" of twenty-five low-income people. A model based solely on this simple derivative of equalization would allocate a fair-share need of twenty-five low-income persons to X municipality.

Besides its simplicity and the social judgment that an economically balanced community is at least "fair," equalization is also used because of a judgment that low- and moderate-income populations reflect past and present exclusionary or non-exclusionary practices.

Employment is perhaps as important as equalization. The location of jobs has traditionally served as an indicator of the appropriate location of residences. Although there have been major changes in the location of employment centers, housing for lower-income employees has not followed jobs—in no small part because of land-use practices and building codes. Many employees, as a result, live at great distances from their places of employment. Municipalities that serve as the employment centers in a region are weighted high for future residential growth. Some municipalities that exclude the poor, however, also have excluded commerce and industry. If this criterion alone were used, such exclusionary municipalities (for example, Far Hills) would have very low allocations.

Available vacant developable land is a factor that puts a greater burden on municipalities that have not yet fully developed from the point of view of physical improvements on land (see discussion below on developing municipalities). Some fair-share plans in New Jersey do not consider this factor at all (Delaware Valley Regional Planning Commission, Gloucester, Mercer).

The obvious reason to consider it is that vacant land is cheaper than improved land and growth pressures for new housing are on the suburban fringe or in pockets of undeveloped land within the metropolitan area. The major reasons for not considering it are: (a) it exempts fully or relatively developed municipalities that may have been exclusionary in the past, and (b) there is, arguably, as much housing development in the reuse of land as there is in the use of vacant land; that is, housing is being built on land not previously vacant and, therefore, availability of vacant land is not the most important factor. Thus, Fort Lee may be the most developing municipality in the state. Nevertheless, the availability of vacant land does attract growth in many areas and may be a relevant factor in particular fair-share calculations.

If this factor is used, caution must be exercised to insure that exclusionists do not misuse environmental factors to underestimate the land available for development. For example, roads, rivers, flood plains bogs and slopes should not be eliminated automatically. *Mount Laurel* severely restricted the use of environmental factors in support of residential restrictions, the Court saying that it was the municipality's heavy burden to prove that a particular restriction was necessary to protect the specific environmental problem.

In line with this mandate, even the exclusion of land that is clearly environmentally undevelopable might not, in certain circumstances, be justifiable. Such land could be used as open space, and has been used as such in planned unit and clustered developments.

The presence of environmentally undevelopable land need not necessarily affect the density of development on a given tract as long as precautions are taken to deal with the environmental problems. In an area zoned at ten units to the acre, even if half of the tract is in a flood plain, ten units per acre of the total tract could be built on the developable half and the flood plain area used as open space. The flood plain would be protected and density maintained. Municipalities have had practice in the land-use technique of clustering, especially when approving industrial park sites, residential clusters, P.U.D.'s and even conventional residential developments. If the same vigor is used in circumventing environmental hazards that exist on lower-income residential tracts as has been exhibited in industrial, commercial and upper-income residential tracts, environmental factors may not be a serious problem in the implementation of *Mount Laurel*.

Relative wealth is a simple concept to use; municipalities are compared and weighted with their tax base being used as the criterion. An assumption here is that current wealth is an indicator of past and present exclusionary practices and, as such, the concept is really another form of equalization. Another consideration is that the wealthier community can better afford to pay for the services necessitated by new development. Also, to the extent that a payment-in-lieu-of-taxes approach is necessary for subsidized housing, wealthier communities may better afford this indirect subsidy.

PROJECTIONS INTO THE FUTURE

Just as planning and zoning are dynamic processes requiring constant reevaluation, so fair-share models must be updated, must incorporate new and changing data and be checked against the realities of the passage of time. Projections of future population trends are necessary since the fair-share model must accommodate future housing needs. Planners have been projecting for years with some success and some failure. Frequent updating will minimize the potential damage of any miscalculation.

"DEVELOPING" VERSUS "DEVELOPED"

Since *Mount Laurel*, many municipalities have scrambled to shelter under the umbrella of "being developed." Indeed, it is hard to find a municipality that will admit to "developing." Some analysts argue that the decision has exempted municipalities that do not have a substantial quantity of available, vacant, developable land.

The assumption here is that, in using the term "developing," the Court was referring to the availability of such land and, moreover, that municipalities without such land are exempt from the fair-share obligation. These assumptions are entirely specious and must be discredited thoroughly as being not only contrary to the letter and spirit of the decision, but also contrary to past and present realities of land use and reuse.

My position is that the fair-share methodology used will determine each municipality's numerical "obligation" and only municipalities that have met that obligation can be said to be exempt from the Court's mandate. I have claimed that development through reuse of existing developed land may be as much of a factor or even a greater factor in residential growth than the development of vacant land. There is a growing sentiment, especially in light of environmental and energy factors, that future growth will have to take place in already developed urban-suburban areas.

In any event, it should be clear that the term "developing" cannot relate solely to available vacant developable land; it just doesn't make sense. Fully "developed" municipalities have experienced enormous population growth due to reuse of previously developed land. Haddonfield, for example, recently permitted the reuse of land that had been a used car lot for the construction of luxury condominiums; it also used other, previously developed land for office buildings. Exactly when in the history of Boston, New York, Philadelphia or Washington could these cities be said to be fully developed?

In my opinion, the Court's use of the term "developing municipality" refers to something else. It refers to growth pressures; that is, a municipality is "developing", if it experiences pressure for development. Under the fair-share concept, it is experiencing such pressure as long as it has not met its fair share of low- and moderate-income housing.

The *remedy* will be different, and that is the key to understanding the emphasis in *Mount Laurel* on available vacant developable land. Mount Laurel Township has a lot of such land. Clearly, in such a township, approaches to fulfilling a fair-share obligation will rely, in large part, on the proposed use of the vacant land.

In a municipality that has little vacant land, emphasis may be on reuse, upgrading conditions in existing substandard dwellings or areas, or using subsidy programs that enable the poor to be relocated into existing standard housing.

My point is that, although the availability of vacant developable land is one factor to consider in evaluating a municipality's resources to accommodate its fair share, it is only one factor.

"INCLUSIONARY" ZONING

The Supreme Court has given some guidance as to which land-use practices are suspect and which are acceptable. Large single-family homes on large lots with wide frontage plus prohibition of multi-family units constitute the bedrock of exclusion zoning. In *Mount Laurel*, the Court mandated small dwellings on very small lots (having found quarter-acre lot sizes, 110 square foot interior floor space, and seventy-five- and one hundred-foot frontage requirements excessive) and multi-family housing, without bedroom or similar restrictions.

It should be noted that the fact that Mount Laurel had approved planned unit developments consisting of "at least 10,000 sale and rental housing units" was not found conclusive since the Court found these units designed for middle- and upper-income occupants. Thus, the mere existence of multi-family units or zones is of not great consequence. The test is whether they are available for the poor.

Furthermore, the Court spoke of low-cost housing of other types, as opposed to single-family or multi-family homes. This, along with other language in the opinion, strongly suggests that the Court is leaning toward a review of previous holdings dealing with mobile homes [5] and mobile-home parks. [6]

The Court attacked overmapping for commercial and industrial uses. It also stated that planned unit developments must not involve unreasonable restrictions and should include a reasonable amount of low- and moderate-income housing in its residential mix.

Various writers have suggested ways in which a municipality could zone for low- and moderate-income housing. I think that the bottom line is this: land-use and building-code restrictions should enable a developer to construct a unit that will qualify for subsidies under federal and state subsidy programs.

Furthermore, the township must relate to the class of people who are ineligible for the subsidy programs but who could afford housing built conventionally under relaxed land-use and building-code restrictions. To the extent such people are in need, the restrictions must be minimized. There can be no justification for requiring improvements in excess of the absolute minimum necessary to protect the health, safety and general welfare as long as people are in need of less expensive units. Middle-class values as to what is "minimal" must not prevail when the effect is that those less fortunate are given no alternative to living in substandard or over-crowded conditions or in housing they simply cannot afford.

It should also be clear that zoning a small parcel at a high density will not do the trick. The result will be an immediate increase in the price of land for that parcel, and a higher-priced unit. If a specific parcel is chosen, then restrictions must be included to insure its use for low- and moderate-cost housing.

A better approach would be the "floating zone" technique; that is, provide special exceptions to any developer within a designated large zone who commits an area to low- or moderate-income use. This would have a minimal or zero impact on land cost while creating a greater potential for activity, since more developers will have the opportunity to choose to build for the poor.

Maxi-mini techniques could be used to insure a lower-cost unit. An ordinance might require a certain maximum (rather than just a minimum) interior-square frontage; for example, require 750 minimum and 950 maximum. The same could be done for density (e.g., sixteen-unit minimum); frontage (maximum of fifty feet); etc.

Density restrictions should prevail over lot-size restrictions. The ordinance could establish a specific density and permit, with some limitation, any use; for example, clustered single-family, townhouse, multi-family, etc. The ordinance could require a minimum percentage of low- or moderate-cost housing in any major subdivision or development.

This does not exhaust the possibilities. New techniques must be tried as they are developed and as we gain experience with present techniques. The point is that we are seeking a technique or approach that will work. If one or more exist, it is incumbent upon us to find them.

NECESSARY AND ADVISABLE

The Court was clear that reforming land-use and building restrictions was not enough; additional action is required to encourage the fulfillment of the municipality's fair share.

Such additional action might include: creating a housing authority (or adopting a resolution permitting an outside housing authority to operate in the municipality); adopting a resolution of need; accepting a payment-in-lieu-of-taxes agreement; applying for state or federal funds for code enforcement, rehabilitation, water and sewer improvements; purchasing land for lower cost housing; and relaxing reporting requirements such as unnecessary studies on project impact. A housing authority may be essential since certain federal programs (such as the "existing housing" Section 8 program) require a local public agency.

The emphasis here is on a single word in *Mount Laurel*: "encouraging." The Court called for additional action encouraging the fulfillment of a municipality's fair share. The hope, however idealistic, is that a municipality committed to meeting its constitutional obligation will seek out ways in which to do so. This is, perhaps, too much to expect, but in this, the Bicentennial year, who can foresee what changes in attitudes may occur?

Conclusion

In conclusion, I reiterate that every municipality could comply immediately. There is no legal or planning obstacle. Techniques exist to create the opportunity for housing for those in need—to build new housing, to upgrade substandard housing and to use existing housing in standard condition.

The issue is not whether we can do it and not whether we are obligated to do it. We can and we are. Only the spirit is weak. The spirit may also be in contempt of the Court's mandate. If it will take litigation to insure compliance, so be it.

The fact that *Mount Laurel* had to be brought in the first place is a sad testament to the policies heretofore followed at various levels of government. The fact that additional litigation may be necessary—even after a unanimous Supreme Court ruling that followed almost two years of deliberation—is also sad, but hardly surprising.

NOTES

1. *Southern Burlington County NAACP v. Township of Mount Laurel,* 67 N.J. 151 (1975).
2. 128 N.J. Super. 438 (Law Div. 1974), certif. granted (argued, awaiting decision).
3. 131 N.J. Super. 195 (Law Div. 1074), rev'd. unreported Appellate Division decision, certif. granted 10/14/75, Docket No. 11745 (awaiting argument).
4. Unreported Law Division and Appellate Division decisions, certif. granted 10/14/75, Docket No. 11748 (awaiting argument).
5. *Napierkowski v. Twp. Comm. of Gloucester Twp.,* 29 N.J. 481 (1959).
6. *Vickers v. Twp. Comm. of Gloucester Twp.,* 37 N.J. 232 (1962).

Judicial Remedies

Arnold K. Mytelka

Introduction

Those interested in land use planning have analyzed *Mount Laurel*,[1] decided March 24, 1975, with keen excitement,[2] while waiting for the other shoe to drop. The opinion sparkles with kinetic potential, suggesting revolutionary change. But important questions are left unanswered. One is the issue of remedy.[3]

Implicitly recognizing the desirability of comity among the several branches and levels of government,[4] the *Mount Laurel* court invited voluntary compliance by municipalities[5] and remedial action by the legislature.[6]

> The municipality should first have full opportunity to itself act without judicial supervision. We trust it will do so in the spirit we have suggested, both by appropriate zoning ordinance amendments and whatever additional action encouraging the fulfillment of its fair share of the regional need for low and moderate income housing may be indicated as necessary and advisable.[7]

In the meantime, the court stayed its hand:

> It is not appropriate at this time, particularly in view of the advanced view of zoning law as applied to housing laid down by this opinion, to deal with the matter of the further extent of judicial power in the field or to exercise any such power. See, however, *Pascack Association v. Mayor and Council of Township of Washington,* 131 N.J. Super. 195 (Law Div. 1974).[8]

The question of remedy awaits decision in two cases pending in the New Jersey Supreme Court. One is *Pascack,* an innovative remedial determination at the trial level, cited with apparent approval in the passage quoted from *Mount Laurel* above. There, Judge Gelman, faced with municipal intransigence, rezoned on the basis of a report prepared by court-appointed experts.[9] Subsequent to and notwithstanding the *Mount Laurel* citation of *Pascack,* the Appellate Division reversed in an unreported decision,[10] holding that the municipality there involved was not a "developing community." The New Jersey Supreme Court granted certification,[11] and oral argument has been held.

The other pending appeal is *Oakwood at Madison, Inc. v. Township of Madison,*[12] a pioneering anti-exclusionary decision by Judge Furman. The case has been in the courts since 1971,[13] and was re-argued around the time of this symposium. Prior to reargument, the New Jersey Supreme Court posed 18 written questions to the litigants and requested supplementary briefs in response.[14] The questions probed deeply into the details of region, fair share, and income categories, into innovative zoning concepts such as density bonus provisions and phased zoning, into the economics of the situation, and into remedial issues, such as the specificity of relief and the possibility of a Special Master "to consult with the municipality and frame specific zoning guidelines." Indeed, the Court invited the litigants "to submit an outline of the basic contents of a zoning ordinance, including specific provisions governing residential zones, which in their opinion would satisfy the *Mount Laurel* case."

It will be interesting to see whether the New Jersey Supreme Court utilizes *Pascack* and *Oakwood* as vehicles to resolve the unanswered questions opened by *Mount Laurel.* Will the court write opinions like wills or contracts, seeking to anticipate all contingencies? Or will it simply resolve the issues before it, perhaps with broad guidelines to aid lower courts and the bar? The common law method, taken together with considerations of comity, suggests the latter approach will be adopted.

In any event, as in any complex socio-legal problem area, judicial opinions—no matter how well-crafted—will undoubtedly require further elucidation and articulation. The aim of this presentation is to assist in the process by exploring several significant aspects of the issue of remedy.

Objectives

The aim of *Mount Laurel* is to obtain construction of low- and moderate-income housing on a fair share basis, while preserving the amenities and limiting adverse fiscal consequences.[15] It is to expedite housing without recreating slums in new locations.[16]

Thus, in administering remedies, courts should "look with a jaundiced eye at any attempt to avoid the intent and spirit" of *Mount Laurel* "through the use of legal technicalities . . . "[17] On the other hand, there should be sensitivity to legitimate aesthetic, historical, fiscal, and environmental considerations.[18] Balanced remedies and expert planning advice is required.

Ideally, the process should be delegated to regional or statewide planning (or at least review) agencies.[19] But experience suggests that the ideal is unlikely to be achieved. If the courts do not act, the goals of *Mount Laurel* will be lost. While less than ideal, it is submitted that judicial remedies can accomplish the desired results.

> Substantial justice can often be accomplished by the granting of conditional, experimental or substitutional relief or any equitable combination thereof . . . Within very broad limits, the court is free to adjust the interests of the plaintiffs, the defendants and the public by devising an individually tailored remedy to fit the particular case.[20]

Definitive Relief

The key to progress lies in definitive relief. While the initial step should almost always be to give a municipality reasonable time to bring its ordinances into conformity with *Mount Laurel*,[21] the courts should not be reluctant to rezone, with expert help, if the proper result is not forthcoming. This was the remedy fashioned by Judge Gelman in *Pascack*, citing desegregation and reapportionment precedents.[22] It was the implication in the New Jersey Supreme Court's invitation to litigants in *Oakwood* to submit draft ordinances for the court's consideration.[23] And it is a species of relief which, with some semantic variations, has been established as an appropriate remedy in Connecticut, Florida, Illinois, Pennsylvania, Virginia, and the federal courts.[24]

The practical problems arising from invalidation of exclusionary zoning, without more, were well stated by Justice Schaeffer of the Illinois Supreme Court:

> The municipality may rezone the property to another use classification that still excludes the one proposed, thus making further litigation

necessary as to the validity of the new classification . . ., [or] a decree which was induced by evidence which depicted a proposed use in a highly favorable light would not restrict the property owner to that use, and he might thereafter use the property for an entirely different purpose.[25]

If the court rezones, "the relief awarded may guarantee that the owner will be allowed to proceed with that use without further litigation and that he will not proceed with a different use.[26]

With *Mount Laurel* now on the books, any municipality which does not comply before litigation or during litigation or within a reasonable time after judgment, should not be heard to complain of judicial zoning. As Professor Krasnowiecki observed in an article in the University of Pennsylvania Law Review; "Obviously, if judicial review of local zoning action is to result in anything more than a farce, the courts must be prepared to go beyond mere invalidation and grant definitive relief."[27]

Plaintiff's Remedy

It is certainly neither fair nor conducive to implementation of *Mount Laurel* to present a successful plaintiff with a pyrrhic victory. A developer who establishes a *Mount Laurel* violation should be permitted to build his project, absent compelling considerations to the contrary. Of course, the court may require modifications in the project, for example, to preserve community amenities. But the municipality should not be allowed to rezone, in the course of litigation or during the period after judgment, in such a way as to defeat the plaintiff's project. Here, too, definitive relief should be the remedy.[28]

The Zoning Amendment Shuffle

A related subject—"the zoning amendment shuffle"—is the not uncommon municipal tactic of avoiding an adverse trial decision by rezoning on appeal. The rezoning excludes plaintiff's property from the area opened for development and often gerrymanders the new development area so as to avoid substantial construction in the near term. For example, multi-family uses may be permitted in a zone which is inaccessible to mass transit or to shopping or to major roads; or the designated zone may be owned by institutions which have no present intention of developing their property for housing purposes.

The objective of this shuffle is twofold. First if the amendment ultimately passes muster, the plaintiff who was ready with a project is thwarted; other developers are scared off; and the high density zone will remain on paper for years to come. Second, even if the amendment is subsequently invalidated, there is substantial delay.[29]

The delay is often fatal. Few landowners or developers can wait years and endure the expense of continuing litigation. Options and conditional contracts run out; mortgage commitments expire; the cost of labor and materials zooms; and, like Pavlov's dogs, developers are trained to build what municipalities want, rather than what the public needs.

The solution is that amendatory afterthoughts should not be considered, at least between the municipality and the litigant who succeeded at trial. Both Illinois and Pennsylvania have so held. A contrary decision, as the Pennsylvania Supreme Court pointed out;

> would effectively grant the municipality a power to prevent any challenger from obtaining meaningful relief after a successful attack on a zoning ordinance. The municipality could penalize the successful challenger by enacting an amendatory ordinance designed to cure the constitutional infirmity, but also designed to zone around the challenger. Faced with such an obstacle to relief, few would undertake the time and expense necessary to have a zoning ordinance declared unconstitutional.[30]

New Jersey's 1964 *Tidewater Oil* case,[31] which holds that "in respect of zoning uses, the law in effect at the time an appellate court decides a cause generally governs the disposition thereof, not the law prevailing when the case was decided in the trial court," [32] should be overruled in the face of the housing emergency referred to in *Mount Laurel*.[33]

Independent Experts

Land use planning is a delicate art. In the *Mount Laurel* context, the trial court must pass upon or delineate regions, decide fair share, weigh ecological and other defenses, and provide for low and moderate income housing without gutting communities or destroying amenities. In fashioning the tailored remedy,[34] the court needs expert help. Often, because of partisanship or litigation economics or poor lawyering, the litigants' expertise leaves much to be desired. In such cases, the trial judge should neither bow to the plan presented by one of the partisan witnesses, nor try to compromise or find his own way. Rather, an independent expert should be appointed by the court, at the expense of the litigants, or, if a state agency planner is deemed objective, at public expense. As Justice Pashman said in *Mount Laurel*:

> It may well be appropriate for the court to appoint independent experts or consultants for its assistance [citations omitted], or to invite participation by the Department of Community Affairs as *amicus curiae*.[35]

As noted, earlier, in *Pascack*, Judge Gelman appointed planning experts and rezoned on the basis of their report.

Indeed, where expertise is lacking, or where expert witnesses are highly partisan and far apart, it may not only be appropriate, but mandatory, for the court to appoint an independent expert. Thus, in *Tp. of Wayne* v. *Kosoff*,[36] a condemnation case, the Appellate Division reversed an award and remanded for new trial on the ground that since the valuation experts were far apart and obviously partisan, the trial judge should have appointed an independent expert.

Compliance With Other Land Use Regulations

Once the court has exorcised a municipality's exclusionary practices, the question arises whether the developer should be permitted to proceed with his project without further ado, or whether he should be required to comply with other land use regulations. By and large, compliance has been compelled.[37] If final plans have been submitted to the municipality at the outset, the court can expedite matters by passing upon them as well as ruling on the constitutional challenge,[38] or by adopting conditions (in whole or in part) set by the local zoning agency.[39]

The bad faith municipality presents the usual problem of delay. Subdivision controls, building codes, environmental reviews, and the like, can be used to delay construction of needed housing. Still, there is the objective or preserving amenities, and expediency is no answer.

Several solutions may be suggested. The court can retain its own planning expert, as in *Pascack*, to review the developer's plans and recommend modifications and conditions, which can be implemented by court order. Alternatively, to short-circuit delay, the court could proceed summarily, by order to show cause requiring the municipality's various land use agencies to set forth any objections or conditions they believe are warranted. This proceeding could take place as part of the settlement of the form of order implementing the court's decision to invalidate the exclusionary ordinance. Finally, proof of arbitrary or bad faith tactics can (and should) result in a simple order requiring issuance of the necessary permits.[40]

Do Courts Build Housing?

In *Mount Laurel*, Justice Hall flatly stated that "Courts do not build housing nor do municipalities."[41] A few lines later, however, he said that "there is *at least* a moral obligation in a municipality to establish a local housing agency pursuant to state law to provide housing for its resident poor now living in dilapidated, unhealthy quarters."[42] And earlier in the

opinion, there is the recognition that low- and moderate-income housing
will generally require some form of governmental assistance.[43]

If zoning changes fail to produce needed housing, it seems reasonably
certain that courts will enjoin municipalities to take the steps necessary to
obtain federal and state aid so as to comply with fair share requirements.[44] While it is doubtful that the courts are presently of a mind to go
further and order the expenditure of municipal funds for housing construction,[45] even that remedy may be reached as a last resort.[46] The federal courts have gone furthest in this direction.[47]

In a recent trial decision implementing *Mount Laurel*, Judge Furman
invalidated exclusionary zoning in eleven Middlesex County communities,
directed rezoning, and took one (but not the final) additional step:

> Whether single-family housing is attainable for moderate-income
> households may hinge upon land and construction costs. The 11
> municipalities should pursue and cooperate in available federal and
> state subsidy programs for new housing and rehabilitation of substan-
> dard housing, although it is beyond the issues in this litigation to order
> the expenditure of municipal funds or the allowance of tax abate-
> ments. See *Hills* v. *Gautreaux*, ___ U.S. ___, 96 *S. Ct.* 1538, 47 *L. Ed.*
> 2d ___ (1976), holding that a federal district court has the authority to
> order the Department of Housing and Urban Development to under-
> take a regional plan for low-income and integrated housing to remedy
> housing discrimination fostered by H.U.D. practices in a central city,
> with the consent of suburban municipalities.[48]

Other Remedies

It may be helpful to complete this presentation with a brief outline of
other remedies suggested in Judge Furman's recent ruling, and in plead-
ings which have come to the writer's attention. Besides the pursuit of
federal and state subsidy programs, Judge Furman declared:

> In implementing this judgment the 11 municipalities charged with fair
> share allocations must do more than rezone not to exclude the possibil-
> ity of low- and moderate-income housing in the allocated amounts. Ap-
> provals of multi-family projects, including Planned Unit Developments,
> should impose mandatory minimums of low and moderate-income
> units. Density incentives may be set. Mobile homes offer a realistic
> alternative within the reach of moderate and even low-income house-
> holds.[49]

Additional remedies might include a restraint on further non-residential
and upper income residential development until low- and moderate-
income housing is built; a requirement that a deficient municipality share
its tax revenues with neighboring municipalities which have provided

their fair share of regional housing needs; an injunction against occupancy of a new non-residential facility (e.g., an office building or industrial plant) until provision is made for employee housing; and mandatory use of tax revenue increments derived from a new non-residential facility to fund a local housing authority's construction of low- and moderate-income housing or to finance the infrastructure needed for such housing e.g., schools and roads).

Conclusion

Mount Laurel was decided over a year and a half ago. As yet, the practical impact has been limited. Substantial implementation requires greater concentration on judicial remedies designed to achieve results. "In exclusionary zoning cases the measure of whether the remedy is working should be actual production of low and moderate income housing."[50]

NOTES

1. *Southern Burlington County N.A.A.C.P.* v. *Township of Mt. Laurel,* 67 N.J. 151, *appeal dismissed,* 96 S. Ct. 18, 46 L. Ed. 2d 28 (1975).
2. *E.g.,* N. Williams, *American Planning Law* § 66. 13b, pp. 3-4 (Addendum 1975) ("the most important zoning decision since Euclid").
3. Others include the meaning of "developing community," "fair share," and "region," discussed elsewhere in this volume.
4. *Cf. Asbury Park Press, Inc.* v. *Woolley,* 33 N.J. 1, 19-22 (1960). Note the tortuous history of *Robinson* v. *Cahill*: 62 N.J. 473 (1973); 63 N.J. 196 (1973); 67 N.J. 35 (1975); 69 N.J. 133 (1975); 69 N.J. 449 (1976); 70 N.J. 155 (1976).
5. *Mount Laurel, supra* n. 1, 67 N.J. at 191-93.
6. *Id.,* 67 N.J. at 188, n. 21, and 189, n. 22.
7. *Id.,* 67 N.J. at 192.
8. *Id.,* 67 N.J. at 192. Justice Pashman disagreed, stating that he "would have the Court go farther and faster in its implementation of the principles announced today."
   Id., 67 N.J. at 194 (concurring opinion).
9. *Pascack Association* v. *Mayor and Council of Township of Washington,* 131 N.J. Super. 195 (Law Div. 1974).
10. Nos. A-3790-72, A-1841-73 (June 25, 1975).
11. 69 N.J. 73 (1975).
12. 117 N.J. Super. 11 (L. Div. 1971), *certif. granted,* 62 N.J. 185 (1972), *remanded* No. A 9/10 (N.J. Sup. Ct., Jan. 14, 1974), *on remand,* 128 N.J. Super. 438 (L. Div. 1974), pending in N.J. Sup. Ct.
13. Ironically, two unrelated cases involving the same municipality permitted trial level relief while *Oakwood* remained undecided, See *Brunetti* v. *Mayor, Coun., Tp. of Madison,* 130 N.J. Super. 164 (L. Div. 1974); *Urb. League New Brunswick* v. *Mayor & Coun. Carteret,* 142 N.J. Super. 11 (Ch. Div. 1976).
14. *Letter,* Sept. 25, 1975, Clerk of the Supreme Court to parties.
15. *E.g., Mount Laurel, supra* n. 1, 67 N.J. at 190-91.

16. *Id.*, 67 N.J. at 212 (Pashman, J., concurring).
17. *Cf. Van Ness* v. *Borough of Deal*, 139 N.J. Super. 83, 101 (Ch. Div. 1975).
18. *E.g.*, by careful phasing and siting of development. *Cf. Mount Laurel, supra* n. 1, 67 N.J. at 188, n. 20.
19. *See.* R. Mytelka and A. Mytelka, "Exclusionary Zoning: A Consideration of Remedies," 7 Seton Hall L. Rev. 1, 5-13 (1975).
20. *Township of Hanover* v. *Town of Morristown*, 108 N.J. Super. 461, 486-87 (Ch. Div. 1969); see *Hecht Company* v. *Bowles*, 321 U.S. 321, 329-30 (1944).
21. Ninety days would seem sufficient. Cf. Mount Laurel, supra n. 1, 67 N.J. at 191. One year, *Middle Union Associates* v. *Zoning Bd. of Adjustment of Twp. of Holmdel*, No. L-1149-72 P.W. (L. Div. 1975), is too long.
22. *Pascack, supra* n. 9.
23. *Supra* n. 14.
24. *Supra* n. 19 at 7 Seton Hall L. Rev. 26-29.
25. *Sinclair Pipe Line Co.* v. *Village of Richton Park*, 19 Ill. 2d 370, 378, 167 N.E. 2d 406, 411 (1960) (citations omitted).
26. Id., 19 Ill. 2d at 379, 167 N.E. 2d at 411.
27. 120 U. Pa. L. Rev. 1029, 1082 (1972).
28. By analogy, courts sometimes limit the retroactive effect of novel decisions, Usually, however, they carve out an exception for the plaintiff "for unless the immediate litigant can hope to gain, there would be no incentive to challenge existing practices or prior holdings which, in the public interest, ought to be reviewed." *Goldberg* v. *Traver*, 52 N.J. 344, 347 (1968).
29. See; *e.g.*; *Oakwood at Madison, Inc.* v. *Township of Madison, supra* n. 12.
30. *Casey* v. *Zoning Hearing Board of Warwick Township*, 328 A. 2d 464, 468 (1974).
31. *Tidewater Oil Co.* v. *Mayor and Council of Carteret*, 84 N.J. Super. 525 (App. Div. 1964), *aff'd*, 44 N.J. 338 (1965).
32. *Id.*, 84 N.J. Super. at 530.
33. *Mount Laurel, supra* n. 1, 67 N.J. at 158-59.
34. *Supra* n. 20.
35. *Supra* n. 1, 67 N.J. at 216.
36. 136 N.J. Super. 53 (App. Div. 1975), *certif. granted*, 69 N.J. 77 (1975).
37. See: *e.g.*, *Dailey* v. *City of Lawton*, 296 F. Supp. 266, 269 (W.D. Okla. 1969), *aff'd*, 425 F. 2d 1037 (10th Cir. 1970); *Casey* v. *Zoning Hearing Bd.*, 328 A. 2d 464, 469-70 (Pa. 1974).
38. See: *Casey* v. *Zoning Hearing Bd.*, 328 A. 2d 464, 469-70 (Pa. 1974).
39. See: *Duggan* v. *County of Cook*, 60 Ill. 2d 107, 114-16, 324 N.E. 2d 406, 410-11 (1975).
40. See: *e.g.*: *Kennedy Park Homes Ass'n.* v. *City of Lackawanna*, 436 F. 2d 108, 113-15 (2d Cir.), *aff'g* 318 F. Supp. 669, 697-98 (W.D.N.Y. 1970), *cert. denied*, 401 U.S. 1010 (1971).
41. *Supra* n. 1, 67 N.J. at 192.
42. *Id.*, emphasis added.
43. *Id.*, 67 N.J. at 188, n. 21.
44. See, *e.g.*, L. Rubinowitz, *Low-Income Housing: Suburban Strategies* (1974).
45. Compare *Robinson* v. *Cahill*, 70 N.J. 155 (1976); *State* v. *Rush*, 46 N.J. 399 (1966).
46. See: *Mount Laurel, supra* n. 1, 67 N.J. at 211 (Pashman, J., concurring); Williams, *supra* n. 2, § 66.13n.

47. *See*: *Crow* v. *Brown*, 332 F. Supp. 382, 395-96 (N.D. Ga. 1971), *aff'd*, 457 F. 2d 788 (5th Cir. 1972); *Kennedy Park Homes Ass'n.* v. *City of Lackawanna*, 318 F. Supp. 669, 697 (W.D.N.Y.) *aff'd*, 436 F. 2d 108 (2d Cir. 1970), *cert. denied*, 401 U.S. 1010 (1971); *Southern Alameda Spanish Speaking Organization* v. *City of Union City*, 357 F. Supp. 1188, 1199 (N.D. Cal. 1970).
48. *Urban League of Greater New Brunswick* v. *Mayor & Council of Carteret*, 142 N.J. Super. 11, 39 (Ch. Div. 1976).
49. *Id.*, 142 N.J. Super. at 38-39.
50. *Supra* n. 44 at p. 211.

Zoning Litigation and Housing Production

Alan Mallach

It is almost a truism that the implications of a major court decision become apparent only after subsequent courts have used, or misused, that decision in other related cases. Since March of this year [1975], when the New Jersey Supreme Court handed down its decision in *Southern Burlington NAACP v. Township of Mount Laurel*[1] this has become apparent. A series of decisions at the trial and appellate level, most of which are, in the author's opinion, misguided at best, have clarified to a remarkable degree the questions and the problems implicit in the *Mount Laurel* decision, which will now have to be resolved by the courts or the Legislature if that decision is to become more than a symbolic victory for the advocates of housing opportunity. Three closely related problems whose resolution will determine whether or not that is to be the case will be discussed here. This article will also focus on some of the questions raised by recent post-*Mount Laurel* decisions, and suggest some directions for the future growing out of the paramount concern of providing genuine housing opportunity.

Housing Construction

The "developing municipality" problem. As is well known, the court in *Mount Laurel* referred to that community as a developing municipality; subsequently trial courts and the Appellate Division have ruled against a series of challenges to local zoning ordinances on the grounds, as in the *Wenonah*[2] case, that "Wenonah cannot be regarded as one of the developing communities of "sizeable land area" to which the requirements imposed by *Mt. Laurel* apply."[3] In the subsequent *Camden National Realty, Inc. v. Township of Cinnaminson*,[4] the trial court held that Cinnaminson was "substantially developed", in view of the fact that 17.8 percent of the township's land area, or 856 acres, remained vacant and buildable.[5] Other cases have arrived at similar conclusions.[6]

The rationale used by the court in *Cinnaminson*, and by the Appellate Division in many of its cases, would exclude well over half the municipalities in New Jersey from any obligation whatsoever under the *Mount Laurel* principle. Furthermore, it would lead to an absurd situation from a social, economic, and environmental standpoint:

> 1. It would exclude most of those municipalities that have adequate infrastructure (sewer, water, municipal and school facilities) to accommodate new development, and nearly all municipalities with excess capacity.
>
> 2. It would exclude most of those municipalities that have reasonable access to public transportation, and provide the locale for most blue-collar employment.
>
> 3. It would encourage precisely that form of sprawl; i.e., 'leapfrogging' that has been shown consistently to be most dangerous environmentally and most costly, in terms of both classical costs and social costs.

It also ignores the realities of development, which show considerable volume of construction in municipalities that fail to meet the criteria apparently used by the Appellate Division or the trial courts. A 1973 survey showed that three of the four New Jersey municipalities issuing the most permits for multifamily housing would not be considered "developing municipalities" by the Appellate Division.[7]

Thus, one must conclude that subsequent court decisions are attempting to interpret *Mount Laurel* in a manner that is both inimical to housing production in general, and to socially and environmentally sound development in particular. A more rational approach—which in fact was suggested by Justice Pashman in his concurring opinion in *Mount Laurel*[8] (and, it would appear, subsequently ignored)—is to vary the nature of the remedy, or the scope of the obligation, on the basis of development characteristics, such as the amount of vacant land, the degree to which development can take place without "grossly disturbing existing neighborhoods"[9] and so on. To the degree that municipalities do, or can, develop, they should provide housing opportunities. To focus on arbitrary quantities, as the court appear to have done, is irresponsible.

The Nature and Scope of the Municipal Obligation

If one can resolve the "developing municipality" question, and establish that housing opportunity is not to be limited to a handful of communities, many questions remain concerning the *nature* of the obligation specified in *Mount Laurel*. The language of the court in that case, although strong, is phrased in general terms. The absence of *specific* standards made it possible for the court in the *Cinnaminson* case to arrive at a preposterous conclusion, finding that the Township had met its fair share, despite the absence of any multi-family housing whatsoever, and a housing stock substantially more expensive than the county average. This may not be significant, since, as was pointed out above, the court in this case had already found that Cinnaminson was not, in its eyes, a developing municipality. A more significant decision on this point was that in *Taberna Corporation v. Township of Montgomery*.[10] In this case the court held that:

> the present apartment / townhouse zone is sufficiently large to meet the Township's obligations as projected in the above two approaches [two alternative 'fair share' plans submitted by defendant's expert]. Consequently, the Court finds that the defendants have carried their burden and have shown that Montgomery has met its fair share of the regional need for low and moderate income housing.[11]

Although the court acted with apparent good intentions, the result, in the realistic economic context of development, is a patent absurdity because:

> 1. The municipal ordinance provides no encouragement or conditions of any sort designed to lead to production of low- and moderate-income housing, thereby providing no basis for a developer to forego the greater profits of luxury housing.
> 2. The size and location of the multi-family zone strongly suggest that land prices within this zone will rapidly rise to the point where it is not economically feasible to construct anything but luxury units in the zone.[12]

Both of the above points are based on the most elementary economic principles. The tract in question is located in Somerset County, an area in which land zoned for multi-family housing is rare, and it is immediately adjacent to Princeton, an area in which luxury housing demand is great. To believe that low- and moderate-income housing will come into being in large numbers in such an area, *without explicit provision for such housing by the municipality,* is to believe in fairies.

Low- and moderate-income housing does not just *happen*—it must be brought into being by a series of municipal assists, including resolutions of need, tax abatement provisions, and waiver of standards in favor of state and federal program standards. Even if one argues that some of these provisions, such as tax abatement, do not fall strictly within the realm of *Mount Laurel* (a zoning decision, after all), the fact remains that there are many zoning-related tools which can be directed toward low- and moderate-income housing production. Montgomery Township has, to the best of the author's knowledge, used none of them.

This case presents the distinction between a meaningless symbolic remedy and a substantive one in clear form. Although the tortured logic of the *Montgomery* decision arrives at the conclusion that the Township *could* meet its fair share of regional housing needs, reality makes clear that it *will* not, unless compelled. For example, the most straightforward means in the compass of classical zoning to encourage low- and moderate-income housing is to provide for it as a special exception, or conditional use. Other tools include density bonus provisions, the so-called "MPMPDU" ordinances (minimum percentages of moderately priced dwelling units), and establishment of maximum standards in zoning ordinances.[13] All of these tools can be made relevant to the economics of housing production.

The emphasis placed in *Mount Laurel* on the importance of housing opportunity and the right to shelter, strongly suggests that the phrases used must be interpreted in a broad social and economic context, and not in an abstract and narrowly legalistic manner.

> The presumptive obligation arises for each such municipality affirmatively to plan and provide, by its land use regulations, the reasonable opportunity for an appropriate variety and choice of housing, including of course low and moderate cost housing.[14]

This suggests, in turn, that *land use regulations should, to the degree feasible, provide for low- and moderate-income housing opportunity, when subjected to scrutiny in the context of the social and economic realities of the particular time and place involved.* Although it is clear that zoning in and of itself cannot provide the needed housing, even with all available land use control innovations, the fact remains that it *does*, to an overwhelming degree, create the conditions under which that housing will or will not be constructed.

The Fate of the Plaintiff

In all of the cases cited, with the exception of the seminal *Mount Laurel* case, the plaintiff has been an individual or corporation involved with the development of a particular site. Many of the cases arose out of municipal denial of use variances under 40:55-39(d), applications which were made to permit multi-family housing in zones permitting only single-family dwellings or permitting no residential uses at all.[15] Although in a few cases, developer-plaintiffs have been successful in the limited sense that the court overturned the municipal zoning ordinance under attack, in no case that has stood so far has the court granted a remedy specifically directed at enabling the plaintiff to develop his or her land.[16] In *Holmdel* the court accepted plaintiff's contention that the Township was exclusionary, and ordered a rezoning of the Township on the basis of "fair share" calculations prepared by plaintiff's expert witness. Nonetheless, the court affirmed the Township's denial of the plaintiff's variance request. It is a reasonable surmise that, at such time that the Township presents its revised zoning ordinance to the court, plaintiff's land will not be among the tracts rezoned for multi-family housing development. Something very much to that effect took place in Washington Township; in response to the initial court order to rezone for multi-family housing, the Township created a thirty-four acre multi-family zone, within which only one parcel, of roughly five acres, was at all potentially developable for multi-family housing.[17] Plaintiff's parcel was excluded from this multi-family zone.

This pattern raises serious questions regarding the effect of this litigation on housing production. Although one would not suggest that successful challenge of a zoning ordinance should lead automatically to an order to grant developer-plaintiff a building permit, the converse should not apply either. At present, the evidence suggests that municipalities, even those found in violation of the *Mount Laurel* principles, are free not only to prevent a successful plaintiff from building, but to frame with impunity a response capable of discouraging housing production in general. This is the logical conclusion from the Appellate Division ruling in *Washington*, or the trial decision in *Montgomery*.

The principal argument in favor of including developer-plaintiffs in court-ordered remedies in *Mount Laurel*-derived cases is a straightforward one. Generally, a developer-plaintiff is in a position to build housing on the tract for which he has applied for a variance; he has acquired an interest in the land, conducted the necessary engineering and planning activities, submitted plans, and obtained the necessary mortgage financing. In the absence of reasonable assurance that it will be possible to

build, few developers assume the expense required to make a case for a
(d) variance, and litigate the denial of the variance request. Given these
considerations, the likelihood is great that an order to grant a permit to a
developer-plaintiff will result, in a fairly short period, in the construction
of housing. No other remedy available to the court can have such a direct
effect. Even if the court requires affirmative steps of the nature discussed
immediately above, substantial gaps may remain between the remedy and
the production of housing.

The issue is even more pronounced in the case of relatively modest
housing—housing that will meet a need not at present being met in the
community or region in which the case takes place. In the *Cinnaminson*
case, the judge asserted that the plaintiff had to prove not only housing
needs in general, but an unequivocal need for housing of the precise
price range and type proposed by plaintiff—thereby virtually requiring a
detailed market analysis—and dismissed the evidence submitted as
"generalities." [18] The argument of the *Brunetti* case, in which the trial
judge held that the *DeSimone* [19] principle, (provision of low- and
moderate-income housing was a special reason justifying a (d) variance
could be extended to conventional housing for people of modest income,
has not been pursued. [20] Instead the courts appear to have imposed an
added standard, requiring an extensive burden of proof on the developer. [21]

Another argument used by the courts to deny a remedy to a
developer-plaintiff is found in *Fobe v. Demarest*, in which the Appellate
Division held:

> Given the zoning ordinance of the municipality, which completely
> excludes multifamily dwellings from within the municipality, no board
> of adjustment or governing body could find with any degree of candor
> or legal propriety that the grant of a variance to construct a complex of
> multi-family dwellings "will not substantially impair the intent and pur-
> pose of the zone plan and zoning ordinance" *N.J.S.A. 40-55:39(d)*. [22]

This is remarkable. Since no responsible planner or architect will assert
that multi-family and single-family housing are inherently incompatible
from a physical standpoint, the only interpretation that can be given to
this holding is that, if the intent of an ordinance is exclusionary, then any
attempt to remedy that exclusionary stance is suspect under the language
of Sec. 39(d). [23]

Although we would not argue that successful *Mount Laurel*-related litigation should guarantee a developer-plaintiff a building permit, we do
believe that serious consideration of such a step should accompany any
such decision. It should be noted that if the municipality were not

exclusionary in the first place the need to apply for a (d) variance may well not have arisen. Thus, the reliance on Section 39(d) with its greater burden on plaintiff is a direct result of the previously exclusionary policy of the municipality. We would suggest that, in the event a court finds a municipal zoning ordinance exclusionary, the developer-plaintiff have at least the opportunity to argue that approval of his development be included in the remedy, and that the developer be able to make that argument on neutral ground,[24] with the burden of proof shifted entirely or in part, to the defendant municipality. Municipalities have long used the presumption of validity as a shield behind which to hide zoning ordinances that were superficial and irresponsible, and administrative practices that were equally so. Although it is useful for municipalities to claim that granting a variance would impair their plan, the fact is that most municipal 'plans' are of such inadequacy that it is often impossible to tell which developments were the result of variances and which took place by right. A finding that a municipality has engaged in exclusionary zoning practices should be adequate to justify suspending any presumption that that ordinance, and its administrative enforcement, be valid.

There are, of course, pitfalls in the use of the (d) variance. It should under no circumstances come to be seen as an *alternative* to the careful rezoning, and framing of affirmatively inclusionary policies, that are the principal long-term remedies for housing exclusion. Similarly, with regard to the shifting presumption, we believe that far greater weight should be given those developers, and their developments, who propose to meet the housing needs of some group demonstrably in need of improved housing opportunities. The developer of three-bedroom townhouses to sell for $25,000 is demonstrably serving a more significant public purpose than the developer of one-bedroom luxury condominiums to sell for $45,000. In the event, however, that a developer and his experts can demonstrate a non-negligible generalized unmet need for the housing he proposes, it is gratuitous for a judge to set arbitrarily high standards of proof. There is enough need for modestly priced housing, by any reasonable standard, to justify allowing builders to build. Finally, any substantive objections by the municipality that should objectively be given weight in opposition to the grant of a variance, can be given full scope through such hearings as are proposed above.[25]

It should be noted that a by-product of such a procedure would be to increase the stakes, particularly with regard to the municipality, in exclusionary zoning litigation. It is not unlikely that the existence of a remedy of this sort, as a complement to the remedies of rezoning and affirmative action, would be a spur to encourage greater municipal responsiveness to the principles enunciated by the courts in *Mount Laurel*.

There is no question that many municipalities directly affected by *Mount Laurel* have been dragging their feet in anticipation, encouraged by many of the court decisions described in this essay that they may be able to defer indefinitely any substantive response to *Mount Laurel*. Put differently, they have come to believe that the court's dictates will be satisfied by symbolic actions, or, under more auspicious circumstances, by no action at all. Were the possibility of direct intervention more plausible, the inclination of some municipalities to undertake voluntary affirmative and inclusionary programs might be increased.

Conclusion

Early in 1975, the author published an article with the unnecessarily tendentious title of "Do lawsuits build housing?"[26] The conclusion that was reached, needless to say, was that they do not. Since then, however, a corollary has become apparent, which was not yet visible prior to the *Mount Laurel* decision. Although lawsuits do not build housing, lawsuits can prevent housing from being built. It is the argument of this piece, in part, that the post-*Mount Laurel* decisions cited, if allowed to stand, will have a deterrent effect on housing production by narrowing the circumstances under which recourse may be had to the courts, and by limiting the remedies available in those few situations where the courts will feel free to intervene. The cumulative effect of the decisions made by the Appellate Division in *Washington, Demarest,* and *East Brunswick,* as well as the trial decisions in *Montgomery* and *Cinnaminson,* can only be to allow local government obstructiveness a free hand in the great majority of situations.

It is the author's contention that, although one cannot ask more from the judiciary than it can give, the tone and content of the *Mount Laurel* decision strongly suggest that judicial action must be cognizant of the realities of the housing development process. Instead, it appears that some judges are engaging in semantic quibbles as a means of letting municipalities "off the hook", while others are establishing gratuitously high hurdles over which plaintiffs must jump in order to obtain relief. The author is hopeful, however, that this is a temporary aberration, and that the thrust of the line of cases culminating in *Mount Laurel* will soon be restored.

NOTES

1. 67 N.J. 151.
2. *Segal Construction Co. v. Borough of Wenonah,* A-797-73, App. Div. decided May 5, 1975.

3. *Id.* at 3.
4. No. L-37016-73 N.J. Super. Law Div. Burlington Co. decided July 8, 1975).
5. *Id.* at 5.
6. There are three additional Appellate Division opinions: *Wilann Assoc. v. Borough of Rockleigh* (A-3224-72, decided May 29, 1975), *Pascack Association, Ltd. v. Township of Washington* (A-3790-72, A-1841-73, decided June 25, 1975), and *Fobe Assoc. v. Borough of Demarest* (A-1965-73, decided July 2, 1975). These last two are on appeal to the Supreme Court as of this writing.
7. New Jersey County & Municipal Government Study Commission, *Housing & Suburbs: Fiscal and Social Impact of Multifamily Housing* (Trenton, New Jersey, 1974), pp. 110-111. The municipalities in question are Fort Lee (4,207 units), Hackensack (4,111 units), and Lindenwold (3,819 units) during the period from 1965 to 1972.
8. 67 N.J. 193.
9. *Id.* at 218.
10. No. L-699-73 P.W. (N.J. Super. Law. Div., Somerset County, decided July 29, 1975).
11. *Id.* at 6.
12. Under the current subsidy programs, in particular the New Jersey Housing Finance Agency and the Federal Section Eight program, it is for all practical purposes not feasible to develop housing on land costing more than $1,500 per dwelling unit, and often no more than $1,000 to $1,200 per unit.
13. Extensive literature on the subject is beginning to emerge. See in particular Kleven, "Inclusionary Ordinances—Policy and Legal Issues in Requiring Private Developers to Build Low Cost Housing", *21 UCLA Law Review 1432* (1974), and Franklin, Falk & Levin, *In-Zoning: A Guide for Policy Makers on Inclusionary Land Use Programs*, Washington, D.C., 1975.
14. 67 N.J. at 179.
15. Among cases cited above, *Rockleigh, Wenonah, Washington, Demarest, Cinnaminson,* and *Montgomery.* Also, see *Showcase Properties, Inc. v. Township of East Brunswick,* (A-2256-73, App. Div. decided June 9, 1975) and *Middle Union Associates v. Township of Holmdel,* (L-1149-72 P.W., NJ Super. Law Div. Monmouth County, decided May 15, 1975).
16. The trial court in *Washington, supra.,* 131 N.J. Super.195, ordered the Township to grant a building permit to plaintiffs. This was reversed by the Appellate Division; case certified to the New Jersey Supreme Court, November, 1975.
17. 131 N.J. Super. 195 at 198. The ordinance amendment adopted by the municipality, in addition to the inadequacy cited above, contained a series of egregiously exclusionary standards; e.g., floor area requirements of 1,000 sq. ft. for one-bedroom units, a requirement that each unit have two parking spaces, and that 25 percent of all parking be enclosed, required central air conditioning, etc. All in all, the conclusion of bad faith on the part of the municipality was rather apparent; all the more amazing, therefore, that the Appellate Division appeared not to notice, or to care.
18. *supra.,* at 12-14, 16.
19. *DeSimone v. Greater Engelwood Housing Corp.* 56 N.J. 248.
20. *Brunetti v. Township of Madison,* 130 N.J. Super. 164. This case was not appealed.

21. *See also: Showcase Properties, Inc. v. Township of East Brunswick supra.* note 15.
22. *supra.* at 2.
23. The suggestion made by the court in *Fobe v. Demarest,* that the appropriate route in such circumstances is through amendment of the zoning ordinance, is hardly a realistic alternative in most cases.
24. To remand a proposal back to the municipal zoning board of adjustment, after having found the municipality in violation of *Mount Laurel* standards, is unlikely to result in a fair hearing for a developer, to say the least.
'5. In the interest of brevity, the issues involved in this question have necessarily been oversimplified. There are many questions, such as those associated with developer good faith, with the feasibility of obtaining binding commitments to provide the units at the costs specified in the litigation, etc., that must be dealt with in detail at some future point.
26. "Do Lawsuits Build Housing: The Implications of Exclusionary Zoning Litigation" 6 *Rutgers-Camden Law Journal* 653 (1975).

The Mandatory Percentage of Moderately Priced Dwellings Ordinance

Jerome G. Rose

At the same time that most suburban communities are utilizing various techniques of exclusionary zoning, such as large lot districts, minimum floor space requirements, apartment restrictions, controlled sequential development, etc.,[1] a few local governments have adopted a new statutory technique that seeks to provide housing for low- and moderate-income families within the community. It is not clear whether the statute is a response to recent judicial admonitions that municipal planning and zoning must provide for a balanced community[2] or to the combined political pressure of newlyweds, empty-nesters, local employers, and those who, for idealistic reasons, seek a more balanced socio-economic mix in the community. Whatever the reason, the Mandatory Percentage of Moderately Priced Dwelling (MPMPD) ordinance is now a fact of life that should be noted and understood by the real estate industry.

An MPMPD ordinance has been adopted by Fairfax County (Virginia) and Montgomery County (Maryland)[3] and it is being studied by other local governmental agencies, including the Regional Planning Board of Princeton (New Jersey), as a possible method of overcoming the high

170

costs of construction that are putting unsubsidized housing beyond the reach of low- and moderate-income families.

Purpose of the
MPMPD Ordinance

The Montgomery County Council found, and the MPMPD legislation recites,[4] that a severe housing problem existed within the county due to an inadequate supply of housing for residents with low and moderate incomes. Studies had shown that there was a rapid increase in the number of residents of, or approaching, retirement age, who either had reduced or fixed incomes; that there was a growing proportion of young adults of modest means forming new households; and that there were numerous employees of government, commerce, and industry within the county whose services were necessary to support the existing and expanding economic base of the county. The supply of moderately priced housing was inadequate to meet the needs of these people. Consequently, many of those working within the county had to commute from outside the county to their places of employment, thereby overtaxing existing roads and transportation facilities and significantly contributing to air and noise pollution.

The Montgomery County Council found that approximately one-third of the county's projected labor force over the next ten years would require moderately priced dwelling units. In spite of this need, the concurrent high level of demand for higher profit potential luxury housing discouraged developers from offering a more diversified range of housing. The Council also determined that the private sector is best equipped and has the necessary resources and expertise to provide moderate-income housing. The only problem was the high cost of land and construction which reduced the profit incentives to build such moderately priced housing. This led the Council to conclude that private developers could be persuaded to build moderately priced housing if they were given adequate profit incentives by permitting greater zoning density and by relaxing some building and subdivision regulations.

The underlying principle of the MPMPD statute is simple: Give a housing developer a bonus in terms of zoning density and the relaxation of building code requirements in return for his agreement to build a proportion of the units within the range of the moderate-income (or low-income) market. Although the principle is simple, the administration of the program is complicated and there are numerous unresolved legal issues.

Administrative Problems

To administer an MPMPD program it will be necessary to posit policy decisions and establish guidelines to resolve the following issues:

1. What percentage of the total number of units built must be allocated to the moderate- (or low-) income market?
2. What range of tenant or purchaser incomes should the mandatory percentage be designed to meet?
3. What kind of administrative mechanism is necessary to adjust rents to changing economic circumstances?
4. If dwelling units are to be sold, what mechanisms are necessary to retain the economic advantages for future purchasers?

THE MANDATORY PERCENTAGE

There are at least two different views for determining the mandatory percentage of low and moderate units. Pragmatists would probably urge that the percentage be based upon market and economic studies to determine the extent to which the developer may effectively pass on the increased costs of subsidizing the lower priced units and the extent to which the market for the higher priced units would be adversely affected by the presence of lower income occupants. Idealists would urge that the mandatory percentage be based upon housing need or the goal of an "ideal" socio-economic mix within the community. Whatever percentage is adopted would, very likely, reflect a compromise between the two points of view.

THE RANGE OF INCOME

Determining this issue will also involve reconciling a number of divergent viewpoints. Pragmatists will argue that the program can succeed only if the market for the higher priced units is maintained. Consequently, they will urge that only the moderate income market be serviced by the program. Idealists will urge that at least some percentage of units be made available to low-income families. If such families cannot be serviced by subsidizing part of the rent, they will urge that some units be offered to the local housing authority under one of the federal public housing leasing programs.

ADMINISTRATION OF RENT REGULATION

Administration of the program must be assigned to a governmental agency with authority to adjust rents. Such adjustment is necessary to achieve the objectives of the program and at the same time to enable the landlord to obtain a fair return on investment. Changing costs of maintenance and fluctuating market demand for higher priced units will require rental adjustments for the subsidized units. The need for continual rent regulation is probably, from the developer's point of view, one of the most serious objections to the program. Zoning density bonuses and the easing of building code standards will have to be substantial to overcome the burdens of rent negotiations with a governmental agency that is subject to increasing political influence of tenant organizations.

ADMINISTRATION OF SALES REGULATION

If the developer agrees to build townhouses or condominiums instead of rental housing, then the MPMPD program will continue to achieve its objectives, if, but only if, each purchaser of a subsidized unit, when he sells, is required to sell at a price that is within the means of low- or moderate-income purchasers. This means that purchasers of subsidized units may have to relinquish all, or part, of the appreciated value of the dwelling when it is sold. Thus, a government agency will have the task of developing principles and administering a program which establishes unit selling prices and selects qualified purchasers.

Legal Problems:
The Need for Enabling Legislation

MPMPD ordinances face two serious legal problems—(a) questions of statutory authorization and (b) questions of constitutional validity. In the short history of this program, the first ordinance of its kind was challenged and found to be invalid on both counts. In *The Board of Supervisors of Fairfax County v. DeGroff Enterprises, Inc.*,[5] the Virginia Supreme Court held invalid a Fairfax County ordinance that required a developer of fifty or more dwelling units to commit himself, before site plan approval, to build at least 15 percent of dwelling units as low- and moderate-income housing. The court held that the ordinance exceeds the authority granted to the local governing body by the enabling act because it is directed to *socioeconomic objectives* rather than *physical characteristics* authorized by the state statute. Furthermore, the court said, the ordinance is invalid because it requires the developer or owner to rent or sell 15 percent of the dwelling units at rental or sale *prices not fixed by a free market*. Such a scheme, the court held, violates the state constitutional provision that no property be taken or damaged for public purpose without just compensation.

In spite of this initial setback, proponents of MPMPD ordinances argue that these ordinances will be upheld in those jurisdictions where the courts have held that the validity of a zoning ordinance depends upon its ability to "promote the general welfare."[6] They argue that these courts will hold that the "general welfare" requirement imposes the obligation upon municipalities to provide for a variety of housing choices. Consequently, it is argued, the courts will determine that not only is the MPMPD ordinance within the scope of zoning enabling legislation, but there is an affirmative duty on the part of local governments to adopt techniques such as MPMPD to provide that housing choice.

In those states that adopt the reasoning of the *Fairfax County* decision, enabling legislation will be necessary. But in either case, the proponents urge, the MPMPD ordinance is alive and well, and gathering support for the next onslaught upon the citadel of suburban zoning practices.

NOTES

1. See: Rose, "New Directions in Planning Law: A Review of the 1972-1973 Judicial Decisions," 40 *J. Amer. Inst. Planners*—(July 1974).
2. See: Rose, "The Courts and the Balanced Community: Recent Trends in New Jersey Zoning Law," 39 *J. Amer. Inst. Planners* 265 (July 1973).
3. For an excellent analysis of the Montgomery County, Maryland legislation see The Potomac Institute, Inc., Memorandum 73-11, Nov. 28, 1973.
4. Montgomery County Code, Chapter 25A, title, "Housing, Moderately Priced," (1973).
5. 214 Va. 235, 198 S.E.2d 600 (1973).
6. E.g., New Jersey, Pennsylvania.

Complaint in
Mount Laurel No. 2

Department of the Public Advocate

In May, 1976 the New Jersey Department of The Public Advocate brought a second suit against the Township of Mount Laurel alleging that the township failed to comply with the March 24, 1975 decision of the New Jersey Supreme Court in *Mount Laurel I*. This later lawsuit asks the court, among other things, to determine the township's fair share of the present and future regional housing need for low- and moderate-income persons and to order the use of specific land to meet such need. The court is also asked to enjoin the township from using funds derived from its municipal taxing and borrowing powers for purposes that benefit middle and upper income persons until it implements an approved program to improve the living conditions of low and moderate income persons.

The text of the complaint is re-printed here.

Southern Burlington County N.A.A.C.P.

v.

Township of Mount Laurel

Amended Complaint in Lieu
of Prerogative Writ

175

Plaintiffs, by way of amended complaint, allege and say:

Prefatory Statement

1. This amended complaint is filed pursuant to the decision of the New Jersey Supreme Court rendered on March 24, 1975 and the Order of this Court signed on February 13, 1976. The Supreme Court decision required that the defendant undertake certain action and provided that plaintiffs should proceed by supplemental pleading if they desired to challenge the defendant's lack of compliance with the Supreme Court's mandate as contained in said decision.

2. The defendant has failed to comply with the aforementioned decision and has persisted, instead, to continue the pattern and practice of economic discrimination and exclusion first condemend by this Court in its decision on May 1, 1972.

3. Said pattern and practice of discrimination and exclusion includes, but is not limited to, the defendant's:

a. failure to properly assess its fair share of the regional need for housing for low and moderate income persons;
b. failure to provide, through land use regulations, for a fair share of the regional need for housing for low and moderate income persons;
c. failure to plan for and to provide for the needs of its indigenous low and moderate income citizenry;
d. failure to take such other action, over and above amending land use regulations, which is necessary and advisable to the satisfaction of the aforementioned housing needs; and
e. continued use of Federal, State, County and local finances and resources solely for the betterment of the wealthy and to the exclusion and detriment of low and moderate income persons.

4. Plaintiffs seek a declaration by this Court that the defendant has failed and refused to act in good faith to comply with the letter and spirit of the Supreme Court decision. Plaintiffs further seek an order containing within it the necessary elements which will insure that plaintiffs' rights under the Constitution and laws of this State and the United States are protected and that compliance with the aforementioned decision is obtained. Said order must include:

a. a determination of the defendant's fair share of the local and regional housing needs of low and moderate income persons;
b. specific remedial land use provisions to enable the satisfaction of such needs forthwith; and
c. injunctive relief ordering specific other action which is necessary and advisable to insure the satisfaction of said needs and, further, to insure that all citizens enjoy equal opportunity in the future use of land in the

township and that Federal, State, County and local finances and resources are administered by the defendant in a non-discriminatory
manner.

Facts

5. The original complaint in this action was filed five years ago on
May 3, 1971.

6. Said complaint (which is incorporated herein as if repeated at
length detailed a history of neglect and abuse suffered by the plaintiffs at
the hands of the defendant municipality.

7. Four years ago, on May 1, 1972, this Court, after a trial on the
merits, rendered its decision. *Southern Burlington County N.A.A.C.P. v.
Township of Mount Laurel,* 119 N.J. Super. 164 (Law Div. 1972). This
Court held, in part, that:

> the patterns and practices clearly indicate that defendant municipality
> through its zoning ordinances has exhibited economic discrimination in
> that the poor have been deprived of adequate housing and the oppor-
> tunity to secure the construction of subsidized housing; and has used
> Federal, State, County and local finances and resources solely for the
> betterment of middle and upper-income persons.

8. This court declared Mount Laurel's zoning ordinance invalid, ordered a determination of the housing needs of residents, present and projected employees, and former residents, and ordered the development of
a plan to satisfy those housing needs. The defendant was given ninety (90)
days to comply. Said time, if not stayed would have expired on July 30,
1972.

9. However, said decision and order were stayed pending appeal.
Three years later, after two oral arguments and extensive briefs, the Supreme Court of New Jersey, on March 24, 1975, rendered its decision
essentially upholding this Court decision while granting plaintiffs' cross-
appeal as to the defendant's obligation for a regional fair share of low and
moderate income housing needs. *Southern Burlington County
N.A.A.C.P. v. Tp. of Mt. Laurel,* 67 N.J. 151 (1975). The Supreme Court
held, in part, that the defendant must:

> [B]y its land use regulations, presumptively make possible an approp-
> riate variety and choice of housing . . . [I]t cannot foreclose the oppor-
> tunity of the classes of people mentioned for low and moderate income
> housing and in its regulations must affirmatively afford that opportun-
> ity, at least to the extent of the municipality's fair share of the present
> and prospective regional need therefor.

10. The Court, in its discussion of exclusionary land use techniques, explicitly cited minimum lot area, frontage and building size requirements as well as the overmapping for industrial uses, the designing of Planned Unit Developments for the affluent and the lack of low cost multi-family housing and housing of other types and varieties. The Court stated:

> Mount Laurel must, by its land use regulations, make realistically possible the opportunity for an appropriate variety and choice of housing for all categories of people who may desire to live there, of course including those of low and moderate income. It must permit multi-family housing, without bedroom or similar restrictions, as well as small dwellings on very small lots, low cost housing of other types and, in general, high density zoning, without artificial and unjustifiable minimum requirements as to lot size, building size and the like, to meet the full panoply of these needs.

11. The Court went on to say that housing opportunities must be provided for the poor and for present and prospective employees, that a planned unit development "must include a reasonable amount of low and moderate income housing in its residential 'mix'" and that industrial mapping must be "reasonably related to the present and future potential for such purposes." In conclusion the Court partially voided the ordinance, ordered the township to comply with its decree

> . . . both by appropriate zoning ordinance amendments and whatever additional action encouraging the fulfillment of its fair share of the regional need for low and moderate income housing may be indicated as necessary and advisable.

12. The Supreme Court stated that, prior to judicial intervention, the defendant should have the opportunity to determine its own method of compliance. It gave the township ninety (90) days to comply which, if not extended, would have run on June 22, 1975. This Court was given the authority to extend the ninety (90) day period, if necessary, to give the defendant time to comply.

13. Mindful of the need to insure that the defendant was given every opportunity to comply voluntarily, plaintiffs consented to numerous requests by the defendant for extensions of time. This was done in spite of the fact that at the end of the initial ninety (90) day period the defendant had done virtually nothing to fulfill the Supreme Court's mandate.

14. The defendant sought and received five extensions of time to comply. These were granted on June 20, 1975, July 14, 1975, August 1, 1975, November 14, 1975 and February 13, 1976. The compliance time was ultimately moved back from the original date of June 22, 1975 to April 20,

1976; that is, approximately ten (10) months. In all, the defendant had almost thirteen (13) months to effectuate compliance with the judicial mandate.

15. Finally, on April 20, 1976 the defendant submitted an amendment to its zoning ordinance which submission was offered as its total compliance with the Supreme Court's decision. The amendment contained:

> a. fair share calculation of only 515 units for low and moderate income persons through the year 2000 (phased at a permissible 103 limit in the first year and a ceiling of 17 units per year thereafter);
> b. the provision of an infinitesimal amount of land to be used for housing low and moderate income persons in three new zones which purport to but, in fact, do not create the opportinuty for such housing; and
> c. numerous "controls" and restrictions on development and impositions exclusively on developers of housing for low and moderate income persons.

16. Despite the direction of the Supreme Court that the defendant should take all other "necessary and advisable" action, the defendant has not undertaken any action other than the adoption of the amended zoning ordinance, to encourage the fulfillment of its fair share of the regional need for housing for low and moderate income persons.

17. The defendant knew, or should have known, prior to and at the time of its submission to this Court, that the aforementioned amended ordinance was inadequate and did not satisfy the mandate of the Supreme Court.

18. The fair share plan of only 515 units for housing for low and moderate income persons was designed for a single purpose: to derive the lowest conceivable figure. The figure is an insignificant percentage of the present and projected total population of the defendant municipality. The methodology used is indefensible, the calculations incorrect and the result patently unreasonable.

19. The zoning amendments are inadequate. Their infirmities include, but are not limited to: (1) a lack of incentives to developers to build low or moderate cost housing; (2) virtually no land zoned at standards established by the Supreme Court; (3) insignificant elimination of industrial overmapping; (4) the failure to provide for mobile homes or modular housing construction; (5) the retention and addition of unnecessary restrictions, controls and specifications which add to the cost of housing and which are not required as promoting the public health, safety and general welfare and (6) the delineation of sites for the construction of housing for low and moderate income persons which are totally unsatisfactory.

20. Throughout the past five years, since the filing of the original complaint and despite this Court's decision and that of the Supreme Court,

the defendant has done virtually nothing to alter the condemned pattern and practice of discrimination and exclusion or to take numerous actions which are both necessary and advisable to the provision of adequate housing for the poor residing within its borders and a fair share of those in the region. This includes, but is not limited to:

> a. for two consecutive years the defendant has refused to cooperate with Burlington County in this county's application for revenue-sharing funds under the Housing and Community Development Act of 1974, 42 U.S.C. 5301, *et seq.* These are grant funds and would have been available at no cost to the defendant. Said federal community development funds to Burlington County have been lessened due to Mount Laurel's refusal to cooperate. More importantly, residents of the township are excluded from the opportunity to participate in the county community development programs, such as: loans and grants for housing rehabilitation and for water and sewer hook-up fees, as well as potential special local projects to serve the needs of the poor such as the acquisition of sites for low and moderate cost housing. The defendant's refusal to participate in this program is unjustifiable and an intentional effort to deprive its own low and moderate income residents of the benefits of this federal grant program;
>
> b. the defendant has failed to adequately plan for or sufficiently engage in any systematic program to upgrade the living conditions of its resident poor. The most tenured residents of this municipality continue to live in deplorable conditions completely lacking or with minimal public services, while the newest residents receive all of the amenities offered by the township;
>
> c. the defendant has continuously let it be known publicly that it will not cooperate with developers of housing for low and moderate income families, will not itself undertake to create a local public agency to facilitate the construction of such housing, will not itself apply for funds to provide for such housing, and will not assist projects by providing for necessary payments in lieu of taxes pursuant to state law; and
>
> d. the defendant has failed to undertake an effective code enforcement program or to develop a workable relocation assistance plan to assist its own residents who reside in substandard conditions.

21. Despite the explicitly stated assumption by the Supreme Court that the defendant would act in good faith to comply with its mandate, no attempt was made to do so. The most important factor is this: the plaintiffs and the class they represent continue to have their basic needs ignored by the defendant and their rights violated while the defendant encourages and provides a decent, safe and sanitary living environment for persons of middle and upper income.

Legal Allegations

22. The plaintiffs represent a class of low and moderate income persons in Mount Laurel and in the regional area who are in need of housing

opportunities in Mount Laurel but who have been foreclosed from obtaining said opportunity by the action and / or inaction of the defendant. This is an appropriate class action pursuant to R. 4:32-1, *et seq.*

23. The aforementioned actions and / or inactions by the defendant do not comply with the mandate of the Supreme Court of New Jersey and violate the Constitution and laws of the State of New Jersey and the United States.

WHEREFORE, plaintiffs request that this Court:

1. Declare that the defendant has failed to comply with the mandate of the New Jersey Supreme Court;

2. Declare that the defendant's zoning ordinance, as amended, other pertinent land use ordinances and provisions, and provisions of the Agreements covering the approved Planned Unit Developments are unlawful and invalid insofar as they operate to exclude the poor;

3. Determine the defendant's proper fair share of the present and projected regional need for housing for persons of low and moderate income; said determination to remain in force until such time as the defendant presents an acceptable plan of its own to this Court;

4. Determine and order the use of specific land use provisions to enable the opportunity for the construction of housing for persons of low and moderate income to satisfy the defendant's fair share obligation; said provisions to remain in force until such time as the defendant presents an acceptable amended ordinance of its own to this Court;

5. Order the defendant to undertake other necessary and advisable action to insure the satisfaction of the aforementioned housing needs and the creation of a proper living environment for low and moderate income present and future residents;

6. Order the defendant to cease and desist from continuing to discriminate against the resident poor in the use of Federal, State, County and local finances and resources and to affirmatively act to correct the imbalance created by its prior history of discrimination;

7. Enjoin the defendant from using, applying for, receiving or accepting any non-constitutionally mandated grant, loan or guaranty from the Federal, State or County Government unless and until it demonstrates to this Court a willingness to use, apply for, receive and accept from said sources such grants, loans and guarantees as are available for the benefit of the resident and future poor;

8. Enjoin the defendant from using its own resources derived through municipal taxation or the bonding power for the purpose of improving or otherwise maintaining areas of industry and middle and upper income persons unless and until the defendant submits to this Court a satisfactory affirmative plan of action and implements a program to utilize said re-

sources to improve and otherwise maintain the living conditions in residential areas of low and moderate income persons;

    9. Certify that this is an appropriate class action;

   10. Retain jurisdiction of the case; and

   11. Grant such other relief as may be just and equitable.

STANLEY C. VAN NESS
PUBLIC ADVOCATE

By: [signed]
   CARL S. BISGAIER
   DEPUTY DIRECTOR
   DIVISION OF PUBLIC INTEREST ADVOCACY
   DEPARTMENT OF THE PUBLIC ADVOCATE
On The Complaint:
   Kenneth E. Meiser, Esquire
   Peter A. Buchsbaum, Esquire
   Peter J. O'Connor, Esquire, Of Counsel
Date: May 6, 1976

Is the Decision
Based on
Wishful Thinking?

Jerome G. Rose

"The people of New Jersey should welcome the result reached by the Court in this case, not merely because it is required by our laws, but, more fundamentally, because the result is right and true to the highest American ideals." With these words, Justice Pashman, in his concurring opinion, set forth the New Jersey Supreme Court's underlying assumption in its decision to make the validity of municipal zoning dependent upon a new and complex standard. First, I will analyze the components of this newly created judicial standard of validity of municipal zoning; then I will examine the issue of whether this standard is likely to achieve its laudable objectives or whether its chances of success will be limited by political realities that conflict with the noble ideals upon which the decision is based.

Components of the Decision

The majority opinion, written by Justice Hall as his swan song after a brilliant career on the New Jersey Supreme Court, contains a contrived and carefully written collection of principles of planning and land-use law. Although all the principles are related to the extent that they seek to achieve a common objective, they are nevertheless separable into individual, distinct components, each of which is significant by itself and each of which may very well create a life of its own in the line of decisions certain to follow.

THE CONCEPT OF "FAIR SHARE"

The court has adopted the concept of "fair share" for allocating municipal responsibility for low- and moderate-income housing. There are at least four different criteria for defining "fair share":

1. Allocation of an *equal share* of the obligation to each municipality;
2. Allocation of responsibility for housing based upon *need*;
3. Allocation of housing to achieve *economic and racial integration*; and
4. The *suitability* of the jurisdiction to accommodate the housing.[1]

Although the court does not reject the possible use of any of the other three criteria of "fair share," it does require that at least the regional *need* for housing be considered. What the result may be where the regional *need* for housing in a given municipality conflicts with the *suitability* of that municipality to accommodate that need remains an unanswered question.

THE CONCEPT OF "REGION"

Municipal responsibility for housing goes beyond its own boundaries and includes the "region." The court does not define "region" except to say that its meaning will vary from situation to situation and that confinement of "region" to the county appears not to be realistic. By this determination, the Supreme Court has adopted the principle suggested by Judge Furman in the *Oakwood at Madison* [2] case that each municipality has a responsibility to meet the need for housing, not only for its own citizens but also for non-residents living within the region who would like to move into the municipality. However, the Supreme Court has not adopted Judge Furman's suggestion that region be defined in terms of "the area from which in view of available employment and transportation, the population of the township would be drawn absent invalidly exclusionary zoning . . . ", i.e., trip time to work.[3]

THE SPECIFIC MUNICIPAL ACTION REQUIRED: "TO AFFIRMATIVELY AFFORD AN OPPORTUNITY"

Municipal attorneys and officials will be asking the question, "What does the court require us to do?" The court's answer to this question is,

"Adopt a zoning ordinance that 'affirmatively affords an opportunity' for low- and moderate-income housing to be built within the jurisdiction." The court readily concedes that "courts do not build housing nor do municipalities." However, municipalities do have the responsibility to "make realistically possible the opportunity" for a variety and choice of housing for all categories of people who may desire to live there, including those with low and moderate incomes. The decision lists some of the requirements and proscriptions of a zoning ordinance that fulfills this responsibility: A valid zoning ordinance *must* permit multi-family housing; it *must* allow small dwellings on very small lots; it *must* permit high density zoning. A valid zoning ordinance *may not* impose bedroom or similar restrictions on multifamily housing; it *may not* impose "artificial and unjustifiable" minimum requirements as to lot size, building size; it *may not* zone for the benefit of the local tax rate (i.e., fiscal zoning is prohibited).

THE TEST OF "PRESENT AND PROSPECTIVE REGIONAL NEED"

A valid zoning ordinance must seek to meet the "present and *prospective* regional need" for low- and moderate-cost housing. The *present* need for low- and moderate-cost housing can be estimated reasonably accurately from existing data relating to population size, family income, number of existing units, vacancy rate, etc. However, the prediction of *prospective* (i.e., future) housing need is much more difficult. The accepted technique, adopted by Rutgers Center for Urban Policy Research [4] and the National Association of Housing and Redevelopment Officials [5] requires an initial prediction of the amount and type of commerce and industry that will move into the area. The income distribution of new residents is then based on the expected wage and salary levels of the jobs to be created by those employers. The number of housing units needed and the rent and cost range is, in turn, based upon that determination of income distribution. Even assuming that all of these calculations are performed with precision and accuracy, the final computation of *prospective housing need* can be no more accurate than the original prediction of the amount and type of commerce and industry that will move into the area. This prediction would seem to be a flimsy and debatable premise to base the validity of a municipal zoning ordinance. [6]

REQUIREMENT OF A RELATIONSHIP BETWEEN RESIDENTIAL AND INDUSTRIAL / COMMERCIAL ZONES

For many years, proponents of open housing have argued that there is a municipal obligation to permit the construction of housing for the employees of the industries that provide the ratables. This argument was rejected in a recent federal district court decision that is presently being appealed.[7] The *Mount Laurel* decision, however, adopted this argument and determined that when a municipality zones for industry and commerce, it must zone to permit adequate housing for the employees who will work there. The difficulty with this concept is similar to the previous problem of predicting future housing needs. Both projections are dependent upon the accuracy of the prediction of the amount and type of industry and commerce that will in fact move into the area. However, as the officials of developing communities know well, the mere fact that land is zoned for commerce and industry is no assurance that such land will be used for those purposes within any foreseeable period of time. Does the obligation to permit housing arise upon the adoption of the ordinance designating industrial and commercial uses or does this obligation arise only when such land is *in fact* put to such uses? There are significant planning implications in either case, but this question is now answered by the decision.

STATE CONSTITUTIONAL BASIS FOR THE DECISION

The majority opinion bases its decision upon state constitutional law, i.e., the state constitutional requirements of substantive due process and equal protection of the laws inherent in Article I, paragraph 1 of the New Jersey Constitution[8] and in the constitutional requirement that all police power regulations must promote the "general welfare." The state constitutional basis for the decision has two legal consequences: (a) It minimizes the possibility of appeal to the United States Supreme Court. It is possible, but unlikely, that the United States Supreme Court would determine that a federal question arises because of the interpretation of the meaning of "due process" and "equal protection," both of which are concepts originating in the United States Constitution. (b) It forecloses the possibility of having the decision overridden by the state legislature. If the decision were based upon a statutory interpretation of "general welfare,"[9] the New Jersey legislature, which is responsive to its substantially suburban constituency, could by simple majority supersede the decision by amending the zoning enabling legislation. This strategy, by which the court substitutes its political judgment in the place of the elected legislature, raises a fundamental issue to be discussed later in this article.

THE JUDICIAL REMEDY

Although the high court sustained the trial court's ruling that the municipal ordinance is invalid, it modified the trial court's judgment in two important respects: (a) The court did not declare the zoning ordinance invalid *in toto*. Only those provisions of the zoning ordinance that are inconsistent with the opinion are invalid. The apparent purpose of this modification is to avoid a state of zoning anarchy that could put the municipality at the mercy of "voracious land speculators and developers." However, as each application for a building permit is made for construction which is not consistent with the zoning provisions, a litigable issue will arise whether the zoning provision in issue is or is not consistent with the opinion. (b) The court specifically vacated the trial court's judgment ordering the municipality to prepare and submit a housing study, and it thereby withdrew the judicial power, at this time, from the process of enforcing the above principles.[10] The court left compliance up to the municipality, initially, with the unexpressed threat of judicial intervention at a later stage if required.

Moral and Political Bases of the Decision

The eloquent opinions of Justices Hall and Pashman are based upon moral and political judgments that American ideals of equal opportunity and equality before the law are more than catchy platitudes to be resurrected and recited at quadrennial inaugural ceremonies and bicentennial independence celebrations. Both opinions have assumed that the suburban electorates and their municipal and state elected officials have forgotten these principles. Therefore, they need only be reminded by the judiciary of the historical and constitutional commitment to these principles and they will, with diligence—if not fervor—renounce their former transgressions and reaffirm these ideals. Simply put, the court has assumed that the suburban electorate—many of whom, at great cost and expense, have fled from the perceived and real dangers of city living to find relative safety and comfort in their socially homogeneous communities—will respond to the judicial mandate with the question, "What do we have to do to comply with this decision?"

Undoubtedly, there will be many who will respond in this manner. The judiciary performs the dual role of articulator of prevailing morality and at the same time is a formulator of emerging moral principles. In both roles, it imposes its principles with authority and persuasion in a law-abiding society. Many suburban communities will indeed respond sincerely and diligently with efforts to comply with this decision.

However, to much of the suburban community, the stakes are high, the perceived risks are great, and the impact of this decision is personal and direct. It remains to be determined what proportion of suburban residents will ask *not*, "How do we comply?" but rather, "How do we postpone, avoid, or even defy this decision?" This group will seek and find devices and techniques to protect its self-interest by avoiding the intended result of economic and racial integration.

It is much too soon to compile an exhaustive list of techniques that may be used to frustrate the goals of the *Mount Laurel* decision. However, a number of devices are self-evident.

STATISTICAL WARFARE

The implementation of this decision requires studies and reports based upon interpretations of such indeterminate and ambiguous concepts as "fair share," "region," "future housing need," and "presumptively realistic efforts to make possible an appropriate variety and choice of housing." Each concept must be quantified, for each municipality, in terms of numbers of housing units. This computation will be based upon underlying premises and theories of extrapolation about which competent and honest professional planners may differ. These differences in professional judgment can cause a wide disparity in the proposed number of housing units necessary to meet the requirements of the decision. It will be possible for a municipality to argue that with a minimum contribution of new housing, its zoning ordinance has met the prescribed standard of validity. A developer restricted by the ordinance will disagree, and the statistical issues will be joined and argued in the courts. The process of litigation has rarely been an inducement to housing construction.

ABETTING ECONOMIC REALITIES

One of the many economic obstacles to the construction of housing for low- and moderate-income families is the fact that the land most appropriate for such residents is land that ideally should be within walking distance of shopping and public transportation. In developing communities, this land is frequently expensive because of these characteristics. However, even without such amenities, once an area is zoned for high-density development, its market value will rise to reflect its development potential. By careful and adroit planning and zoning, it would be possible to meet the requirements of the decision but at the same time designate land for multifamily dwelling use that becomes too expensive to build housing for low- and moderate-income families without substantial outside subsidies.

INEFFECTUAL EFFORTS TO OBTAIN SUBSIDIES

At some stage of every discussion of the effect of "exclusionary zoning" upon the supply of housing for low- and moderate-income people, it becomes necessary to recall the fact that the removal of land-use restrictions alone will not result in the construction of such housing. Under prevailing costs of land, materials, labor, and financing, it is not possible in many areas to build housing that low- and moderate-income families can afford without some form of federal or state subsidy. The amount of funds available for these subsidies has traditionally been extremely limited and requires dedicated, diligent, and persistent efforts on the part of municipal officials to succeed in each application. Even after an application for funds is made and a "presumptively realistic effort to make possible an appropriate variety and choice of housing" is evidenced, that effort may fail as a result of an imperceivable (and difficult to prove) reduction in the diligent processing of the application. How long a period of failure in applications will be necessary before a court can conclude that a municipality's efforts have not been "presumptively realistic"?

SUBTERFUGE AND CUNNING

The validity of a zoning ordinance of a developing community will depend upon evidence of its efforts to make low- and moderate-cost housing possible within the community. One recent proposal to provide such housing *without an outside subsidy* is the mandatory percentage of moderately priced dwelling (MPMPD) ordinance.[11] By the provisions of this type of ordinance, a developer is given a bonus in zoning density in return for his agreement to build a proportion of the units within the range of the moderate- and low-income market. Adoption of this type of ordinance would appear to be evidence of the kind of affirmative effort required by the decision. However, by skillful and crafty adjustment of the details of this program, it would be possible to raise the percentage of subsidized units, lower the income level of eligible tenants, provide for effective rent control of future leases, and otherwise administer the program in such a manner that would foreclose any possibility that the program will be utilized by any developer whose incentives include profit and investment protection.

ECOLOGICAL CONSTRAINTS

The opportunity for the use of ecological or environmental factors to justify limitations of housing development arises from the equivocal statements on the subject that appear in the opinion. On one hand, Justice Hall found that the environmental factors in Mount Laurel did not provide a sufficient excuse in itself to limit housing to single-family dwellings on large lots. But then he added, "This is not to say that land-use regulations should not take due account of ecological or environmental factors or problems. Quite the contrary. Their importance, at last being recognized, should always be considered." The state of the art of analysis and presentation of ecological and environmental evidence is at an early stage in its development. Professional planners are just now perfecting techniques and standards to describe the impact of various kinds of development on flooding, water supply, water pollution, air pollution and which cause other damage to the environment. This type of ecological information will provide the basis of arguments by idealistic and responsible members of the community for opposition to proposed housing construction.

TIMED GROWTH DELAYS

A plan by which the sequential development of a community is programmed is not, per se, a device to frustrate the goals of the *Mount Laurel* decision. In fact, in the *Ramapo* decision in which a timed growth plan was upheld, the New York high court specifically found that the program was not intended to exclude population growth. However, the system does provide a device which can be used to postpone housing development until completion of capital improvement programs intended to serve the needs of future residents. Further extensions of time could be expected upon a showing of unanticipated problems. Ultimately, if low- and moderate-cost housing is not in fact produced, the program might be declared invalid or otherwise abandoned. But a substantial period of time could have elapsed before that happens, and the purposes of its advocates will have been served.

The availability of these and other devices that can be used to outmaneuver the judicial process suggests that the solution of this problem must come from an instrumentality of government other than the judiciary. What is needed is a responsive administrative mechanism that can issue regulations that remove ambiguities and close loopholes. This administrative agency would have to be empowered to define the "region," to determine "fair share," and to prescribe the range of land-use choices of each municipality. This agency would have to derive its authority from the state legislature, which is the only legitimate and effective instrumentality of government that has the mandate to make the kinds of policy judgments on which the *Mount Laurel* decision is based. If the state legislature is unable to create a workable consensus by the political processes of negotiation and accommodation of conflicting interests to resolve the underlying policy issues, then it is fair to ask whether the underlying goals of the *Mount Laurel* decision are presently achievable or whether they are based upon the wistful hopes of an idealistic but credulous court.

NOTES

1. For a discussion of the problems created by each of these criteria for defining "fair share," see Rose, "Some Unresolved Issues of Exclusionary Zoning and Managed Growth,"—Rutgers Camden L.J.—(Spring 1975).
2. *Oakwood at Madison, Inc. v. Madison Township*, 117 N.J. Super. 11, 283 A.2d 353 (1971), *on remand* 127 N.J. Super. 438, 320 A.2d 223 (1974), *appeal docketed.*
3. For a discussion of some of the problems involved in using the "trip-time to work" definition of "region," see Rose, note 1 *supra.*
4. *See:* James & Hughes, *Modeling State Growth: New Jersey 1980* (Rutgers Center for Urban Policy Research 1973).
5. *See:* Alexander & Nenno, *A Local Housing Assistance Plan: A NAHRO Guidebook* 27 (National Association of Housing and Redevelopment Officials 1974).
6. For a discussion of some of the problems involved in the methodology for the computation of prospective housing need, see Rose, note 1 *supra.*
7. *Metropolitan Housing Dev. Corp. v. Arlington Heights*, 373 F. Supp. 208 (N.D. Ill. 1974), *appeal docketed.*
8. It is interesting to note that this provision of the New Jersey Constitution does not expressly contain the phrases "due process" or "equal protection of the laws." The section referred to by the court provides as follows:
   All persons are by nature free and independent, and have certain natural and unalienable rights, among which are those of enjoying and defending life and liberty, of acquiring, possessing, and protecting property, and of pursuing and obtaining safety and happiness.
   N.J. Const. Art. I, ¶ 1.
9. Justice Mountain wrote a short concurring opinion in which he said that he reaches the same conclusion as the majority but he bases his decision on the interpretation of "general welfare" as it appears in the zoning enabling legislation, rather than on the state constitution.
10. Justice Pashman wrote a long concurring opinion in which he said that he differs with the majority only in that he would have preferred to have the Court implement the principles contained in the majority opinion.
11. For a discussion of this technique see Rose, "The Mandatory Percentage of Moderately Priced Dwelling Ordinance (MPMPD) Is the Latest Technique of Inclusionary Zoning," 3 Real Estate L.J. 176 (1974).

IV
Reactions
to the
Decision

From the Environmentalists:

The General Welfare
and
Environmental Considerations

Nicholas Conover English

In the now famous case of *Southern Burlington County N.A.A.C.P. v. Township of Mt. Laurel,* the New Jersey Supreme Court thoroughly documented the housing crisis, and held that the general welfare required each developing municipality to make provisions for its fair share of the regional housing needs for low- and moderate-income persons. The Court however recognized that a developing municipality's obligation to provide such housing might be modified by environmental considerations; thus, the Court states:

> "This is not to say that land use regulations should not take due account of ecological or environmental factors or problems. Quite the contrary. Their importance, at last being recognized, should always be considered."[1]

It is a truism, and has become a cliche, that *Mt. Laurel* created more issues than it solved. One such issue involves the nature and extent of the environmental concerns that must be considered, and their relationship to the municipality's fair share of regional low- and moderate-income housing. Another issue is the definition of the region whose housing needs the municipal zoning plan must recognize. It is submitted that the "region" must include the ecological region and not merely the home-job region.

New Jersey is the most densely populated state in the union. Hence, it is subject to the most intense pressures of public policy regarding land use. One of the main forms of such pressure grows out of the need for additional housing, particularly for low- and moderate-income persons. The principal counter-pressure arises from the need for protecting the natural environment although the tax system and the construction of public works produce their own pressures on land use.

It is high time that those who make or influence land use decisions — whether municipal officials, judges, or planning, engineering and legal consultants — be aware that the natural resource base in New Jersey has definite limitations and that this cannot be ignored without serious consequences to the state and its people.[2]

The focus of environmental considerations in zoning litigation can perhaps be most conveniently centered upon water quality and flooding. These are matters of prime public importance.[3] Indeed, available water resources may put an ultimate ceiling on the population of New Jersey.[4] In the vital matter of water supply, it was stated in April 1975:

> The Hackensack River basin is the most densely populated, and is now using more than its maximum safe annual supply determined on the basis of the most recent drought in the mid 1960s. The only reason that this region has escaped problems in recent years is that the rainfall in the area has been above average.*** Turning to the Passaic River basin we find that, at the present time, the safe dependable water yield of the Passaic River basin has been completely allocated.*** The safe yield of the Raritan River basin has not yet been completely developed and it therefore has a potential surplus of water.[5]

In June 1973, the County and Municipal Government Study Commission reported:

> Water is a basic resource; it is necessary for sustaining life. The use of rivers, streams and bays as sewers for dilution and transport of wastes negates their use as a source of water supply, as a base of recreational activity, as a habitat for fish and wildlife. In the extreme it may mean the survival of the State's economic base. . . . In summary, New Jersey's extensive water pollution is probably the most serious problem currently imperilling the quality of our physical environment.[6]

Some if the characteristics of streams, and some of the effects of human activities thereon, may be noted. In recent years, flooding has become a major problem in many areas of New Jersey.[7] In 1972, the Legislature enacted a law regulating land use in flood hazard areas.[8]

When a pervious surface (e.g. woods, pastures or fields) is changed to an impervious surface (e.g. roofs and paved areas), the quantity of surface water runoff into the streams is increased because the water cannot soak into the ground as readily and the time of concentration of the runoff at the stream is reduced. The result is a tremendous increase in the quantity of water that enters the stream in a given space of time and the inevitable result is flooding.

It has been judicially declared to be "common knowledge that impermeable surfaces, specifically, roofs and streets, increase surface water runoff.[9] In another case the court found on the facts before it: "For open lands, 20 to 35 percent of the rain-fall reaches the Brook as runoff whereas, for roof and paved areas, the runoff ranges from 70 to 95 percent of the rainfall."[10]

The "assimilative capacity of streams" refers to a stream's ability to "digest" waste materials that enter it and to transform them into animal or plant forms in a way that maintains water quality.

> An aquatic ecosystem has a substantial but finite capacity to assimilate the wastes which result from human use of the land in its watershed. As the land is developed more extensively, or more intensively, and the area of undisturbed open space decreases while population density increases, the assimilative capacity may be exceeded. The resulting ecological disturbance and eventual environmental degradation affect many uses and may cause public health problems. Diminishing quality of the water for water supply, increasing treatment costs, destruction of aquatic life, and loss of recreational or aesthetic value are among the probable results.[11]

Non-point sources contribute approximately half of the total pollution entering streams. Non-point or non-recorded sources of pollution are those which cannot be precisely identified; they would include surface water runoff and ground water seepage.

A study by the Water Resources Research Institute at Rutgers University of the organic pollution of the Upper Passaic, Upper Raritan and Millstone River Basins discloses:

> Even though water quality in these basins' data was rather incomplete; there seems little doubt that the organic loading of each of the three river systems is much greater than the organic loading from recorded effluents. For the Passaic River, for which there is far more data than for the other two, and where a much greater effort at surveillance and enforcement has been made, the recorded effluents account for 39 percent of the total organic loading entering the river system. In the Millstone Basin, a comparable figure is 24.3 percent. In the Raritan Basin the proportion of the organic loading attributable to recorded effluents is only 7.3 percent, a figure so low as to suggest either a

serious deficiency in the records used, or a lack of control of major
sources of pollution in the Raritan Basin.[12]

The Institute has further reported:

> The findings of this preliminary examination raise serious questions
> as to the usual basis on which water quality plans are prepared. It
> would be relatively unproductive to plan advanced waste treatment for
> effluents, if an equal or larger organic loading were uncontrolled, and
> growing with the population and industry of the basin. In view of the
> findings in this paper, it should not be assumed that treatment of re-
> corded effluents is sufficient to achieve any desired water quality
> standard, without also looking into the occurrence of untreated organic
> loadings.[13]

In the last few years there has been developed a growing body of research into non-point pollution resulting from urbanization, and a recognition that desired water quality standards cannot be achieved without consideration of nonpoint pollution.[14] As the New Jersey Commissioner of
Environmental Protection, David J. Bardin, stated in 1975:

> We will be spending in excess of one billion dollars in New Jersey
> within the next several years to control point source pollution. We
> know where those sources are and basically how to control them. . . .
> What we do not know enough about is the identification of the sources
> and magnitude of nonpoint and urban runoff pollutants and their physi-
> cal, legal and institutional means of control. We are aware that point
> source control will not be adequate to clean our streams.[15]

Land use is a significant factor in nonpoint pollution.[16]

Stream pollution increases with a population increase in a river basin,
notwithstanding continuing improvement in waste water treatment. A
study of the Upper Passaic, Upper Raritan and Millstone Rivers found:
"Statistical analysis indicates that over the period of investigation, the
gross pollution for these streams has increased about 0.54 percent for each
1.0 percent increase in population."[17]

A study published by the Center for Urban Policy Research, Rutgers
University, in April 1972, and based upon analysis of data pertaining to
the Raritan River Basin stated:

> Present water quality standards cannot be met in all reaches of the
> basin — even if effluent standards are rigorously enforced — unless
> regional development in *both* population and industrial growth is not
> only restricted, but reversed so as to diminish both industrial activity
> and population density.
> Our study of pollution suggests that the traditional commitment of
> our society to continued economic growth (as in the case of the Raritan

Basin) has produced its own antithetical need to limit and even to reverse growth lest the cumulative ecological deterioration of our environment proceed to a level where dangerous and irreversible damage is done.[18]

Sewerage treatment plants do not guarantee clean rivers. There are many reasons for this.

In the first place, there are many kinds of pollutants. These include organic or oxygen demanding wastes, nutrients, (both of foregoing are produced by domestic sewage), minerals, salts and acids from industrial and agricultural processes, toxic substances, disease-causing agents, and sediments.[19] Limited amounts of sewage can be purified by dilution, if the stream is big enough.

Primary treatment will generally remove about 60 percent of the suspended solids and about 30 percent of the BOD in raw sewage. Secondary treatment is a biological process that normally removes up to 90 percent of the BOD.[20]

It is important to note however, that secondary treatment does not remove all of the nutrients; additional processes are required for that purpose. Further treatment beyond secondary can become expensive and usually involves a separate process for each kind of pollutant. The nature and degree of advanced waste water treatment, and the concomitant cost, will depend, of course, upon the kinds of pollutants in the wastes to be treated and also upon the uses to which the stream water is to be put farther down. Where, as in most major New Jersey rivers, the same stream is used both to dilute and carry away treated sewage effluent and to provide water for public drinking purposes, a high degree of treatment is required. How high a degree of treatment required will depend upon the size or volume of flow in the stream in relation to the volume of treated effluent, in order to provide dilution of the effluent within the limits of the assimilative capacity of the stream. The extent of pollution from other sewage treatment plants along the same stream must also be considered. And allowance must be made for the nonpoint sources of pollution in addition to that caused by the sewage treatment plants.

Large sewage systems may have an adverse effect upon water quality in two respects. First, by transporting waste water away from a given area, the system restricts groundwater recharge that could be accomplished by septic systems or spraying of effluent. Secondly, large sewerage plants tend to concentrate a large volume of effluent at a point where the stream may be too small to assimilate it.

Groundwater is a natural resource deserving adequate protection. As previously stated, groundwater flows into streams and, if polluted, will contaminate the stream. Similarly, a polluted stream can contaminate groundwater. Moreover, groundwater is extensively used, by means of wells, as a source of water supply.

Groundwater is the source of water supply in many parts of the State, and is the principal source of supply in the coastal plain area of New Jersey. Unwise land use controls can affect the purity and quantity of the supply.

Once polluted, groundwater is extremely difficult, if not impossible, to purify.[21] Excessive pumpage or curtailment of recharge may so lower the water table as to cause danger of salt water intrusion in coastal areas, or to cause wells to go dry in upland areas, and waste disposal in excess of the soil's capacity to handle it may cause outright contamination.

Many students of water resources have concluded that water quantity and quality are inseparable from land use. From what has already been said, it should be clear that flooding problems and water pollution problems result from the nature and intensity of land usage.

In April 1975, the Governor's Commission to Evaluate the Capital Needs of New Jersey reported:

> Water Pollution — The current state of New Jersey's waters are the result of unplanned and uncontrolled expansion of population, combined with inadequate waste treatment facilities in some of the older cities and industrial plants whose waste water treatment methods are based upon the dilution principle.[22]

Even though the courts will issue injunctions and award damages in cases of stream pollution,[23] and even though there are statutory penalties for stream pollution,[24] the fact remains that New Jersey's rivers are polluted. The Passaic River and Arthur Kill have the dubious distinction of ranking among the 10 most heavily polluted rivers in the nation. Clearly, statutes and judicial remedies have proved inadequate to ensure the quality of water in New Jersey's rivers that the future will require. Even if technology can purify anything — even New Jersey's sewage and industrial wastes — there is a real question whether the public will pay the financial costs required. The fiscal woes of New York City, the defeat of the proposed bond issues in New Jersey in November 1975, and the growing demand for less government spending, all suggest that technology is no more of an answer than statutes and judicial decrees.

The County and Municipal Government Study Commission pointed out three years ago the connection between land use in upstream areas and the degraded water quality in New Jersey rivers. The Commission said:

> Urban growth, suburban sprawl, and industrial development have accelerated the deterioration of water quality. As a consequence of the expanding and competing demands, fresh water must be used and re-

used many times throughout the State. In the Passaic River, for example, the Passaic Valley Water Commission (PVWC) takes 75 million gallons daily from the river at Little Falls to supply over 400,000 people in sixteen municipalities. Sewage treatment facilities located above Little Falls discharge 50 million gallons of treated domestic and industrial wastes daily. This means that during the summer months when the river's flow is 100 million gallons daily, the PVWC actually supplies at least 25 mgd of reused water.[25]

It is submitted that the only effective solution to the problem lies in appropriate land usage.[26]

Regional needs extend to matters other than housing, and include environmental concerns such as water supply, waste disposal and flooding.

In *Mount Laurel*, the Supreme Court clearly established that local zoning must take due account of regional needs in the field of housing. Prior to that decision, it was held that local zoning regulations, in the promotion of the general welfare, may validly consider regional needs for a mental hospital,[27] or for educational institutions,[28] or, apparently, for senior citizens housing.[29]

Land use in the upper part of a river basin affects downstream communities in respect to flooding and water quality. In certain cases, land use may contaminate groundwater used elsewhere for public consumption.

Quite obviously the "region" cannot be realistically defined in terms of political boundary.[30] On the facts before it, the Court in *Mount Laurel* appears to conceive of the region primarily in terms of the home-job relationship. So did Judge Furman in *Oakwood at Madison v. Township of Madison.*[31]

Victor J. Yannacone, Jr. defines ". . . the Regional Ecological System as the overall area in which any effect attributable to the actions under consideration can be perceived or measured."[32] He goes on to say:

> Successful land use legislation depends upon determination of the highest and best use of land and natural resources in terms of intrinsic suitability for, and natural constraints upon, development. . . . Any planning effort which fails to fully evaluate the effects of proposed land use or development activity on the overall ecological integrity of the Regional Ecological System affected is an inadequate plan at best. . . Any zoning law or land use regulation — local, state or federal — based upon such inadequate evaluation must fail.[33]

The installation of sewers in certain areas without regard to other environmental conditions and concerns is contrary to the general welfare.

In an effort to seek a reasonable balance between the sometimes conflicting social imperatives of housing and of protecting natural resources

and the environment, the following statement in *Mount Laurel* requires
further analysis:

> "It is said that the area is without sewer or water utilities and that
> the soil is such that this plot size is required for safe individual lot
> sewage disposal and water supply. The short answer is that, this being
> flat land and readily amenable to such utility installations, the township
> could require them as improvements by developers or install them
> under the special assessment or other appropriate statutory proce-
> dure." [34]

The court was properly making the point that unsubstantiated environmental concerns do not justify exclusionary zoning. But if the court
means that the housing aspect of the general welfare requires, as a matter
of law, the construction of sewerage systems wherever the terrain permits, such a holding must be challenged as contrary to the general welfare. The concern should focus not so much on the engineering feasibility
of sewering a particular site, but rather on the regional and environmental
effects of sewers — and the consequent size of the population — at the
particular location.

Land values in New Jersey being what they are, it may be assumed
generally that low cost housing cannot be provided except by multi-family
housing at densities that will require a sanitary sewerage system. The fact
of the matter is that there are many areas in New Jersey where sewerage
systems readily *could* be installed but where they *should not* be.

The need to clean up New Jersey's polluted rivers is unquestioned. The
magnitude and urgency of the task exceed presently available resources.
Recent studies advocate using the resources that are available to upgrade
sewerage systems in existing urban areas rather than to utilize such funds
to extend sewerage systems into new areas. [35]

The matter of further expenditures for sewerage treatment plants has to
be considered in the light of the Federal Water Pollution Control Act
Amendment of 1972. [36] This legislation declares that: (a) it is the national
goal that the discharge of pollutants into the navigable waters to be eliminated by 1985; and (b) it is the national goal that wherever attainable, an
interim goal of water quality which provides for the protection and propa-
gation of fish, shellfish, and wildlife and provides for recreation in and on
the water be achieved by July 1, 1983. The states are required to make
plans to accomplish these goals. A discussion of some of the effects of this
legislation is found in *Natural Resources Defense Council* v. *Train*, from
which it appears that the states must make plans to meet the federal
requirements, and the plans must deal with both point as well as certain
non-point sources of pollution. [37]

New Jersey has not yet completed its plans, so it is impossible to determine at present the effect which the federal legislation would have on the land use plans of any particular municipality, or, conversely, the effect which land usage in particular areas would have upon the State's ability to meet the federal guidelines. To achieve the federal mandate for recreationally clean waters in New Jersey by 1983, or the elimination of the discharge of pollutants, whether from point or nonpoint sources, by 1985, would seem to be an extraordinarily difficult task at best. If it is made even more difficult by a rule of law mandating sewer systems where they should not be placed, the general welfare will most definitely not be promoted.

The general welfare requires protection of natural resources and the environment. Land use regulation is encompassed within the state's police power. That the police power encompasses preservation of the natural environment was recently made clear by the Supreme Court in *Hackensack Meadowland Development Commission* v. *Municipal Sanitary Landfill Authority*, wherein the court, speaking unanimously through Justice Mountain, said:

> The Supreme Court has recognized that the protection of public health through the preservation of the environment is a valid, and indeed primary, objective of the police power. *Huron Portland Cement Co.* v. *Detroit*, 362 U.S. 440, 442, 4L.Ed. 2d 852, 855 (1960). Today it cannot possibly be questioned that the preservation of the environment, and the protection of ecological values are, without more, sufficient to warrant an exercise of this power. See for example, *Adams* v. *Shannon*, 7 Cal. App.3d 427, 432, 86 Cal. Rptr. 641, 644 (Ct. App. 1970); Garton, *Ecology and the Police Power*, 16 S.D.L. Rev. 26 (1971).

And at 68 N.J. 476: "We know too and are constantly becoming more acutely aware that the environmental resources as well as ecological and human values that have become so endangered upon this 'plundered planet,' insistently demand every reasonable protection that can possible be recruited." [38]

The new Municipal Land Use Law states the purpose of the act, which include:

> d. To ensure that the development of individual municipalities does not conflict with the development and general welfare of neighboring municipalities, the county and the State as a whole;
> e. To promote the establishment of appropriate population densities and concentrations that will contribute to the well-being of persons, neighborhoods, communities and regions and preservation of the environment;

f. To encourage the appropriate and efficient expenditure of public funds by the coordination of public development with land use policies;

g. To provide sufficient space in appropriate locations for a variety of agricultural, residential, recreational, commercial and industrial uses and open space, both public and private, according to their respective environmental requirements in order to meet the needs of all New Jersey citizens; [39]

A county master plan is to contain the county planning board's ". . . recommendations for . . . the general location and extent of forests, agricultural areas, and open development areas for purposes of conservation, food and water supply, sanitary and drainage facilities . . . ." [40]

In recent years the New Jersey Legislature has imposed restrictions on land use in environmentally sensitive areas. [41] It has also authorized municipalities to create Environmental Commissions, having power to recommend "plans and programs for inclusion in a municipal master plan" and "to study and make recommendations concerning open space preservation, water resources management, air pollution control, solid waste management, noise control, soil and landscape protection, environmental appearance, marine resources and protection of flora and fauna." [42]

Courts have upheld drastic land use restrictions in order to protect natural environmental features in a variety of situations. [43]

Against this background, how do environmental concerns affect a developing municipality's fair share of regional housing needs?

The first thing to do is to determine the maximum population which the environmental constraints will permit to live in the town without adverse effect within or without the municipal boundaries. Indeed, this seems to be called for by the new Municipal Land Use Law. It is now ordained that a zoning ordinance "shall be adopted after the planning board has adopted the land use plan element of a master plan." [44] The land use plan element of a municipal master plan is to take into account "natural conditions including, but not necessarily limited to, topography, soil conditions, water supply, drainage, floodplain areas, marshes, and woodlands." The master plan is also to include a conservation plan element. It should also be pointed out that the legislature has provided for municipal environment commissions which have powers of recommendation. [45] One member of the environmental commission shall be a member of the planning board. Thus the legislature has tried to ensure that environmental factors be reflected in the master plan. Moreover, a zoning ordinance must "either be substantially consistent with the land use element of the master plan or designed to effectuate such plan element," or the reasons for not doing so must be stated in the minutes. [46] In short, a zoning ordinance is now supposed to be based, among other things, upon environmental constraints.

The process of preparing a natural resource inventory and a master plan based thereon, should result in the identification of such areas of undeveloped land that are unbuildable because of steep slopes, floodplain, marshland, or publicly-owned open space. It should also identify any areas that should remain undeveloped in order to protect the public water supply,[47] or otherwise further the general welfare. This process will, in effect, define the areas which remain available for development. The acreage thus determined as developable, and the application of the considerations listed in N.J.S.A. 40:55 D-2 will suggest appropriate limits on future population growth, and hence the ultimate maximum population of the municipality.

It is important to check the projected future population growth against available water supply and sewage disposal capacity. The state of New Jersey is presently embarking upon the preparation of a state-wide master plan of water supply, which, when completed, may suggest allocations of water that will not permit unrestrained population growth everywhere in the state.

Pursuant to the Federal Water Pollution Control Act Amendments of 1972, planning in accordance with 33 U.S.C.A. § 1288 and § 1313 is underway in New Jersey, but not yet completed. It is apparent, however, that the planning process when combined with the permit system for controlling discharges into streams,[48] will result in waste load allocations being assigned to sewerage treatment plans which will in effect limit the size of such plants and hence the number of people who can be served thereby.[49] These limitations may well be drastic in the case of municipalities located in the headwaters of the Passaic and Raritan river basins and in areas located over aquifers or where wells are readily susceptible to pollution. In particular situations, these limitations may curtail further population growth in the municipality to the extent that what would otherwise be regarded as its fair share of regional housing needs will have to be reduced.[50]

For municipalities located in the pinelands or in certain coastal areas, a formulation of fair share that is based upon housing and job relationships may have to be modified in order to comply with the regional planning required by N.J.S.A. 13:18-3; 13:18-9; 13:18-13; and 13:19-16, so as to protect what the legislature has declared to be important environmental interests.

The general welfare requiring consideration of regional environmental needs as well as housing needs finds direct support in the opinion in *Mount Laurel:*

> Proper planning and governmental cooperation can prevent over-intensive and too sudden development, insure against future suburban

sprawl and slums and assure the preservation of open space and local beauty. We do not intend that developing municipalities shall be overwhelmed by voracious land speculators and developers if they use the powers which they have intelligently and in the broad public interest.[51]

This result can come about only if the necessary ecological facts are presented to municipal bodies and to the courts, and only if municipal bodies and courts exercise foresight and judgment.

What sort of a New Jersey are we to bequeath to the next generation? "A prudent man forseeth the evil and hideth himself but the simple pass on, and are punished."[52]

NOTES

1. 67 N.J. 151, 33G A.2d 731 (1975).
2. *Hackensack Meadowlands Development Commission* v. *Municipal* Sanitary Land Fill Authority, 68 N.J. 451, 476, 348 A.2d 505, 518 (1975); *AMG Associates* v. *Township of Springfield*, 65 N.J. 101, Note 4 at p. 112, 319 A.2d 705, 711 (1974); *Future Land Use* (Eds. Burchell & Listokin), Center for Urban Policy Research. Rutgers University (1975), pp. 35 and 39.
3. Note the volume and complexity of the legislation contained in N.J.S.A. Title 58 "Waters and Water Supply."
4. See paper entitled "New Jersey's Future: Goals and Plans" prepared for Bureau of Statewide Planning, Division of State and Regional Planning, Department of Community Affairs for Forum on the Future of New Jersey, Bicentennial Celebration, Rutgers - The State University, sponsored by the Urban Studies Center, Dec. 8, 9, 1967.
5. Vol. 2, Research Report of The Governor's Commission to Evaluate the Capital Needs of New Jersey, April 1975, pp.38, 41.
6. "Water Quality Management: New Jersey's Vanishing Options", June 1973, County and Municipal Government Study Commission, at p.2.
7. L. 1971, c. 110, § 2, N.J.S.A. 58:16B-2 states: "The Legislature hereby finds that: (a) The safety, economic vitality and general welfare of the residents of the Passaic River Basin region are threatened due to reoccurring flooding conditions causing loss of life, damage to public and private property and to natural resources amounting to in excess of $150 million."
8. L. 1972, c. 185, N.J.S.A. 58:16A-55, et seq.
9. *Oakwood at Madison, Inc.* v. *Township of Madison*, 117 N.J. Super. 11, 21, 283 A.2d 353, (LAW Div. 1971). *Divan Builders* v. *Planning Board, Township of Wayne*, 66 N.J. 582, 334 A.2d 30, (1975). See also facts stated in *Armstrong* v. *Francis Corp.* 20 N.J. 320, 323; 120 A.2d 4, 6, (1956).
10. *Cappture Realty Corp.* v. *Board of Adjustment, Elmwood Park*, 126 N.J. Super. 200, 206, 313 A.2d 624, (Law Div. 1973); aff'd. 133 N.J. Super. 216, 336 A.2d 30, (App. Div. 1975).
11. "Upper Raritan Watershed Water Quality Survey, 1972, for the Upper Raritan Watershed Association" p. 1, Academy of Natural Sciences, Philadelphia, Pa., March 1974.
12. "Preliminary Mass Balance of BOD on Three New Jersey Rivers" by William Whipple, Jr., Water Resources Research Institute, Rutgers University, October 1969.

13. "BOD Mass Balance and Water Quality Standards" by William Whipple, Jr., Vol. 6, No. 3, "Water Resources Research", June 1970.

14. Some of the results are reported in a volume entitled "Urbanization and Water Quality Control" edited by William Whipple Jr., American Water Resources Association, Minneapolis, 1975.

15. *Id.* p. 178.

16. *Id.* pp. 10, 265, 268, 272.

17. "Predicting Future Growth of Organic Pollution in Metropolitan Area Rivers", M. Marcus and Wm. Whipple, Jr., Water Resources Research Institute, Rutgers University, Feb. 1970, p. 20.

18. "Urbanization, Water Pollution and Public Policy", Carey, Zobler, Greenberg and Hordon, April 10, 1970, p.6.

19. "A Primer on Waste Water Treatment", pp. 10-13, U.S. Environmental Protection Agency, March 1971.

20. "A Primer on Waste Water Treatment", supra, p.4. See description of process in *Borough of Westville* v. *Whitney Home Builders,* 40 N.J.Super. 62, 71, 122 A.2d 233, (App. Div. 1956).

21. Vol. 2, Research Report of the Governor's Commission to Evaluate the Capital Needs of New Jersey, April 1975, p.43.

22. Summary Report, p. 18.

23. See New Jersey cases reviewed in Hanks, "The Law of Water in New Jersey", 22 Rutgers Law Review 621, 667-687. For a discussion of private groundwater pollution controversies, see Hanks, "The Law of Water in New Jersey", 24 Rutgers Law Review, 621, 661-670. Cities have been held liable in damages, or else enjoined, from dumping inadequately treated sewage into waterways, at suit of downstream riparian owner. *City of Walla Walla* v. *Conkey,* 6 Wash. App. 300, 492 P.2d 589 (1971); *People* v. *City of Port Huron,* 305 Mich. 153, 9 N.W.2d 41 (1943); *Freitas* v. *City of Atwater,* 196 Cal. App. 2d 289, 16 Cal. Rptr. 393 (1961); *Crane* v. *Brintnall,* 29 Ohio Misc. 75, 278 N.E.2d 703 (Com. Pl. 1973); *Cf. Weston Paper Co.* v. *Pope,* 155 Ind. 394, 57 N.E. 719 (1900); *Westville* v. *Whitney Home Builders, Inc.,* 40 N.J.Super. 62; 122 A.2d 233 (A.D. 1956).

24. N.J.S.A. Title 58, Chaper 10.

25. "Water Quality Management: New Jersey's Vanishing Options", *supra,* p.1.

26. "Water Quality Management: New Jersey's Vanishing Options", *supra,* at p.6: "Land use and community development planning continues to be incoherent as long as water quality is not viewed as an equal basic factor in decision making."

27. *Kunzler* v. *Hoffman,* 48 N.J. 277, 287; 225 A.2d 321 (1966).

28. *Andrews* v. *Ocean Township Board of Adjustment,* 30 N.J. 245, 251; 152 A.2d 580 (1959); *Roman Catholic Diocese* v. *Ho-Ho-Kus Borough,* 47 N.J. 211; 220 A.2d 97 (1966).

29. *Borough of Roselle Park* v. *Township of Union,* 113 N.J.Super 87; 272 A.2d 762 (L.Div. 1970).

30. *Duffcon Concrete Products* v. *Cresskill,* 1 N.J. 509, 513; 64 A.2d 347 (1949); *Mount Laurel, supra,* 67 N.J. 189, Note 22.

31. 128 N.J.Super. 438, 441; 320 A.2d 223 (L. Div. 1974). *See also:* "Defining 'Fair Share' of 'Regional Need'," 98 N.J.L.J. 633, and critique thereof in letter to the Editor, 98 N.J.L.J. 684.

32. "Future Land Use," *supra,* p.150.

33. *Id.* p.162.

34. 67 N.J. at 186. Apparently there was no evidence in Mount Laurel of environmental damage likely to occur to surface waters or aquifers as the result of development. See also *Oakwood at Madison v. Township of Madison, supra* at 117 N.J. Super. 2 1; 283 A2d 359, and 128 N.J. Super. 447; 320 A2d 227.

35. Vol. a, Research Report of The Governor's Commission to Evaluate the Capital Needs of New Jersey, April 1975, pp. 19, 36, "Secondary Impact of Regional Sewerage Systems, Vol. 1", N.J. Department of Community Affairs, June 1975.

36. Illuminating statements as to the 33 U.S.C.A. § 1251, *et seq.* purpose and nature of this complex legislation are found in *E.P.A.* v. *California*, U.S. _____, (June 7, 1976), 8 E.R.C. 2089; *American Frozen Food Institute v. Train;* _____ F.2d _____, (U.S. Ct. App. Dist. Col., May 11, 1976); in concurring opinion of Judge Adams in *American Iron & Steel Institute v. E.P.A.*, 526 F.2d 1027, 1073 (3rd Cir. 1975); and in *Town of Sutton v. Water Supply etc. Commission,*355 A.2d 867 (S. Ct. N.H. 1976).

37. 396 F. Supp. 1386 (D.C. D.C. 1975).

38. 68 N.J. 451, 348 A.2d 505 (1975). 68 N.J. at 473-476. See also *AMG Associates v. Springfield*, 65 N.J. 101, 319 A.2d 705 (1974), note 4, p. 112.; *Sands Point Harbor, Inc.* v. *Sullivan*, 136 N.J. Super. 436, 346 A.2d 612, (1975).

39. L. 1975, c. 291, N.J.S.A. 40:55 D-1, *et. seq.* in §2.

40. N.J.S.A. 40:27-2. See also N.J.S.A. 13:1B-5.1 (b).

41. See, for example PL 1970, c. 272, N.J.S.A. 13:9A-1 *et seq.* — Coastal Wetlands; PL 1971, c. 417, N.J.S.A. 13:18-1 *et seq.* — Pinelands Environmental Council; PL 1972, c. 185, N.J.S.A. 58:16A-50, *et seq.* — Flood Hazard Areas; PL 1973, c. 185, N.J.S.A. 13:19-1 *et seq.* — Coastal Areas Facility Review Act.

42. N.J.S.A. 40:56A-1, *et. seq.* State aid for these activities has been authorized by N.J.S.A. 13:1H-1, *et seq.*

43. Dune Ordinance: *Spiegle* v. *Beach Haven*, 46 N.J. 479, 492, 218 A.2d 129, 137 (1966); *cert. den.* 385 U.S. 831.
Preventing the filling in of wetlands: *Dooley* v. *Town Plan, etc. Com'm. of Fairfield*, 151 Conn. 304, 197 A2d 770 (S.Ct. 1964); *Zabel v. Tabb*, 430 F.2d 199 (5 Cir. 1970), *cert. den.* 401 U.S. 910; *Golden v. Board of Selectmen of Falmouth*, 358 Mass. 519, 265 N.E. 2d 573 (S. Ct. Mass. 1970); *Potomac Sand & Gravel Co.* v. *Governor of Maryland*, 266 Md. 358, 293 A.2d 241 (C. of A. 1972); *Just v. Marinette County,** 56 Wis.2d 7, 201 N.W.2d 761; (S.CT. 1972); *Sibson v. State*, 336 A.2d 239 (S. Ct., N.H. 1975).
Prohibiting building in floodplains: *Turnpike Reality Co.* v. *Dedham*, 284 N.E.2d 891 (S.Jud. Ct. Mass. 1972); *cert. den.* 409 U.S. 1108; *Turner v. County of Del Norte*, 24 Cal. App. 3d 311, 101 Cal. Rptr. 93 (Cal. App. 1972).
Restricting density of residential development in order to prevent water pollution: *Salamar Builders Corp.* v. *Tuttle*, 29 N.Y.2d 221, 275 N.E. 2d 585, 325 N.Y.S. 2d 933 (C. of A. 1971) (upheld change from 1 acre to 1-1/2 acre lots to reduce number and proximity of septic systems); *Nattin Realty, Inc.* v. *Ludewig*, 67 Misc.2d 828, 324 N.Y.S.2d 668 (S.Ct. 1971); aff'd without op. 40 A.D.2d 535, 334 N.Y.S.2d 483 (A.D. 1972); aff'd 32 N.Y.2d 681, 296 N.E.2d 257, 334 N.Y.S.2d 360 (C. of A. 1973) (upheld rezoning for single family houses after Planning Board approval of 342 garden apartments); *Walsh v.*

Spadaccia, 73 Misc.2d 866, 343 N.Y.S.2d 45 (S. Ct. 1973) (reversed approval of site plan for apartment houses for failure to consider effect upon water quality of nearby Lake Mohegan).

Enacting a moratorium on development pending preparation of zoning regulations designed to protect the environment: *Cappture Realty Corp.* v. *Board of Adjustment, Elmwood Park*, 133 N.J. Super. 216 (A.D. 1975); *State* v. *Superior Court of Orange County*, 12 Cal.3d 237, 115 Cal Rptr. 497, 524 P.2d 1281 (S.Ct. 1974); *CEEED* v. *California Coastal Zone Conservation Com'm.*, 118 Cal. Rptr. 315, 43 Cal. App.3rd 306 (Cal. App. 1974); cf. *Silva* v. *Romney*, 473 F.2d 287 (1 Cir. 1973).

§Wherein the court said at 201 N.W.2d 768:

"An owner of land has no absolute and unlimited right to change the essential natural character of his land so as to use it for a purpose for which it was unsuited in its natural state and which injures the rights of others. The exercise of the police power in zoning must be reasonable and we think it is not an unreasonable exercise of that power to prevent harm to public rights by limiting the use of private property to its natural uses."

44. N.J.S.A. 40:55 D-62a.
45. The "how to" of preparing a natural resource inventory and of relating the data therein to land use planning, may be found in such publications as "Handbook for Environmental Commissioners", N.J. Department of Environmental Protection; and a series of papers on "The Process of Environmental Assessment - Options and Limits", published by New Jersey Conservation Foundation, 300 Mendham Road, Morristown, NJ 0796.
46. N.J.S.A. 40:55 D-62a.
47. Cf. "The Pequannock Watershed Conservation and Development Plan" prepared by the Newark Watershed Conservation and Development Corporation, June 1, 1975.
48. This is the NPDES, or National Pollutant Discharge Elimination System, 33 U.S.C.A. §1342; see also *Town of Sutton* v. *Water Supply etc. Commission*, *supra*, footnote 35.
49. The integrity of the regional plan prepared under 33 U.S.C.A. §1288 will require that any private package plants either be included in the plan or else forbidden. It has been held that forbidden private septic systems, when such prohibition is part of a county comprehensive sewerage and water plan, does not deprive an owner of his property without due process of law, *Smoke Rise, Inc.* v. *Washington etc. Commission*, 400 F. Supp. 1369, 1390 (D. Md. 1975).
50. The assumption is that multi-family housing for any income level will require sewerage treatment rather than on-site disposal.
51. 67 N.J. 151, 191; 336 A.2d 713, 733.
52. Proverbs 22:3.

From the Courts:

The Trickle Before the
Deluge from *Mount Laurel*

Jerome G. Rose

In March 1975 the New Jersey Supreme Court held, in *Southern Burlington County NAACP* v. *Township of Mount Laurel*,[1] that a zoning ordinance of a developing municipality must provide for a fair share of the present and prospective housing needs of the region of which the municipality is a part. In the months that followed, decisions began to trickle down from the trial courts and lower appellate courts, attempting to interpret the *Mt. Laurel* decision and apply it to varying factual situations. In the decisions to date the lower courts in New Jersey have interpreted the decision strictly and narrowly, and it appears that the lower courts have not been overcome by the "spirit of *Mount Laurel*."[2] There is every likelihood that this trickle of decisions will grow into a flood as municipalities begin to defend their zoning plans against attack by developers and open-housing groups whose goals and objectives are not consistent with the local land-use policies adopted by the local governing bodies.

So far, most of the lower court decisions have turned on the "developing municipality" question: Is the municipality within the meaning of the

Mount Laurel decision and therefore subject to its mandate?[3] A few decisions have begun to deal with the difficult issues of "region" and "fair share." No decision has yet dealt in any detail with the complex problem of the computation of "prospective housing needs" or with the precise action required to "affirmatively afford the opportunity" for low- and moderate-income housing.[4]

What Is a Developing Municipality?

A number of decisions deal with the question of whether a municipality is a developing municipality within the meaning of *Mount Laurel*. In May 1975 the Appellate Division held[5] that the Borough of Wenonah, with an area of only one square mile, is not a municipality of "sizeable land area." Consequently, its contribution to the housing needs of the county would be only a minor one. The court observed that "requiring multi-family use of this last sizeable parcel of developable land within this tiny borough would thus subject Wenonah to a judicially created explosive growth phenomenon for which it may be ill equipped to deal." The court noted also that, when the minor contribution of the municipality to the housing needs of the county is compared to the major impact upon the municipality resulting from providing for those needs, there is no constitutional or statutory requirement of the municipality to provide such housing.

Later in May 1975 the Appellate Division held[6] that the *Mount Laurel* decision was not intended to apply to a community like the Borough of Rockleigh, which occupies less than one square mile, houses only 300 people in forty-six single-family houses, has not experienced significant growth, and can be characterized as "a tiny substantially developed community of settled and long-standing character with only rudimentary utility and transportation facilities and none for public education. Constitutional considerations do not, in our view, require the creating or enlarging of present public services to accommodate the relatively small number of persons who could be housed in judicially mandated multi-family units on the few remaining acres available for that kind of development. . . ."

In June 1975 the Appellate Division reversed[7] the decision of Judge George Gelman that had ordered Washington Township (Bergen County) to issue a building permit for multiple-family dwelling units subject to specified density, bedroom, parking, and floor-space requirements that had been recommended by the trial court's planning consultants.[8] The Appellate Division determined that the *Mount Laurel* decision is limited in application to "developing municipalities" with "sizeable land area" and is inapplicable to Washington Township, a small and almost completely developed municipality. Appeal of this decision is pending before the New Jersey Supreme Court.

In July 1975 the Appellate Division upheld[9] the Demarest Board of Adjustment denial of a use variance for multifamily dwellings in a municipality whose zoning ordinance excludes multifamily dwelling use. The court found that such a variance would impair the intent and purpose of the municipal zoning plan, and said that if such change is to be made it should be accomplished by amendment and not by variance. The court held that the principles of *Mount Laurel* were inapplicable because Demarest is a small municipality consisting of only 1,345 acres, with only 2.5 percent of that amount still undeveloped.

Also in July, trial Judge Paul R. Kramer in Burlington County (the same county that includes Mount Laurel) upheld[10] the Cinnaminson Board of Adjustment denial of a use variance for 100 condominiums on a ten-acre tract, based upon evidence that the property was ill suited for the proposed project because of topographical and drainage problems. The court found that Cinnaminson is "substantially developed," although 17.8 percent of the land (after subtracting flood-prone land) is undeveloped.

In November 1975, trial Judge Irving I. Rubin held[11] that North Haledon is not a "developing municipality" within the meaning of *Mount Laurel.* Plaintiff sought an order to compel the Borough to permit part of its land to be used for multifamily purposes. North Haledon is a municipality with 3.5 square miles, a population of 7,614 people, a total employment of 240 full-time and 243 part-time employees, with only two shopping centers built in the past twenty years and no new industries in the last forty years. Plaintiff alleged that 40 percent of the land is vacant. The court found that the "available" vacant land is less than 15 percent and that there was insufficient evidence to project future employment and housing needs.

No decision to date contains a comprehensive analysis of each of the six components of the definition of "developing municipality" set forth in the *Mount Laurel* decision. Those components are: (a) sizable land area; (b) location outside the central city and older built-up suburbs; (c) loss of rural characteristics; (d) great population increases since World War II; (e) incomplete development; (f) location in the path of inevitable future growth.[12] It is still unclear from decisions to date whether the *Mount Laurel* decision is to be applied only to a limited number of municipalities that are similar to Mount Laurel "with but relatively insignificant variation in details,"[13] or whether a municipality must meet all of the six components of the definition. On the other hand it has been argued that the carefully prescribed definition of "other municipalities . . . like Mount Laurel" set forth in the majority opinion is mere dicta and was not intended to limit the application of the *Mount Laurel* principles to only those municipalities that fit that definition.[14] It is hoped that some of these questions will be answered by the New Jersey Supreme Court in the *Washington Township* case currently on appeal.[15]

What Is the Region?

One of the most significant of the contributions of the *Mount Laurel* decision to the principles of land-use law is the judicial determination that the validity of municipal zoning depends upon the affirmative effort by the municipality to fulfill the housing needs of the *region*. Having taken this step, the court must be prepared to define "region" with some precision or face a deluge of suits in which the definition of "region" will be litigated. The New Jersey Supreme Court seems to have adopted the latter alternative. The court dismissed the problems arising from this issue with the statement that

> "The composition of the applicable 'region' will necessarily vary from situation to situation and probably no hard and fast rule will serve to furnish the answer in every case. Confinement to or with a certain county appears not to be realistic, but restriction within the boundaries of the state seems practical and advisable. . . ."[16]

The lower courts have begun to face the complexities of this issue on a case-by-case basis.

Judge Furman was one of the first to recognize the difficulties involved in this definition, in *Oakwood at Madison*,[17] where he observed that in that case, limiting the region to the *county* would not be realistic. He suggested that the appropriate region for the municipality to consider when assessing housing needs is that region from which, in view of available employment and transportation, the population of the municipality would be drawn absent invalid exclusionary zoning.[18]

In May 1975, trial Judge Merritt Lane, Jr. determined[19] that the county is the appropriate region to consider for the purpose of determining the obligation of the Township of Holmdel to provide for low- and moderate-income housing. He based this decision on the fact that 70 percent of the residents of Holmdel work in Monmouth County and, consequently, the people of Holmdel have an obligation under the *Mount Laurel* decision to help meet the needs for rental housing within that county.

In June 1975 the Appellate Division[20] dealt with the issue of region in an indirect way. The case involved a recommendation by the East Brunswick Board of Adjustment for a use variance for 250 multifamily dwelling units. The East Brunswick Township Council denied the application. The trial court reversed the township council and upheld the action of the zoning board. The Appellate Division reversed the trial court on the grounds that there was insufficient evidence to justify a finding of "special reason" required by the enabling legislation for a use variance. The issue of "region" is involved only indirectly because most of the evidence upon which the argument of public need for multifamily housing was based was derived from statistics taken from the Middlesex County Master Plan. Although this issue was not raised specifically, it seems to have been assumed by all parties and by the trial and appellate courts that the county is the appropriate region for determining the public need for multifamily housing.

In July 1975, trial Judge Arthur G. Meredith found it necessary to define "region" in an action in which the Montgomery Township zoning ordinance was attacked as exclusionary and unconstitutional.[21] The court adopted the township's designation of Somerset and Mercer Counties as the "region." This determination was based upon the fact that over 80 percent of the work-trip destinations of township residents are within the two counties. The court observed that county borders provide convenient areas for statistical and administrative purposes. The court also noted that this approach permits flexibility and allows each municipality to determine its own distinctive region even though it may be included in a different region adopted by another municipality.

The New Jersey Supreme Court has indicated its awareness of the multiplicity of reasonable theories by which "region" may be defined. In its order for reargument in the *Madison Township* case,[22] it requested all attorneys to file supplementary briefs on a list of eighteen issues, the first of which is:

> "1. Is it necessary, for fair share purposes, for the Court to fix a specific 'region', or may the municipality zone on the basis of any area which it reasonably may regard as an appropriate region?"

It is hoped that the decision in the *Madison Township* case will help to clarify this unresolved issue.

What Is a Fair Share of Regional Housing Needs?

After it is determined that a given municipality is a "developing municipality," and after the "region" of which it is a part is delineated, it then becomes necessary to compute the "fair share" of the housing needs of that region to be allocated to that municipality. But "fair share" might be computed on six different bases: (1) the allocation to each municipality of an *equal share* of the obligation to provide low- and moderate-income housing; (2) the allotment of responsibility for this housing based upon the *need* of local populations; (3) the allocation of this housing to achieve *economic and racial integration;* (4) the *suitability* of the municipality to accommodate the residents of low- and moderate-income housing; (5) the allocation of new units of low- and moderate-income housing to *avoid any reduction in existing proportions* of such housing in the municipality; (6) a minimum obligation of each municipality to *"take care of its own"* population, i.e., those who are a part of the community and who ought to be able to live there.

Most of the lower court decisions to date have adopted the second theory, i.e., allocation based upon *need.* Although this theory addresses only a part of a large and complex planning problem, the lower courts have probably been guided by the discussion of "fair share" in the *Mount Laurel* decision in which the court advises:

> "We may add that we think that, in arriving at such a determination, the type of information and estimates, which the trial judge (119 N.J. Super. at 178) directed the township to compile and furnish to him, concerning the housing needs of persons of low and moderate income now or formerly residing in the township in substandard dwellings and those presently employed or reasonably expected to be employed therein, will be pertinent." [23]

The definition of "fair share" adopted by Judge Merritt Lane, Jr. in the *Holmdel* case [24] is based upon the *Mount Laurel* suggestion. In *Holmdel* the court held that the township's "fair share" of the low- and moderate-priced housing units needed in the county should be based upon the township's percentage of jobs in the county. The court adopted the testimony of the plaintiff's planning expert [25] that there is a present need for 30,000 moderate- and low-priced housing units in the county and that Holmdel has 7 percent of the jobs in the county. The court ordered the township to amend its zoning ordinance to provide for reasonable areas where 2,100 units (i.e., 7 percent of 30,000) of low- and middle-income housing units could be built.

In the *East Brunswick* case [26] the Appellate Division dealt with the "fair share" issue only indirectly. The court upheld the governing body's rejection of the zoning board's use variance recommendation and found that the governing body was justified in rejecting the public need for multifamily housing and other factors as a special reason for a use variance. The court noted, with implied approval, that the township council did not give "dispositive or determinative weight" to the county's population projections or to the testimony as to the needs for additional rental units. Furthermore the court found that the evidence failed to show that the township had not provided its "fair share" of housing to meet the regional needs.

In the *Cinnaminson* case,[27] Judge Paul Kramer found that the township had more than met its "fair share" of housing during the previous twenty years. Based upon expert planning testimony[28] the court determined that there currently exists a desirable cross-section of incomes and housing (i.e., 20.5 percent of the population earned less than $10,000 a year) and a good balance between areas zoned for industry and areas zoned for residences. In determining the extent of the housing need (upon which "fair share" is based), the court rejected the principle that housing need is to be based upon the proportion of municipal population to regional population because this principle would penalize the municipality that permitted growth during the period of the past twenty years.

The most detailed and complex computation of "fair share" to date was made by Judge Arthur Meredith in the *Montgomery Township* case.[29] Based upon expert planning testimony,[30] the court established a two-step procedure for computing "fair share." In the first step, housing need of the township was computed as that percentage of the housing need of the region as the township land zoned for employment-generating uses (i.e., industrial and commercial) bears to the total amount of land zoned for such uses in the region. (In this case, the region was found to be Somerset and Mercer Counties.) The court accepted the expert testimony that the township should provide 7 percent of the total need because it has 7 percent of the employment-generating land of the entire region. The need for new housing in the region for the period between 1970 and 1985 was projected at 56,900 new households, Consequently, it was determined that the township share should be 7 percent of 56,900, or 3,983 new units. Of that amount, 67.5 percent or 2,689 units should be designated for multifamily use because 67.5 percent of the families of the region have incomes below $15,000 per year. Thus the "fair share" obligation of the township was determined to be 2,689 units for the fifteen-year period from 1970 to 1985, or 178 units per year.

However, the court recognized that complete reliance upon the above method could lead to abuse by municipalities because the analysis relies too heavily upon *present* land-use patterns. Thus a developing municipality that is currently upper-income residential in character could maintain its character and avoid its "fair share" obligation by limiting the amount of land zoned for commercial and industrial uses. Consequently the court suggested a second step or concurrent method of analysis and computation of the "fair share" obligation.

The second method is based upon population projections for the area. The court adopted the testimony that the population projection for the township for 1985 is approximately 13,000 people, less 1,000 in group quarters. It assumed household occupancy of 3.5 persons per unit as the basis of a computation of a need of 3,430 dwelling units. To this amount, the court added 137 units to cover a 4 percent vacancy rate, providing a total need of 3,567 units in 1985. There was testimony that 1800 units already existed, leaving a need for 1,767 additional units over the next ten years, or 177 units per year. Using the same figure of 67.5 percent to represent the percentage of families of the region having an income under $15,000 per year, the court determined that the "fair share" allocation of the township under the second method would be 119 units per year. The court then concluded that the existing zoning law provided a sufficiently large area to meet the township's obligations under both methods of computation.

The underlying weakness of the assumption that *housing need* may be used as the exclusive theory on which "fair share" is to be computed is illustrated by the Appellate Division's decision in the *Washington Township* case.[31] The specific holding of that case is that the *Mount Laurel* decision is inapplicable to Washington Township, which is a small, almost completely developed municipality. As part of the reasoning on which the conclusion was based, the court noted that the proposed development would increase the township's population approximately 20 percent, more than its "fair share" of the housing needs of the region. The court also noted that Washington Township has no industry and little commerce whereas other communities in the region have both.

The misconception upon which the Appellate Division decision is based is the assumption that *housing need* is the only standard by which "fair share" is to be measured. The court rejected the recommendation of the planning consultants[32] appointed by Judge George Gelman, that there is a need for apartment rental units to serve the township's own population, i.e., young married couples and older people who wish to remain in the community but who cannot or do not want to maintain large single-family residences. The planner's recommendation was based upon an assumption that there is an obligation of *every municipality,* whether a developing municipality or not, to provide in its zoning law for the allocation of land to meet the needs of its own citizens. The "fair share" obligation of a *developing municipality* may extend to the region; but this should not foreclose the responsibility of *all municipalities* to permit a reasonable and appropriate amount of land to be used to meet the needs of its own citizenry.

Furthermore, it may be argued that the New Jersey Supreme Court would have been wiser to have adopted in the *Mount Laurel* decision, the "take-care-of-your-own" standard of zoning validity rather than the "fair-share-of-regional-housing-needs" standard. It is clear that the take-care-of-your-own standard would have had greater political acceptance and economic viability. For these reasons, it may be argued that more housing could be built in the suburbs in the long run, under a politically acceptable and economically feasible standard of zoning, than will be built under the more idealistic but contentious standard.

Litigation in the Pipeline

The cases described above are just the beginning of the torrent of litigation that will flow out of the *Mount Laurel* decision. At the time of this writing, the New Jersey Supreme Court has before it the long-delayed appeal of the *Oakwood at Madison* decision and the more recent appeal of the *Washington Township* decision. Many municipal attorneys and counsel for developers are anxiously waiting for the latest pronouncement of judicial codification of planning theory to emerge from those cases.

In the meantime, other suits are being threatened, prepared, or are currently pending before the trial courts. In Essex County a suit has been brought against the Borough of North Caldwell [33] by the owners of two tracts to declare the zoning ordinance invalid and to permit multifamily development on the tracts. After the *Mount Laurel* decision was rendered, the township served a third-party complaint against eighteen other municipalities "to aid the court in adjudicating" such questions as: (1) Does the plaintiff have standing to sue and to raise *Mount Laurel* arguments on behalf of persons, not parties to the suit? [34] (2) Is the Borough of North Caldwell a "developing municipality"? (3) What is the applicable "region"? (4) What is the "fair share" of each of the municipalities? (5) What is the present and prospective regional need for low- and moderate-income housing?

In Middlesex County a suit has been brought [35] by the Urban League of Greater New Brunswick and individual plaintiffs representing a class of all low- and moderate-income persons in the north-eastern New Jersey area. The defendants are twenty-three of the twenty-five municipalities in Middlesex County. The other two were added as third-party defendants. Plaintiffs challenge the zoning and other land-use policies of defendants which, by effectively excluding housing that plaintiffs can afford, prevent them from residing in these municipalities. Plaintiffs have requested injunctive relief to prevent the continuation of the defendants' alleged exclusionary policies and practices. Plaintiffs also have requested affirmative relief to facilitate racially and economically integrated housing within the means of plaintiffs and the class they represent.

The above review of the growing litigation arising out of the *Mount Laurel* decision gives some credence to the jocular observation, frequently repeated at planning conferences, that the *Mount Laurel* decision is New Jersey's Full Employment Act for planners and land-use lawyers. Although this is a facetious characterization of an important decision, it nevertheless focuses attention upon the fact that the underlying policy judgment upon which *Mount Laurel* is based does not have the approval and support of the suburban constituents upon whom it will be invoked. It remains to be seen whether municipal officials will comply in good faith with this judicially proclaimed constitutional mandate or whether they will resist the decision as a perceived judicial usurpation of legislative prerogative and local home rule. In either case there will be numerous opportunities for planners, lawyers, and judges to transform untested theories and postulates of urban planning into binding principles and canons of land-use law.

ADDENDUM

During the period between the writing and publication of this article several additional post-*Mount Laurel* decisions have "trickled-on-down."

1. *Freehold Development Co. v. Township of Freehold,* (Law Div., Monmouth County, Dkt. No. L-25360-72 P.W. and L-34971-72 P.W., April 6, 1976).

Judge Merritt Lane Jr. held that *Mount Laurel* is not applicable to Freehold Township and the facts of the case. The opinion also contains observations on "region" and "fair share."

2. *Davanne Realty Co. v. Township of Montville,* (Law Div., Morris County, Dkt. No. L-292-74 P.W., April 14, 1976).

Judge Jacques H. Gascoyne "remanded" the case to the municipality with a time table within which to comply with the requirements of *Mount Laurel.*

3. *Urban League of Greater New Brunswick v. Borough of Carteret,* (Chancery Div., Middlesex County, Dkt. No. C-4122-73, May 4, 1976).

Judge David Furman applied *Mount Laurel* principles to 11 of 23 defendant municipalities, imposed conditions for a "consent dismissal" of 11 others and dismissed one municipality because of its small size and other reasons. This is an important decision containing interesting application of the concepts of "region" and "fair share."

4. *Southern Burlington County NAACP v. Mount Laurel,* (Law Div., Burlington County, Dkt. No. L-25741-70-P.W.)

On May 6, 1976 the Public Advocate filed an amended complaint in the *Mount Laurel* case alleging that the amended zoning ordinance and other non-action of the municipality fails to comply with the *Mount Laurel* decision and seeks numerous judicial remedies.

5. *Nigito v. Borough of Closter,* (App. Div., Dkt. No. A-943-74, A-1139-74, June 2, 1976).

The Appellate Division sustained a municipal denial of a use variance for garden apartments and also held that the *Mount Laurel* decision is not applicable to the Borough of Closter because it is not a "developing municipality of sizable land area."

6. *Landmark Development Co. v. Rocky Hill,* (Law. Div., Somerset County, Dkt. No. L 21706-72 P.W. (S 9777), June 4, 1976).

In an appeal from a denial of a use variance to build condominiums in an office-research district, Judge B. Thomas Leahy held the ordinance invalid because it left plaintiff with no reasonable use of the land. Judge Leahy also offers observations about "the spirit of *Mount Laurel*," "fair share," and "developing municipalities."

NOTES

1. 67 N.J. 151, 336 A.2d 713 (1975).
2. Both former Justice Frederick Hall (now retired) and Justice Morris Pashman have talked about the "spirit of Mount Laurel." Justice Hall made such statement as principal speaker at the convention of New Jersey's League of Municipalities in Atlantic City. Evening Times, Nov. 20, 1975 at B 11. Justice Pashman referred to the "spirit of Mount Laurel" during reargument of the *Madison Township* case. Evening Times, Nov. 19, 1975, at B 1.
3. For a full discussion of the "developing municipality" issue see Rose & Levin, "What is a 'Developing Municipality' Within the Meaning of the *Mount Laurel* Decision?" 4 Real Est. L.J. 359 (1976).
4. For a discussion of some of the problems involved in these issues, see Rose, "Exclusionary Zoning and Managed Growth: Some Unresolved Issues," 6 Rutgers-Camden L.J. 689, 709-720 (1975); Rose, "The *Mount Laurel* Decision: Is It Based on Wishful Thinking?" 4 Real Est. L.J. 61, 62-64 (1976).
5. *Segal Constr. Co. v. Borough of Wenonah,* 134 N.J. Super. 421, 341 A.2d 667 (App. Div. 1975).
6. *Wilann Assoc. v. Borough of Rockleigh,* Dkt. No. A-3224-72 (App. Div. 1975) (unreported).
7. *Pascack Ass'n Ltd. v. Township of Washington,* 131 N.J. Super. 195, 329 A.2d 89, *rev'd* Dkt. No. A-3790-72, A-1841-73 (App. Div. 197t), *cert. granted* (1975).
8. For a discussion of this case from the perspective of the consultants, see Levin & Rose, "The Suburban Land Use War: Skirmish in Washington Township, New Jersey," Urban Land 14 (May 1974).
9. *Fobe Assoc. v. Borough of Demarest,* Dkt. No. A-1965-73 (App. Div. 1975) (unreported).
10. *Camden Nat'l Realty v. Township of Cinnaminson,* Dkt. No. L-37016-73 (L. Div. 1975) (unreported).
11. *Urban Farms, Inc. v. Borough of North Haledon,* Dkt. No. L-16324-72 P.W. (L. Div. 1975) (unreported).

12. 67 N.J. 151 at 160, 336 A.2d 713 at 717 (1975).

13. *Id.*

14. This is the position taken by the New Jersey Department of the Public Advocate in an amicus curiae brief submitted in the *Washington Township* case.

15. Note 7 *supra.*

16. *Southern Burlington County NAACP v. Township of Mt. Laurel*, note 1 *supra*, at 189.

17. *Oakwood at Madison, Inc. v. Madison*, 117 N.J. Super. 11, 283 A.2d 353 (L. Div. 1971), *on remand* 128 N.J. Super, 438, 320 A.2d 223 (L. Div. 1974), *cert. granted* 62 N.J. 185, 299 A.2d 720 (1972).

18. *Id.*, 117 N.J. Super. at 20-21, 283 A.2d at 358.

19. *Middle Union Associates v. Township of Holmdel*, Dkt. No. L-1149-72 P.W. (L. Div. 1975) (unreported).

20. *Showcase Properties, Inc. v. Township of East Brunswick*, Dkt. Nos. A-2256-72, A-2634-73, A-2733-73 (App. Div. 1975) (unreported).

21. *Taberna Corp. v. Township of Montgomery*, Dkt. No. L-699-73 P.W. (S-10199 P.W.) (L. Div. 1975) (unreported).

22. Letter from Florence R. Peskoe, clerk of the New Jersey Supreme Court, to attorneys of record in *Oakwood at Madison v. Township of Madison*, Sept. 25, 1975.

23. *Southern Burlington County NAACP v. Township of Mt. Laurel*, 67 N.J. at 190, 336 A.2d at 733.

24. *Middle Union Associates v. Township of Holmdel*, note 19 *supra.*

25. Expert testimony was provided by Harvey S. Moskowitz, P.P., A.I.P., and member of the faculty of the Department of Urban Planning, Rutgers University. For an interesting discussion of the technique of using planning experts, see Moskowitz, "How to Use Experts Effectively in Land Regulation Proceedings," 3 Real Est. L.J. 359 (1975).

26. *Showcase Properties, Inc. v. Township of East Brunswick*, note 20 *supra.*

27. *Camden Nat'l. Realty v. Township of Cinnaminson*, note 10 *supra.*

28. Expert testimony was provided by William Queale, P.P., A.I.P.

29. *Taberna Corp. v. Township of Montgomery*, note 21 *supra.*

30. Expert testimony was provided by Carl Lindbloom, P.P., A.I.P. For an excellent discussion of the details of this testimony, see Lindbloom, "Defining Fair Share of Regional Need: A Planner's Application of *Mt. Laurel*," N.J.L.J. 1 (July 24, 1975).

31. *Pascack Ass'n Ltd. v. Township of Washington*, 131 N.J. Super. 195, 329 A.2d 89, *rev'd* Dkt. Nos. A-3790-72, A-1841-73 (App. Div. 1975).

32. The court-appointed planning consultants were Jerome G. Rose and Melvin R. Levin, both professors of urban planning at Rutgers University.

33. *Cypress Constr. Co. v. Borough of North Caldwell*, Dkt. No. L-35493-72 (L. Div. Essex County) (*pending*).

34. For a discussion of the legal issues raised under this question, see *Taberna Corp. v. Township of Montgomery*, note 21 *supra; Construction Indus. Ass'n of Sonoma County v. City of Petaluma*, 522 F.2d 897 (9th Cir. 1975), *cert. denied;* Warth v. Seldin, 422 U.S. 707 (1975).

35. *Urban League of Greater New Brunswick v. Borough & Council of Cartaret*, Dkt. No. C-4122-73 (L. Div. Middlesex County (1973)).

From the Courts:

Oakwood at Madison:
A Tactical Retreat
By The New Jersey
Supreme Court To Preserve
The *Mount Laurel* Principle

Jerome G. Rose

After six years of litigation, the New Jersey Supreme Court, on January 26, 1977, finally rendered its decision in *Oakwood at Madison v. Township of Madison*. In a four to three decision, written by Justice Conford and with separate opinions written by Justices Clifford, Mountain, Pashman and Schreiber, the court made a tactical decision to withdraw its troops (i.e. the trial courts) from the losing battle of "statistical warfare" involved in the legislative-administrative process of defining "region" and allocating a "fair-share" of regional housing needs to municipalities involved in *Mount Laurel* litigation.

The *Oakwood at Madison* decision is New Jersey Supreme Court's latest word in the litigation that gave rise to the concept of a municipal obligation to provide for a fair-share of regional housing needs adopted by the court in *Mount Laurel*. The litigation started in September 1970 when the plaintiff developer brought an action challenging the validity of the Madison Township zoning ordinance. After trial, Judge David Furman held the zoning ordinance invalid on the grounds that "it failed to promote reasonably a balanced community in accordance with the general welfare." The decision also said that in defining a "balanced community, a municipality must not ignore housing needs, that is, its fair proportion of the obligation to meet the housing needs of its own population and of the region." This decision was appealed to the New Jersey Supreme Court and was scheduled for argument in March, 1973 and again in January, 1974, together with oral argument in the *Mount Laurel* case. However, because Madison Township had adopted a major amendment to the zoning ordinance, the New Jersey Supreme Court remanded the *Oakwood at Madison* case to the trial court for a ruling on the effect of the amended ordinance, and proceeded with and then rendered a decision in the *Mount Laurel* case.

After a hearing on remand, Judge Furman held that the Township's obligation to provide its fair-share of the housing needs of its region is not met unless its zoning ordinance approximates in additional housing unit capacity the same proportion of low-income housing as its present low-income and moderate-income population. The court found that the amended ordinance does not meet this test and therefore the entire ordinance is invalid. In defining "region," the housing needs of which must be met by the Township, the court said that the region is not coexistensive with the county. "Rather it is the area from which in view of available employment and transportation the population of the township would be drawn absent invalidly exclusionary zoning."

Upon return of the appeal to the Supreme Court, oral argument was presented twice with emphasis placed upon the effect the *Mount Laurel* decision that had been rendered in the intervening period. The Supreme Court affirmed the judgment with modifications. In the majority opinion, written by Justice Conford, the legal issues of the case were broken down into three questions:

1. Is the zoning ordinance exclusionary?
2. Should the trial court demarcate the "region" and determine the "fair share" of regional need? and
3. What is the proper judicial remedy?

Is the Ordinance Exclusionary?

In answering the first question, whether the zoning ordinance is exclusionary, the court made it clear that a zoning ordinance is "exclusionary" if it "operates in fact to preclude the opportunity to supply any substantial amounts of new housing for low and moderate income households now and prospectively needed in the municipality and in the appropriate region" whether or not such effect was intended. Thus the New Jersey Supreme Court has taken a position that squarely contravenes the position taken by the United States Supreme Court a few weeks earlier in *Village of Arlington Heights* v. *Metropolitan Housing Development Corp.* _____ U.S. _____ (Jan. 11, 1977). In the *Arlington Heights* case, the U.S. Supreme Court upheld the refusal of a municipality to zone to permit subsidized multi-family housing even though such refusal would have a racially discriminatory *effect* because there was insufficient evidence to show a racially discriminatory intent. In *Oakwood at Madison*, the New Jersey Supreme Court held that a zoning ordinance may be "exclusionary" without a showing of exclusionary *intent*.

The test established by the court is whether the zoning ordinance operates *in fact* to preclude the opportunity for the requisite share of low- and moderate-income housing to be built. Under this new test it is not necessary for the municipality to devise specific formulae for estimating a precise fair-share allocation of lower-income housing needs for a specifically demarcated region. Nor is it necessary for a trial court to make such findings. What is necessary under the *Oakwood at Madison* test is a *bona fide* effort by the municipality toward the elimination or minimization of undue cost-generating requirements in the zoning ordinance. In the language of the court:

> "To the extent that the builders of housing in a developing municipality like Madison cannot through publicly assisted means or appropriately legislated incentives . . . provide the municipality's fair share of the regional need for lower income housing, it is incumbent on the governing body to adjust its zoning regulations so as to render possible and feasible the 'least cost' housing, consistent with minimum standards of health and safety, which private industry will undertake, and in amounts sufficient to satisfy the deficit in the hypothesized fair share."

Role of the Courts

The primary contribution of the *Oakwood at Madison* decision may be its admonition to the trial courts to withdraw from the process of "demarcating the region" and determining the "fair share" of the municipality. The court observed that this process "involves highly controversial economic, sociological and policy questions of innate difficulty and complexity. Where predictive responses are called for they are apt to be speculative or conjectural." In a statement that may have only limited significance, the court articulated the constitutional truism that this process "is much more appropriately a legislative function rather than a judicial function to be exercised in the dispostion of isolated cases." Nevertheless, after indicating its awareness of the existence and importance of the fundamental principle of separation of powers in our legal system, the court stated:

"But unless and until other appropriate governmental machinery is
effectively brought to bear the courts have no choice, when an ordinance is challenged on *Mount Laurel* grounds, but to deal with this
vital public welfare matter as effectively as is consistent with the limitations of the judicial process."

These preliminary statements alone would leave unanswered the question of how the trial courts will deal with the concepts of "region" and
"fair-share" when the validity of the municipal zoning ordinance is challenged in an action before them. However, the opinion goes on to provide some guidelines. Generally, the court concluded that "there is no
specific geographical area which is necessarily the authoritative region as
to any single municipality in litigation." The objective of the trial courts is
to determine whether the zoning ordinance "realistically permits the opportunity to provide a fair and reasonable share of the region's need for
housing for the lower income population." The technical details of the
basis for fair-share allocations of regional goals among municipalities are
not as important "as the consideration that the gross regional goals shared
by the constituent municipalities be large enough fairly to reflect the full
needs of the housing market of which the subject municipality forms a
part." The court then indicated its approval of Judge Furman's definition
of "region" as "the area from which, in view of available employment and
transportation, the population of the township would be drawn absent
exclusionary zoning." The court also reaffirmed the statement by Justice
Hall in the *Mount Laurel* opinion that "confinement to or within a certain
county appears not to be realistic, but restriction within the boundaries of
the state seems practical and advisable." The opinion predicted that an
official fair-share housing study of a group of counties or municipalities
conducted under the auspices of the regional agency pursuant to the governor's Executive Order No. 35 would be entitled to *prima facie* judicial
acceptance.

On the question of the computation of the "fair-share" allocation for the
defendant municipality, the court was equally circumspect. It recognized,
(in a footnote) that "because of the conjectural nature of such calculations,
utilization of the court as the forum for determining a municipality's fair
share may result in 'statistical warfare' between the litigants." Nevertheless, the court recognized (in another footnote) that "fair share studies by
expert witnesses may be of substantial evidential value to a trial court."
The opinion summarized the court's conclusion on this issue with the
statement that:

"Fair share allocation studies submitted in evidence may be given
such weight as they appear to merit in the light of the two statements
above. But the court is not required, in the determination of the mat-

ter, itself to adopt fair share housing quotas for the municipality in
question or to make findings in reference thereto."

After setting forth these general principles relating to the fair-share allocation to municipalities, the court directed its attention to the specific
issue of the relevance of ecological and environmental considerations in
this process. Evidence had been offered at the trial relating to the adverse
environmental impact of the proposed development upon the surrounding
area. Judge Furman had declined to consider this evidence because there
was a substantial amount of other land free from such environmental impact available in the municipality with which the fair-share of its regional
housing needs could be met. The Supreme Court ruled that the trial
court had erred in not receiving in evidence and considering these environmental factors. The court said:

> "It is not an answer to say there is ample other land capable of being
> deployed for lower income housing. The municipality has the option of
> zoning areas for such housing anywhere within its borders consistent
> with all relevant considerations as to suitability. . . "

To prevent future litigants from generalizing too broadly from this
statement, the court repeated its statement in the *Mount Laurel* decision
that although ecological and environmental factors may be considered in
zoning, "the danger and impact must be substantial and very real (the
construction of every building or the improvement of every plat has some
environmental impact) — not simply a makeweight to support exclusionary housing measures or preclude growth. . . "

The Judicial Remedy

To prospective developers of higher density housing in suburban communities the most significant part of the *Oakwood at Madison* decision
may be the order of the court directing the issuance of a permit for the
development of the housing project proposed by the developer-plaintiff.
However, this order is made subject to the condition that the developer
comply with its representation that it will guarantee the allocation of at
least 20 percent of the units to low- or moderate-income families. However, the court did subject the enforcement of the order to the supervision of the trial court to assure completion with local regulations and to
determine whether the developer's land is environmentally suited to the
degree, density and type of development proposed.

In addition, the court ordered the municipality to submit to the trial
court for its approval a revised zoning ordinance that would, among other
things, allocate more land for single family houses on small lots, allocate

more land for multi-family units, eliminate provisions resulting in bed-room restrictions and eliminate undue cost-generating requirements. The trial court is specifically authorized, in discretion, to appoint an impartial zoning and planning expert or experts, to assist in the process.

Significance of the Decision

The full significance of an important judicial decision is not always readily discernible immediately. Frequently, it is necessary for some period of time to elapse before the many complex ideas can be assimilated and interrelated with each other and with the realities of the world to which they will be applied. However, some first impression observations may be of interest.

REAFFIRMATION OF THE MOUNT LAUREL PRINCIPLE

The Oakwood at Madison decision reaffirms the *Mount Laurel* principle that the zoning ordinance of every developing municipality must afford the opportunity for the municipality's "fair-share" of the present and pro-spective regional need for low- and moderate-income housing. Although the role of the trial courts is to be more constrained, the test of validity of a municipal zoning ordinance will continue to be based upon the answer to such questions as: (a) What is the "region?" (b) What is "fair-share?" (c) What is the present housing need?" (d) What is the prospective hous-ing need?"

JUDICIAL RESTRAINT

The New Jersey Supreme Court has paid homage to the constitutional principle of separation of powers and to the concept of judicial restraint. It has recognized the impropriety of having judges engage in the legisla-tive and administrative processes necessary to define "region" and calcu-late "fair-share." However, it has at the same time made it clear that it intends to retain such judicial power as is necessary to protect and pre-serve the integrity of the judicial process. Having found that exclusionary zoning violates the state constitution in *Mount Laurel*, the court does not intend to abandon the judicial power to enforce its ruling. The *Oakwood at Madison* decision should not be interpreted to be a weakening of the court's resolve to outlaw exclusionary zoning. Rather, this decision is based, in part, upon a tactic designed to consolidate the judicial forces into a position in which they will be less vulnerable to direct attack.

It is also interesting to note that most of the admonition relating to the court's participation in the process of demarcating the region and computing "fair-share"is more applicable to Judge Furman's decision in *Urban League of Greater New Brunswick, v. Carteret* than Judge Furman's decision in *Oakwood at Madison*. Although the *Urban League* case was not before the court there is little doubt that the members of the court were aware of its existence and aware of the extent to which a trial judge could become emeshed in the intricacies of the planning process.

AMBIGUITY OF THE STANDARD OF VALIDITY

The decision fails to provide an unambiguous standard for municipal officials to determine, with some assurance, whether their zoning ordinances will be upheld, short of completely abandoning all programs of rational and comprehensive community planning. On one hand, the decision states that it is not necessary for a municipality, whose zoning ordinance is challenged, to devise specific formulae for estimating their precise share of the housing needs of the region. Rather, the municipalities and the courts should make *bona fide* efforts toward the elimination of undue cost generating requirements. On the other hand, when a zoning ordinance is challenged, the court will evaluate "fair-share" allocation studies submitted in evidence (although the court will not adopt a "fair-share" housing quota for the municipality). Thus, it would appear that a municipality could made a *bona fide* effort toward the elimination of undue cost generating requirements in the zoning law but still be vulnerable to attack on the grounds that is has not fulfilled its "fair-share" housing quota. Consequently each municipality and each developer-challenger of zoning validity will have to prepare its own study to support its position and the statistical warfare will continue to be fought in the courtrooms. The only difference, after *Oakwood at Madison*, is that the trial court will remain aloof from the proceedings and only evaluate the alternative methodologies but will not prescribe one for the municipality.

IMPLEMENTATION OF THE MANDATORY PERCENTAGE OF MODERATELY PRICED DWELLINGS (MPMPD) REQUIREMENT

The court ordered the issuance of a building permit to the developer-plaintiff subject to the condition that the developer guarantee the allocation of at least 20 percent of the units to low- or moderate-income families. The court did not deal in any way with the complex and difficult problem of administering the procedure by which the benefits of low and moderate income housing units would be preserved over a period of time for succeeding generations of occupants. This issue creates a difficult dilemma. If no attention is given to this matter the first occupant of each of up to 20 percent of the units will benefit from the court ordered obligation imposed on the developer. However, as costs rise and property values increase, subsequent occupants will have to pay the increased non-subsidized costs of occupancy. On the other hand, to avoid the short-lived benefits to only the first occupant, a system of administration would have to be established that would control the rents of apartments or control the selling prices of sales units. Either mechanism would subject the developer to a form of regulation that would constitute a significant disincentive to development.

THE DUAL REQUIREMENTS OF LAND AND SUBSIDIES

At some point in every comprehensive discussion of exclusionary zoning it becomes necessary to remind all participants that there are two separate and distinct questions that must be resolved if low- and moderate-income families are to have an opportunity to live in suburban communities. The first question is: Is land available in the community that can be used for "least cost" housing? The second question is: Are subsidies available to close the gap between the cost of housing construction and the amount that low- and moderate-income families can afford to pay? The *Oakwood at Madison* decision focused attention upon the duality of these issues and reaffirmed the principle that the state constitution requires each developing municipality to make land available for "least cost" housing. However, in response to the second question the court was unwilling to impose an affirmative obligation on developing municipalities to help to subsidize construction costs. Although the *amicus* brief of The Public Advocate had suggested various forms of affirmative municipal action to help subsidize these costs, the New Jersey Supreme Court deferred this issue to another day.

From the Courts:

A New Test for Exclusionary Zoning: Does it "Preclude the Opportunity" for "Least Cost" Housing?*

Jerome G. Rose

The New Jersey,[1] Pennsylvania,[2] New York,[3] Colorado,[4] California,[5] and federal courts,[6] among others, have in the past few years rendered landmark decisions dealing with the question of the validity of municipal land use regulations that tend to limit development and exclude people from suburban communities. More specifically, municipal ordinances that prohibit or make no provision for multifamily housing, allocate insufficient land for housing on small lots, or impose cost-generating requirements for housing developments have been challenged as invalid "exclusionary zoning."[7]

One of the troublesome legal problems involved in all of these cases is the question of the criteria by which a land use regulation may be evaluated for the purpose of determining whether it is "exclusionary" and therefore vulnerable to attack. The New Jersey Supreme Court has recently proposed a new test by which this determination may be made. In *Oakwood at Madison v. Township of Madison*[8] the New Jersey court has

---

* This article will appear in the *Real Estate Law Journal* (Fall 1977).

proposed that a land use regulation is "exclusionary" if it "operates in fact to preclude the opportunity to supply any substantial amounts of new housing for low- and moderate-income households now and prospectively needed in the municipality and in the appropriate region," [9] whether or not such effect was intended. This new judicial formula, couched in language that is more legislative than judicial in style, contains several elements, each of which raises new legal issues for further litigation to resolve. Among the new issues are:

1. What is the definition of "preclude the opportunity" and will the new test succeed in replacing the "fair share" test?
2. Is it realistic to include new housing for *low* as well as *moderate* income persons in the test and what is the definition of "least cost" housing to be provided for this purpose?
3. Is it feasible to include *prospective* as well as *present* housing need in the test?
4. Is the test of exclusionary *effect* rather than exclusionary *intent* too broad and inclusive?
5. Does the test involve an evaluation that is within the scope of the judicial process?

"Preclude the Opportunity"— Will It Replace "Fair Share"?

The new test proposed by the New Jersey Supreme Court calls for evidence relating to whether the land use regulation will "preclude the opportunity" for the described types and amount of housing. This is a great improvement over the test previously prescribed by the court. Under the previous test,[10] a developer could challenge a municipal zoning ordinance by merely showing that the land use regulations have not made *realistically possible* a variety and choice of housing—including low- and moderate-income housing.[11] Once having established that the land use regulations fail to make such housing "realistically possible" the burden of proof under the old test would shift to the municipality to establish a valid basis for the law. The misconception on which the old test was based is that land use regulations *do not and cannot* make low- and moderate-income housing "realistically possible." However, land use regulations can and sometimes do "preclude the opportunity" for low- and moderate-income housing to be built within a municipality and consequently the new test is a more accurate reflection of the economic realities of the housing construction industry.

Although it was easy for the New Jersey Supreme Court to substitute the "preclude the opportunity" standard for the "realistically possible" standard, it is questionable whether the "preclude the opportunity" standard will be able to replace the "fair share of regional housing needs" test of whether a municipal ordinance is exclusionary. One of the purposes of the "preclude the opportunity" test proposed in *Oakwood at Madison* is to extricate the trial courts from the process of "demarcating the region" and calculating the municipality's "fair share" or regional housing needs.[12] The Court correctly observed that this process "involves highly controversial economic, sociological, and policy questions of innate difficulty and complexity. Where predictive responses are called for they are apt to be speculative or conjectural."[13] The Court also recognized (in a footnote) the danger that "because of the conjectural nature of such calculations, utilization of the court as the forum for determining a municipality's fair share may result in 'statistical warfare' between the litigants."[14]

It would seem that one of the purposes of the new test is to enable a trial court to determine whether a municipal zoning ordinance is exclusionary without having to engage in the "controversial," "speculative," or "conjectural" calculations required to determine "fair share" allocations of regional housing need. However, it seems unlikely that a trial court will be able to determine whether a given zoning ordinance "precludes the opportunity" for the required types and amounts of housing without evidence relating to fair share of regional housing needs. For example, would a municipal zoning ordinance be characterized as "exclusionary" where evidence establishes that: (1) there is a significant amount of existing housing for low- and moderate-income persons; (2) there are zoning districts in which some multifamily housing can be built; (3) there are districts in which some single-family housing can be built on small and moderate sized lots; (4) there are some districts in which cost-generating requirements are reduced; (5) the plaintiff-developer's land is not in any of the above districts; (6) there are other districts for which high cost single-family dwellings are contemplated.

It is very likely that a trial court would not be able to determine whether such a zoning ordinance is "exclusionary" unless it receives evidence relating to the amounts and relative proportions of the types of housing possible under the existing ordinance. This information will have only limited significance unless the court also receives evidence relating to regional housing needs for each of the categories of housing authorized by the ordinance. Thus it remains to be seen whether it will be possible to determine whether a municipal zoning ordinance is "exclusionary" without implicating the trial courts in the statistical warfare involved in calculating the fair share allocation of regional housing needs.

New Housing for Low As Well As Moderate Income Persons: "Least Cost" Housing

Under the new test, a land use regulation is exclusionary if it precludes the opportunity for *new* housing for *low-* as well as moderate-income persons. There are at least two debatable economic and public policy issues assumed in this part of the test: (1) Is *new* housing economically feasible for low-income persons? and (2) Is there an obligation for all (developing) municipalities to allocate land for low-income persons regardless of suitability of the municipality for low-income persons to reside there?

The question whether it is realistic and economically feasible to provide new housing for low-income persons is debatable at best. The underlying difficulty with this principle is that current costs of housing construction in most areas of the country put the sales or rental price of new housing far beyond the reach of low-income persons. To close the gap between the costs of new housing and the ability of low-income persons to pay, substantial subsidies to reduce the costs of housing and/or to supplement the income of low-income persons are necessary. Experience has indicated that the nation is prepared to allocate only a limited amount of its resources to this purpose. For this reason it may be argued that more low-income persons can be benefited if the limited subsidies are applied to lower the costs of older, rather than new, housing for low-income persons. Apparently the sense of inequity of prescribing older and therefore a lower minimum standard for low-income persons, and other manifestations of socioeconomic philosophy, appear to have entered into the reasoning of the New Jersey Court when it formulated this part of the new test.

The New Jersey Court has responded to this issue by creating a new addition to the litigable issues of exclusionary zoning, called "least cost" housing. Where builders of housing cannot, with public assistance and incentives, provide for the municipality's fair share of the regional housing need for lower income housing the court has declared that "it is incumbent on the governing body to adjust its zoning regulations so as to render possible and feasible the 'least cost' housing, consistent with standards of health and safety. . . ." [15] In a footnote, the court explained that the concept of "least cost" housing does not contemplate the construction of housing that could easily deteriorate into slums. Health and safety standards should be maintained. However, innovation and economy in construction and the elimination of regulations that unnecessarily increase construction costs should be used to reduce housing construction costs as low as possible, consistent with health and safety standards. [16]

The court stated expressly that nothing less than zoning for "least cost" housing will satisfy the judicial mandate.

However, after making this declaration the court did concede that compliance with this requirement may not provide *new* housing for *all* lower income persons. Nevertheless the "least cost" requirement would assist the lower income population by increasing the total supply of housing available to it through the "filtering down" (also known as the "trickle-down") process, defined as the movement of upper-, moderate-, or middle-income families to newly constructed housing, leaving their former housing available for families lower in the income scale.[17]

The second assumption made by the court in formulating the new test for exclusionary zoning is that *all* (developing) municipalities have an obligation to house low-income persons regardless of the suitability of the municipality for such persons. It can be argued that a municipality that has few jobs, no public transportation, insufficient educational, medical and social services, and a high property tax, or a combination of the above, would be inappropriate for low-income persons[18] and that failure to provide for low-income housing should not be a reason to characterize the land use regulations as "exclusionary." In spite of this argument, any (developing) municipality whose land use laws preclude low-income housing will be characterized as "exclusionary" without regard to suitability.

Future As Well As Present Housing Needs

Land use regulations are "exclusionary" under the new test if they preclude the opportunity for housing needed in the future as well as at present. The requirement to provide for future housing needs is surprising in view of the Court's interest in eliminating difficult, complex, conjectural, and speculative calculations from the judicial process.[19] Estimating the present housing needs of a municipality is difficult and conjectural but possible within an acceptable margin for error. Present housing need may be estimated by considering such factors as vacancy rates, extent of dilapidation, extent of overcrowdedness, number of low-income families paying over 25 percent of income for housing, and estimating the extent of overlap of the factors used in the computation.[20]

The estimation of future housing need of an area is much more speculative. Planning experts may select one of several alternate methodologies for this purpose. The following methodology was adopted by the New Jersey Division of State and Regional Planning to determine future housing needs:

> Step 1. Predict the population for a given date in the future.
> Step 2. Predict the average household size at that date.

Step 3. Divide the predicted population by the predicted average household size. The quotient is the predicted number of households at the given date.

Step 4. Subtract present number of households from predicted future number of households. The difference is the total household growth for the period.

Step 5. Predict the percentage of future households that will have low or moderate income.

Step 6. Multiply the predicted household growth for the period by the predicted percentage of low- and moderate-income households. The product is the predicted prospective housing needs for low- and moderate-income households at the given date in the future.[21]

Although separate submethodologies are available for each of the predictions required in the above steps, critical policy decisions are involved in these methodologies. For example, in predicting future population growth, the New Jersey Department of Labor and Industry has proposed four different population projections for estimating future levels of growth.[22] The projections make different assumptions about fertility/birth rates, mortality rates, and in/out-migration. There are also different assumptions relating to long-term trends, economic events, etc. The projections for each group of assumptions may be characterized as: (1) slow growth; (2) current trends; (3) long-term trends; and (4) maximum growth. Each of the assumptions differs significantly and the selection of one rather than another will have a significant effect upon the prediction of future housing needs. Similar variations will result from the selection of other assumptions (e.g., future average household size) in the process of computation. Thus the requirement that future housing needs be considered in the process of determining whether a municipality's land use regulations are "exclusionary" will involve the courts in battles of statistical warfare that the New Jersey Supreme Court had hoped to avoid.

Regional As Well As Local Housing Needs

The new test for exclusionary zoning raises the issue whether the municipal zoning ordinance precludes the opportunity for regional as well as local housing needs. Thus, under the test a zoning ordinance that provides for land for housing to meet the needs of its own residents will nevertheless be characterized as "exclusionary" if it precludes the opportunity to provide for housing to meet the needs of persons living outside the municipality but within a "region." The difficulties with this test is that it becomes necessary to demarcate the appropriate "region" and to calculate the housing needs for that "region." Where conflicting evidence is presented, a court will have to make a finding of fact on these issues.

The New Jersey Supreme Court has offered some suggestions to assist the trial courts. With respect to the definition of "region," it indicated approval of Judge David Furman's definition as "the area from which, in view of available employment and transportation, the population of the township would be drawn absent exclusionary zoning."[23] The court also reaffirmed the observation of Justice Frederick Hall that "confinement to or within a certain county appears not to be realistic, but restriction within the boundaries of the state seems practical and advisable."[24] It should be readily apparent that neither definition is sufficiently precise to enable a trial court to select the appropriate region from among the many delineations of region that may be made and offered in evidence, within the vague guidelines of the two judicial statements.

The second part of a regional housing needs test makes it necessary to calculate the housing needs of the newly delineated region. This process can become extraordinarily complicated and conjectural, particularly where Judge Furman's definition is adopted. Under this definition the region will very frequently assume an amoeba-like shape with fingerlike protrusions along major highways. The size and shape of the region under this definition will also depend upon a very basic but debatable assumption relating to travel time to work. An assumption that time to work should be one-half hour will produce a very much smaller region than an assumption that many suburban residents are willing and do in fact travel up to two hours each way to and from work. Many alternate sizes and shapes of regions are possible with other assumptions.

Because of the many serious problems involved in a judicial demarcation of a region, the courts of most states other than New Jersey,[25] New York,[26] and California[27] have not adopted a *regional* test for the validity of municipal zoning. The federal courts, particularly, have avoided becoming involved in this issue, taking the position that "the federal court is not a super zoning board and should not be called on to mark the point at which legitimate *local* interests in promoting the welfare of the community are outweighed by legitimate *regional* interest. . . ."[28] (emphasis added)

Is the Test of Exclusionary Effect Rather Than Intent Too Broad and Inclusive?

Under the new test, if a zoning ordinance has the effect of excluding low-income households, even though this effect was not *intended*, the ordinance is nevertheless characterized as "exclusionary." It should be readily apparent that the burden of proving exclusionary effect is much easier than the burden of proving a legislative intent to keep low-income persons out of the jurisdiction. The test also invites the temptation and risk of attributing to zoning laws the impact of the maladjustment of housing construction costs in the general economy that have the effect of precluding the opportunity of low-income persons to purchase or rent housing in most parts of the country.

The danger of adopting an "effects" test of exclusionary zoning is that it may be too broad and inclusive for at least two reasons: (1) in a complex economic system many economic forces interact to cause an effect; this test attributes to only one cause the impact of many causes; (2) zoning ordinances are particularly but unfairly vulnerable to an "effects" test because the primary purpose of zoning laws is to have the effect of restricting and excluding.

For these and other reasons, the United States Supreme Court and the Court of Appeals, Ninth Circuit, have rejected the "effects" test. In a case involving a similar issue, the Supreme Court has held that the refusal of a suburban municipality to change its zoning laws to permit low-income housing does not violate the provisions of the United States Constitution even though the *effect* of the municipal zoning ordinance is to exclude members of racial minorities from the community.[29] In the Court of Appeals decision, the court held that even where the *express purpose* and actual effect is to exclude substantial numbers of people who would otherwise elect to move to that municipality the zoning ordinance is not invalid. The court observed that "practically all zoning restrictions have as a purpose and effect the exclusion of some activity or type of structure or a certain density of inhabitants."[30]

Is the Test Appropriate to the Judicial Process?

The proposed test is designed to establish the criteria by which a trial court may determine whether a municipal zoning ordinance is exclusionary. To make this determination, a trial court will have to hear evidence on such issues as: (1) What is the present housing need of the municipality? (2) What is the future housing need of the municipality? (3) What is the appropriate region of which the municipality is a part? (4) Is the region delineated by the municipality a reasonable one? (5) Is the region delineated by the plaintiff a better one? (6) What is the present housing need of the region? (7) What is the future housing need of the region? (8) What are the assumptions on which the region's growth are based? (9) What are the alternative assumptions on which regional growth may be predicted? (10) Is it economically feasible to build new housing for low-income families? (11) What are the kinds and characteristics of "least cost" housing in the municipality and the region? (12) Is the allocation of land in the ordinance for multifamily housing reasonable or sufficient? (13) Is the allocation of land in the ordinance for single-family dwellings on small and moderate sized lots reasonable or sufficient? (14) Are the cost-generating requirements of the land use regulations reasonable in view of ecological and other factors? (15) To what extent should the suitability of low-income housing in the defendant municipality be considered?

The evidence required for these and other issues of fact that must be determined under the test will tend to make the trial a long, drawn-out, and expensive procedure that will be based upon "highly controversial economic, sociological, and policy questions of innate difficulty and complexity." The evidence will be based upon the testimony of "experts" whose responses are "apt to be speculative or conjectural." This is just the kind of process the New Jersey Supreme Court indicated it would like to avoid.[31]

The future of the new test is very much in doubt because of its questionable utility and because its administration would conflict with the purpose of the *Oakwood at Madison* decision to extricate the trial courts from a process involving policy decisions. The New Jersey Supreme Court cast additional doubt upon the viability of the new test within two months after its formulation in the *Oakwood at Madison* decision. In March, 1977 the Court rendered its decision in the *Washington Township*[32] and *Demarest*[33] cases and made the following statements in dicta not required for either decision:

> "But the overriding point we make is that it is not for the courts to substitute their conception of what the public welfare requires by way of zoning for the views of those in whom the Legislature and the local electorate have vested responsibility. . . ."[34]

> "In short [the judicial role] is limited to the assessment of a claim that the restrictions of the ordinance are patently arbitrary or unreasonable or violative of the statute, not that they do not match the plaintiff's or the court's conception of the requirements of the general welfare, whether within the town or the region. . . ."[35]

> "We are, of course, not insensitive to the current social need for larger quantities of affordable housing of all kinds for the general population. . . . A possibility of some relief in that regard is contained within the statutory special exception or variance process. . . . But insofar as review of the validity of a zoning ordinance is concerned, the judicial branch is not suited to the role of an *ad hoc* super zoning legislature, particularly in the area of adjusting claims for satisfaction by individual municipalities of regional needs, whether as to housing or any other important social need affected by zoning. . . ."[36]

These statements of the New Jersey Supreme Court made so soon after the formulation of the test for exclusionary zoning in the *Oakwood at*

Madison decision would seem to argue against the use of the judicial process for the administration of the test it had so recently created. If this is true, the prognosis for the successful implementation of the new test is very much in doubt.

NOTES

1. Southern Burlington County NAACP v. Township of Mount Laurel, 67 N.J. 151, 336 A.2d 713, *cert. denied*, 423 U.S. 808 (1975).
2. Township of Willistown v. Chesterdale Farms, Inc.,_____ Pa. _____, 341 A.2d 466 (1975); Firsh Appeal, 437 Pa. 237, 263 A.2d 395 (1970).
3. Berenson v. Town of New Castle, 38 N.Y.2d 102, 378 N.Y.S.2d 672 (1975).
4. Robinson v. Boulder, 547 P.2d 228 (Colo., 1976).
5. Associated Home Builders of the Greater Eastbay, Inc. v. Livermore, _____ Cal. _____, P.2d _____, Dkt. No. S.F. 23222, (1976).
6. Construction Industry Ass'n. of Sonoma County v. City of Petaluma, 522 F.2d 897 (1975) *cert. denied* 96 S.Ct. 1148 (1976).
7. See Buchsbaum, "The Irrelevance of the 'Developing Municipality' Concept—A Reply to Professors Rose and Levin," 5 *Real Estate Law Journal* 280 (1977); Kelly, "*Robinson v. Boulder*—A Balance to *Ramapo* and *Petaluma*," 5 *Real Estate Law Journal* 170 (1976); Rose, "The Trickle Before the Deluge from *Mount Laurel*," 5 *Real Estate Law Journal* 69 (1976); Rose & Levin, "What Is a 'Developing Municipality' Within the Meaning of the *Mount Laurel* Decision?" 4 *Real Estate Law Journal* 359 (1976); Rose, "The Mount Laurel Decision: Is It Based on Wishful Thinking?" 4 *Real Estate Law Journal* 61 (1975); Kelly, "Will the Housing Market Evaluation Model Be the Solution to Exclusionary Zoning?" 3 *Real Estate Law Journal* 373 (1975); Mandelker, "Downzoning to Control Growth Draws a Close Look from the Courts," 3 *Real Estate Law Journal* 402 (1975); Rose, "The Mandatory Percentage of Moderately Priced Dwelling Ordinance (MPMPD) Is the Latest Technique of Inclusionary Zoning," 3 *Real Estate Law Journal* 176 (1974); Listokin, "Fair Share Housing Distribution: Will It Open the Suburbs to Apartment Development?" 2 *Real Estate Law Journal* 739 (1974).
8. Oakwood at Madison, Inc. v. Township of Madison, _____ N.J. _____, _____ A.2d _____, Dkt. No. A-80/81 Sept. Term. At the time of preparation of this article the decision was not formally reported, and all citations are to the Slip opinion.
9. *Id.*, Slip opinion at 12.
10. Southern Burlington County NAACP v. Township of Mount Laurel, 67 N.J. 151, 336 A.2d 713, *cert. denied*, 423 U.S. 808 (1975).
11. See 67 N.J. at 187, 336 A.2d at _____, where the court said:
    "By way of summary, what we have said comes down to this. As a developing municipality, Mount Laurel must, by its land use regulations, make realistically possible the opportunity for an appropriate variety and choice of housing for all categories of people who may desire to live there, of course including those of low and moderate income. . . . ."
12. See Rose, "*Oakwood at Madison*: A Tactical Retreat By the New Jersey Supreme Court to Preserve the *Mount Laurel* Principle," 13 *Urban Law Annual* _____ 1977).

13. Oakwood at Madison, Inc. v. Township of Madison, Slip opinion at 66.
14. *Id.* Slip opinion at footnote 39.
15. *Id.* Slip opinion at 36.
16. *Id.* Slip opinion at footnote 21.
17. *Id.* Slip opinion at 38.
18. See Rose, "Fair Share Housing Allocation Plans: Which Formula Will Pacify the Contentious Suburbs?" 12 *Urban Law Annual* 3, 16-18 (1976).
19. Oakwood at Madison, Inc. v. Township of Madison, Slip opinion at 67-68.
20. *New Jersey's Present Housing Needs*, New Jersey Division of State and Regional Planning, Draft Report (1976).
21. *Prospective Housing Needs Report*, New Jersey Division of State and Regional Planning, Draft Report (1976).
22. *Official State Projections, New Jersey Population 1980–2020*, Division of Planning and Research, N.J. Dept. of Labor and Industry (1975).
23. Oakwood at Madison, Inc. v. Township of Madison, Slip opinion at 71.
24. *Id.*
25. Southern Burlington County NAACP v. Township of Mount Laurel, 67 N.J. 151, 336 A.2d 713, *cert. denied*, 423 U.S. 808 (1975).
26. Berenson v. Town of New Castle, 38 N.Y.2d 102, 378 N.Y.S.2d 672 (1975).
27. Associated Home Builders of the Greater Eastbay, Inc. v. Livermore, _____ Calif. _____, _____ P.ed _____ Dkt. No. S.F. 23222, (1976).
28. Construction Industry Assoc. of Sonoma County v. City of Petaluma, 522 F.2d 897 (9th Cir. 1975) at 906.
29. Village of Arlington Heights v. Metropolitan Housing Development Corp. _____ U.S. _____, 97 S.Ct. 555 (1977).
30. Construction Industry Assoc. of Sonoma County v. City of Petaluma, 522 F.2d 897 (9th Cir. 1975) at _____.
31. At the time that the New Jersey Supreme Court rendered its decision in *Oakwood at Madison* there was pending before the Appellate Division an appeal of another of Judge Furman's decisions, Urban League v. Mayor & Council of Borough of Carteret, 142 N.J. Super. 11, 359 A.2d 526 (Ch. 1976). In the *Urban League* case an action was brought against twenty-three municipalities in Middlesex County alleging that "the policies and practices of all defendant municipalities, taken together, bar plaintiffs from securing housing and employment opportunities throughout a major and expanding market area." The court demarcated the region as the county and established a procedure for allocating to each of eleven of the twenty-three defendant municipalities its fair share of regional housing for low- and moderate-income persons.
32. Pascack Association, Ltd. v. Township of Washington, _____ N.J. _____, _____ A.2d _____, (Dkt. A-130, 1977).
33. Fobe Associates v. Demarest, _____ N.J. _____, _____ A.2d _____, (Dkt. A-129, 1977).
34. Oakwood at Madison, Inc. v. Township of Madison, Slip opinion at 19.
35. *Id.* Slip opinion at 20.
36. *Id.* Slip opinion at 23.

From the Courts:

After the Recent
New Jersey Supreme Court Decisions:
What Is the Status
of Suburban Zoning?*

Jerome G. Rose

M any municipal officials are confused, with good reason, about the law that will determine the validity of their zoning ordinances. Ever since the *Mount Laurel*[1] decision in March, 1975 they have heard, from attorneys, planners, developers, public advocates, and others, that their zoning ordinance will be held invalid unless it provides for apartments and other forms of housing for low- and moderate-income persons. During the past two years many officials have become reconciled to the prospect of having to amend their zoning ordinance to provide for such housing or face the possibility of having their ordinance held invalid under the *Mount Laurel* principle.

However, during the past year, the New Jersey Supreme Court has handed down a number of decisions that have begun to create doubts about the impact and effectiveness of the *Mount Laurel* requirements. The first hint of things to come appeared in September, 1976 in the Court's decision in the *Weymouth Township* case.[2] On its face, this deci-

---

*This article appeared in *New Jersey Municipalities* (May, 1977).

sion held only that a municipal ordinance that created a mobile home park district for the elderly is valid. However, many legal eyebrows were raised because the net result of this decision (in spite of the elaborate judicial rationale) was that the Court upheld a provision of a zoning ordinance that had the *effect* of excluding young married with children from the zoning district.

Then, in January, 1977 the New Jersey Supreme Court decided the *Oakwood at Madison* [3] case and determined that the trial courts will no longer engage in the process of "demarcating the region" or calculating the "fair share" of regional housing needs that the municipal zoning ordinance must provide for. There was also some hint of a changing judicial attitude in the Court's statements that controversial economic, sociological, and policy questions are more appropriately a legislative than a judicial function.

And while the municipal officials and attorneys were still reeling under the influence of the heady effects of the potential significance of the *Oakwood at Madison* decision, the New Jersey Supreme Court rendered two more decisions in the *Washington Township* [4] and *Demarest* [5] cases. In its narrowest sense, these cases held only that (1) the *Mount Laurel* principle applies only to "developing municipalities" (hardly a surprise to those who read the *Mount Laurel* decision carefully), and (2) there were sufficient grounds for the Demarest Board of Adjustment to deny a use variance for multifamily residential units. However, these decisions, taken together, have begun to make many municipal officials begin to wonder whether the New Jersey Supreme Court has expressed something more important than the narrow holdings of those cases. There is reason to believe that there may be a change in the court's attitude about the propriety of judicial intervention in the planning and zoning process. It is difficult to ignore the potential import of such statements as the following that were included in the *Washington Township* decision:

> But it would be a mistake to interpret *Mount Laurel* as a comprehensive displacement of sound and long established principles concerning judicial respect for local policy decisions in the zoning field. What we said recently in this regard in *Bow and Arrow Manor v. Town of West Orange*, 63 N.J. 335, 343 (1973), is worth repeating as continuing sound law: "It is fundamental that *zoning is a municipal legislative function, beyond the purview of interference by the courts* unless an ordinance is seen in whole or in application to any particular property to be clearly arbitrary, capricious or unreasonable, or plainly contrary to fundamental principles of zoning or the statute. . . ." [6] (emphasis added)

> But the overriding point we make is that it is not for the courts to substitute their conception of what the public welfare requires by way

of zoning for the views of those in whom the Legislature and the local electorate have vested responsibility. . . .[7]

In short [the judicial role] is limited to the assessment of a claim that the restrictions of the ordinance are patently arbitrary or unreasonable or violative of the statute, not that they do not match the plaintiff's or the court's conception of the requirements of the general welfare, whether within the town or the region. . . .[8]

We are, of course, not insensitive to the current social need for larger quantities of affordable housing of all kinds for the general population. . . . A possibility of some relief in that regard is contained within the statutory special exception or variance process. . . . But insofar as review of the validity of a zoning ordinance is concerned, the judicial branch is not suited to the role of an *ad hoc* superzoning legislature, particularly in the area of adjusting claims for satisfaction by individual municipalities of regional needs, whether as to housing or any other important social need affected by zoning. . . .[9]

After evaluating the recent decisions in the light of these statements, municipal officials have begun to ask: What are the obligations of my municipality to provide for housing for low- and moderate-income persons? If there are insufficient zoning provisions for such housing will the ordinance be vulnerable to a use variance application?

To answer these questions with any sense of assurance municipal officials, and their legal and planning advisers, are going to have to undertake a multistep analysis of their municipality and zoning ordinance. The following is an outline of the steps that should be useful in such an analysis:

Step One: Determine whether your municipality is a "developing municipality" within the meaning of the *Mount Laurel* decision.
  a. If the municipality is not a developing municipality, go directly to Step Three.
  b. If the municipality is a developing municipality, go to Step Two and Step Three.

Step Two: Determine whether the zoning ordinance is "exclusionary."
  a. If the zoning ordinance is "exclusionary," consider the amendments necessary to change that characterization.
  b. If a challenge to the zoning under the *Mount Laurel* principle is expected, undertake the studies necessary to defend the validity of the ordinance.
  c. Go back to the primary question of Step Two and reconsider the conclusion in light of action taken under Step Two, a and b.

Step Three: Determine whether the zoning ordinance is vulnerable to a use variance application by a high density developer.

To make this determination, answer the following questions:
a. Is a regional need for multifamily housing a "special reason" for granting a use variance?
b. Will a multifamily development impair the intent and purpose of the zone plan?

Step One: Is Your Municipality a "Developing Municipality" within the Meaning of the *Mount Laurel* Decision?

The *Mount Laurel* decision determined, and the *Washington Township* and *Demarest* decisions reaffirmed, that the obligation imposed by *Mount Laurel* (that a municipal zoning ordinance must provide for its fair share of the housing needs of the region) is limited to "developing municipalities." Thus, if a municipality is not a "developing municipality" its zoning ordinance will be upheld even if it does not provide for its fair share of the regional housing needs, unless it is arbitrary, unreasonable, or results in a confiscatory taking of the owner's property. It therefore becomes essential for every municipality to determine whether it is, or is not, a "developing municipality." The *Mount Laurel* decision sets forth the criteria for this determination.[10] Under the standards established in that decision, there would appear to be three categories of municipalities:

1. *Developing* municipalities like Mount Laurel
2. *Developed* municipalities like Washington Township and Demarest
3. *Undeveloped* municipalities that are still rural and likely to remain so for some time yet.

To determine whether your municipality is a "developing municipality" or whether it fits into one of the other two categories, it will be necessary to examine each of the following characteristics of a "developing municipality."[11]

Sizeable Land Area. A developing municipality is one that has "sizeable land area." Thus, it will become necessary to determine whether the land area in your municipality is, in fact, "sizeable." This determination will be based upon a comparative judgment after considering the relative size of the 567 municipalities in the state. The land area of New Jersey municipalities ranges from tiny Shrewsbury Township with only .09 square miles to Hamilton Township with over 113 square miles. The median size of municipalities in the state is 4.3 square miles. The average (arithmetical mean) size is 13.2 square miles. The Court has determined that Mount Laurel's 22 square miles is sizeable; Washington Township's approximately 3 square miles and Demarest's approximately 2 square miles are not sizeable. It would be reasonable to argue that a municipality with land area substantially under the average of 13.2 square miles and certainly one with less than the median of 4.3 square miles is not sizeable. As the land area of a municipality approaches the arithmetical mean of 13.2 square miles in size it becomes susceptible to the characterization of having "sizeable land area."

Location outside Central City and Older Built-up Suburbs. A developing municipality is one that is outside the central city and older built-up suburbs. There are probably a number of reasons why the Supreme Court adopted this characteristic as a standard. It seems clear that the Court intended to exempt the central city and older built-up suburbs from additional responsibilities to provide for the housing needs of the region. Thus, the *Mount Laurel* obligation applies only to the newer and more recently developed or developing municipalities. This result is consistent with the underlying purpose of the decision: to open up the suburbs to migration by low- and moderate-income persons currently trapped within the central cities and older suburbs. Additional housing facilities within the central cities would help meet the housing needs of the region but would not help to achieve the Court's other purpose of fostering economic and racial integration within the state.

Loss of Rural Characteristics. A developing municipality is one that has "shed its rural characteristics." This is a somewhat subjective criterion. However, there are at least two factors that are relevant when the question arises whether a formerly rural community has in fact changed its characteristics. Those factors are significant changes in population density and significant changes in land use. A report by the Regional Plan Association observed that, at about 100 persons per square mile, the rural feeling begins to change.[12] A population of approximately 2,000 to 4,000 persons per square mile is a fairly typical density for a suburban area.

The standards for comparison of the proportions of various land uses for a rural area are less precise. A typical rural community would have predominantly agricultural or undeveloped land, with a minimum of commercial and industrial use. A municipality begins to shed its rural characteristics when it *begins to use* increasing proportions of its land for nonagricultural purposes. The *Mount Laurel* opinion seems to indicate that rural characteristics are also shed when the municipality begins to zone substantial amounts of its area for commercial and industrial uses. The basis for such a position would be that the designation of a large amount of area for commercial and industrial uses raises a suspicion that the municipality is under pressure for residential development and is trying to avoid its regional obligations by zoning an unrealistically large amount of its land for industrial purposes.

Great Population Increases Since World War II. A developing municipality is one that has had great increases in population in the period since 1940. The significance of an analysis of population figures during this period may be to distinguish the three categories of municipalities, as follows:

1. *Developing municipalities.* The population in the 1940s was relatively small. During the period since 1940 the proportionate population increase has been significant and the incremental trend will continue up to the time of analysis, providing evidence for a projection of continuing growth and development of the municipality.

2. *Developed municipalities.* The population increase during the period from 1940 to the present may or may not indicate significant growth but recent population counts would indicate a slowing or a termination of previous growth. This category would include both those municipalities that had substantial population in the 1940s that have not grown substantially since that time and also those communities that have grown substantially during this period but have reached a peak and are no longer in a period of growth or development.

3. *Pre- or nondeveloping municipalities.* The population in the 1940s was relatively small. During the period from 1940 to the present there were relatively insignificant increases in population, indicating that the municipality remains relatively small and undeveloped, and has had a population growth that is not significant enough to use as a basis for projecting future population increases.

The significance of changing population growth statistics is subject to conflicting interpretation and will probably become the basis of future litigation. On one hand, it may be argued that a dramatic decrease in population growth is evidence that a municipality has reached its saturation point and therefore is no longer "developing." On the other hand it may also be argued that a decreased population growth rate is evidence of the exclusionary zoning practices that the *Mount Laurel* decision is intended to eliminate, and that if those exclusionary zoning obstacles were removed, the municipality would continue to develop.

Incomplete Development. A developing municipality is one that is not completely developed. In determining whether a municipality is completely developed it will be necessary to examine *both:* (1) the *amount* of land undeveloped and (2) the *characteristics* of that land. The amount of undeveloped land is significant in terms of both its relative size, i.e., its proportion of all the land in the municipality (and possibly in the region), and its actual size. In the *Mount Laurel* case, 65 percent of the land in the municipality was undeveloped. In the *Demarest* case, approximately 3 percent of the land was undeveloped, and the court held that Demarest is not a developing municipality. The difficult cases will involve proportions between those figures.

However, the *quantity* of undeveloped land taken alone could provide a misleading index of whether the municipality has reached its limits of development. The Appellate Division, in the *Washington Township* case, astutely identified this issue when it characterized the *nature* of the land to be considered as "readily and quickly available for development." There are many reasons why some land remains undeveloped after most of the other land in the municipality has been developed. Among the reasons why some land is not "readily and quickly available for development" are: (1) land assembly problems; (2) agricultural use; (3) part of a large private estate; (4) part of public parks, playground, country clubs, camps, college campus, or other institutional use; (5) unavailability of water, sewer, or other utilities; (6) soil, topography, drainage, or other high-cost-of-development problem.

If, for any of the above or other reasons, land in a municipality is not readily available for development, it is debatable (and litigable) whether such land should be included in the amount of land to be considered for the purpose of determining whether a municipality is "not completely developed" within the definition of a developing municipality.

Location in the Path of Inevitable Future Growth. A developing municipality is one that is in the path of inevitable future residential, commercial, and industrial demand and growth. The concept of a "path of inevitable future growth" is even more imprecise, vague, and amorphous than the concept of "region." The path of inevitable future growth in the northeast region of the country would include a hugh swath from Boston to Washington, D.C. If so defined, the "path" would be too broad and inclusive to serve any useful purpose. On the other hand, if all of the many pockets and interstices of non-growth are to be excluded, the analysis will become too complex and intricate to serve any useful purpose. Nevertheless, the path of inevitable growth is one of the factors to be considered in determining whether a municipality is developing for the purpose of imposing the *Mount Laurel* requirements of zoning validity.

After applying the above standards, if a municipal official determines that his municipality is a "developing municipality" then it becomes necessary to proceed to the next step.

Step Two: Is Your Municipal Zoning Ordinance "Exclusionary" Within the Meaning of the *Oakwood at Madison* Decision?

To determine whether your municipal zoning ordinance is "exclusionary" it is necessary to examine the ordinance and analyze its effect upon the ability of a developer to build "least cost" housing in the municipality. More specifically, it is necessary to apply the new test established in the *Oakwood at Madison* case, namely, does the zoning ordinance "operate in fact to preclude the opportunity to supply any substantial amounts of new housing for low and moderate income households now and prospectively needed in the municipality and in the appropriate region." [13] Although the application of this new test is difficult and complex, in many cases it may be possible to resolve the issue quickly by asking the following questions:

> Does the ordinance provide for substantial areas for single-family dwellings on very small lots?
> Does the ordinance provide for substantial areas for single-family dwellings on moderate sized lots?
> Does the ordinance provide for substantial areas for multifamily dwellings?
> Does the ordinance not discourage the construction of apartments with two or more bedrooms?
> Does the ordinance not create undue cost-generating requirements that would discourage "least cost" housing construction?

Unless the answer to all of the above questions is clearly and conclusively, "yes," there is a risk that the ordinance may be characterized as "exclusionary." Consequently, it will be necessary to amend the ordinance in an effort to eliminate the "exclusionary" characterization and/or undertake studies to defend the validity of the ordinance when it is challenged by a developer seeking the right to build housing at a location and at a density not in accordance with the zoned plan. It would be advisable for every municipality that cannot, with assurance and certainty, answer "yes" to each of the above questions to direct its planning staff or planning consultant to undertake studies to provide responsible and credible answers to the following questions:

1. *What is the present housing need of the municipality?* The report should include an analysis of such factors as vacancy rates, extent of dilapidation, extent of overcrowdedness, number of low-income families paying over 25 percent of income for housing, and an estimate of the extent of overlap of the factors used in the computation.

2. *What is the future housing need of the municipality?* This report will include an analysis of population projections for a future date, household size, number of households, and predictions of proportion of low- and moderate-income households in the municipality at that future date.

3. *What is the appropriate "region" of which the municipality is a part?* This report will include an analysis of each of the many possible demarcations of "region" that may arguably be appropriate for the municipality together with persuasive reasons for the adoption of the demarcation of "region" selected.

4. *What is the present housing need of the "region" selected?* The report will include the items discussed in question number 1 above.

5. *What is the future housing need of the "region" selected?* The report will include the items discussed in question number 2 above.

6. *What are the alternative assumptions upon which regional growth may be predicted?* The report will analyze the various assumptions upon which regional population projections may be based and will provide the reasons why adopted rate of population growth was selected instead of alternate assumptions and theories.

7. *What are the types and characteristics of "least-cost" housing that may be built in the municipality and region?* This report will contain an analysis of the various forms of least-cost housing, including methods of construction, size, and lot size, and will include an analysis of the costs of construction and maintenance costs, including property taxes and the amount of income required to maintain such housing.

8. *Is the allocation of land in the ordinance for multifamily housing reasonable or sufficient?* This report will make a "fair share" allocation of regional needs and provide the reasons to support the adopted theory of "fair share" allocation.[14]

9. *Is the allocation of land in the ordinance for single-family housing on small and moderate sized lots reasonable or sufficient?* This report will include items discussed in question number 8 above.

10. *Are the cost-generating requirements of the land use regulations reasonable in view of ecological and other factors?* This report will analyze ecological, esthetic, fiscal, and other constraints that may justify "cost-generating" requirements.

To the municipal official who balks at the length, complexity, and expense of the reports required to answer the above questions, the most telling response is that if he or she fails to respond satisfactorily to these questions then the ordinance will be vulnerable to attack under the *Mount Laurel* and subsequent decisions.

To make matters even worse, a satisfactory response to all of the above questions does not guarantee that the legislative policy decisions about the character and development of the community will prevail. Even if the zoning ordinance withstands the attack of being "exclusionary," the zoned plan may be disrupted by the granting of a use variance application.

Step Three: Is Your Zoning Ordinance Vulnerable to a Use Variance Application by a High Density Developer?

Under the New Jersey Municipal Land Use Law[15] the zoning board of adjustment may grant a use variance to allow a structure or use in a district restricted against such structure or use upon showing "special reasons" therefor and upon showing that such a variance can be granted "without substantial detriment to the public good and will not substantially impair the intent and purpose of the zone plan and zoning ordinance," i.e. the so-called "negative criteria." The two questions that arise from this provision are: (1) Is a regional need for multifamily housing a "special reason" within the meaning of the use variance provision? and (2) Will the court uphold a finding that granting a use variance for multifamily housing in a single-family district fails to meet the "negative criteria" requirement because of substantial detriment and impairment of the intent and purpose of the zone plan?

Is a regional need for multifamily housing a "special reason"? The question of what is a "special reason" that will justify granting a use variance is a complex one. In general, a "special reason" is one that promotes the health, morals, or general welfare. Consequently, variances have been upheld for public and semipublic uses, such as parochial schools, telephone equipment, private hospitals, and semipublic low-income housing outside a ghetto area. However, since almost every legal use of property would in some way serve the "general welfare," the New Jersey Supreme Court has held that merely showing that the proposed use would serve the general welfare is insufficient.[16] In addition to serving the general welfare, a court will find that a "special reason" exists if the proposed use either (1) is one that "inherently" serves the general welfare, such as a school or a hospital, where the use per se constitutes a special reason for a variance, or (2) is *"peculiarly fitted to the particular location"* for which the variance is sought.

In applying the above principles the Court has held that "variances to allow new nonconforming uses should be granted only sparingly and with great caution since they tend to impair sound zoning."[17] In the *Demarest* case, the Court recited criticism of a recent trial court decision that upheld a variance for construction of garden apartments on the grounds that such housing constitutes a special reason. The cited criticism argued that this decision "would lead to subverting rational land use planning" and "inevitably result in even greater misplanning in New Jersey suburbs."[18] The *Demarest* opinion also cited Justice Hall's statement in *Mount Laurel* that "while the special exception method . . . is frequently appropriate for the handling of such uses, it *would indeed* be *the rare case* where proper 'special reasons' could be found to validly support a [use] variance for such privately built housing. . . ." (emphasis added by the Court).[19]

After directing attention to this important issue and after raising the question whether a variance to provide private rental housing in a region that plainly needs it is "inherently" for the general welfare, the New Jersey Supreme Court decided in the *Demarest* decision "to leave definitive resolution of this knotty problem to a future case which will compel it; the instant one does not."[20]

Thus, after the latest word from the New Jersey Supreme Court, it is not possible for municipal officials to determine whether the courts will decide that an application for a variance for rental housing will meet the "special reasons" requirement for a use variance.

Will multifamily housing in a single-family district meet the "negative criteria" requirements of a use variance? The *Demarest* decision upheld the decision of the board of adjustment to deny granting a use variance for multifamily housing upon a finding that the grant would substantially impair the intent and purpose of the zone plan and zoning ordinance. The Court recognized that the board of adjustment has authority to weigh all the evidence, consider the arguments pro and con and then exercise its discretion in deciding whether to grant or deny a variance application. Consequently the courts will not disturb the variance decision of the board of adjustment as long as that determination is not arbitrary or capricious. Having found that there was substantial evidence for the determination of the board of adjustment, the Court upheld the board's decision.

The lesson that municipal officials may learn from the *Demarest* case is that if a decision to deny a use variance for a multifamily development is to be made bx the board of adjustment and sustained by a court it will be necessary to provide evidence for the record that would support the denial. Such evidence may be provided by the testimony of a planning consultant retained by the planning board to analyze the issue and report the findings of such a study. Failure to provide such evidence may result in a record that cannot support a denial of the variance.

Conclusion

After the recent New Jersey Supreme Court decision, the status of suburban zoning is still very much in doubt and subject to conflicting judicial principles and statements. On one hand, the state Supreme Court has reaffirmed the *Mount Laurel* principle that requires the zoning ordinance of a developing municipality to provide for its fair share of the regional housing needs for low- and moderate-income persons. On the other hand, the Court has withdrawn the trial courts from the process of "demarcating the region" or calculating "fair share." In addition, the Court has more recently expressed the need for judicial restraint and for judicial respect for the legislative and administrative processes. The Court has held that the *Mount Laurel* requirements are limited to "developing municipalities" and that those principles apply only if the municipality's zoning ordinance is "exclusionary." The problem of how to determine whether or not the ordinance is "exclusionary" is still unresolved, as are the problems of "demarcating the region," calculating "fair share," determining "present housing need" and predicting "future housing need" for the municipality and the region.

There are enough unresolved issues to occupy the time and energies of municipal officials and courts for many years to come. However, it is very likely that the New Jersey Supreme Court will adopt a policy that will result in an abatement of the flurry of zoning decisions by the Supreme Court for a substantial period of time to provide opportunity for state and local policymaking bodies to respond to the social, economic, political, and constitutional requirements of the state.

NOTES

1. Southern Burlington County NAACP v. Township of Mount Laurel, 67 N.J. 151, 336 A.2d 713, *cert. denied,* 423 U.S. 808 (1975).
2. Taxpayers Ass'n. of Weymouth Township, Inc. v. Weymouth Township, 71 N.J. 249, 364 A.2d 1016 (1976).
3. Oakwood at Madison, Inc. v. Township of Madison, _____ N.J. _____, _____ A.2d _____, (Dkt No. A-80/81, 1977).
4. Pascack Ass'n., Ltd. v. Township of Washington, _____ N.J._____, _____ A.2d _____, (Dkt. A-130, 1977).
5. Fobe Associates v. Demarest, _____ N.J. _____, _____ A.2d _____, (Dkt. A-129, 1977).
6. Pascack Ass'n., Ltd. v. Township of Washington, Slip opinion at 13.
7. *Id.* at 19.
8. *Id.* at 20.
9. *Id.* at 23.
10. The *Mount Laurel* decision defined "developing municipality" in the following paragraph (67 N.J. at 160, 336 A.2d at 717):
    As already intimated, the issue here is not confined to Mount Laurel. The same question arises with respect to any number of other municipalities of sizable land area outside the central cities and older built-up suburbs of our North and South Jersey metropolitan areas (and surrounding some of the smaller cities outside those areas as well) which, like Mount Laurel, have substantially shed rural characteristics

and have undergone great population increase since World War II, or are now in the process of doing so, but still are not completely developed and remain in the path of inevitable future residential, commercial and industrial demand and growth. Most such municipalities, *with but relatively insignificant variation in details,* present generally comparable physical situations, courses of municipal policies, practices, enactments and results and human, governmental and legal problems arising therefrom. It is in the context of communities now of this type or which become so in the future, rather than with central cities or older built-up suburbs or areas still rural and likely to continue to be for some time yet, that we deal with the question raised. [Emphasis added.]

11. Much of the material in this section was derived from Rose & Levin, "What Is a 'Developing Municipality' within the Meaning of the *Mount Laurel* Decision," 4 *Real Estate L. J.* 359 (1976), reprinted in *After Mount Laurel: The New Suburban Zoning* (New Brunswick, N.J.: Rutgers University, Center for Urban Policy Research, 1977).

12. See "Regional Plan Association Report," N.Y. Times, June 16, 1975, p. 17.

13. Oakwood at Madison, Inc. v. Township of Madison, slip opinion at 12. For an extensive discussion of this new test and its application, see Rose, "A New Test for Exclusionary Zoning: Does It Preclude The Opportunity for 'Least Cost' Housing," 6 *Real Estate L.J.* (Fall, 1977), printed also in *After Mount Laurel: The New Suburban Zoning* (New Brunswick, N.J.: Rutgers University, Center for Urban Policy Research, 1977).

14. For a discussion of the various techniques of "fair share" housing allocation, see Rose, "Fair Share Housing Allocation Plans: Which Formula Will Pacify the Contentious Suburbs?" 12 *Urban Law Annual* 3 (1976), reprinted in *After Mount Laurel: The New Suburban Zoning* (New Brunswick, N.J.: Rutgers University, Center for Urban Policy Research, 1977).

15. N.J.S.A. 40:55D-70d.

16. Kohl v. Mayor and Council of Borough of Fair Lawn, 50 N.J. 268 (1967).

17. *Id.* at 275.

18. Fobe Associates v. Demarest, slip opinion at 21, footnote 4. The decision criticized therein is Brunetti v. Mayor, Council, Township of Madison, 130 N.J. Super. 164 (Law Div. 1974).

19. *Id.* at 21, citing *Mount Laurel* at 181-182.

20. *Id.* at 23.

From the Legislature:

A Legislative Response
To The Problem
Of Exclusionary Zoning

Martin L. Greenberg
and Spiros Caramalis

On the day the New Jersey Supreme Court handed down its landmark decision on exclusionary zoning in *Southern Burlington County N.A.A.C.P.* v. *Township of Mount Laurel,* I introduced in the Senate of the New Jersey State Legislature a bill entitled the "Comprehensive and Balanced Housing Plan Act."[1] The bill was subsequently revised in accordance with testimony rendered at public hearings on the bill held by a joint committee of the New Jersey Legislature and reintroduced in the 197th session of the New Jersey Legislature as Senate Bill 1227. The purpose of this article is to: state some of the reasons for introducing Senate Bill 1227; describe some of the key provisions and objectives of the bill;[2] and, discuss some of the possible negative consequences of housing allocation legislation.

It is not the intention of this article to go over well-trodden ground. A large and growing body of specialized literature has already ably documented the scope, magnitude and some of the consequences of exclusionary zoning and other restrictive practices.[3] Similarly, the *Mount Laurel* decision has drawn considerable attention in recent law journal articles.[4] It is, however, necessary to briefly touch upon some of these same points in setting out some of the more salient arguments which predispose me to pursue a legislative remedy to the problem of exclusionary zoning.[5]

First, exclusionary zoning has exerted a disequilibrating and disruptive effect on the long-term processes of spatial dispersion of population, industry and commerce which discernibly intensified during the 1950s and 1960s. The result has been the unbalanced growth and a growing disparity in the fiscal capacities of diverse municipalities, while the patterns of development encouraged by such zoning practices have given rise to extravagant and wasteful use of land and other natural and capital resources of the State and its residents.[6]

Second, the present system of taxation and land use regulation encourages and rewards a predatory type of behavior commonly referred to as fiscal zoning. According to the calculus of narrow self-interest inherent in the concept and practice of fiscal zoning, a municipality's interests are best served by a land use policy which encourages the location of developments with a high, positive benefit-cost ratio (favorable ratables) while discouraging developments with low or negative ratios (unfavorable ratables). The logic of this position further dictates the externalization, or imposition on neighboring municipalities, of any of the avoidable negative spillover effects or consequences (pollution, vehicular traffic, capital and social service investment, adequate housing opportunities for work force, etc.) generated by the location of otherwise favorable ratables.

Third, by delimiting the availability of adequate site locations, particularly for certain types of development, and in imposing excessive lot size, floor space and other related requirements, restrictive zoning practices add appreciably and unnecessarily to the already high costs of housing construction.[7]

Fourth, a growing body of literature is serving to undermine many of the fiscal arguments for exclusionary zoning.[8] The evidence seems to indicate that certain types of multiple dwellings units and cluster developments do not per se impose insuperable fiscal burdens on municipalities. Indeed, from the standpoint of generating new revenues and requiring additional capital and service expenditures, certain types of dwelling units and cluster developments may, in fact, constitute more favorable ratables for a municipality than most detached single-family dwelling units.

Fifth, while court decisions have served to identify and dramatize the nature and consequences of exclusionary zoning practices, and have even traced the outlines of a constructive solution to the problem, these decisions also render more urgent early legislative action. The broad and general nature of the court majority's decision in Mount Laurel, and the diversity of approaches employed by or suggested to the lower courts which are charged with the onerous burden of applying general precepts to specific controversies,[9] have tended to compound the confusion of municipalities seeking guidance as to what may or may not be reasonably and legally required of them in the wake of the *Mount Laurel* decision. Furthermore, the vagaries of the judicial process, burdened by a case-by-case approach and the selectivity with which complaints or appeals are filed, do not augur well for the early resolution of the many problems posed by *Mount Laurel*.[10]

Sixth, having delegated to municipalities their land use powers and defined the limits of such planning and zoning powers through enabling legislation, the Legislature has the principal burden of grappling with the issues raised by *Mount Laurel* and providing guidance thereon to the municipalities of the State. Moreover, the issues involved are too important and too far reaching to be left to executive or, for that matter, judicial fiat.[11]

Senate Bill 1227

Although drawn separate and apart from one another, the legal standards used by the court majority in Mount Laurel in adjudging the constitutionality and legality of municipal land use regulations can, as well, serve as a statement of principles for Senate Bill 1227. According to the Court majority, every developing municipality — or, in the case of Senate Bill 1227, every municipality — has a positive obligation to adopt land use regulations which:

> make realistically possible an appropriate variety and choice of housing. More specifically, presumptively it cannot foreclose the opportunity of the classes of people mentioned for low and moderate income housing and its regulations must affirmatively afford that opportunity . . . these obligations must be met unless the particular municipality can sustain the heavy burden of demonstrating peculiar circumstances which dictate that it should not be required so to do. (p.174)

A statement of policy principles and objectives is, however, only to pose the essential problem on another, more programmatic or practical level. In this latter respect, the majority's decision raises as many problems as it resolves. Furthermore, despite the court's efforts to sketch out general standards for zoning standards, its primary responsibility, reflected in the decision, was to decide the immediate issue in controversy and to afford, if it so found necessary, affirmative relief to the plaintiffs from the unlawful municipal exercise of the zoning power. In contrast, the formulation of legislative policy is subject to a different set of contextual constraints and legislative policy must meet the tests of equity, uniformity or universality, and effectiveness and practicability, which depend on the forging of a delicate balance among a wide range of overlapping, oftentimes conflicting values, interests and policy goals.

The Comprehensive and Balanced Housing Plan Act was introduced partly on the assumption that it met many of the above tests, and partly in the expectation that it could and would be improved by being passed through the filter of public scrutiny and debate. Senate Bill 1227 is a result of the partial working of such a filtering process. The remedies proposed constitute neither the only possible strategy, nor will they necessarily yield optimal results. It may not even fully accord with all of the dicta set forth in the Mount Laurel decision; it most certainly does not provide the regional type solution to the problem suggested by the court.[12] Yet, the allocational approach proposed in Senate Bill 1227 does have the virtues of conceptual and methodological simplicity and flexibility, dealing with the exclusionary in an uncluttered and straightforward manner, and telling municipalities what they must know, allowing them to assess in advance the consequences of their actions and assuring them considerable continued control over the pace and patterns of their future development.

Senate Bill 1227 establishes a mechanism, procedure and standards for determining housing needs of each municipality and requires each municipality, if necessary, to plan for the accommodation of its housing needs. The State is charged with the responsibility, in the first instance, (a) to determine, in accordance with legislative standards, each county's share of its regional needs, based upon developments outside a county which exert a direct and appreciable effect on the housing needs of the county, and (b) to prepare advisory guidelines on each county's total housing needs. Each county planning board will then conduct an independent survey of the county's housing needs and determine the numbers and types of dwelling units required in each municipality to meet such needs, to which sum shall be added each municipality's share of the county's regional housing obligation.[13] Upon state certification of the housing survey and municipal allocations, each municipality is charged with amending its land use regulations and taking such other measures as may be necessary to facilitate the realization of its allocation.[14] State guidelines and county and municipal housing allocations are to be updated or revised on a periodic basis.[15]

Having established an intergovernmental framework for determining housing needs and goals, Senate Bill 1227 decidedly opts for a municipally-based rather than, as advocated by the court majority in *Mount Laurel,* a regionally-based strategy. The reasons for such a focus are severalfold. First, recent ventures in developing a regional approach to land use planning have been distinguished by a singular lack of success.[16] Second, municipalities have traditionally borne and continue to bear the primary, if not sometimes exclusive responsibility in the area of land use controls. There thus already exists a well established and well articulated system of municipal land use control which, whatever its other deficiencies, has served the interests of local communities and their residents reasonably well. Third, the diversity of local circumstances and interests dictates a continuing need for highly flexible planning structures accommodative of such diversity. Fourth, land use controls are the essential means by which municipalities ultimately shape the nature and quality of life within their boundaries. Fifth, the vitality of local self-government is itself a measure of the health and vitality of a democratic polity. Sixth, the success of any allocational scheme must, unless a radical change is made in the existing institutional order, ultimately depend upon the cooperation of those units of government responsible for its implementation.

Accordingly, what is required at this point in time is not the diminution or weakening of local institutions as instruments of self-governance, but a clearer articulation and more vigorous assertion of State and regional interests and goals. It is not to supplant but to build upon the existing system of land use planning and regulation, to broaden the vistas and accountability of local decisionmakers, and to render local units of government more effective instruments for the mediation, reconciliation and effectuation of State and local policies, which is to say, to better realize those very purposes for which local governments were created.

Senate Bill 1227 abridges municipal authority only to the extent that policy objectives require objectivity, equity and uniformity, and the balancing of the differing interests of neighboring municipalities, which is to say, in those policy areas requiring a broader areal perspective. Yet, even in such instances, municipalities are afforded some representation at higher levels of decisionmaking[17] or have ample avenues of appeal from county or state bodies. The detailed nature of the bill's planning provisions are also designed to assure maximum accountability on the part of all levels of government. Otherwise, municipalities are granted wide discretion in the planning and implementation of their housing allocations.[18]

Nowhere is the municipal emphasis of the bill more clearly manifested than in the proposed formula for determining a municipality's housing allocation, with its heavy emphasis on the spatial linkage of employment and residential opportunities and on high growth centers.[19] An underlying assumption and policy objective of an employment-growth center strategy is that a municipality or county should, to the maximum extent possible, have the primary responsibility for satisfying housing needs gen-

erated by its development policies.[20] A corollary presumption is that orderly and balanced community growth requires an essential harmony between a municipality's housing subplan and the other subplan elements of
the master plan.[21]

The allocation formula gives secondary weighting to a municipality's responsibility for accommodating the housing needs of its current residents. A tertiary set of factors, primarily of a locational and local capacity
nature, are also to be given weighted consideration, including: the existence of adequate land area for development or redevelopment; geographical proximity and accessibility to public transportation, major employment centers or high growth areas; the availability and capacity of
existing and planned community facilities and the overall (public and private) capacity to accommodate additional housing units; relative fiscal
capacity; and the need to expand and improve housing opportunities
within the region and the county, while avoiding excessive spatial concentrations of low income and subsized dwelling units.[22]

Having received its certified municipal housing allocation, each municipality is then required, if necessary, to make appropriate changes in its
land use regulations to accommodate its two six-year housing allocations.
Municipalities are also encouraged to adopt, in accordance with statutory
standards and guidelines set forth in sections 23 and 24, a housing development plan outlining a proposed course of public action for implementing its allocation. Municipal obligations under such a plan do not go
beyond a municipality's present responsibilities for properly planning and
accommodating additional growth within its boundaries.

A municipality may submit its land use regulations and housing development plan to the county planning board for review and certification
in accordance with uniform state standards. Upon receipt of local regulations or plans, the county planning board may provide unqualified certification, qualified approval or reject either or both the regulations and
plan as failing to satisfy the certified housing allocation of the municipality.[23]

In recognition of the desirability of locational specialization in certain
instances or in instances where allocations are too sparse or land costs too
high, a municipality may enter into joint agreements with any other contiguous municipality for the purpose of drafting joint land use regulations
or a joint housing development plan. Such agreements may also include
cost or tax sharing formulas. All such agreements shall be submitted to
the county planning board or boards for approval.[24] Encouragement is
also given to smaller municipalities to enter into service contracts with the
county for the preparation of appropriate land development regulations or
a housing development plan.[25]

Sections 21 and 22 utilize the "presumption of validity" test, suggested in the *Mount Laurel* decision for zoning ordinances, as an inducement for municipal compliance with the requirements of Senate Bill 1227. The burden for establishing the invalidity of local land use regulations falls most heavily on the developer where a municipality has obtained certification of its land use regulations and housing development plan. The burden of proof gradually shifts in accordance with the degree of municipal action or inaction, with the primary burden falling on the municipality if the municipality fails to take appropriate action within a reasonable time after receipt of its certified housing allocation. Upon finding that the municipality has failed to take sufficient action and that the development application will help the municipality satisfy its housing allocation, the court shall direct the municipality to approve the application. To avoid further litigation of the same problem, the court shall also require the municipality to approve any future applications for development that serve to meet the municipality's housing allocation, unless or until the municipality either submits to the court certified land use regulations and a housing development plan or approves the required number of dwelling units to satisfy its certified housing allocation.

Finally, Senate Bill 1227 attempts to eliminate any inconsistencies between the legislative goals contained in the Comprehensive and Balanced Housing Plan Act and related state aid programs. In so doing, it is hoped to create some additional incentives for more active municipal cooperation.

Conclusion: A Summation and a Prologue

Senate Bill 1227 is designed to provide a constructive remedy to a problem which has troubled municipalities even before *Mount Laurel;* that decision has only lent new urgency to the question of what is or is not an appropriate use of the zoning power. In *Mount Laurel,* the New Jersey Supreme Court held that not only may a municipality not use its land use regulations "to make it physically and economically impossible to provide low and moderate income housing in the municipality" but that, indeed, a (developing) municipality has a positive obligation to "make realistically possible the opportunity for an appropriate variety and choice of housing for all categories of people who may desire to live there. . . ."

Senate Bill 1227, for its part, seeks to provide municipalities with clearer guidance on the legal use of the zoning and other regulatory powers, as well as to what may be legally and reasonably be required of municipalities in fulfilling their local and regional responsibilities to provide adequate and appropriate locational opportunities to satisfy their present and prospective housing needs. In so doing, Senate Bill 1227 proposes standards and guidelines by which a municipality can: reasonably assess and predict the housing and other related consequences of alternative development strategies; more rationally select a development strategy that best accords with its perceived interests, needs and goals; and better anticipate and properly plan for the orderly implementation of its development policy in a manner which will serve to preserve if not upgrade its qualities as an "attractive and viable" community.

Although there is no dearth of appropriate methodologies for determining housing needs or making housing allocations, nor is experience therewith lacking, Senate Bill 1227 does constitute a pioneer effort at a mandatory statewide allocation system the consequences of which cannot be fully anticipated. Thus, for example, while the proposed allocational scheme has the intended objective of upgrading the quality and expanding the scope of the municipal planning process, the ultimate effect of such a scheme may be to overload the present local planning system or otherwise further expose some of its already manifest inadequacies. On the other hand, municipal efforts to effectuate the objectives of Senate Bill 1227 may well dictate greater intermunicipal cooperation, thereby generating a push below for a more regional approach to the site location problems of housing and other land development. Through such regional initiatives, municipalities may begin to get a handle on a host of land use problems which have hitherto defied the individual efforts of any single municipality.

Another serious potential problem of housing allocation legislation is endemic to the "problem-solving" nature of legislation. The proposal of a "legislative solution" to a problem requires reduction of the targeted problem to definable and manageable proportions, which is to say, the reduction of a universe of complex, interrelated, multicausal phenomena to an isolated and simple cause-and-effect relationship. Once the relationship is established, the policy agent then intervenes on the causal side of the relationship or equation in order to bring about the desired policy results. Yet the actual results are not always the intended results in that the targeted problem is only one segment of the total problem, and because of the unforeseen and unintended consequences of said policy on other related policy areas.

Nowhere is this problem more evident than in the area of land use policies. In the past several years, numerous measures have been enacted which deal with the problems of air and water pollution, sewage and solid waste disposal, open spaces and recreational areas, resource conservation, the protection of ecologically sensitive areas, economic development, housing and transportation, and capital expenditures therefor. Each of these measures exert, in varying degrees, an impact on and thereby help to shape the resource and growth, including land use, policies of the State. In short, for want of a coherent and comprehensive resource and growth policy, such policies are, in fact, being formulated in a piecemeal, somewhat onesided, oftentimes conflicting manner.

This too is an inherent danger of housing allocation legislation. Such legislation may, in fact, undesirably tip the scales in favor of accelerated development, notwithstanding the other collateral objectives set forth in section 1 of Senate Bill 1227, to wit: encourage a "greater diversity and the better distribution of housing opportunities . . . consistent with environmentally sound and well planned community development and the efficient use" of the State's resources. Recognizing these dangers, it is my fervent hope that enactment of Senate Bill 1227, or of a similar housing allocation measure, will provoke a comprehensive legislative review of the resource and growth policies of the State, and of the planning and operative structures for effectuating such policies.

NOTES

1. Several earlier court decisions presaged the main outlines of the court majority's decision in *Mount Laurel*. See, for example: *Vickers v. Gloucester Tp. Comm.*, 37 N.J. Super 232 (1962); *Molino v. Mayor and Council of Borough of Glassboro*, 116 N.J. Super. 195 (1971); *Oakwood at Madison, Inc. v. Madison Tp.*, 117 N.J. Super. 11 (1971); *Southern Burlington County N.A.A.C.P. v. Tp. of Mount Laurel*, 119 N.J. Super. 164 (1972); *DeSimone v. Greater Englewood Housing Corp. No. 1*, 56 N.J. 428 (1970). In the preparation of the bill draft, close attention was given to in-State and out-of-State decisions on exclusionary zoning, the literature on fair share allocations, and the abortive Voluntary Balanced Housing Plan Act, introduced in the State Assembly in 1972 as Assembly Bill 1421.
2. The sections of the bill cited below refer to the original printed copy of Senate Bill 1227.
3. The staff of the Center for Urban Research at Rutgers University have explored and documented in considerable detail the situation in New Jersey. The Center's staff have developed and further elaborated on the basic themes contained in three seminal works on New Jersey: N.J. Department of Community Affairs, *The Housing Crisis in New Jersey* (1970); ibid, *Land Use Regulation, The Residential Land Supply* (1972); and Norman Williams, Jr. and Thomas Norman, "Exclusionary Land Use Controls: the case of North-eastern New Jersey," *Syracuse Law Review*, 1971, Vol. 22, 476.
4. See for example: "Symposium on Exclusionary Zoning," *Rutgers Camden Law Journal*, Spring 1975, Vol. 6, No. 4; the addendum to Chapter 66 of Norman Williams, Jr. *American Planning Law*, 1975, Vol. 5; Jerome G. Rose, "The Mount Laurel Decision: Is It Based on Wishful Thinking?", Real Estate Law Journal, Summer 1975, Vol. 4, No. 1, 61-70; ibid, "From the Courts: The Trickle Before the Deluge from Mount Laurel", *loc. cit.*, Summer 1976, Vol.

5, No. 1, 69-79; Jerome G. Rose and Melvin Levin, "What is a Developing Municipality Within the Meaning of Mount Laurel," *loc. cit.*, Spring 1976, Vol. 4, No. 4, 359-86; Rosaling M. Mytelka and Arnold K. Mytelka, "Exclusionary Zoning: A Consideration of Remedies," *Seton Hall Law Review*, Fall 1975, Vol. 7, No. 1, 1-32.

5. Exclusionary zoning does not encompass all of the restrictive practices used by municipalities to limit or control the types of growth within their boundaries. Neither is the term meant to include well-conceived and impartially implemented restrictive practices which accord with legitimate, or statutorily prescribed, planning standrads and goals.

6. Council on Environmental Quality, *The Costs of Sprawl*, 1974, 2 vols.

7. One important school of thought considers futile and illusory any housing legislation, and particularly housing allocation schemes, which fails to address the basis problem of high construction costs. Two counter-arguments can be conjured up in favor of the allocational scheme contained in Senate Bill 1227. First, the housing problem is as much a matter of adequate site locations and environmental quality as it is of housing and construction and rehabilitation. Second, the high costs of housing construction do not appear susceptible to a single dramatic solution, but instead seem to require a series of incremental steps on a wide variety of fronts, such as building codes, land costs, construction and mortgage financing, labor productivity, etc. By increasing the availability of site locations and abating unnecessarily restrictive zoning and building requirements, Senate Bill 1227 may end up exerting a stabilizing influence, if not downward pressures, on rising land costs.

8. See George Sternlieb, et al., *Housing Development and Municipal Costs* (1973); New Jersey County & Municipal Government Study Commission, *Housing & Suburbs, Fiscal & Social Impact of Multifamily Development* (1974.).

9. *See* Rose and Levin, *"What is a Developing Municipality,"* and Rose, *"The Mount Laurel Decision."*

10. For example: what is a municipality's fair and equitable "share of present and prospective regional need"? How is the region to be defined? What is an "appropriate variety and choice of housing for all categories of people"? Or, what should be the extent or limits of a municipality's obligations in realizing the foregoing ends? And, how can these pious phrases be translated into housing construction or rehabilitation?

11. Otherwise and except for some tactical differences, I have no serious quarrels with the substance of Executive Order No. 35 (1976), pursuant to which Governor Brendan Byrne directed the State Department of Community Affairs to undertake a survey of the housing needs of New Jersey and assign numerical housing goals to the various counties. But the Governor's action cannot discharge the Legislature of its heavy and ultimate responsibility for setting policy on this matter.

12. *Mount Laurel*, 188-190 and footnote 22.

13. Sections 4, 6, 10 and 13.

14. Sections 20 thourgh 24.

15. Sections 4 and 29.

16. The substance of these recommendations may be found in: Division of State and Regional Planning (Department of Conservation and Economic Development), *The Setting for Regional Planning in New Jersey* (1961); the horizon

planning studies conducted by the Division in 1965-1966; Senate Bill 803 (1969) and Assembly Bill 1422 (1972).

17. Sections 8, 11, 14 and 16.
18. Sections 20 through 23.
19. Compare this approach with that set forth in *Urban League of Greater New Brunswick v. Mayor and Council of the Borough of Cartaret, et. al.,* N.J. Super (Chancery Div.), Docket No. C-4122-73 (1975).
20. Subsection 2d of the New Jersey Municipal Land Use Law (C.40:55D-2d) declares it to be an essential objective of the act to "ensure that the development of individual municipalities does not conflict with the development and general welfare of neighboring municipalities, the county and the State as a whole." See also *Mount Laurel*, 178-81.
21. See C.40:55D-2 and 28.
22. Sections 6, 10 and 24.
23. Section 25.
24. Section 26.
25. Section 28.

From the Legislature:

Housing in New Jersey:
A Realistic and Comprehensive Approach

Alvin E. Gershen
and Richard T. Coppola

Within the past year, much consideration has been given to the effect of recent court decisions upon planning and zoning in New Jersey. Since the various decisions have been rendered, many citizens of the state have looked to the Legislature to resolve the unanswered questions. Recently, the Senate Committee on County and Municipal Government held hearings on the proposed "Comprehensive and Balanced Housing Act."

Senate No. 3100 is an attempt to "establish a new planning framework within which local units of government rationally plan for the housing needs of their residents, while simultaneously acting as responsible partners and instrumentalities of the state in helping the state meet its responsibilities to all of the residents of New Jersey." [1] Essentially, however, the proposed legislation would allow the state and the counties to formulate a specific housing allocation program without the formal input of the state's municipalities.

More specifically, Senate No. 3100 directs the Commissioner of the State Department of Community Affairs to:

1. Prepare standards and guidelines for the determination of municipal housing allocations by County Planning Boards;
2. Prepare rules and regulations relating to the manner in which the survey reports submitted by the counties will be evaluated;
3. Prepare standards and guidelines for the housing development programs to be adopted by the municipalities;
4. Identify high-density and high-growth areas in the state and determine their impacts on regional housing needs;
5. Identify areas of critical housing needs throughout the state;
6. Prepare standards for determining feasible and desirable density levels and recommended models of alternative patterns;
7. Identify and delineate geographical areas with high development potential based upon existing development and available service and infra-structure facilities;
8. Compile and distribute relevant information on federal and state housing programs to the counties and municipalities of the state; and
9. Coordinate all public housing programs.

While there is no quarrel with the general concept of the proposed legislation specifically that there should exist throughout the state of New Jersey a diversity of housing opportunities to satisfy a total spectrum of housing needs, exception is taken with the proposed legislation on three grounds.

1. Legislation already exists in the state of New Jersey providing the authority for the state to act now to solve the housing problems addressed in Senate No. 3100; thus, there is no need for additional legislation;
2. Municipalities must have a significant and clearly prescribed role in the housing allocation process;
3. Regardless of the specific framework of municipal zoning controls, the mere act of zoning cannot insure that affordable housing will be supplied to all economic ranges.

The very fact that housing produced in the private market does not fill the needs of a wide segment of New Jersey's society strongly suggests that if a housing program is to fulfill its goals, then housing must be built with the assistance of state and federal funds. A most important consideration for the State Legislature is to insure that such funds are available.

These three points require brief elaboration.

1. Title 52, Article II, Chapter 27C-18 of the Revised Statutes of the State of New Jersey provides, among other things, that the Department of Conservation and Economic Development (the department from which was established the existing State Department of Community Affairs which inherited these functions) shall have the authority and responsibility to:

c. Investigate living, dwelling and housing conditions and into the means and methods of improving such conditions; determine where slum areas exist or where there is a shortage of decent, safe and sanitary dwelling accommodations for persons of low income; make studies and recommendations relating the problems of clearing, replanning and reconstructing of slum areas, and the problem of providing dwelling accommodations for persons of low income; and cooperate with any public body in action taken in connection with such problems; and engage in research, studies and experimentation on the subject of housing.[2]

These provisions not only permit, but apparently require the Executive Branch of our state government to prepare studies as outlined in the nine points above which form the basis of Senate 3100. When coupled with the new requirements of the recent Supreme Court decision, commonly referred to as *Mount Laurel*,[3] it seems that our executive branch of government should not be in the process of doing these studies without waiting for additional legislation to be adopted. Creative administration mandates the reading of existing laws in light of new Supreme Court decisions and acting in an imaginative and forthright way. It is not necessary for our legislative branch of government to respond with specific legislation when existing legislation, directly to the point, already exists.

2. Municipal home rule can and must be preserved. Our state administrators should bring local units of government directly into the decision-making process, even though the framework of that process may change from time to time. The recent *Mount Laurel* decision has mandated that the framework of local land use decision-making be changed; however, that decision has not mandated that municipal Planning Boards should no longer be a viable part of the decision-making process.

3. Even if Senate 3100 were enacted today and its provisions were meticulously followed, or even if the administrative process advocated here were pursued and concluded quickly and effectively, still not one new unit of housing would be produced. For in order to produce decent, safe and sanitary housing, whether new or rehabilitated, at costs affordable by most of our people, particularly our lower-middle-, moderate- and low-income families and elderly citizens, additional state subsidy programs must be enacted and made operative.

The recent *Mount Laurel* decision must be viewed as the most auspicious of and single land-use edict of government on New Jersey within recent memory, primarily for two reasons: (a) The decision rendered by the Supreme Court is now the law of our state; and (b) The decision is comprehensive and far-reaching.

The housing issues raised in the *Mount Laurel* decision can be reduced to the contention that there is a "presumptive obligation" for a municipality to provide the opportunity for housing production directed at the needs of a total spectrum of socio-economic levels. More specifically, the court stated that: (a) In determining its obligation and responsibility to provide a diversity of housing, a municipality must consider the region of which it is part; and (b) A municipality must not prevent development of housing through its laws, but must act "affirmatively" to provide housing for all socio-economic needs.

The *Mount Laurel* finding, however, did not specify how and what a municipal jurisdiction must do to insure conformance with the decision. A number of items remain unresolved:

1. What is the region and how analytically is it defined?
2. Must every "developing municipality" provide every possible type of physical housing unit for the various socio-economic age groups?
3. Who defines the housing needs for a municipality?
4. What specific relationship, if any, between job opportunities in a municipality versus housing opportunities should be established? and
5. Isn't the "timing" of development still the whole rationale behind the concept of planning?

On April 4, 1975, the Senate Committee on County and Municipal Government heard testimony on proposed Senate No. 3054, the "Municipal Land Use Law." Mr. Gershen stated then that while we are in need of updated land use enabling legislation, we must attempt to draw together and coordinate the overall land development process rather than continue a piece-meal approach which results in a total ambiguity and lack of coordination in the statute provisions and detrimentally affects everyone associated with the planning and development process.

The basic question is, What do we need to do to provide for the production of housing within New Jersey for our people? Do we need to prescribe a process of housing allocation formulation to insure that the law of our state as decided in the *Mount Laurel* case, as enacted in the statutes and as may be augmented and modified by subsequent Supreme Court Decisions, will be effectuated? The answer is "yes." Do we need to have Senate 3100 enacted in order to proceed? The answer is "no." The New Jersey State Department of Community Affairs already has the authority to perform a study delineating the state-wide housing needs.

There is an administrative process that can be followed now using the findings of the *Mount Laurel* decision and existing legislation as found in Title 52, Article III Chapter 52:27C-18 of the state's Revised Statutes. This process, which should be modified as new decisions are rendered by our courts or as new information becomes available, can be creatively and effectively handled by our executive branch without recourse to further legislation.

As an example, using the above Statute, the Department of Community Affairs can cause a housing inventory and need allocation study to be made. The information would be compiled on a state-wide basis using all of those factors necessary to ascertain state-wide trends and needs. Naturally, this state-wide analysis will have to be broken down into component regions within the state.

What would be used for "regions"? What are logical planning regions for our state and how do we arrive at concensus? This study of the state and its delineation into component regions was previously undertaken and discussed in a December 1961 publication of the State Department of Conservation and Economic Development, the forerunner of today's Department of Community Affairs. The study, entitled "The Setting for Regional Planning in New Jersey,"[4] defined regions employing data which indicated the relative importance of the various urban centers and the relative influence of the centers over outlying areas, without regard to existing political boundaries. Such data included a number of considerations including daily newspapers, weekly newspapers, retail sales, banks, hospital service areas, telephones, high schools, labor market areas, radio communications, joint chambers of commerce, traffic and transportation, and social organizations. Coupled with additional considerations such as natural features, physiographic features, productive lands, watersheds and man-made physical elements, a summary map of suggested planning regions was formulated.

Using the 1961 state study or, preferably, a modification and update of that study, it would be the state's responsibility within the Department of Community Affairs to stipulate the specific housing needs by regions after compiling state-wide housing needs. Within this process, the state would consider and coordinate the following:

1. Demographic characteristics
2. Housing characteristics
3. Physical land characteristics
4. Community facility characteristics
5. Traffic circulation characteristics
6. Market characteristics
7. Employment opportunities and characteristics

The state-wide housing needs study at this point would, therefore, be reduced to a regional basis. However, there are no regional governmental units in New Jersey, and we would need a governmental unit in order to complete our process of fair share allocation and ultimate land use determination and zoning delineation. It is therefore suggested that these regional findings be broken down and reassembled on a county basis.

In other words, it is suggested that although with one or two possible exceptions most land areas in any one county fall within more than one region, the basic housing information gathered on a regional basis can be summarized for administrative purposes on a county basis.

The county is the most viable and logical existing governmental entity to serve as the intermediary between the gross figures established by the state and the unique ability of a municipality to deal with its own specific characteristics of land development. Thus, the county would have the benefit of a definitive housing need study and would be responsible to implement its specific share of the overall regional housing need as determined in the study made by the state. This would be done *in conjunction* with the member municipalities of the county with consideration given to the same list of items as was undertaken by the State Department of Community Affairs, except that these considerations would be at the local level. Added to this list, however, would be specific considerations as to the unique character differences between the municipalities within the county. Thus it would be possible to relate the general regional trends coming from above, down to the municipality, to the specifics of the municipality, which would rise to influence the allocation of housing within the county.

The final municipal responsibility would be to effectuate its share of the housing allocation need through its zoning provisions as reflected in modified zoning mapping and text procedures. The type of housing unit and the conceptual form of development would be determined and justified by the municipality.

What remains for us to consider is the nature of the enforcement process. What process is called for to insure that counties and municipalities would do their "thing" in the general administrative machinery for fair share allocation? How are the findings of such a study to be enforced?

Clearly, the state must have the responsibility and effective tools to insure conformance at the county and municipal levels with its original findings. It must, first of all, be recognized that the state's study would be the most comprehensive and most expensive study heretofore performed and that opponents of the study would find themselves in a position of having to formulate another study of equal credibility. This is unlikely. Moreover, the study, once issued, would be used by Planning Boards, professional planners, developers, the courts, attorneys, housing advocacy groups, and other individuals and groups in their efforts on behalf of and against municipal zoning codes. We are facing a period of protracted court actions. We need, as quickly as possible, a definitive state-wide housing inventory and needs study prepared by the executive branch of our state government for the guidance of our courts and our legislative as well as our local Planning Boards and governing bodies. The mere presence of this study would add much to the enforcement process.

The study would have defined regions. The study would have defined the concept of a "developing municipality." The study would have defined socio-economic age groups. The study would have defined housing needs. And the study would have defined the permissible "timing" of development. Albeit, some of us may quarrel with certain of the findings of such a study; but a basis for rational decision-making will have been formulated.

However, the most straightforward and effective way of insuring municipal and county compliance with the state's analysis would be for the Commissioners of the various departments of state government to withhold recommendation for federal and state financial assistance to the local governments unless the substance of the state's regional housing analysis was agreed to and responsively effectuated by the county or municipal jurisdiction. As with the authority of the State Department of Community Affairs to undertake the housing study, this authority of the state government is already in the laws of the state of New Jersey. No additional legislation is necessary.

Under Title 52, Article IV, Chapter 27C-31, the Commissioner of Community Affairs has the following authority:

> "52:27C-31. No Federal aid unless commissioner has
>   opportunity to recommend
>
> Notwithstanding any other legislation heretofore enacted, no Federal financial assistance may hereafter be paid to or accepted by any political subdivision, special district or ad hoc authority of this State for a public improvement project unless and until the commissioner has had a reasonable opportunity to make recommendations with respect thereto and certifies that the public body sponsoring the project has complied with the requirements of this chapter, with respect to the filing of project descriptions, correspondence, agreements and documents." [5]

This function and power was exercised as long ago as 1959 in the former "Assistance For Public Works Planning Program (702)." In a manual describing that program, it was stated that:

> "3.2 State Requirements
>
> Though the Advances for Public Works Planning is solely a Federal program for assistance, State law in New Jersey (NJSA 52:27C-28: Article 4: Public Works Reserve) requires approval by the Department of Conservation and Economic Development as to whether the application for advances complies with all pertinent State legislation and meets the approval of other interested State agencies." [6]

Clearly, then, the state government may use this existing statute to effectuate the laws of our state, namely the findings of the *Mount Laurel* decision.

We do need new legislation, however, to insure that once the opportunity is provided for housing construction in the state of New Jersey, that such housing will be built and that this housing is geared to the needs of all socio-economic levels. We have a collection of programs which is, generally speaking, not functioning to fulfill the particular housing need which now exists. To some extent, these programs are not functioning because there is a severe lack of funds provided for their implementation. We need a new financing system for housing delivery and this can only be accomplished by state legislative action, primarily geared to providing funds to supplement and augment federal housing subsidy programs where they are unevenly applied to our state's problems due to their national scope and to providing new funding mechanisms where no federal programs now exist. It is these areas that should be most intensively investigated as a means of trying to reduce rents and costs to satisfy the growing demand for housing for all of our families and older citizens.

NOTES

1. Senate No. 3100, State of New Jersey, introduced March 24, 1975, by Senator Greenberg, p. 2, lines 29 through 34.
2. N.J.S.A. 52:27C-18c.; Article III: Physical Planning, Housing Urban Rehabilitation.
3. *Southern Burlington County N.A.A.C.P. v Township of Mt. Laurel*, March 24, 1975.
4. "The Setting for Regional Planning in New Jersey", published by the State of New Jersey: Department of Conservation and Economic Development, December 1961.
5. N.J.S.A. 52:27C-31; Article IV: Public Work Reserve.
6. Procedural Guide: Program of Assistance for Public Works Planning, published by the State of New Jersey, Department of Conservation and Economic Development: Division of State and Regional Planning, July 1961, pg. 3.

From the State Administration:

State of New Jersey Executive Department

Executive Order No. 35

Introduction

On April 2, 1976 Governor Byrne of New Jersey issued an executive order that directed the head of the state's Division of State and Regional Planning to determine the state housing goal for each county and to allocate each county goal among the municipalities therein. The order sets forth the criteria for the formulation of county housing needs and for the allocation of the "fair share" to each municipality. The executive order directed state officials to penalize municipalities that do not take action to meet their fair share by withholding state financial assistance and to encourage compliance by giving priority to those municipalities that do. Shortly thereafter, two state legislators filed a complaint against Governor Byrne in State Superior Court alleging that the executive order exceeded the powers of the governor under the state constitution.

On December 8, 1976 the state agency released its detailed report containing an allocation of low and moderate income housing for all of the municipalities within the state. Upon its release Governor Byrne immediately indicated his dissatisfaction with the report and ordered the state agency to revise it during the following year. The projected date for the release of the revised report would be after the gubernatorial and legislative elections.

WHEREAS, there exists a serious shortage of adequate, safe and sanitary housing accommodations for many households at rents and prices they can reasonably afford, especially for low and moderate income households, newly formed households, senior citizens, and households with children; and

WHEREAS, it is the policy of the State of New Jersey, as reflected in numerous acts and programs, to alleviate this housing shortage; and it is the law of the State of New Jersey that each municipality, by its land-use regulations provide the opportunity for the development of an appropriate variety and choice of housing for all categories of people, consistent with its fair share of the need for housing in its region; and

WHEREAS, it is the policy of the State that local government should be the primary authority for planning and regulating land-use and housing and housing development; and that the State shall provide appropriate assistance to local governments so that municipalities can meet their obligation to provide an opportunity for the development of an appropriate variety and choice of housing for all categories of people, consistent with the municipality's fair share of the need for housing in its region; and

WHEREAS, the laws of the State of New Jersey (P.L. 1944, c. 85; P.L. 1961, c. 47; P.L. 1966, c. 293; P.L. 1967, c.42) authorize the Division of State and Regional Planning to conduct comprehensive planning, to plan for housing needs, and to provide planning assistance to local governments; and

WHEREAS, continuation of financial assistance by the federal government to the State for comprehensive planning under section 701 of the Housing Act of 1954, as amended by the Housing and Community Development Act of 1974, is contingent upon the Division of State and Regional Planning carrying out an ongoing comprehensive planning process, including, as a minimum preparation of a housing element and land-use element by August 22, 1977;

NOW, THEREFORE, I, BRENDAN BYRNE, Governor of the State of New Jersey, by virtue of the authority vested in me by the Constitution and by the statutes of this State, do hereby ORDER and DIRECT that:

1. The Director of the Division of State and Regional Planning, in accordance with the provisions of this Order, shall prepare State housing goals to guide municipalities in adjusting their municipal land-use regulations in order to provide a reasonable opportunity for the development of an appropriate variety and choice of housing to meet the needs of the residents of New Jersey.

2. The Director shall allocate housing goals pursuant to this Order, as expeditiously as feasible, but no later than 10 months from the date of this Order and no later than 2 years after each future decennial cen-

sus. Periodically the Director may reevaluate the adequacy of the current State housing survey and may make appropriate changes in housing goal allocations.

3. The Director shall complete a housing needs study which takes into account:

    (a) the existence of physically substandard and over-crowded housing in the State;

    (b) the existence in the State of households paying a disproportionate share of income for housing; and

    (c) other factors as may be necessary and appropriate.

4. All agencies of State Government shall cooperate with the Director and furnish such copies of any data, reports or records as may be required by the Director to discharge the responsibilities under this Order and as may be available in accordance with applicable law and regulations.

5. The State housing need as determined by the housing needs study shall serve as the basis upon which the Director shall formulate a "State Housing Goal" and allocate this goal to each county or group of counties. The formulation of the State housing goal, to the extent the Director deems appropriate, shall take into account the capacity of the public and private sector to ameliorate the State housing need within a reasonable time period. The Director also may announce the State housing goal in time stages.

6. a. The Director, in allocating this goal to each county or group of counties, shall take into account the following:

    (1) The extent to which housing need exists in each county or group of counties.

    (2) The extent to which employment growth or decline has been experienced in each county or group of counties.

    (3) The extent to which the fiscal capacity to absorb the housing goal exists within each county or group of counties.

    (4) The extent to which appropriate sites to provide for the housing goal exist within each county or group of counties.

    (5) Other factors as may be necessary and appropriate.

    b. Consistent with these standards, the Director may suballocate the housing goal or goals of a county or group of counties to groups of contiguous municipalities comprising major geographic areas of a county or group of counties.

7. The housing goal allocated to each county shall specify a minimum number of housing units economically suitable for different segments of the population for which an adequate range of appropriate sites should be made available within the county. Appropriate sites include any land or

residential structure that is suitable or amenable to providing a location for housing development, redevelopment, rehabilitation, or program of assistance for existing housing.

8. The Director, except as provided in Section 9 of this Order, shall allocate each county housing goal among the municipalities in a county and each housing goal for a group of contiguous municipalities selected pursuant to Subsection 6 b. of this Order among the municipalities within such a group. This allocation of a county housing goal among municipalities in a county or a group housing goal among the municipalities in a group of contiguous municipalities selected pursuant to Subsection 6 b. of this Order shall take into account the following factors.

   (a) The existence at the municipal level of physically substandard and overcrowded housing.
   (b) The existence at the municipal level of households paying a dispro-portionate share of income for rent.
   (c) Past, present and anticipated employment growth and relative ac-cess to these employment opportunities by low and moderate in-come workers.
   (d) Relative availability of appropriate sites for housing on a municipal basis.
   (e) Relative capacity of municipalities to absorb additional housing units as measured by fiscal capacity.
   (f) Relative municipal shares of low and moderate income households, and anticipated change in such households.
   (g) Past, present and anticipated residential and non-residential munic-ipal growth patterns.
   (h) The existence of a county development plan as it relates to fair share housing needs in that county.
   (i) Other factors as may be necessary and appropriate.

9. The Director may delegate to a county planning board the authority to allocate the county housing goal among the municipalities in the county and any housing goals for groups of contiguous municipalities selected pursuant to Subsection 6 b. of this Order among the municipalities within such groups. Such county planning board allocation shall conform to the standards in Section 8 of this Order and appropriate guidelines provided by the Director. If a county planning board does not allocate the munici-pal housing goals in a reasonable period of time, as determined by the Director and consistent with the time periods of Section 2 of this Order, or if the Director determines that the allocations do not conform to the standards in Section 8 of this Order and the guidelines provided by the Director; then the Director, consistent with the standards of Section 8, shall perform the housing goal allocation which had been delegated to the county planning board.

10. (a) The Director may promulgate the allocations required pursuant to Section 8 of this Order and may authorize a county planning board to promulgate allocations pursuant to Section 9 of this Order in time stages which give a priority to the promulgation of allocations for developing municipalities.

(b) The Director may promulgate the allocations required pursuant to Section 8 of this Order and may authorize a county planning board to promulgate the allocations required pursuant to Section 9 of this Order by initially promulgating collective allocations to small groups of contiguous municipalities which individually would receive relatively low allocations pursuant to Section 8 of this Order.

11. The Director shall provide opportunities for the public, other agencies of State government; and regional, county, and municipal planning agencies to comment on the determinations of housing need and the allocation of housing goals pursuant to this Order.

12. State officials administering state and federal programs providing grant and loan aid and technical assistance to municipalities and counties for open space preservation, sewerage improvements, community development, local program management and comprehensive planning, housing development and demonstration projects, housing finance, interlocal services; and the construction, repair, and maintenance of municipal and county roads and bridges; local street lighting projects, and programs supporting public transportation shall, in accordance with existing law and for purposes of providing incentive aid consistent with the objectives of this Executive Order, give priority where appropriate to municipalities which are meeting or are in the process of meeting a fair share of low and moderate income housing needs. State officials participating in regional planning activities and regional clearinghouse review and comment decisions on municipal and county applications for federal funding shall take into account whether a municipality or group of municipalities is meeting or in the process of meeting a fair share of low and moderate income housing. Any municipality in which a disproportionately large share of low and moderate income households resides and which is making an effort to improve housing conditions shall not be assigned a lower priority under the provisions of this section.

13. The Director may establish procedures and guidelines for determining whether a municipality has reasonably accommodated its municipal housing goal, as determined pursuant to this Order, and may report periodically on the progress of municipalities in complying with their respective allocations.

14. The Director of the Division of State and Regional Planning shall continue to prepare comprehensive housing and land-use plans for guid-

ing development decisions in this State. This comprehensive planning activity, consistent with the fair share housing objectives of this Order, shall continue to be a part of the housing and land-use programs of this State.

> GIVEN, under my hand and seal this 2nd day of April, in the year of Our Lord, one thousand nine hundred and seventy-six of the Independence of the United States the two hundredth.

/s/   Brendan Byrne

GOVERNOR

ATTEST:

/s/   John J. Degnan

Executive Secretary to the Governor

From the Developers:

There's a Long, Long Trail Awinding — Mount Laurel From The Developers' View

William L. Brach

For that practical breed of men and women who would build housing and make money, *Mount Laurel* is a promise and not a delivery system.[1] Land development for apartments or for less expensive homes on smaller lots has become increasingly difficult since the early 1970s as community after community has sought to confine new housing to expensive single family dwellings in small numbers on large lots. Since 1973, housing development in New Jersey has fallen below half and multi-family construction has dropped to one-third or one-fourth of what it was just five years ago. The graph and table on the next page tell part of the story.

Concededly, it is an oversimplification to suggest that the sharp curtailment of housing construction is solely a consequence of exclusionary zoning. Financing, environmental constraints, market, inflation and recession have all played and continue to play a part. But what the cynics say about money can be said about the causes of the drop in production. Exclusionary zoning as a cause is way ahead of whatever factor is in second place. Coupled with the steep rise in construction costs, large lot zoning has simply priced most families out of the new housing mar-

Authorized Resdidential Building Permits—1970-1976 [2]

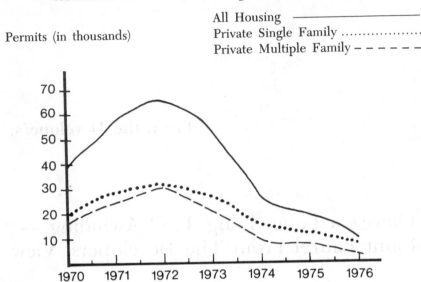

Permits (in thousands)

All Housing ──────────
Private Single Family ....
Private Multiple Family – – – – – –

Among the counties exhibiting exclusionary zoning the following table is indicative of the practice:

Percent of Vacant Land Zoned for Residential Use [3]

	One-half Acre Plus	One Acre Plus	Multi-Family
Bergen	76.6	55.1	.6
Hunterdon	99.2	97.1	.2
Middlesex	85.9	38.7	.5
Monmouth	95.0	84.6	.4
Morris	95.5	82.9	1.2
Somerset	99.3	85.4	0.0
Passaic	66.4	44.1	4.6

ket. *Mount Laurel* promises to cut away an obstacle to producing housing. Landowners, home builders and housing sponsors should be cheering from rooftops built and to be built. Yet in terms of housing provided, the *Mount Laurel* impetus to judicial removal of development barriers has been disappointing. Of seven communities that have been the subject of pro-housing *Mount Laurel* decisions, the results in terms of immediate or early housing production has not been impressive. Consider the following:

Community	Date of Decision			Status of Developer as of Sept. 1976
Mt. Laurel	March	24,	1975	On remand - no construction
Cranbury	April	18,	1975	On appeal - no construction
Holmdel	May	15,	1975	On appeal - no construction
Bedminister	Oct.	17,	1975	On appeal - no construction
Marlboro	Apr.	7,	1976	On appeal - no construction
Montville	Apr.	14,	1976	On appeal - no construction
Middlesex County	May	4,	1976	On appeal - no construction

There is a time lapse generally of from three to five years from the time of the filing of the Complaint to the time of the decision.[4]

Those municipalities which construe the precepts of *Mount Laurel* as something to be resisted, hopefully defeated[5] or at least delayed, have drawn together a kit of Development Frustrators. Topping the list is: "Who me?" Already there is a string of municipalities which have won exemptions on the ground that they are not developing communities, including Winonah, Closter, Demarest, Rockleigh, Washington Township, North Haledon and Livingston. It is like Goldilocks and her porridge; one town is too small, the next too developed, the third too rural. It is as if the Supreme Court intended to confine the impact of *Mount Laurel* to a select few municipalities which have precisely the right combination of factors to qualify.

Another Frustrator is: "Let's stop everything and plan." The new Municipal Land Use Law[6] recognizes, and in this sense codifies existing case law, the right of a municipality to enact interim zoning ordinances for one year, with an extension available for an additional year.

The next Frustrator is the change of ground rules — a matter of zoning amendments which keep the regulations fluid and the developer off balance. This runs up the cost of preparing plans for submission and makes it easy to reject a proposal on the ground that it fails to satisfy the most recently enacted ordinances. The tactic is supported by decisions holding that courts will only review the validity of the restrictions in effect at the time of decision.[7]

Other Frustrators can be listed simply to show the variety available if the intent is to head off a development proposal encouraged by *Mount Laurel*. The presumption of legislative validity continues to provide temporary hiding places for the municipal rear guard with their battle slogan, "if you want to build, you got to beat down the doors first." Of course, *Mount Laurel*, at 181 shifted the presumption of validity when an exclusionary pattern was shown. However, with the great variety of restrictive ordinances which do not evince an exclusionary purpose per se, the burden and the task still falls to the challenger.

Defendants also recognize, particularly where the owner or developer is of limited means, that time is on the side of the municipality. The hope here is that he (the developer) may drop dead. The table of favorable decisions shows how years are lost. Carrying costs pile up. For example: Twenty acres to support 200 units of garden apartments may be worth $600,000. Assuming a carrying cost for interest on a mortgage and return on capital of 10 percent per year, and adding taxes and insurance, five years of litigation, maneuvering and delay can compel the owner or developer to invest half the total value of the land into front-end carrying costs without any real assurance of recoupment. Small wonder that municipalities feel "time is on my side" and that litigation, even if ultimately lost, may well bring victory through attrition.

The developer who pursues *Mount Laurel* may also find out that the reward for diligence is that the rezoning, if compelled, will accrue to the benefit of his competitor and lastly, if ever, to him.[8] A recalcitrant community usually finds some way to communicate this sentiment to those who would urge assumption of *Mount Laurel* responsibilities.

This does not exhaust the list. There is token compliance. An Essex County community zoned for multi-family one of its choice landlocked sites where the highway extension was still five years away. Also, there is the concern for environmental protection, as recognized in *Mount Laurel* itself. Here, the understandable apprehension that development may cause damage to flood plains, waterways and natural habitats forms a legitimate barrier to some development. It is difficult to evaluate whether the concerns are sincerely and justifiably expressed or whether they are the stalking horse for perpetuating exclusionary zoning practices under a more socially acceptable label.

Finally, and perhaps most critical of all, is the plaint that the community lacks some aspect of the developmental infrastructure, such as sanitary sewer capacity, water supply, or an adequate road network.[9] *Mount Laurel*, provides some suggestion that there may be judicial impatience when this turns out to be a dodge.[10] However, the last word has not been spoken on the extent to which a community can hold off necessary public improvements to make development possible, or concomitantly, to what extent a developer can insist that this be done. The Municipal Land Use Law prohibits refusal of zoning approval on the grounds of any prohibition by a State agency such as a sewer ban. However, it does leave open the right of a municipality to condition its approval on the removal of any such legal impediment.[11]

Mount Laurel itself falls short of meeting the concerns of the landowner-developer in four prime regards. It was written essentially in terms of redefining "general welfare" to meet prevailing social needs for housing. It was not directed to providing relief for builders and landowners whose desire to build coincided with the "general welfare" as now interpreted.

The first failing was the suggestion that there may be municipalities not embraced by the term "developing community" and that consequently are entitled to zone without regard to the *Mount Laurel* considerations. This has triggered the race to the exit and disrupted the overriding need for a comprehensive plan of development for the State and its regions without holes punched into the geographic fabric. The court may yet reinterpret the "developing communities" concept and reconcile the application of *Mount Laurel* to a comprehensive Statewide plan. Its consequence has been to encourage litigation and delay, permitting perpetuation of "favored" municipalities not sharing the common responsibility for housing low- and moderate-income families, and exacerbating the impact on those communities which are not exempted.

Second, the court failed to define the status of the owner-developer who would seek to use land for the "general welfare" purposes embraced in *Mount Laurel*, (*e.g.* multi-family housing). The decision strongly suggested rezoning as appropriate in those communities making no provision for such housing, and noted that it would be "a rare case indeed" when the variance procedure would be proper. The owner-developer then, following the rezoning route occupies the unenviable position of attacking the municipality and its officials and then hoping that his site among the various potential sites will be selected by these very same officials when forced into a general revision of the Zoning Ordinance. Such a challenge, given its cost in money and extensive time, and with uncertain benefits even if the case is won, requires a plaintiff with strong determination or a keen sense of injury.

Akin to this is failing number three, hopefully to be answered in the pending decision of *Oakwood at Madison*: namely, that with the victorious establishment of rights against exclusionary community, the court is far less strong and clear about the remedy.[12] The remand with directive to rezone within three months is a notoriously ineffective device. *Mount Laurel* itself demonstrated that the return to the drawing boards did not produce a workable blueprint, at least in the plaintiff's view. From the developer's perspective, each such round entails six months to a year of lost time. Again, for an owner of twenty acres hoping to build 200 units of housing, the fruitless remand procedure alone would mean an additional $50,000 to $75,000 in carrying costs.

Failing number four embraces the unresolved substantive areas which directly affect the ability to develop. *Mount Laurel,* while speaking in terms of housing vareity and choice beyond the needs of low- and moderate-income families, sketched out in the remedial section of the opinion the delineation of a region and the determination of a fair share solely in terms of low- and moderate-income housing. What about the other forms of housing which may not be subsidized? The very real prospect of the continuing consumption or remaining and available land in large lots (see vacant residential land table) suggests that denser land use will not come about on any scale unless the court is willing to intervene on behalf of unsubsidized (middle-luxury) multi-family housing as well as for low- and moderate-income housing. The readiness of courts to do just that where little housing choice is evidenced in the zoning plan remains to be resolved in the post-*Mount Laurel* era. Also, to effectuate housing for low-moderate income families more municipal action is required than simply the appropriate rezoning of land, as critical as this first step is. The recent oral opinion of Judge Lane in *Prime Feather and Down v. Zoning Bd. of Ad., Tp. of Marlboro,* requiring the establishment of an official body to facilitate low income housing recognizes that something akin to an affirmative action program is necessary.[13] The community effort cannot stop with the first faltering step. Financing aid through the State moderate-income housing program cannot be obtained until the municipality adopts a resolution of need.[14] The *Mount Laurel* court readily recognized that low- and moderate-income housing would not be forthcoming unless such special subsidized financing was available. It follows that a *Mount Laurel* remedy must be coupled with the acknowledgement that rezoning for low and moderate income families constitutes the finding of a "need for moderate-income housing projects". Of equal importance is the securing of an agreement to make payments in lieu of taxes as permitted under N.J.S.A. 55:14J-30(b). Here, too, local opposition can defeat a project just as surely as if the necessary zoning had never been provided. Thus, the delivery system to redeem the pledge of *Mount Laurel* has to be directed at all the necessary municipal action to assure the financing and applicable tax considerations alluded to but not resolved in the *Mount Laurel* opinion itself.

Beyond the perspective of landowner and developer, *Mount Laurel* has brought in its wake the confusion of conflicting interpretations by different courts in deciding what is the region for various localities, how fair share is to be calculated and similar questions of implementations. The limitations of judge-made law come into play here as courts are ill-designed to fashion a planning scheme through individual cases which can embrace large geographic areas, and to do so in a way that gives fair consideration both to the immediate litigants and to the vast number of interested public and private parties inevitably affected by the decision. This simply highlights the urgency of locating a more appropriate vehicle to carry out the planning implications of *Mount Laurel*. The courts are singularly without appropriate means and resources.

These deficiencies and weaknesses in the *Mount Laurel* format, evident in the *Mount Laurel* aftermath, afford no real cause for optimism that the decision and its progeny can resolve the inherent conflict between those who wish to build and those who would stop them in the interest of maintaining the status quo. Exclusionary zoning is a political problem. As land becomes more scarce and environmental considerations rule out use of much of our current vacant land, a rational policy for what remains becomes a matter of such urgency that provincial constraints must give way to the overriding demands of public necessity. Lots of at least one-half acre and individual houses costing at least $75,000 are now zoned into approximately 85 percent of the available land in the 16 counties, according to *Land Use Regulations, The Residential Land Supply*, cited earlier. This state of affairs as a fact of life cannot persist forever. Events and public awareness have a way of catching up with such distortions of local power.

But something more than *Mount Laurel* and a slow evolution of our approach to zoning is needed. Land-use decisions in the form of development could take place on much of what remains before responsible planning catches up with events. A decade or even two could be lost while the slow but deliberate process of education and restructuring persuades those that have local control to permit the general welfare to be served. Meanwhile, the poplulation in need of housing remains unaided.

A few jurisdictions, principally Massachusetts, have, by legislation, compelled all of their municipalities to accept a limited responsibility for low- and moderate-income housing. Under the Massachusetts law 10 percent of dwelling units, or 1½ percent of the municipal land area, must be set aside to meet this need. There is an avenue of appeal both from a refusal to honor this requirement and from an effort to impose conditions or regulations which render construction uneconomic. The City of Hartford, Connecticut, is suing to block federal grants for its more affluent neighbors who have failed to provide for their share of low- and moderate-income families. The Pennsylvania legislature has specifically provided judicial relief to developers who must face the evasive tactics of recalcitrant exclusionary municipalities. The Pennsylvania Planning and Development Laws, empower a court to direct that a developer's specific land use plan be approved, subject to those further conditions and supplemental approvals as the court might see fit to impose. In New Jersey, by Executive Order No. 35, April 2, 1976, a priority is to be given to sewer and water grants to communities which have evidenced a concern to meet these responsibilities.

To be effective, a legislative solution would have to include in the planning, and at least in the review of zoning, a jurisdictional authority higher than the municipal level to assure that vacant land most suitable for more intensive housing development, including low- and moderate-income housing, is not improperly zoned. Further, it must have remedies and sanctions that are sufficiently expeditious to insure that correction of improper zoning is no longer just a promise without practical means of redemption. Also, the legislation must embrace all portions of the State and not tolerate exceptions and exemptions which preclude orderly planning. Finally, it must build in a mechanism for research and study so that the overriding planning and zoning concept will take into account population shifts, employment trends, changes in transportation patterns, environmental decisions affecting land use and similar circumstances. In short, the *ad hoc* determinations brought on by *Mount Laurel* have to be replaced with a more rational and more comprehensive decision-making process.

As a practical matter landowners and developers cannot be expected to wait until the millenium arrives in the form of well-conceived legislation. They have a right to build, at least to the extent that the "general welfare" dictates. Court remedies should be shaped and designed to provide the owner and developer a reasonable opportunity to secure, if justified, this right. This means, in the absence of a legislative solution, a way of obtaining in court not only the negative remedy of invalidating an ill-conceived ordinance, but the positive response which alone has meaning: the right to build for low- and moderate-income families and, beyond this, the right to offer a "housing choice", that is, to build other forms of housing than single-family detached dwellings on large lots. The courts must begin to invoke remedies that go beyond simply negating existing zoning. They must view a housing project in its totality and include in their directives provisions to make financing and tax relief possible as part of the elements of a project. And finally, tactics of delay should not be rewarded by letting time be consumed, costly to the owner and developer but advantageous to the municipality, which would defer an undesired change by them as long as possible. For the developer who proves his case, the municipality should be taxed with the cost which the developer would otherwise by compelled to absorb. It may be that these costs (taxes and carrying charges) should be directed back into reducing the land cost for the ultimate development so that it would be a consumer benefit. In any event, delay which drives up the investment in land and dims the chances of building for low- and moderate-income families should, where caused by local intransigence, be the burden of that community. There should be a disincentive to protracted litigation, and a price paid in the form of damages for engaging in it.

In the first instance, courts must build into their decisions and applicable orders that which will truly implement the policy enunciated in *Mount Laurel.* Having picked up the cudgel of *Mount Laurel,* the courts cannot disown the delivery system. High souding principles can be turned into ashes by simple obstructive tactics. Our judicial system, having written the recipe, should aid those who would attend to baking the cake. While the complete solution lies elsewhere with the legislature, interim court action by its firm resolve that *Mount Laurel* be implemented is the surest and best catalyst to bringing a legislative decision to pass.

NOTES

1. *Southern Burlington NAACP* v. *Tp. of Mt. Laurel,* 67 N. J. 151 (1975) hereinafter *"Mt. Laurel".*
2. State of New Jersey, *Residential Construction Authorized by Building Permits,* Annual Summary, 1970-1973, N.J. Dept. of Labor & Industry, Office of Business Economics; State of New Jersey, *Residential Building Permits,* 1974 Summary, N.J. Dept. of Labor & Industry, Division of Planning and Research; State of New Jersey, *Residential Building Permits,* Data for June, 1976, N.J. Dept. of Labor & Industry, Division of Planning and Research.
3. State of New Jersey, *Land Use Regulation, The Residential Land Supply,* N.J. Dept. of Community Affairs, Division of State and Regional Planning (April, 1972) Tables V and VII.
4. The movement to place public housing in the suburbs has been frustrated even more than the effort to build private and subsidized houwing. In 1966, black residents of Chicago filed a suit to compel Chicago Housing Authority to build housing outside the ghetto. They achieved early victory and Judge Austin of the U. S. District Court projected a figure of 1,500 units of low rent housing to be built outside the ghetto. This April, 10 years later, the U.S. Supreme Court in *Hill v. Gautreaux* (Docket # 74-1047) directed Hud to take steps to encourage projects on a Metropolitan regional basis. In the intervening decade 62 units were built.
5. Allies in the legislature have introduced a proposed Constitutional amendment, Concurrent Resolution No. 140, which would amend our State Constitution with a paragraph which in one breath affirms non-discrimination in zoning while expressly authorizing zoning provisions which exclude users who have "insufficient financial resources."
6. L1975, c. 291, effective August 1, 1976, N.J.S.A. 40:55D-1 *et seq.*
7. *Tice* v. *Borough of Woodcliff Lake,* 12 N.J. Super 20 (App. Div. 1951).
8. *See e.g., Township of Williston* v. *Chesterdale Farms, Inc.,* 341 A2d 466 (S. Ct. Pa. 1975).

9. *See e.g., Pascack Assoc. Ltd.* v. *Washington Tp.*, (L 36048-70; S.Ct., L.Div. Bergen Co., 1972); 131 N.J. Super 195 (L.Div. 1974); rev'd. in an unreported decision of the Appellate Division, 1975.
10. 67 N.J. at 186.
11. N.J.S.A. 40:55D-22.
12. *Oakwood at Madison* v. *Township of Madison*, 117 N.J. Super 11 (L. Div. 1971) on remand 128 N.J. Super. 439 (L. Div. 1974) currently on appeal before the Supreme Court A80/81-75 (A-52/53-74).
13. *Prime Feather and Down* v. *Zoning Bd. of Ad.*, *Tp. of Marlboro*, L-6843-73 P.W. (August 4 1976).
14. N.J.S.A. 55:14J-1 *et. seq.*

V
Implications of the Decision
Outside New Jersey

Mount Laurel, Economics, Morality And The Law

George Sternlieb

There are a number of ways to view the *Mount Laurel* decision. It can be described facetiously and we have heard comments along those lines—the lawyer's full-employment act, the planner's retirement act. Certainly it will generate new talents and approaches. Not the least of these will be the demand for the "slow-pitch planner"—the planning consultant who "happens" to be *very* methodical in preparing a master plan—for towns can now employ such a planner and thereby stall their responses to *Mount Laurel*. The immediate responses to *Mount Laurel* have been numerous, but rarely more positive than planning 100 units of housing for the elderly, while hiring the best firm of environmentalists one can find to prove that the area can not, or should not, support additional development. This is to view the response in the most narrow context. The kitchen middens of the nineteenth century are presented as rare archeological treasures, and aquifers lie dangerously underfoot. In a broader view, *Mount Laurel* is an artifact of our society, reflecting that society and telling us something of the shortcomings, capacities, fears, and desires of that society.

In this context I would suggest that *Mount Laurel* represents a monstrous failure of the legislative process and, obviously, of the democracy which is served by that process. Let me suggest the applicability of the Toynbee model of society's rise and fall. Toynbee suggests that societies rise as they meet challenges and surmount them. They stagnate or fall when they lack either challenges to meet, or the capacity to accommodate new challenges—to adapt to new realities. It seems to me in this context that *Mount Laurel* represents the failure of the broader society. The reason that the court had to voice a decision in this area is not because the judiciary is uniquely able to meet these specific problems. Rather the judiciary made this decision, as it has for a host of other very important social problems, by default of those who are normally responsible for meeting these kinds of problems—the people, the *demos*, as represented by the legislative organs. Regardless of the courts' substantive findings, I would suggest here that instead of criticizing the courts' involvement, one should sadly commend them for at least having the courage to respond to the vacuum. A vacuum, let me repeat, caused by the popular will to avoid problems. We are all liberal, we are all open for action—except in our own backyards, and the sum of all of our backyards is a universe of inertia which must face change.

How is this change to be administered? What are the new ground rules? Since *Mount Laurel* we have had the very interesting set of questions raised by the court in the *Madison Township* case. (Those eighteen questions somewhat remind one of Luther's posting his theses on the church door.) I have the feeling that long after *Mount Laurel* has drifted away to the more obscure reaches of dated casebooks, the subject matter of the eighteen questions will be with us. These questions are dedicated to issues of public policy and public implementation of policy. They are questions which are not, in my judgment, appropriate to judicial scrutiny within the present state of the planning practice and art form. They concern topics which ideally would have been researched in a series of legislative committee meetings. They are questions which in another government would have been at least raised, and possibly even researched by, the executive branch, and then turned over to the legislature for determination. But by default of this essential initiative, we end up with the courts acting essentially as arbitrators in a substantive vacuum. The parallel to the busing and school integration cases, I think, requires no elaboration. The situations are ones in which the court serves as conscience and the legislative elements as reactors—and not necessarily creative ones.

Let me turn very briefly to a couple of these issues. When one looks at the literature on determining a region, about the only thing available on housing is the FHA marketability study, which is based on periodic surveys taken to determine the commercial viability and mortgage feasibility of indentures in certain areas. The FHA's definition is a very simple one—a housing region is that region in which the housing units are mutually competitive. But this rule is far from adequate for many areas. In this collection of speeches and articles with its enlightening comments on regions, we have determined that region, for the moment, relates to journey-to-work. That's all well and good, but a remarkable number of Americans no longer journey to work.

Let me give you a case in point. The Center for Urban Policy Research has just finished a series of studies on rent control, and one of them was in Miami Beach. In the area of Miami Beach being studied, 95 percent of the people do not work. The determination of a vacancy rate, one of the questions raised by *Mount Laurel*, is made in terms of a certain region within certain geographic limits. But what limits? Most of the people in Miami Beach have emigrated from the north. They could have gone to Arizona, or to California, or to a retirement village in southern New Jersey. Is the vacancy-rate regional or national? Or, to put it in a much more limited context, the owners of luxury buildings in Miami Beach sought to be excluded from municipal rent-control. Most of the buildings are on Collins Avenue, bordering the ocean. Is the housing region to be Collins Avenue facing the ocean?

Let me turn to a broader context raised in the course of some work that the Center did on Mahwah, an affluent suburb in northern New Jersey by the New York State line. One piece of the town is cut off by a highway; on this piece sits a very large automobile assembly plant which generates substantial tax revenues to the great benefit of the community. Suit was brought against Mahwah and its neighbors, Saddle River, Upper Saddle River, and Ramsey, to alter their present, substantially large-lot, zoning pattern in order to permit a variety of different housing configurations to be built. Is there a diffference in the levels of housing responsibility between Mahwah, which has the ratable, and a neighborhood which has no commercial facilities—but is almost exclusively zoned for 3-½ acre minimum? In the course of this study, we examined the housing location patterns of 12,000 automobile workers in four different plants, three of them in New Jersey and one of them right across the border in New York State. Each sits in a very different pattern of zoning and housing availability. Yet, interestingly enough, the journey-to-work pattern is not very different. Thus our results would indicate that changing the zoning in and around Mahwah would not greatly change the journey-to-work pattern. This is because changing the zoning won't provide affordable housing.

In terms of the broad picture, I think the court may be well ahead of the legislature not merely because of equity considerations but also, perhaps unfortunately, because of the basic economic realities. From 1960 to 1970 the median rent level paid by Americans and median income made by all Americans were mismatched. The increases in renters' income exceeded the increases in rent. Similarly the income of homeowners grew faster than the price of their housing, based on the median price of all owner-occupied housing and the income of all owners. Sometime around 1970 this changed drastically. Let us turn to figures for the northeast for the moment. (Unfortunately there is no data for New Jersey *per se*, but presumably they would not differ much from the northeast's data generally.) A very sudden and a very sharp imbalance is opening up. Based on the rent paid by everybody living in the northeast and the income of renters, as well as the owner-stated value of all one-family houses, once again you find a very sharp and abrupt gap opening in contrast to the change in income in the three years after 1970. I ended the period in 1973 in order to show that this pattern evolved before the energy business and before the recession hit really hard. The median rent and the median value of one-family housing increased approximately 30 and 38 percent, respectively. During the same three-year period, however, the income of renters and homeowners increased roughly 15 percent. The results of this are evident. An increasing proportion of Americans cannot afford housing whether it be rental housing or one-family housing. And this basic economic reality will ultimately determine the public reaction to *Mount Laurel*. In the shorter run, there are some disturbing questions that must be raised, however. Key among them is the supposed link between zoning and housing costs.

The national data on land reveals a very interesting phenomenon—the median lot size of new housing built in the United States from 1970 to 1973 dropped by slightly more than 20 percent. The value of the lots, however, went up 25 percent. Should our concern be zoning or the cost per buildable lot? The two are not necessarily hitched together. In addition, "making land available" for housing is at best a limited tool. We must face up to the whole web of costs that go into housing: interest for construction and permanent financing, materials, labor, and the like. Changes within zoning patterns may be far less important than subdivision controls, and even the sum of these changes, though they may facilitate new starts, will not generate the millenium.

A study on zoning and housing costs conducted by the Center several years ago examined 153 tract developments with fifty units or more in New Jersey. The developments, which contained 529 house models, either had been completed or were for sale at the time of the study. The study analyzed the scale of the builder's operation, the socio-economic characteristics of the community, the lot size, setback frontage, sewerage requirements, sidewalks—every element that could be nailed down.

Several findings came through. One, and perhaps the most rigorous, was that if you reduced lot size and you reduced the size of the house being built, and you reduced the building requirements, and you speeded up the enormous and very costly lags such as filing times—all at an optimum level—you achieved significant price reductions. Yet the vast bulk of New Jerseyans would still not be able to afford one-family housing. And that was before the influence of increased energy costs. What is clearly required, therefore, is a quantum drop in the standards of construction and the quality of housing that Americans have grown to believe is their right. They can't afford it. They could not afford it before *Mount Laurel*. They will not be able to afford it after *Mount Laurel*. We are presiding over a decline in the real housing standard of Americans. And, let me repeat, these data do not include energy changes or the effects of the recession.

Let me turn for the moment to the recession. In New Jersey we have largely had the attitude, to some degree justified by historic fact, that there were a whole host of growth elements hammering at our walls. We therefore could erect the walls higher and higher, making the admission requirements more and more costly, so that only the elite of the besiegers could climb over. Even with these barriers, there were enough buyers to take care of the building trades, the land speculators, and basic growth. General growth made up for and supported the cost of our land use patterns. Now, however, our state is lagging behind the national economy by roughly 50 percent. It sits in a region which is also lagging behind the national economy by nearly the same percentage. One of the major questions New Jersey must now ask is very simply: is that a bump in the road, a temporary deviation from upwards and onwards? Or does it indicate a new direction rendering obsolete the generalizations, the platitudes about our future?

State planning commissions used to consume their limited resources on grandiose studies—such as New Jersey's with projected populations of 10 million, or 20 million—and go around the state with colored charts indicating "My God, look what it's going to look like." But those days are probably over. We are still attempting to deal with center city versus suburbs, and the flight of jobs from center city to suburbs. But the much more crucial problem is the flow of jobs out of the region to rival areas. Houston's development as the energy capital, for example, or Washington, D.C.'s development as the imperial city, immediately threatens the future of those who live and those who own things in New

Jersey. Up to some twenty years ago, Washington was a sleepy southern town which came to life like Sleeping Beauty the few months a year that Congress kissed its brow. Otherwise there was nothing there. New York was the imperial city; it said so, and it was. Those who wanted to do business came to New York. But now the federal government spends about 30 percent of the gross national product and Washington is where the vast bulk of who gets what is determined. So if you have a trade association, if you represent major industry, if you're a law firm, you go to Washington not New York. And New York's decline affects New Jersey's growth. New Jerseyans have commonly assumed that because most New Jerseyans both live and work in the state, their former dependence on the vitality of New York, or for that matter of Philadelphia, was fading. I have been guilty of the same generalization. Now I think there is fairly clean-cut evidence that we are all going to sink together. And we are going to sink. The outward movement of blue collar jobs and a variety of paper-handling jobs leave only the great growth of service employment. But service employment requires the presence of somebody to pay for the service, and when those somebodies don't exist in your region, the services must also atrophy.

The decline of the major urban nodes of New York and Philadelphia initially generates a spurious demand for facilities which are proximate to the *urbs* yet removed from their attendant crudities. I say "spurious" because it is probably transient. Hoboken would hardly flourish, nor would stock-market traders come to New Jersey, if there wereno New York City.

The great pressures for land development in New Jersey, the unquestioned vitality of just a little while ago are undoubtedly muted. But the mill of the courts grinds on. New Jersey courts with greater or lesser degrees of competency, are filling the role that a state government, if we had one, would be occupying. Now, the *reason* for the courts' actions will probably bear little relation to the results of *Mount Laurel*. The poor, and increasingly those of moderate income, will continue to be housed for the next several years as they have been historically—in hand-me-downs. Without deep and widespread subsidies, *Mount Laurel* will enrich many landholders while making it possible to accommodate more of the middle class. The latter is certainly far from a trivial award. Indeed, the most efficient way to house families of limited means is to rehouse the over-facilitated elderly, those living in large-scale units by default of any other reasonable choice. And *Mount Laurel* has begun to generate these kinds of alternatives. But to say that the scope of judicial remedies is limited is far from saying that it is trivial. Our problem is how to make this state once again fit and ready for a variety of growth, and I think *Mount Laurel* shows a great intuitive grasp of this problem.

The future of governmental initiatives follows several parallel streams. One of them is the enormous potency of the A95 review requirement. The language of A95 gives the review agency a competency Congress was unable to give metropolitan planning or statewide planning agencies *per se*. It packages all the goodies—the water, the sewerage, just about all the lump forms of federal subsidy—and sets up an agency with sign-off powers that have great potential leverage. Basically before any of these goodies are given out the agency must make sure that the ultimate recipient is flying right on a variety of grounds. And one of those grounds is housing allocation.

Presently the enforcement elements and detailed scrutiny are limited in practice. But though I am no student of administrative process and administrative reality, let me suggest that this kind of administrative reality, this kind of juggernaut-moving can lead to things undreamed of by its original sponsors. This month (November, 1975) two major New Jersey counties came to the Center to ask for preparation of the housing-need and fair-share component required by their HAP filing. Yet if any of the county planning officers had, until recently, uttered the term "fair-share" without a sneer, he probably would have gotten fired.

So the wheels are turning. The problems of getting them to turn responsively are enormous. We are dealing now with a new generation of Americans—Americans who are much more scared of losing what they've got than of gaining anything new. There is an old saying among crapshooters—and it has considerable wisdom—that scared money never wins. An enormous degree of political backlash is a serious problem.

A perceived threat to territoriality can cause the discontinuance of housing subsidy approaches that make it feasible. Certainly much of the decline in the funding of public housing is caused by scattered-site requirements. A requirement to house low- and moderate-income families might well generate an equivalent response. The demographics, however, and the basic imbalance between income for housing and the costs of housing—the latter in part a function of present land use regulation—are enormously potent.

The term "housing"—a simple seven-letter word—was a powerful political phrase during the latter part of the forties and the fifties. It took a brave man indeed to be against it. But sometime in the sixties, that same seven-letter word became politically reprehensible—"my tax rate," "those people moving in here," and the like. It will shift again, however. We are now developing a broad-based constituency that needs housing, that wants to buy housing, and that cannot find housing.

It is uniquely incumbent upon our society, a materialistic society, to deliver the goods—that's what we do best. Capitalism is not lovable, but it has been productive. For the sake of this productivity it cannot long tolerate keeping out the prospective buyer. It can do so when those prospective buyers are a small minority, or when they are an ethnic group singled out by society. But it really can't do it when these prospective buyers represent the broad masses of society as a whole. So I think *Mount Laurel* is here to stay.

Inclusionary Programs
and the
Larger Public Interest

Herbert Franklin,
David Falk,
and Arthur J. Levin

Most of the vast literature in the field of exclusionary land use is addressed to the extraterritorial or metropolitan problems caused by local exclusionary policies rather than to the problems experienced by exclusionary jurisdictions themselves. Accordingly, the benefits to be gained from an inclusionary policy are usually spelled out in regional or metropolitan terms.

The idea that a better distribution of lower income housing in metropolitan areas will help to ameliorate problems of poor housing, urban education, and the like are supported by reports from many national commissions, such as the 1968 National Commission on Urban Problems (the "Douglas Commission"), the 1968 President Committee on Urban Housing (the "Kaiser Committee"), the 1968 Report of the National Advisory Commission on Civil Disorders, and other groups. The American Society of Planning Officials has asserted, for example, that a balanced housing supply is an important condition for improved community planning and growth. The American Institute of Planners has set forth professional guidelines, adopted in 1972, which includes a statement that the planner as part of his professional responsibilities must urge the alteration of policies, institutions and decisions that militate against expanded choice and opportunities for disadvantaged persons.

There is extensive literature analyzing metropolitan housing and land use problems but relatively scanty literature evaluating affirmative efforts to deal with them. The policymaker thus has a large volume of literature and reports that uniformly agree on the desirability of assuring that local policies address regional needs. Any local legislation that acts on these premises will thus be founded on a unanimous body of opinion that supports such affirmative action to improve the general welfare of all citizens. This part outlines these larger public interest considerations, and describes certain changes in national policy, as embodied in federal housing and community development legislation, that impose inclusionary responsibilities on localities as a condition of eligibility for federal community development subsidies and, in addition, evaluates two state approaches that have attempted to achieve them and as to which there is some analysis in the literature at this date.

Inclusionary Programs and Metropolitan Benefits

BETTER ACCESS TO EXPANDING JOB OPPORTUNITIES FOR LOWER INCOME WORKERS

A major theme common to all literature on the subject is that opening suburban housing opportunities for lower income workers would enable them to gain better access to expanding job opportunities in such locations.[1] The extent to which jobs open to lower income workers have increased in suburban areas in relation to central city areas has received greater attention in the New York and Washington metropolitan areas than elsewhere.[2] The U.S. Civil Rights Commission has also documented the negative impact of the suburbanization of federal employment in the Washington, D.C. area on minority employment opportunities.[3] Other studies, not limited to given metropolitan areas, suggest that it is possible to exaggerate the extent to which the exodus of lower income employment opportunities is a universal phenomenon that is bound to continue at past rates.[4]

In any event, promoting housing in the suburbs as a means of enhancing job accessibility for lower income workers does not appear to be a policy susceptible of "fine tuning" unless industrial employers build housing for their workers. Simply increasing incrementally the supply of lower income housing provides no assurance that such housing would be occupied by persons who are newly employed nearby and who moved from a previous central city location. Only a vast increase of the supply could in practice work effectively in this direction. If lower income housing opportunities are developed at a modest scale in urbanizing jurisdictions, it seems far more likely that such housing will be occupied primarily by lower income households already in or near the jurisdiction who now reside in inadequate housing, or that such housing will be occupied by moderate income persons familiar with the jurisdiction because they already are employed there.

Virtually every commentator on this subject has nevertheless drawn a connection between the need for lower income housing in suburban and urbanizing jurisdictions and the plight of the central city worker faced with the out-migration of job opportunities. The basis for this linkage has been the impact on minorities of *job relocation* to the suburbs. In the Washington metropolitan area, the out-migration of governmental jobs has led to the documented loss of the existing jobs to low-income, central city minorities. For example, between February and July 1966, the National Bureau of Standards facilities were moved from the District of Columbia to a new location in Gaithersburg, Maryland. This relocation was the subject of a report prepared for the United States Commission on Civil Rights.[5] The report showed the relocation to have caused a large shift in the residence of white employees to the Gaithersburg area without comparable shifts in the black sector of the work force. This disparity the report attributes to the inaccessibility of the job site to blacks rather than a desire on their part to remain in former residential locations.

The job/housing matching concept has led some commentators to suggest an economic self-interest to support a local inclusionary land use policy on the part of new growth areas. They question whether a jurisdiction will be able to attract tax base-enhancing manufacturing firms if the "blue collar" workforce cannot live close enough to such work places to avoid costly journey to work expenditures.[6] Conceivably this separation of the home from the work place can even affect the ability of a suburban government itself to attract public employees—e.g., fire and police personnel and teachers—if people in these wage brackets are not able to live close enough to their places of work to avoid excessive transportation costs. In sum, this reasoning asserts that a recognition of the actual needs of business and local government should enter into the planning for future growth by assuring that the potential workforce should be able to reach the work place conveniently. If a preponderant majority of the net new jobs created in the United States continues to be located in the nation's suburbs, as seems likely, it is conceivable that a sizeable locality providing a more balanced housing supply may succeed in attracting a better industrial or commercial tax base than its exclusionary neighbors. A locality, of course, does not have to wait until empirical data show that it has lost out to competing jurisdictions before it takes corrective action. Consequently, local legislation could adopt inclusionary goals as a means of competing for a better tax base and a competent public work force even in the absence of any convincing empirical data on this point.

In terms of the racial impact of suburban job location, some commentators have suggested that the location by an employer of the work place in an area that is inaccessible to minority personnel may constitute a violation of Title VII of the Civil Rights Act of 1964 because the employer is in effect offering jobs to relatively nearby potential white workers on terms and conditions differing from those offered more distant minority persons.[7] In 1972 Title VII was amended to apply to the employment practices of local government,[8] thus raising the same issue with respect to whether a locality violates the Act if its land use policies in effect prevent minorities from convenient access to its workforce.

It should also be noted that federal housing and community development legislation described later in this Part adopts the principle that localities should provide a supply of housing adequate to meet the needs of those employed or anticipated to be employed in the locality. There is no indication, however, that this principle would involve any effort to match the occupants of such housing to jobs in the locality.

What, then, is the relevance to the policy-maker of the job/housing linkage? The strongest potential link exists in the case of central city-based industry that seeks a suburban location. Here a case can be made that the relocation of such jobs to an area without an adequate lower income housing supply can have a disadvantageous impact on lower income and minority workers; but the corrective action would involve preventing the relocation, not in developing the housing (unless it is company-owned and managed and limited to employees). In any other context the job/housing link emerges as a generally accepted urban planning principle that the work place and the home should be physically closer as metropolitan development proceeds, in the hope that this will improve job accessibility and reduce long commuting costs and time in the long run. It also appears to be aimed at achieving a rough tax base equity objective: that is, that a locality with the presumed benefits of a commercial and industrial tax base ought to house, and provide the requisite urban services for, the workers in such employment centers. In addition, with public policy possibly moving in the direction of trying to limit vehicle miles travelled in order to reduce gasoline consumption and air pollution, a local policy of linking jobs and housing through land use regulation may draw on these bases for support. But this connection does not appear to be developed in the literature.

In summary, then, any local legislative effort intended to increase the supply of low- and moderate-income housing in suburban locations is consistent with the universal view of commentators that such an objective is desirable. The mismatch between the location of housing and employment opportunities under prevailing urban development patterns has given rise to federal legislation described later in this Part. In the absence of some mechanism that assigns occupancy of housing to families on the basis of where the primary wage-earner works, such an objective must be regarded as a general, overall urban planning, environmental and social equity goal rather than an effective tool for reducing unemployment or underemployment.

HIGHER QUALITY SCHOOLING FOR DISADVANTAGED CENTRAL CITY CHILDREN

Some of the literature emphasizes that the flight of white (and increasingly black) middle class households from the central city will leave lower income minority children in the central city dependent on reduced financial resources for public education and a racially segregated educational environment. The U.S. Supreme Court has not accepted the argument that disparities in educational expenditures between affluent and poor districts constitutes a denial of equal protection of the law under the U.S. Constitution.[9] And in its recent opinion in *Milliken v. Bradley*[10] the Court, by the same 5-4 majority, has ruled that ordering busing across central city/suburban school district lines to desegregate a central city school system is not permissible except in extraordinary circumstances even though the diminishing number of white students in the central city system may mean that a remedy limited to the central city would not accomplish desegregation.

To the dissenters in *Milliken*, the majority decision was, in the opinion by Justice Marshall, "more a reflection of a perceived public mood . . . than it is the product of neutral principles of law. In the short run, it may seem to be the easier course to allow our great metropolitan areas to be divided up into two cities—one white, the other black—but it is a course, I predict, our people will ultimately regret."[11]

In a separate concurring opinion, Justice Stewart, whose vote makes a majority on either side, noted that the decision was based on practical considerations of framing effective relief rather than a question of substantive constitutional law. An interdistrict remedy, he observed, may be proper and necessary in other factual situations. "Were it to be shown, for example, that state officials had contributed to the separation of the races . . . by purposeful, racially discriminatory use of state housing or zoning laws, then a decree calling for transfer of pupils across district lines or for restructuring of district lines might well be appropriate." [12]

The likelihood of any litigant being able to show that housing and zoning laws have been used *purposefully*, as indicated in Part I, is not high. Nevertheless, the interrelation between housing and zoning policies and the desegregation goals in public education are recognized in this key opinion. An inclusionary land use policy can therefore be legislatively premised on a state's constitutional obligation to assure equal educational opportunity.

ACHIEVING QUANTITATIVE GOALS FOR NEWLY-CONSTRUCTED LOWER INCOME HOUSING

Vacant land for low- and moderate-income housing in central cities is generally far more expensive than vacant land in outlying locations. Moreover, suitable vacant land in central city locations is harder to find without costly acquisition and clearance for redevelopment. It is also likely that less land will be made available for low- and moderate-income housing construction under the provisions of recently enacted federal housing and community development legislation (see Emerging National Inclusionary Policies, which follows), which generally calls for the dispersal of central city concentrations of low-income people.

Although federal legislation has veered away from its earlier emphasis of new construction as the primary means for meeting national housing goals, it is apparent that most metropolitan areas will simply not be able to meet minimal needs for new low- and moderate-income housing without significant use of suburban land.[13]

An inclusionary land use program can be legislatively premised, therefore, on meeting quantitive needs for such housing in the state, region and locality without reference to appropriate distribution of such housing in a region. In other words, a locality can move forward on an inclusionary program with adequate general welfare premises even in the absence of a fair share plan as described in Part V.

SOCIAL HETEROGENEITY AS A BASIC VALUE

Another theme frequently found in the literature is that a policy of inclusion serves a basic societal value in preventing cultural and class divisions by permitting people of diverse backgrounds to live and work together.[14] This goal is not one that can be proved or disproved as feasible or infeasible, efficient or inefficient. If this value is accepted, the allocation of land to permit a wide spectrum of persons to live in the community is a matter of equity, something that should be done because it is "right."

This value concerns classifications of racial as well as economic groups. The values inherent in racial heterogeneity are exemplified by a recent ruling of the U.S. Supreme Court; the social value of economic heterogeneity is adopted by recent federal housing and community legislation. In the case of *Trafficante v. Metropolitan Life Insurance Company*,[15] two tenants of an apartment complex filed complaints with the Secretary of Housing and Urban Development alleging that their landlord discriminated against nonwhites, thereby depriving the plaintiffs of the social benefits of living in an integrated community, causing them to miss business and professional advantages that would have accrued from living with members of minority groups, and stigmatizing them as residents of a "white ghetto." A lower court had held that the complaining tenants were not within the class of persons entitled to sue for relief under the Civil Rights Act of 1968. The Supreme Court reversed, and in its opinion recognized that "The alleged injury to existing tenants by exclusion of minority persons from the apartment complex is the loss of important benefits from interracial associations." In this case, the Court noted, the Civil Rights Act of 1968 protects "not only those against whom a discrimination is directed but also those whose complaint is that the manner of managing a housing development affects 'the very quality of their daily lives'."[16]

As described later in this Part, congressional findings that led to the enactment of the Housing and Community Development Act of 1974 included, for the first time, specific language on the desirability of opening up housing opportunities for persons of lower income. Localities are asked, moreover, to prepare housing assistance plans to implement this objective.

A distinction has been noted in the literature between homogeneity on the neighborhood scale and homogeneity on the scale of the entire community, so that space for lower income housing may achieve municipal heterogeneity but not necessarily socioeconomic mixing at the neighborhood level. (See Part IV.) In theory, the general objective of opening up suburban housing opportunities to lower income households may be independent of striving for heterogeneity within neighborhoods.

The new federal housing assistance program appears to adopt the goal of encouraging economic heterogeneity at the project scale. The purpose of the new leased housing program, enacted in 1974 and described later in this Part, is described as aiding lower income families in obtaining a decent place to live and of promoting economically mixed housing.

MAKING POSSIBLE THE IMPROVEMENT OF
ADVERSE CONDITIONS IN THE CENTRAL CITY AREAS

The thesis here is that conditions in racially concentrated areas of the central city ghetto are closely linked to events in the outlying parts in the same metropolitan areas, and that no strategies for improving central city conditions will work in the long run without opening up the suburbs to low- and moderate-income households.[17] This theory proceeds logically as follows: for central cities to recapture the middle class will require renovation of many residential areas, displacing poor households now living there and these households will move either into adjacent neighborhoods or take advantage of subsidized housing dispersed throughout the metropolitan area. Their movement into adjacent neighborhoods in large numbers may initiate deterioration, which means that dispersal strategies are essential to rebuilding the central city. In a few decisions, courts have evaluated density allowances or restrictions on the basis of whether they made possible the alleviation of undue concentrations of population *elsewhere*, a principle that would support a local inclusionary program.[18]

Virtually every legal and planning commentary on the question of exclusionary land use controls agrees implicitly or explicitly with this thesis of suburban-central city interrelationships. The rulings of federal courts with respect to the operation of the federal housing subsidies also implicitly or explicitly accept this thesis, as do some state courts in articulating zoning principles. And Congress, in enacting the Housing and Community Development Act of 1974, apparently accepted the thesis when it adopted the goals of the legislation as explained below.

Consequently, the adoption of an inclusionary land use policy by a locality can serve generally recognized vital large public interests of importance to the state, which interests are compatible with the narrower interests of the locality. The existence of a regional housing allocation plan, as described in Part V, enables a locality to adopt inclusionary objectives in the knowledge that it is not taking all metropolitan problems on its own shoulders. If a locality adopts an inclusionary land use policy but its neighbors do not do so, it can protect itself from carrying more than its "fair share" of needed residential growth by merely assuming that its neighbors will meet a regional standard.

Emerging National Inclusionary Policies

The federal Housing and Community Development Act of 1974 (Public Law 93-383) (hereinafter referred to as the 1974 Act) became effective August 22, 1974.[19] This Act substantially restructures federal housing and community development assistance in ways that could threaten exclusionary localities with the loss of community development grants. At the same time, it gives communities new flexibility and new responsibility in carrying out housing and community development programs.

COMMUNITY DEVELOPMENT POLICY

Community Development Grants. The 1974 Act creates a new system, beginning January 1, 1975, of 100% formula-allocated block grants to local communities to replace previous categorical grants that required local contributions. The former categories are now merged into a new community development (CD) program grant, thereby allowing great flexibility to localities in determining the specific purposes of federally funded CD programs. The 1974 Act also greatly expands eligible purposes beyond the old categorical purposes.

Eligible activities under a "Community Development Program" may include:

> "(1) the acquisition of real property which is (A) blighted, deteriorated, deteriorating, undeveloped, or inappropriately developed from the standpoint of sound community development and growth; (B) appropriate for rehabilitation or conservation activities; (C) appropriate for the preservation or restoration of historic sites, the beautification of urban land, the conservation of open spaces, natural resources, and scenic areas, the provision of recreational opportunities, or the guidance of urban development; (D) to be used for the provision of public works, facilities, and improvements eligible for assistance under this title; or (E) to be used for other public purposes;" (Section 105(a)(1)).[20]

This greatly expands the authority under federal legislation for land acquisition of undeveloped or inappropriately developed land or acquisiton of land for the "guidance of urban development" or "for other public purposes." These and other provisions move federal community development grants some distance beyond their original connection with the removal of blighted conditions in built-up areas, and provide a potential resource for the advance acquisition of sites for lower income housing, among other public purposes (see Part VI).

In addition, federal CD grants may be used for the:

> "acquisition, construction, reconstruction, or installation of public works, facilities, and site or other improvements—including neighborhood facilities, senior centers, historic properties utilities, streets, street lights, water and sewer facilities, foundations and platforms for air rights sites, pedestrian malls and walkways, and parks, playgrounds, and recreation facilities, flood and drainage facilities in cases where assistance for such facilities under other Federal laws or programs is determined to be unavailable and parking facilities, solid waste disposal facilities, and fire-protection services and facilities which are located in or which serve designated community development areas;" (Section 105(a)(2)).[21]

The same section permits grants to be used for code enforcement, clearance and rehabilitation of buildings and improvements, historic preservation, provision of public services necessary to support other community development activities (such as employment, economic development, crime prevention, child care, etc.), relocation payments, and activities necessary to develop more effective community development planning and management capacity.

City entitlements. Metropolitan cities and urban counties (counties with over 200,000 people in unincorporated areas and possessing community development powers) will be entitled to 100% grants according to a system based on the higher of (1) their formula amount (population, poverty weighted twice, and housing overcrowding) or (2) their "hold harmless" amount, keyed to past program experience. Communities that have received large amounts of federal money in past years under urban renewal and other programs will have full "hold harmless" protection for only three years under the program, and then will begin to phase into the same formula used by all other communities during the following three years. (Section 106.) [22] (A number of large cities ultimately may face substantial decreases in federal funds because of this provision.)

The 1974 Act makes discretionary grants available to non-entitlement communities, but they will be required to submit applications that are similar to those required of entitlement applicants. Such discretionary grants would not be based on formula, nor would they necessarily be for multi-year programs.

Housing assistance plan (HAP) requirements. Formula entitlement communities must apply annually for grants, and HUD must act on such applications within 75 days of receipt or the application will be approved automatically. The 1974 Act requires HUD to approve an application for metropolitan cities and urban counties unless the applicant's statement of community development need is "plainly inconsistent" with available information, the activities proposed are plainly inappropriate to meeting the needs and objectives identified by the community in its application, the application does not comply with the law, or the activities proposed are ineligible under the Act (Sections 104(c) and (f)). [23]

In the application the community must summarize a three-year community development plan, which identifies its needs and strategies for meeting them and specifies "both short- and long-term community development objectives which have been developed in accordance with areawide development planning." The application must formulate a program that includes the activities to be undertaken, together with their estimated costs and general location. The community must thus provide a three-year summary plan with a one-year application for funds specifying activities to be carried out. The most significant part of the application for purposes of this study is the required "housing assistance plan" that:

> 1. accurately surveys the condition of the housing stock in the community and assesses the housing assistance needs of lower-income persons (including elderly and handicapped persons, large families, and persons displaced or to be displaced) residing in *or expected to reside in the community*; [Emphasis supplied.]
>
> 2. specifies a realistic annual goal for the number of dwelling units or persons to be assisted, including (i) the relative proportion of new, rehabilitated, and existing dwelling units, and (ii) the sizes and types of housing projects and assistance best suited to the needs of lower-income persons in the community; and
>
> 3. indicates the general locations of proposed housing for lower-income persons, with the objective of (i) furthering the revitalization of the community, including the restoration and rehabilitation of stable neighborhoods to the maximum extent possible; (ii) *promoting greater choice of housing opportunities and avoiding undue concentrations of assisted persons in areas containing a high proportion of low-income persons;* and (iii) assuring the availability of public facilities and services adequate to serve proposed housing projects;" (Section 104(a)(4)).[24] [Emphasis supplied.]

The House-passed version of this bill, H.R. 15361, is the source of this "housing assistance plan" requirement in the applicant's community development plan, although the Senate bill, S. 3066, had directed HUD to make *housing* subsidies available "in general conformity" with the housing plans of the state and general unit of government. Unlike its House counterpart, however, the Senate bill did not define the contents of such "housing plans." The final conference bill adopted the more detailed House plan provision but made it a condition to eligibility for community development funds rather than to housing subsidies. Under the 1974 Act, it is the only substantive portion of the community development grant application that may not be waived by HUD, thus emphasizing its importance. (Section 104(b)(3)).[25] The authoritative legislative history in this regard is therefore the report of the House Committee on Banking and Currency.

The House Committee report points out that the HAP requirement has an "open community" feature in regard to a locality's relationship to the region, as well as a dispersal feature in regard to the location of assisted housing within a community:

> "The committee wishes to emphasize that the bill requires communities, in assessing their housing needs, to look beyond the needs of their residents to those who can be expected to reside in the community as well. Clearly, those already employed in the community can be

expected to reside there. Normally, estimates of those expected to re-side in a particular community would be based on employment data generally available to the community and to HUD. However, in many cases, communities should be able to take into account planned employment facilities as well, and their housing assistance plans should reflect the additional housing needs that will result . . . "

*   *   *

[The opportunity for communities to make their own judgments is an extremely important innovation in federal housing policy with regard to] "the bill's requirement that housing assistance plans indicate the general locations of proposed assisted housing in the community. This long-overdue requirement recognizes that the location of housing is an integral part of a community's overall physical development plan; that only if local elected officials make location decisions will they be able to coordinate the location of new housing with existing or planned public facilities and services; and that a major objective of such location deci-sions must be the promotion of greater choice of housing opportunities and the avoidance of undue concentrations of lower income per-sons." [26]

The HAP requirement must be read in conjunction with basic legisla-tive findings in the preamble to the 1974 Act.

The first finding of the 1974 Act recites that:

"the Nation's cities, towns, and smaller urban communities face critical social, economic, and environmental problems arising in significant measure from—(1) the growth of population in metropolitan and other urban areas, and the *concentration of persons of lower income in the central cities* . . . " (Section 101(a)(1)) [27] [Emphasis supplied.]

The 1974 Act further indicates that its primary objective:

"is the development of viable urban communities by providing decent housing and a suitable environment and expanding economic oppor-tunities, principally for persons of low and moderate income. Consis-tent with this primary objective, the federal assistance provided in this title is for the support of community development activities which are directed toward the following specific objectives—

*   *   *

"*the reduction of the isolation of income groups within communities and geographical areas* and the promotion of an increase in the diver-sity and vitality of neighborhoods through the *spatial deconcentration of housing opportunities for persons of lower income* and the revitaliza-tion of deteriorating or deteriorated neighborhoods to attract persons of higher income." (Section 101(c)(6)) [28] [Emphasis supplied.]

This marks the first time that congressional findings have been directed to the problem of economic as well as racial segregation.

The passage of this provision by the Congress makes highly relevant the recommendations in the literature (see Part III-C) regarding the need for a local policy statement on inclusionary land use programs. In that Part it is suggested, based on the implications of some literature, that the local legislative body should formulate and formally adopt a statement of policy to guide the application of an inclusionary land use program. Such a policy statement is in many respects similar to the federally required HAP, but it goes beyond the HAP by declaring an intention to encourage needed housing by revision of local codes to permit greater flexibility in housing type and to reduce costs, and an outline of the locality's plans to adopt the land use regulatory techniques discussed in Part IV.

Benefits for low- and moderate-income families. The Senate bill had prohibited more than 20% of an applicant's community development funds from being used for activities not directly or significantly benefiting low- and moderate-income families or blighted areas. The 1974 Act contains in place of this provision, a requirement that the applicant "certify" to HUD's satisfaction that:

> "its Community Development Program has been developed so as to give maximum feasible priority to activities which will benefit low- or moderate-income families or aid in the prevention or elimination of slums or blight." (Section 104(b)(2)).[29]

Nondiscrimination. The 1974 Act includes a provision prohibiting discrimination on the basis of race, color, national origin or sex in carrying out community development programs (Section 109).[30]

Federal review of performance and remedies. In return for reduced federal review of applications and program activities, HUD is given authority to conduct a post-performance review of local programs at least annually and to adjust (or terminate) funding where the program carried out was not that substantially described in the application, the program did not conform "to the requirements of this bill and other applicable laws" or the recipient does not have the continuing capacity to carry out the program in a timely manner (Section 104(d), Section 111).[31]

The remedies for noncompliance enable HUD to terminate, reduce, or limit the use of payments to any locality after a finding, based on notice and opportunity for hearing afforded the affected locality. A locality that has been the subject of such a finding and administrative remedy may within sixty days contest the action in a U.S. Court of Appeals. The court may affirm or modify the administrative action and may order additional evidence taken (Section 111).[32]

Except in cases of serious misuse of funds, HUD would be likely to invoke these procedures only in the case of entitlement communities, which have a multi-year funding eligibility. Non-entitlement jurisdictions eligible for discretionary funding would theoretically be vulnerable only to having their subsequent applications for funding simply rejected on the basis of unsatisfactory performance on earlier HUD-funded CD activities; and this formal procedure would probably not apply.

Regional review of applications. The 1974 Act provides for review by an "A-95" regional agency of applications for community development grant assistance (Section 104(e)).[33] Thus, the statements of housing needs and the "realistic annual goals" for housing assistance required of the local HAP could be the subject of comment by a regional agency on the basis of a previous "fair share" allocation formula. It should be noted, however, that this would be regional review of an overall local housing and community development plan rather than review of specific community development project activities in view of the elimination of categorical community development programs. In theory, review and comment on a local HAP could provide facts to establish whether such a plan is "plainly inconsistent" with real needs of the region and whether the "general locations" proposed by the locality for assisted housing meet the statutory purpose of avoiding concentrations of low-income people.

NEW POLICIES GOVERNING SUBSIDIZED HOUSING

The new Act revises the law governing the low-rent public housing program and authorizes a new lower income housing assistance program. Among the many changes from prior law the following are most relevant:

Local disapproval option. For all subsidized housing programs a new local disapproval option is provided by Section 213.[34] Within 10 days after receipt of an application for housing subsidies HUD must notify the chief executive of the local government of the application. The local government has 30 days from such notification to indicate its disapproval to HUD on the ground "that the proposed housing is inconsistent" with the HAP that each locality must file to obtain community development funds.

HUD can agree with the locality, or can approve the application if it finds that the project is consistent with the local plan; this decision must be made within 30 days of the receipt of an objection. In the absence of a formal local objection within the 30 days, HUD has an additional 30 days on its own to disapprove an application on grounds of inconsistency with the local plan. HUD may also ask a locality that does not have a HAP (e.g., a nonentitlement locality or one that does not wish to have CD funds) to comment on a proposed project. Projects of less than 13 units in HUD-assisted new communities or assisted by state housing agency loans are exempted from the local approval requirement. In the case of state-assisted projects, however, the locality in its HAP can make that exemption inapplicable to the community.

Allocation of housing subsidies. The Act establishes, for the first time, a need-related allocation of housing subsidies on a nationwide basis. HUD is required, so far as practicable, to "consider the relative needs of different areas and communities as reflected in data as to population, poverty, housing overcrowding, housing vacancies, amount of substandard housing" in allocating subsidies. The Act limits nonmetropolitan areas to not less than 20 percent or more than 25 percent of the total amount of assistance (Section 213(d)(1)).[35]

Regulations under Title I of the Act provide that HUD will advise applicants, on request, of housing assistance resources available prior to submission of the HAP by the locality. (24 C.F.R. §570.303(c)(d).) HUD regulations under Title II of the 1974 Act, governing housing assistance payments for new constructions projects, provide that HUD shall, after considering the content of any local HAP, determine the number and types of units to be made available for new construction and substantial rehabilitation in any given geographical area. (24 C.F.R. §1273.201-2.) Moreover, such regulations also state that new construction projects shall be permitted only where HUD determines that there is not likely soon to be an adequate supply of *existing* housing to meet the needs of eligible families. (24 C.F.R. §1273.103.)

The manner in which HUD implements this provision may have serious impact on the extent to which a locality with vacant developable land may be able to carry out a significant inclusionary program. Such a locality may find that available housing subsidies are quite limited because of HUD allocations to build up central city portions of metropolitan areas. Whether such HUD allocations will be affected by regional housing allocation plans (see Part V) remains to be seen.

LOWER INCOME HOUSING ASSISTANCE PROGRAM

The 1974 Act authorizes a new lower income housing assistance program to be implemented not later than January 1, 1975. The new program authority replaces existing authority for assistance with respect to low-income housing in private accommodations. Major features of the new program (contained in Section 8 of the revised U.S. Housing Act of 1937)[36] are as follows:

> 1. Assistance will be provided on behalf of eligible families occupying new, substantially rehabilitated, or existing rental units through assistance payments contracts with owners (who may be private owners, cooperatives, or public housing agencies, which are broadly defined to

include agencies assisting in the development or operation of low-income housing as well as those directly engaged in such activities).

2. Eligible families are those who, at the time of initial renting of units, have total annual family incomes not in excess of 80 percent of area median income, with adjustments for smaller and larger families, and other variations necessary because of prevailing levels of construction costs, unusually high or low family incomes, or other factors. At least 30 percent of the families assisted by HUD on a national basis must be families with gross incomes not in excess of 50 percent of area median income, subject to adjustment by HUD.

3. Major responsibility for program administration is vested in HUD, which can contract directly with owners or prospective owners (which may be public housing agencies) who agree to construct or substantially rehabilitate housing.

4. Assistance payments contracts will specify the maximum monthly rent that may be charged for each assisted unit. Maximum rents generally may not exceed by more than 10 percent a fair market rent established by HUD at least annually for existing or newly constructed rental units of various sizes and types suitable for occupancy by eligible families. (Higher rents necessary to implement an approved HAP may be permitted.)

5. The amount of assistance provided with respect to a unit will be an amount equal to the difference between the established maximum rent for the unit and the occupant family's required contribution to rent. Aided families will be required to contribute not less than 15 nor more than 25 percent of their total family income to rent. Maximum rent levels will be adjusted annually or more frequently, as necessary.

6. Up to 100 percent of the units in a structure may be assisted, upon application of the owner or prospective owner, but in cases involving projects containing more than 50 units that are designed for use primarily by nonelderly and nonhandicapped persons HUD may give preference to projects involving not more than 20 percent assisted units. This "preference" is accorded, under the 1974 Act, only among applications received during 60-day periods, thus perhaps inducing a "bunching effect" with respect to project reviews (see 9 below).

7. Assistance payments for any unit may run for a minimum period of one month and for the following maximum periods: in the case of existing units, payments may be made for as long as 180 months (15 years). In the case of new or substantially rehabilitated units, payments may be made for up to 240 months (20 years), except that if the project is owned by, or financed by a loan or loan guarantee from, a state or local agency, payments may run for as long as 480 months (40 years).

8. Owners of new or substantially rehabilitated assisted units will assume all ownership, management and maintenance responsibilities, including the selection of tenants and the termination of tenancy, but the owner may contract for such services with any entity, including a public housing agency, approved by HUD, for the performance of such responsibilities. Owners of existing units also will select tenants, but public housing agencies will have the sole right to give notice to vacate. Maintenance and replacement with respect to existing units will be in accordance with standard practice for the building concerned.

9. The proposed regulations governing the new construction program establish a processing procedure for housing subsidies. Under this procedure HUD will periodically invite preliminary proposals by number of units and geographical area. The invitation will include specific information, including relevant local HAPs. Developers are to respond with preliminary proposals, which are forwarded to the chief executive of the local government for 30-day review for consistency with the local HAP. In addition HUD will begin its preliminary evaluations and submit those proposals it deems acceptable to A-95 clearance (see Part V). (24 C.F.R. §1273.203-210.) What this means is that localities may be receiving several preliminary proposals at one time, and will be reviewing them concurrently. Presumably the HUD site criteria and the local HAP can be applied more rationally under this "bunching" of preliminary proposals than under past practice, when there was no assurance of where or when separate housing proposals might be made in the community.

NOTES

1. For a resume of such literature, see Rubinowitz, Leonard S., *Low-Income Housing: Suburban Strategies* (Ballinger Publishing Co., Cambridge, Mass., 1974).
2. *See*: National Committee Against Discrimination in Housing, *The Impact of Housing Patterns on Job Opportunities* (New York, NCDH, 1968); New York Regional Plan Association, *Linking Skills, Jobs and Housing in the New York Region* (N.Y.R.P.A., March, 1972).
3. U.S. Commission on Civil Rights, *Federal Installations and Equal Housing Opportunity* (Government Printing Office, 1970).
4. *See*: e.g., Harrison, B., *Urban Economic Development: Suburbanization, Minority Opportunity, and the Condition of the Central City* (The Urban Institute, Washington, D.C., 1974). One study suggests that a respectable absolute rate of job growth has been maintained in the central cities, with sufficient growth in semi-skilled and low-skilled jobs to accommodate the unemployed if, in fact, they had access to those jobs. Fremon, C., *The Occupational Patterns in Urban Employment Change, 1965-67* (The Urban Institute, Washington, D.C., 1970).
5. U.S. Commission on Civil Rights, *supra* note 3.
6. This thesis is developed most fully in Babcock, Richard F., & Bosselman, Fred P., *Exclusionary Zoning, Land Use Regulation and Housing in the 1970's* (Praeger Publishers, New York, 1973), ch. 3.
7. *Id.* ch. 3, note 15. See also Bellman, Richard, *Applicability of Employment Nondiscrimination Laws to Corporate Location and Relocation in Suburbia.* (National Committee Against Discrimination in Housing, Inc.) (undated (mimeo); Blumrosen, A., *The Duty to Plan for Fair Employment: Plant Location in White Suburbia*, 25 Rutgers Law Review 383 (1971).
8. P. L. 92-261, §2(1), amending 42 U.S.C. §2000e.
9. *Rodriguez* v. *San Antonio Independent School Dist.*, 411 U.S. 1 (1973).
10. *Milliken* v. *Bradley*, 41 L. Ed. 2d 1069 (1974).

11. 41 L. Ed. 2d at p. 1131.
12. 41 L. Ed. 2d at p. 1097.
13. This thesis is expounded in Downs, Anthony, *Opening Up the Suburbs, An Urban Strategy for America* (Yale U. Press, New Haven, 1973), at p. 36 ff.
14. Babcock & Bosselman, *supra* note 6, Rubinowitz, *supra* note 1, and Downs, *supra* note 13, all articulate this value.
15. 409 U.S. 205 (1972).
16. 409 U.S. at 211, quoting from *Shannon* v. *Department of Housing & Urban Development*, 436 F. 2d 809 (3rd Cir. 1970), at p. 818.
17. This is central to the Downs strategy, *supra* note 13.
18. *Id.* at pp. 129-30.
19. 42 U.S.C. §5301 *et. seq.* [Further references to the Act and regulations appear in the text.]
20. 42 U.S.C. §5305(a)(1).
21. 42 U.S.C. §5305(a)(2).
22. 42 U.S.C. §5306.
23. 42 U.S.C. §5304(c) and (f).
24. 42 U.S.C. §5304(a)(4).
25. 42 U.S.C. §5304(b)(3).
26. H. Rep. No. 93-1114 (93rd Cong. 2d Sess. 1974), at pp. 7-8.
27. 42 U.S.C. §5301(a)(1).
28. 42 U.S.C. §5301(c)(6).
29. 42 U.S.C. §5304(b)(4).
30. 42 U.S.C. §5309.
31. 42 U.S.C. § §5304(d), 5311.
32. 42 U.S.C. §5311.
33. 42 U.S.C. §5304(e).
34. 42 U.S.C. §1439.
35. 42 U.S.C. §1439(d)(1).
36. 42 U.S.C. §1437. The new "Section 8" program is found at 42 U.S.C. §1437f.

Exclusionary Zoning and Managed Growth: Some Unresolved Issues

Jerome G. Rose

Introduction

Legal scholars and planners have written at length on the subject of exclusionary zoning,[1] analyzing the exclusionary effect of large-lot zoning, multi-family dwelling prohibitions, bedroom restrictions, minimum floor space requirements, low income housing exclusions, building moratoria, refusals to provide municipal services, mobile home prohibitions and environmental impact impediments. Courts have responded to the problems raised by municipal exclusionary zoning techniques with a wide range of judicial solutions.[2] For example, in the most recent decision in this series, *Series Burlington County NAACP v. Township of Mount Laurel,*[3] the New Jersey Supreme Court sustained, with some modification, a lower court holding that a municipal zoning ordinance is invalid because it excludes people of low and moderate incomes.[4] In spite of the extensive scholarly comment and the many judicial decisions on the subject, a number of legal issues remain unresolved. Does the municipal zoning power include the authority to regulate (a) the rate of growth of the com-

317

munity, and (b) the social and economic composition of the population? Does the validity of a zoning ordinance depend upon its ability to accomodate population growth of a size and socioeconomic composition sufficient to meet regional needs? If so, how is that standard of validity to be defined? What is the appropriate role of the judiciary in resolving these issues? This article will examine these questions and will suggest directions in which solutions may lie.

The Municipal Zoning Power: Does it Encompass the Authority to Regulate the Rate of Growth of the Community or the Social and Economic Composition of the Population?

THE RATE OF GROWTH OF THE COMMUNITY

In order to determine whether the zoning power allows for regulation of a community's growth rate, it is necessary to first consider the scope of the typical zoning statute. Section 1 of the Standard State Zoning Enabling Act,[5] on which most state enabling legislation is based,[6] describes the zoning power as the authority

> to regulate and restrict the height, number of stories, and size of buildings and other structures, the percentage of lot that may be occupied, the size of yards, courts, and other open spaces, the density of population, and the location and use of buildings, structures, and land for trade, industry, residence, or other purposes.[7]

The authority to regulate, however, is not unchecked; the regulation must relate to the purposes of zoning. Under section 3 of the Standard Act, the purposes for which the zoning power may be exercised are expressly enumerated as follows:

> to lessen congestion in the streets; to secure safety from fire, panic, and other dangers; to promote health and the general welfare; to provide adequate light and air; to prevent the overcrowding of land; to avoid undue concentration of population; to facilitate the adequate provision of transportation, water, sewerage, schools, parks, and other public requirements . . . [8]

Notwithstanding this limitation, the essence of the zoning power, as described in the standard enabling legislation, is its mandate to exclude and to restrict. From the explicit grant of power to zone for the purposes of preventing the overcrowding of land and the undue concentration of population comes the clear implication that under the typical zoning act a municipality may regulate population growth to achieve these legitimate zoning objectives.

Of course, this finding does not preclude challenges to such regulation. Even if a municipal zoning ordinance is consistent with enabling legislation, it must nevertheless comply with federal constitutional limitations. An otherwide valid zoning regulation cannot stand if it is unreasonable, arbitrary or capricious;[9] if it infringes upon freedom of religion;[10] if it denies equal protection under the law;[11] or if it constitutes an unlawful taking of property.[12]

In addition to these traditional constitutional restrictions, courts recently have begun to focus on the constitutionally protected right to travel as a limitation upon the use of zoning laws to control municipal population growth. The right to travel has been recognized for many years in other contexts. It was first acknowledged as a constitutional principle in 1941 in the case of *Edwards* v. *California*,[13] in which the United States Supreme Court struck down a California statute that imposed criminal liability on anyone bringing an indigent nonresident into the State.[14] The Court held that such a restriction imposed an unconstitutional burden upon interstate commerce.[15] In 1969 the Supreme Court in *Shapiro* v. *Thompson*[16] cited this constitutionally protected freedom to travel as the reason for invalidating a statute that conditioned eligibility for welfare assistance upon a one year residency requirement.[17] The Court held that even though the residency requirement might not have operated as an actual deterrent to travel, the statute was nevertheless invalid if its purpose was to penalize the exercise of the right to travel, unless it could be shown to be necessary to promote a compelling governmental interest.[18] In the 1972 case of *Dunn* v. *Blumstein*,[19] the Supreme Court cited the right to travel as one of the reasons for invalidating a one year residency requirement for voting.[20]

In 1974 the Supreme Court reaffirmed the right to travel principle when it struck down an Arizona statute requiring at least one year's residence in a county as a condition of an indigent's eligibility to receive non-emergency hospitalization or medical care at the county's expense.[21] The Court found that the residency requirement violated the equal protection clause and infringed upon the constitutionally protected right to travel by denying newcomers a basic necessity of life.[22] Because the law penalized indigents in the exercise of the right to travel, it could be justified only if it met the compelling state interest test.[23] In an attempt to meet this standard, the state advanced numerous justifications for the statute:

1. The need to conserve the county's limited fiscal resources;

> 2. the desire to deter indigents from taking up residence in the county solely to utilize medical facilities;
> 3. the protection of the rights of long-time residents who have contributed to the community by the payment of taxes;
> 4. the need to maintain public support for the county hospital by assuring taxpayers that the tax revenues will be used primarily for their benefit;
> 5. the administrative convenience in establishing a clear-cut criterion for bona fide residence;
> 6. the need to predict the scope of services to be rendered by the hospital for budget purposes.[24]

The Court nevertheless held that none of these reasons, singly or in combination, showed a state interest sufficiently compelling to outweigh the restriction on the right to travel.[25]

Basing its decision upon this line of cases, a federal district court in California, in *Construction Industry Association* v. *City of Petaluma*,[26] held that a municipal ordinance designed to safeguard the community's small town character by keeping out newcomers unconstitutionally restricted the right to travel.[27] The ordinance, among other things, limited new construction to 500 houses per year and thus prevented the influx of new residents.[28] The *Petaluma* case is particularly significant because the municipality eliminated any doubt about the objectives of its program by declaring in the preamble of the ordinance, "In order to protect its small town character and surrounding open spaces, it shall be the policy of the City to *control its future rate and distribution of growth* . . . "[29] The city also argued that the zoning power gave it the right to control its own rate of growth and to protect the character of the community.[30] The district court held, however, that a "municipality capable of supporting a natural population expansion [could not] limit growth simply because it does not prefer to grow at the rate which would be dictated by prevailing market demand."[31]

In addition to its reliance on Supreme Court right to travel cases, the *Petaluma* court also adopted the rationale and language of several Pennsylvania Supreme Court cases which invalidated ordinances that sought to exclude newcomers.[32] In *National Land & Investment Co.* v. *Easttown Township Board of Adjustment*,[33] the Pennsylvania court overturned a four acre minimum lot size requirement, stating:

> The question posed is whether the township can stand in the way of the natural forces which send our growing population into hitherto undeveloped areas in search of a comfortable place to live. We have concluded not. A zoning ordinance whose primary purpose is to prevent the entrance of newcomers in order to avoid future burdens, economic and otherwise, upon the administration of public services and facilities can not be held valid.[34]

The holding of *National Land* was reinforced by *In re Kit-Mar Builders, Inc.,*[35] the language of which was also quoted with approval by the *Petaluma* court:

> The implication of our decision in *National Land* is that communities must deal with the problems of population growth. They may not refuse to confront the future by adopting zoning regulations that effectively restrict population to near present levels.[36]

Having concluded that the city's plan was invalid, the district court: (1) permanently enjoined its implementation insofar as it purported to limit the natural population growth of the area; (b) retained jurisdiction to prevent the city from circumventing the spirit of the holding; and (c) declared that, should any controversies arise, it would appoint a special master to supervise the enforcement of the order.[37] If the *Petaluma* case is upheld by the Ninth Circuit,[38] a strong precedent will be established for the principle that the zoning power does not encompass the authority to control a community's population growth.

THE SOCIAL AND ECONOMIC COMPOSITION OF THE COMMUNITY

The second issue raised by an investigation of the scope of the zoning power involves the socioeconomic quality of the population, rather than its quantity or growth rate. For example, is it within the zoning power to prescribe or regulate such socioeconomic characteristics as the age, marital status, family size, or income of the population? An analysis of the relevant judicial decisions indicates that this issue is still unresolved with respect to both indirect and direct forms of such regulation.

Many forms of zoning regulation have an indirect effect upon the social and economic characteristics of the community. Minimum size lots, minimum size lots, minimum floor space requirements, prohibition of or restrictions on apartments and exclusion of mobile home parks are zoning devices that are frequently used to regulate, albeit indirectly, the social and economic composition of the community. Increases in minimum lot size and floor space requirements raise the costs of construction and thereby exclude residents with insufficient income. Restrictions on the construction of multiple dwellings and on the number of bedrooms therein tend to exclude single persons and larger families with lower income. Exclusion of mobile home parks has the same effect. Since a large proportion of low income families in urban areas are members of racial and ethnic minorities, these zoning restrictions fall most heavily upon minority groups and effectively exclude them from many suburban communities.

Initially such restrictions were approved by the courts as legitimate subjects for zoning regulation. In New Jersey, for example, a minimum lot size requirement of five acres was sustained on the grounds that it was an appropriate method of preserving the character of the community;[39] a minimum floor space requirement was upheld as a reasonable exercise of the zoning power;[40] and a prohibition of mobile home use within the jurisdiction was upheld on the basis of aesthetic considerations.[41] The Supreme Court itself has approved as a legitimate device of participatory democracy a state constitutional provision requiring prior referendum approval for construction of subsidized housing.[42]

More recently, the courts in a number of states, particularly Pennsylvania, New Jersey and Michigan, have begun to reexamine the question of whether zoning regulations may be sustained without regard to the indirect consequences on the social and economic composition of the regulated community. The Pennsylvania Supreme Court struck down zoning ordinances prescribing four acre[43] and three acre[44] minimum lot size requirements as an arbitrary and unreasonable use of the zoning power in violation of the fifth and fourteenth amendments because their primary purpose was to "keep out people, rather than [to] make community improvements."[45] The same court has also invalidated a zoning ordinance that failed to provide multi-family dwelling use, except by a variance application.[46] The lower courts in New Jersey, in a series of decisions, have voided several attempts to impose restrictions on construction of low income and subsidized apartments[47] and have overturned a minimum lot size requirement of 40,000 square feet, or almost one acre, for single family houses.[48] In *Mount Laurel*, the New Jersey Supreme Court invalidated a zoning ordinance to the extent that it excluded people of low and moderate incomes.[49] The Michigan lower courts have invalidated zoning exclusion of mobile home parks when the effect of such prohibition would be to exclude a socioeconomic component of the population.[50]

While the decisions of these courts may be indicative of a trend toward the invalidation of indirect regulation of social and economic composition, the issue is still unresolved and will remain so until more federal and state courts are faced with its resolution. Surprisingly enough, there may be greater authority for direct control in light of the United States Supreme Court's recent pronouncements. Although there are a number of cases holding that the only proper concern for zoning laws is the *physical use* of land and the structures thereon and that *socioeconomic objectives* are not within the zoning power,[51] the Supreme Court in *Village of Belle Terre* v. *Boraas*[52] upheld the validity of a municipal zoning ordinance specifically designed to exclude a component of society, *i.e.* groups comprised of more than three unrelated persons.[53] These two conflicting views represent the heart of the exclusionary zoning debate.

The most explicit judicial prohibition of the use of the zoning power for the direct regulation of socioeconomic matters appears in *Board of Supervisors of Fairfax County* v. *DeGroff Enterprises, Inc.*[54] In that case the Virginia Supreme Court struck down a "mandatory percentage of moderately priced dwellings" ordinance.[55] The ordinance required a developer of fifty or more dwelling units to commit himself, before site plan approval, to build at least fifteen percent of the units as low and moderate income housing.[56] One of the grounds on which the Virginia court held the ordinance invalid was that it exceeded the authority granted by the statute to the local governing body because it was directed to *socioeconomic objectives* rather than to *physical characteristics*, as authorized by the state enabling statute.[57]

A number of lower court decisions in New Jersey would seem to support this position. In the 1972 case of *Bridge Park Co.* v. *Borough of Highland Park*,[58] the Appellate Division of the New Jersey Superior Court held that the zoning power could not be used to prevent the conversion of an apartment house into condominium ownership.[59] The court indicated that the zoning power was intended to regulate *physical* use rather than the *economic* nature of the tenure.[60] In 1973 another panel of the same court, in *Taxpayers Association of Weymouth Township* v. *Weymouth Township*,[61] held that the zoning power could not be used to limit residency in a Trailer and Mobile Home District to elderly persons.[62] Likewise, in 1974 a lower court held that a zoning ordinance limiting residency in senior citizen communities to persons 52 years of age or over violated the equal protection clause.[63] The significance of this decision was somewhat diffused, however, by the court's further explanation that while a plan to "provide accommodation for the needs and services to a segment of our society . . . is a valid purpose of zoning . . . "[64] nevertheless "such age qualification bears no realistic relationship to a recognized objective of zoning legislation."[65]

In *Mount Laurel*, however, the New Jersey Supreme Court upheld socioeconomic objectives as proper goals of zoning regulation and rejected the prior distinction between socioeconomic objectives and physical characteristics.[66] Thus this 1975 decision is in direct conflict with the *Fairfax County* case. In *Fairfax County* an affirmative attempt to include low and moderate income residents was invalidated by the Virginia Supreme Court. In *Mount Laurel* it was the failure to make such an attempt that was successfully attacked.

Mount Laurel is also difficult to reconcile with the Supreme Court's decision in *Village of Belle Terre v. Boraas*.[67] This decision is one of the

Supreme Court's rare intrusions into the battle over the validity of local zoning regulation. The *Belle Terre* case involved a small community on Long Island, New York, which contained only 220 homes and 700 people.[68] The village, located in the vicinity of the newly constructed campus of the State University of New York at Stony Brook, adopted a zoning ordinance that prohibited more than three unrelated persons from occupying a "one-family" house.[69] Six unmarried university students, three male and three female, leased a house for their own use and, claiming to be "one family," challenged the validity of the ordinance.[70] The Second Circuit Court of Appeals held that the ordinance was invalid as a violation of the equal protection clause.[71] The Supreme Court reversed, however, holding that the ordinance "bears a rational relationship to a [permissible] state objective."[72] Justice Douglas, writing for the Court, described the scope of permissible state objectives in the regulation of land use in the following terms: "The police power is not confined to elimination of filth, stench, and unhealthy places. It is ample to lay out zones where family values, youth values, and the blessings of quiet seclusion and clean air make the area a sanctuary for people."[73]

Thus, while the United States Supreme Court held that the Constitution did not prevent a municipality from regulating its socioeconomic composition or rate of growth, the New Jersey Supreme Court held that its state constitution prohibited the exclusion of low and moderate income residents.[74] It observed that the state constitutional requirements of substantive due process and equal protection "may be more demanding than those of the federal Constitution."[75]

Does the Validity of a Zoning Ordinance Depend on Its Ability to Accommodate Population Growth of a Size and Socioeconomic Composition Required to Meet Regional Needs?

The preceding section discussed whether a zoning authority *may* regulate population growth. This section confronts the clearly derivative issue of whether a zoning authority *must* provide for future regional needs resulting from an increase in population size and changes in socioeconomic composition. Or, stating the question conversely, does the validity of a zoning ordinance depend upon whether it contains an affirmative plan to meet these regional needs? This question has been answered in the affirmative by Judge Furman writing for the New Jersey Superior Court in *Oakwood at Madison, Inc. v. Township of Madison*,[76] by Justice Hall, writing for the New Jersey Supreme Court in *Mount Laurel*,[77] and by a number of Pennsylvania decisions.[78] On the other hand, several federal court decisions would seem to indicate that there is no such requirement under constitutional and federal law.[79] The *Madison* case first attracted national attention when, in 1971, Judge Furman held invalid the entire Madison Township zoning ordinance on the ground that "it fail[ed] to promote reasonably a balanced community in accordance with the general welfare."[80] The opinion stated that "[i]n pursuing the valid zoning purpose of a balanced community, a municipality must not ignore housing needs, that is, its fair proportion of the obligation to meet the housing needs of its own population and of the region."[81] The decision was appealed to the New Jersey Supreme Court,[82] but, in the interim, Madison Township removed many of the former restrictions by amending its zoning law.[83] When the case reached the New Jersey Supreme Court it was remanded to Judge Furman to determine whether the amendments overcame the earlier objections.[84]

After a hearing on the question of the effect of the zoning amendments, Judge Furman in April 1974 held that the township's "obligation to provide its fair share of the housing needs of its region is not met unless its zoning ordinance approximates in additional housing unit capacity the same proportion of low-income housing as its present low-income population . . . "[85] In defining the region whose housing needs must be met by the Township, the court said that this region was

> not coextensive with Middlesex County. Rather, it is the area from which, in view of available employment and transportation, the population of the township would be drawn, absent invalidly exclusionary zoning.[86]

In response to the argument that because of high land and construction costs, it would not be possible to build single family housing for low income families anyway, the court replied that "[e]ven without governmental subsidies, however, multi-family housing may be provided for low and moderate-income families . . . [by] [i]ncentives . . . such as extra density [allowances] for low and moderate-income units."[87]

Three separate components of this decision should be noted. First, a zoning ordinance is invalid "unless [it] approximates in additional housing unit capacity the same proportion of low-income housing as its presant low-income population . . . "[88] Notice that the verb in this sentence is the word "approximates." It is not clear whether the word "approximate" is intended to mean "permit" or "allow" or is intended to have the more exacting meaning of "assure the construction of." Under this rationale, the validity of a zoning ordinance does not depend upon an assurance by the municipality that such housing will be built, but rather may depend upon the inclusion in the zoning ordinance of provisions that will "approximate" in capacity the prescribed proportions. Secondly, the court's above-quoted test for identifying the region is difficult to apply.[89] Assuming a one hour trip time as a reasonable measure of the acceptable travel time between home and job, the validity of the zoning ordinance may require the municipality to meet the low income housing needs of a major part of the New York-New Jersey metropolitan area. Finally, Judge Furman seems to have recognized that zoning ordinances do not build housing and that some form of subsidy is usually necessary to bring the cost of housing within the reach of low income families.[90] The decision implies, however, that the validity of a zoning ordinance may depend upon whether extra density incentives are provided in the ordinance to encourage the construction of such housing.[91]

Many of the principles articulated in *Madison* were adopted by the New Jersey Supreme Court in *Southern Burlington County NAACP v. Township of Mount Laurel*.[92] The lower court in *Mount Laurel* held that a zoning ordinance which discriminated against the poor by depriving them of adequate housing and the opportunity to secure subsidized housing violated the equal protection clause.[93] It ordered the municipality to evaluate the housing needs of low and moderate income residents and nonresidents working in the township, and to develop an affirmative action program.[94] The State Supreme Court affirmed the judgment, but decided that it was not necessary to nullify the entire zoning ordinance. It held the ordinance invalid only to the extent that it failed to comply with the standards set forth in the opinion.[95] It concluded, in addition, that the municipality should be given the opportunity to reformulate the ordinance prior to judicial intervention.[96]

Mount Laurel is significant in its unequivocal affirmation of the requirement that local zoning ordinances accommodate the regional housing needs of all socioeconomic elements of the population. The court based this conclusion on its interpretation of the concept of the "general welfare," which underlies the state's police power. Thus it stated:

> It is plain beyond dispute that proper provision for adequate housing of all categories of people is certainly an absolute essential in promotion of the general welfare required in all local land use regulation.[97]

It articulated this duty as follows:

> . . . [T]he presumptive obligation arises for each such municipality affirmatively to plan and provide by its land use regulations, the reasonable opportunity for an appropriate variety and choice of housing, including, of course, low and moderate cost housing, to meet the needs, desires and resources of all categories of people who may desire to live

within its boundaries. Negatively, it may not adopt regulations or policies which thwart or preclude that opportunity.[98]

To eliminate any doubt about the extent and nature of the municipal housing obligation, the New Jersey court opined as follows in words which will undoubtedly be cited with great frequency:

> We conclude that every such municipality must, by its land use regu-
> lations, presumptively make realistically possible an appropriate variety
> and choice of housing. More specifically, presumptively it cannot fore-
> close the opportunity of the classes of people mentioned for low and
> moderate income housing and in its regulations must affirmatively af-
> ford that opportunity, at least to the extent of the municipality's *fair
> share* of the present and *prospective* regional need therefore.[99]

Several Pennsylvania cases, *National Land & Investment Co. v. Easttown Township Board of Adjustment*,[100] *In re Kit-Mar Builders*,[101] and *In re Girsh*[102] support this position only indirectly. All three cases voided exclusionary zoning ordinances and each contained strong state-ments that zoning may not be used to exclude people who would want to move into the community. The opinions, however, did not expressly state that the validity of the ordinances would depend upon whether they con-tained affirmative programs to meet regional housing needs. In the land-mark *National Land* case, upon which the other two cases are based, the Pennsylvania Supreme Court said,

> Zoning is a tool in the hands of governmental bodies which enables
> them to more effectively meet the demands of evolving and growing
> communities. It must not and can not be used by those officials as an
> instrument by which they may shirk their responsibilities. Zoning is a
> means by which a governmental body can plan for the future—it may
> not be used as a means to deny the future . . . Zoning provisions may
> not be used . . . to avoid the increased responsibilities and economic
> burdens which time and natural growth invariably bring.
>   It is not difficult to envision the tremendous hardship, as well as the
> chaotic conditions, which would result if all the townships in this area
> decided to deny to a growing population sites for residential develop-
> ment within the means of at least a significant segment of the
> people.[103]

On the other hand, the federal courts have in the last year handed down several decisions which seem to undercut severely these state deci-sions on matters of constitutional law.[104] This group of federal cases in-volves municipal attempts to block the construction of federally subsidized or financed low income housing within the municipal boundaries. The common thread running through these cases is the issue of whether there is a constitutional requirement that municipalities develop affirmative programs to meet regional housing needs. To restate the issue more narrowly, may a municipality bar by ordinance or refuse to accept the construction of federally subsidized housing if its action has the effect of excluding low income persons who would move into the area given suitable housing?

The cases are in agreement that there is no constitutional obligation for a municipality to provide affirmatively for regional housing needs. Zoning ordinances and municipal decisions preventing or rejecting the construction of subsidized low income housing projects are valid if not racially motivated or racially discriminatory in operation. These decisions hold that the municipality's action will be upheld, if the community can present valid objections to the project based on community needs. In addition, the ordinance must withstand judicial scrutiny for racial motivation or effect.

In *United States v. City of Black Jack*,[105] a municipality rezoned a formerly multi-family zone to a single family dwelling zone in order to prevent the construction of a federally financed low income housing project. The federal government challenged the zoning ordinance under the Fair Housing Act of 1968 [106] on the grounds that (a) exclusion of multi-family use throughout an entire municipality was an improper purpose of zoning [107] and (b) the ordinance was invalid because it was clearly motivated by racial prejudice against the inner city blacks, who would be likely to occupy the project.[108] The federal district court first determined that the ordinance's ban on apartment construction was valid under Missouri law and was therefore a proper exercise of the municipality's delegated police power.[109] It then found that there was insufficient evidence to support the charge of racial motivation behind the ordinance, particularly in view of the reasons "advanced for opposition to apartments, among them the character of the community, road congestion, school impaction, property devaluation, and opposition to transient apartment dwellers."[110] The court specifically found these reasons to be community objectives of sufficient merit to justify such a zoning change, within the provisions of the Fair Housing Act.[111] The case was appealed to the Eighth Circuit, which reversed on the ground that the trial court record presented no factual basis for the assertion that any of the claimed community objectives were in fact furthered by the ordinance.[112] The appellate court found the zoning ordinance invalid under the Fair Housing Act because it had the racially discriminatory effect of preventing blacks in metropolitan St. Louis from obtaining housing in Black Jack.[113]

Contemporaneously with the *Black Jack* decision, the Second Circuit faced the same question in a different factual setting and reached the opposite conclusion. In *Citizens Committee for Faraday Wood v. Lindsay*,[114] it affirmed a district court ruling that New York City's rejection of a federally subsidized housing project did not have the effect of preventing blacks from obtaining housing in the area and was not racially motivated. First, the court agreed with the trial court's conclusion that the city terminated the project for political reasons based upon community opposition. It found the termination not to be racially motivated because the local opposition was primarily based upon a fear that the proposed construction of high-rise buildings would overburden community facilities. In addition, the city itself had many other federally subsidized projects scheduled.[115] Secondly, the court observed, as had the district court, that eighty percent of the units in the Faraday Wood project were scheduled to be occupied by middle income families, with an annual income limitation of more than $23,000.[116] The court found that this high income limitation and the lack of disproportionate over-representation of minority groups at the middle income level precluded a finding that the termination of the project had or was designed to have a discriminatory effect upon racial minorities.[117]

In *Mahaley v. Cuyahoga Metropolitan Housing Authority*[118] the Sixth Circuit held that a suburban community is under no obligation to enter into a cooperation agreement for federally subsidized low income housing under the Housing Act of 1937[119] even though its refusal would tend to perpetuate existing de facto racially segregated housing patterns.[120] The appellate court observed that under the Housing Act of 1937 the municipality had the power to decide for itself whether it needed subsidized low income housing.[121] It also found that the municipality's refusal did not have a racially discriminatory effect because the limiting of local low-income housing equally affected both black and white low income groups.[122] The court concluded that since there was no racially discriminatory motive or effect, the municipality's action was not illegal.[123] The decision stands for the proposition that under federal law there is no requirement for affirmative municipal programs to meet regional housing needs. In discussing plaintiff's fourteenth amendment claim, the court concluded:

> In *Lindsey v. Normet* . . . the Court held that no one has a constitutional right to adequate housing. Since a person has no right to public housing in his own city, it follows that he has no such right in a municipality in which he does not reside.[124]

Similarly, in *Metropolitan Housing Development Corp. v. Village of Arlington Heights*,[125] a suburban community with extensive industrial development refused to rezone a local site in a single family residential zone to permit multi-family use by plaintiff, a non-profit corporation which proposed to build a federally funded low income housing project.[126] Plaintiff argued two points: that under the fourteenth amendment the municipality could not zone so as to exclude housing that employees of nearby industries could afford; and that the effect of the municipality's refusal was to prevent low income minorities from working in a community in which jobs were available, but in which they could not find decent low income housing.[127] The federal district court rejected both of these arguments in the following terms:

> The legal issue on this point, therefore, is whether low-income minorities have a constitutional right to live in an area where they work or desire to seek work. Even more broadly, do low-income workers have a constitutional right to low-rental housing either where they work or elsewhere? We know of no such rule of law.[128]

Moreover, the court noted that the refusal to rezone the parcel for multi-family use was supported by a valid planning principle—that multi-family development would seriously damage the value of surrounding single family homes.[129] The court also found that even though some neighborhood opposition to the project may have been based on racial or economic prejudice, nevertheless the Village trustees' zoning decision was valid under the fourteenth amendment because it was based upon a "legitimate desire to protect property values and the integrity of the Village's zoning plan."[130] Appeal of this case to the Seventh Circuit is pending.[131] The rationale of these cases is that while the fourteenth amendment forbids discrimination against racial minorities, it does not forbid discrimination against poor people, notwithstanding that it is within this group that these minority persons are most often found. In the absence of racially discriminatory motive and effect and in the presence of carefully substantiated community objections, the federal courts will sustain a municipality's exclusion of federally subsidized low income housing projects against constitutional challenge. Both the motivation and the justification for the municipality's action, however, will be closely scrutinized.

Although close scrutiny seems to be the rule, the federal courts are divided concerning the weight or deference to be given to justifications for opposition to low income housing projects. For example, to what extent should opposition to low income housing on the ground of degradation of surrounding property values be allowed to justify perpetuation of *de facto* segregated housing patterns? How closely should a court scrutinize the grounds given for the opposition and the evidence offered to show lack of racial motivation, purpose or effect? The Eighth Circuit in the *Black Jack* decision seems to be applying the most intense scrutiny in this type of situation. On the other hand, the dissenting opinion in the *Faraday Wood* decision alleged that the Second Circuit was proposing the following double constitutional standard in housing cases:

> "strict" equal protection if a housing project contemplates a very high percentage of, or exclusively, low income units, and simple "rationality" if it includes a goodly percentage of middle income units—apparently on the theory that middle income housing is for white people and low income housing for nonwhites.[132]

Comparing these federal and state decisions, one possible rationale for the differing attitudes is that absent a clear constitutional violation, such as blatant racial discrimination, federal courts are reluctant to interfere too actively with municipal zoning, since zoning is an exercise of the police power reserved to the states. The state courts are less constricted by feelings of deference, since active review of zoning decisions is well within their authority. Nevertheless, the divergence in constitutional theory has further contributed to the controversy over affirmative action.

If the Validity of a Municipal Zoning Scheme Depends Upon the Achievement of a Prescribed Goal of Population Growth and Composition, What Standard Should be Used to Determine its Validity?

A judicial resolution that communities must affirmatively plan for growth does not reach the heart of the exclusionary zoning dilemma. There remain the issues of the criteria that a governmental agency or a court should use to determine whether a given zoning ordinance has or has not in fact fulfilled its fair share of regional obligations to accommodate population growth and the boundaries of the region for which this obligation arises.

THE CRITERIA FOR ALLOCATION OF FAIR SHARE HOUSING OBLIGATIONS

A number of governmental agencies have formulated criteria for the allocation of a municipality's fair share of the regional need for low- and moderate-cost housing.[133] These criteria have been the subject of careful study by planners.[134] Examination of these studies reveals that the use of most of these criteria involves the application of basic political judgment, complex governmental administration and intricate professional planning skills. These criteria may be classified under one of the following four principles:

1. the allocation to each municipality of an *equal share* of the obligation to provide low- and moderate-income housing;
2. the allocation of responsibility for this housing based upon the *need* of local populations;
3. the allocation of this housing to achieve *economic and racial integration*; and
4. the *suitability* of the jurisdiction to accommodate the low and moderate income housing.

The application of this last principle, in turn, requires a consideration of the amount of available land in the jurisdiction and an analysis of the environmental and fiscal impact of the development of that land and the availability of municipal services and facilities.

The theory underlying the "allocation based on equal share" principle is that *every* community has an *equal* obligation to meet the region's housing needs and therefore every community should provide no less than a prescribed equal percentage of low- and moderate-income housing units. For example, it may be determined that fifteen percent of the housing of every community within the state shall be within the reach of families of low- or moderate-income. To achieve this criteria a governmental agency with extensive powers would have to be created to administer the program. Such an agency might be given the power to override local zoning decisions that prohibit or impede construction of such housing. This is the technique used by the Massachusetts "anti-snob" law.[135] The agency might be authorized to administer a "mandatory percentage of moderately priced dwellings" ordinance similar to the Fairfax County, Virginia ordinance.[136] It might be given powers of development and construction similar to those contained in the New York State Urban Development Corporation Act.[137] It could be designated as a "public housing agency" within the meaning of the Housing and Community Development Act of 1974[138] and thereby become eligible to administer the new assisted housing programs under Title II of that Act.[139] Without an effective governmental agency with broad administrative powers, the mere designation of a percentage that represents an equal share of a municipality's housing obligation would do little to accomplish the goal that the numerical designation represents.

The "allocation based upon need" principle is designed to allocate housing units for low and moderate income families to those areas where there is the greatest *need* for housing by such families. This standard will tend to allocate the greatest obligation for housing to urban areas where there are large numbers of families who cannot afford local rents. The general application of this principle will tend to minimize the obligation of suburban communities to provide for such housing and will tend to defeat the third principle's goal of economic and racial integration. To overcome these objections, the analysis of housing *needs* may include a projection of future population movement into suburban areas and predictions of the income mix of that population.

A guidebook [140] for the preparation of local housing assistance plans [141] prepared by the National Association of Housing and Redevelopment Officials (NAHRO) describes several techniques for predicting housing needs. One technique for making this prediction is to extrapolate the information from existing census data. [142] This method may be reasonably reliable for short periods of a year or two, but it becomes increasingly unreliable as the period of projection is extended. [143] Another technique that is used to predict future population characteristics is based on a prediction of family income that may be derived from anticipated changes in employment opportunities. [144] A third procedure is set forth in detail in the NAHRO guidebook. This technique involves the following computations:

1. Project the income distribution of new residents based on the expected salary of the jobs to be added over the planning period.
2. Survey projected new construction to determine the distribution of rents and house values of new units to be added to the stock.
3. Allow for turnover in existing housing by interviewing bank officials and surveying county records to determine the rent and house value range of older homes for sale.
4. Calculate the needs for additional housing that will not be met by new construction for a turnover in the existing stock; this calculation is simply the difference between total expected demand and total available units.
5. Calculate the rent-income mismatch (the rent gap); this represents the need for subsidies or other assistance necessary to make new construction serve the real demand. [145]

The efficacy of this procedure depends upon the accuracy of the prediction of future job opportunities since it will form the basis for plotting household characteristics which will in turn be converted into housing demand.

In spite of this potential weakness, the NAHRO model is a generally accepted procedure and was adopted in a recent study of population growth in New Jersey. In this major study, undertaken by the Rutgers University Center for Urban Policy Research, [146] the aggregate state employment in twenty-nine industry groups (twenty manufacturing employers, six private nonmanufacturing employers, and three governmental employers) was examined and projected for the entire state and then was distributed among counties within the state. The characteristics of the workers in each occupation were estimated and projected. These characteristics included the number of heads of household, and the amount of earnings and the household income. This information was then converted into housing demand using the NAHRO model technique.

Among the major conclusions of this study was the prediction that "[e]mployment will concentrate increasingly in broad arcs circumscribing the historic central city and core areas of New York City and Philadelphia."[147] Furthermore, the study asserted that "[t]he physical linkage of jobs and homes increasingly becomes a function of zoning [and that] [t]he design of zoning patterns is perhaps the crucial controlling mechanism."[148] This study can be criticized because it concludes that the quantification of housing need is based upon existing zoning decisions. Consequently, if the proposed criterion of housing *need* is then applied to allocate housing obligation among the municipalities, the existing zoning decisions will have to be modified, in some cases drastically. This in turn will change the underlying assumptions upon which the calculation of housing need was originally based. Thus, to the extent that the zoning pattern is in fact changed, the computation of housing need for the area will be inaccurate for any further use.

In spite of the weaknesses in the methodology by which housing need may be computed, however, it is very likely that this procedure will continue to be used widely (and perhaps improved) because of the provisions of the Housing and Community Development Act of 1974.[149] Under this Act, applications for financial assistance for housing[150] or community development[151] must contain a "local housing assistance plan."[152] Grants of federal planning funds to state and local governments must be used to formulate a comprehensive ongoing plan containing a "housing element" and a "land-use element."[153] The development of both a "local housing assistance plan" and a "housing element"[154] will require an analysis and computation of housing needs.

The goal of the third principle is to allocate housing units for low and moderate income families to those areas which have the least representation of low income and racial minority groups within their communities. There is little difficulty in determining the areas to which such allocation would be made. This information is available from census data on income distribution, as well as from other easily obtainable data on location of welfare recipients and subsidized housing units. Most of the subsidized housing would be allocated, under this criterion, to suburban areas.

The most critical aspect of this principle is that it is based upon a fundamental policy decision that requires some manifestation of political support for its successful implementation. Although there have been frequent expressions of the "ideal" of racial and economic integration in federal and state constitutions and in federal, state and local legislation, there is nevertheless some doubt about whether this "ideal" enjoys the support of the residents of the areas to which low income housing would be assigned. This lack of political support is particularly evident where there is a perception by suburban residents (regardless of the accuracy of this perception) that the introduction of subsidized housing will conflict with their community's goals of good schools, low incidence of crime and preservation of the value of their homes.

Where political support for the principle of economic and racial integration exists, the controversy, if any, can be narrowed to the issue of the number of units that should be allocated to a given jurisdiction. This is the type of policy decision that is readily susceptible to resolution by negotiation and compromise. However, the very existence of a legal problem described as "exclusionary zoning" is evidence of the fact that such political support *does not in fact* exist in many suburban communities. Consequently, it seems unlikely that this problem can be resolved by judicial attempts to impose a standard that defies the political realities out of which the problem arises.

The objective of the fourth principle is to allocate subsidized housing units to those areas where the most *"suitable"* sites for housing are available. The skills and judgment of professional planners will be particularly helpful when this standard is used. Planning techniques utilized for this purpose would include: (a) a survey of available land in the jurisdiction; (b) an analysis of the ecological characteristics of the available land and the environmental impact of its development; (c) an analysis of existing municipal services and facilities and an estimate of additional facilities required by proposed development; (d) an estimate of future employment opportunities; and (e) an analysis of the fiscal impact of the development.

A land survey is used to determine the gross amount of land available for development. It will determine the gross number of acres of developable land, the proportion of developable to developed land and the general location and proximity of the vacant developable lands to each other and to the rest of the developed land within the jurisdiction. From this gross figure should be subtracted the amount of vacant land that is not desirable for development because of topography, soil condition, water table or other environmental factors.

Ecological analysis is designed to determine the environmental suitability of the vacant land for development.[155] The information derived from this analysis will supply objective standards for evaluating the relative suitability of vacant land and will provide the basis for the exercise of professional judgment in determining the amount of land that must be subtracted from the gross acreage to calculate the net amount of developable land in the jurisdiction. An analysis of municipal services and facilities will furnish the information necessary to determine the extent to which new facilities will have to be provided.[156]

The suitability of an area also depends upon a determination of the extent to which jobs are available within or near the municipality to which low income housing will be allocated. This analysis is made, not to determine the need for housing within the jurisdiction, as in the second principle, but for the purpose of determining the suitability of a particular municipality for the allocation of such housing. The analysis will include, however, in addition to a survey of existing job opportunities, an estimate of future job opportunities based upon professional judgment of the likelihood that industrial and commercial enterprises will be built within the community. Consequently, the results of this analysis will be subject to the same admonitions of inexactness and attenuated presumption that limit the usefulness of the projections of employment opportunities for the purpose of determining housing need within a community.

In recent years a number of New Jersey courts have indicated that zoning to minimize municipal expenses by excluding people is invalid.[157] Nevertheless, the impact of housing development upon the ability of a municipality to provide essential services is one of the factors to be considered in determining the suitability of any given community for a share of low income housing allocation.[158] The analysis of this fiscal impact must include an examination of both municipal revenue and expenditures; an analysis of existing revenue and the feasibility of alternative sources of revenue; an analysis of existing expenditures and predictions of future expenditures resulting from rising costs and increased levels of service; and an analysis of the impact of development upon the fiscal system. Among the conclusions of a recent study by the New Jersey County and Municipal Government Study Commission is that the level of municipal expenditures per resident is primarily a "function of population size and growth rate."[159]

DELINEATION OF THE "REGION"

If the validity of municipal zoning is to depend upon its fulfillment of regional obligations, it is not only necessary to determine the criteria by which the fulfillment of the obligations may be measured, but also to determine the "region" to which this obligation is owed. Traditionally, zoning laws have been adopted to meet municipal needs. Some legal scholars have placed much of the blame for the harmful consequences of exclusionary zoning upon the delegation of the zoning power to municipal government and the overreliance of municipal government upon the property tax for its revenue.[160] This indictment of municipal zoning has directed attention to the possibilities of allocating responsibility for land use regulation to a region larger than municipal jurisdictions. Proposals have been made to transfer the land regulation power to states or counties, to specially created environmentally critical areas, or to some form of metropolitan region.

Although the role of state government in land use planning and control is growing [161] the only example of an outright assumption of land-use control powers at the state level is Hawaii. [162] In spite of some criticism of the Hawaiian system, [163] greater state participation in land use regulation continues to be recommended by academicians. [164] The proposals, however, have enjoyed only limited support in state legislatures. County regulation of land use has had some success in Oregon [165] fifi Wisconsin [166] where there has been a tradition of effective county government. In New Jersey, however, and in most other states, the legal, fiscal, and administrative inadequacies of county government have prevented them from assuming an effective role in land use regulation. [167] More recently, a number of states have adopted programs by which environmentally critical regions are regulated. [168] The delineations of environmentally critical regions, however, are inappropriate to resolve the social and economic issues raised by exclusionary zoning.

It has been proposed that municipal zoning laws must meet the needs of the metropolitan region of which the municipality is a part. The decision by Judge Furman in *Oakwood at Madison, Inc. v. Township of Madison* [169] was specifically addressed to this issue. The decision suggested that the appropriate region for the municipality to consider when assessing housing needs is that region from which, in view of available employment and transportation, the population of the municipality would be drawn absent invalid exclusionary zoning. [170] The decision acknowledged that the perimeters of a region from which such a population is drawn are generally measured by examining the employment sources in the area and the available transportation facilities. From this information one can compute the boundaries of the region by measuring the time it takes to travel to work and back each day. The *Madison* decision, however, failed to establish the standards by which the length of "journey-to-work" relationship is to be evaluated; nor does it address the problems of interstate metropolitan regions.

The standard of journey-to-work trip time is not difficult to apply for the purpose of delineating a region, once there is agreement about the length of the "trip-time" and the means of transportation. There are debatable value judgments involved in each of these issues, however. Neither the planning profession nor the commuters themselves have been able to agree on the maximum acceptable limits of travel-to-work time— the only agreement is that it should be as short as possible. Professional planners usually consider a half hour to be the optimum limit of travel-time;[171] but this figure has been extended as a result of the willingness of commuters to travel one, two, or even more hours in each direction to and from work. As the period of travel-time is extended, the region for which housing needs must be met by a municipality must be extended also. This elastic principle of delineation is further confused by disagreement about whether public transportation, rather than the use of a private automobile, should be the only method considered in determining the relationship of distance to employment for low and moderate income families.

The use of travel-to-work time as a standard for delineating a region is complicated further in states such as New Jersey, where the major metropolitan areas encompass interstate regions.[172] Jobs in New York City and Philadelphia would create journey-to-work regions including major portions of New Jersey; new employment opportunities in suburban areas of New Jersey would create regions including vast numbers of low income families in New York City and Philadelphia. Under current political and fiscal constraints, it is patently unrealistic to expect any municipal government to assume the responsibility for the housing needs of a region prescribed by this standard.

Recognizing these difficulties, Justice Hall observed in *Mount Laurel* that the definition of "region" will vary from case to case.[173] He agreed with Judge Furman, however, that limiting the region to the county is not realistic, but that restricting the municipality's obligation to housing needs within the state seems "practical and advisable."[174] Yet, Justice Hall added parenthetically, "[t]his is not to say that a developing municipality can ignore a demand for housing within its boundaries on the part of people who commute to work in another state."[175]

V. What is the Appropriate Role of the Judiciary in Resolving the Issues of Exclusionary Zoning?

Many lawyers, planners and others advocate that the courts should resolve the issues of exclusionary zoning by holding such laws to be invalid.[176] More specifically, these proponents argue that exclusionary zoning is invalid because: (a) it is outside the scope of zoning enabling legislation; (b) it violates the due process clause; (c) it violates the equal protection clause; (d) it violates the supremacy clause; and (e) it is not a proper exercise of the police power.[177] Some courts have adopted this position;[178] others have rejected it usually upon a determination of insufficient evidence to support a finding of de facto discrimination upon which those legal arguments are based.[179] Still other courts have deliberated, agonized, postponed and avoided a definitive decision on this issue.

This latter course of action does not constitute an evasion of its judicial responsibility. Rather, it reflects an awareness of the judicial dilemma that would be created by an unequivocal decision on the issue of exclusionary zoning. Once a court determines that such practices violate statutory or constitutional principles, it must *either* provide a remedy to overcome the consequences of the legal violation *or* it must concede that the judiciary is incapable of providing a remedy for this judicially determined wrongful act. The latter alternative would diminish and subordinate the authority of the courts in relation to the other branches of government, thus destroying the balance of power among the branches. The former alternative is equally unsatisfactory because it involves the courts in activities that approach or exceed the limits of justiciability. To provide a remedy in cases involving invalid exclusionary zoning ordinances, the courts must make determinations involving controversial political issues, based upon professional expertise and requiring complex administrative machinery, all of which are more appropriate for the legislative and executive branches of government.

As every novice student of logic knows, the best escape from the horns of a dilemma is to deny the exclusivity of the dual choices by seeking alternative courses of action. This strategy does not always provide a happy solution, but it does increase the number of options and encourages a realistic comparison of the relative merits of each choice. The courts do, in fact, have more than two choices in dealing with the unresolved issues of exclusionary zoning. Each choice has its own advantages and disadvantages. Only the most dogmatic idealist can fail to recognize the existence of a number of viable judicial choices.

One course available to the courts, and adopted by some, is a delaying action using remands, postponements, referrals, and intimations of harsher rulings to come. At first glance this strategy might appear to be a default of the judicial process. The goal of this strategy, however, is to provide time for private or political resolution of the conflict. Admonitions and delay have been traditional devices to encourage settlement of private suits. The same techniques may also be used, to a lesser extent, to encourage legislative action that would be otherwise more difficult to achieve. A legislator who would ordinarily oppose a compromise housing program might support it, if he were able to base his decision upon the fact that he was "required to do so by judicial mandate" or if it were "necessary to avoid more stringent judicial action." Over the long term, the passage of time sometimes results in a change of attitude or community values to conform to a judicial declaration of fundamental moral and legal principles. It is difficult for a court to predict the chances of success with this course of action. Excessive delay, blatant equivocation and unenforced judicial admonitions can undermine the respect for and the integrity of the entire judicial system. On the other hand, additional time for reflection upon alternatives that command strong precedential support in case law can have a persuasive influence upon members of legislative bodies and can avoid a governmental crisis arising from a legislative-judicial confrontation.

The second choice, adopted by some courts, is to determine that the use of the zoning power to regulate the rate of population growth does *not* violate statutory or constitutional principles unless the declared or obvious purpose of such a regulation is to discriminate against persons on the grounds of race or other constitutionally unacceptable bases of classification.[180] Such a holding would rest upon a finding that control of population density is a proper governmental goal within the scope of the police power and the enabling legislation. It would also be based upon a premise, either stated or implicit, that disparities in opportunities for housing and other personal needs are part of the national economic system of distribution of resources and are not inconsistent with prevailing political or constitutional principles. A necessary corollary of such a decision would be the determination that, even though the impact of economic disparities in housing opportunities falls most harshly upon members of racial minorities, this is insufficient, by itself, to invalidate zoning laws that are not intended to effect such discrimination.

This choice, with some modifications, has been the traditional, if not the prevailing, judicial resolution in exclusionary zoning cases. In recent years, Pennsylvania, New Jersey and some federal courts have rejected some of the underlying premises or necessary implications of this decision.[181] Opponents have criticized the naive or hypocritical disregard of the de facto racial and ethnic discrimination that results from this choice.[182] Supporters argue that this choice is consistent with the prevailing moral and political consensus and that any other decision would inject the judiciary into a political controversy that it does not have the authority, the mechanisms or the mandate to resolve.[183]

The third choice, adopted by the Pennsylvania courts,[184] is to declare invalid in its entirety any zoning ordinance that is found to be "exclusionary" in effect. This requires an explicit and careful definition of the criteria for determining what is "exclusionary" and involves the court in the intricacies of planning analysis as described above. While this choice forces the court to make policy decisions with debatable political support, it succeeds in transferring the issue to the legislature, where the political processes of negotiation and compromise operate more effectively.

Proponents of this judicial choice argue that it represents a practical compromise, enabling a court to fulfill its obligation to apply principles of equity and justice incorporated into the equal protection and due process clauses and at the same time allowing it to avoid interference with the legislative process. The primary disadvantage of this choice is the uncertainty of the legislative response. The legislature may fail to respond within the prescribed time limit, as the New Jersey legislature has failed to respond to the judicial mandate to remove the fiscal disparities in education financing ordered in *Robinson v. Cahill*.[185] The legislature may fail to respond satisfactorily, as municipal governments involved in the *Oakwood at Madison, Inc. v. Township of Madison*[186] and *Pascack Association, Ltd. v. Township of Washington*[187] cases have failed to respond to the court's direction to remove the "exclusionary" components of their zoning ordinances. In fact, it may be argued that this judicial choice is predicated upon a naive and unrealistic assumption that the mere imposition of a judicial order will be sufficient to produce a legislative resolution of an issue on which there is widespread and ardent political disagreement. Once having made a judicial determination of the issue in litigation, the court must face the dilemma of legislative inaction by either providing a remedy or by conceding judicial impotence. This may carry the court beyond its originally contemplated scope of activity.

As a fourth option, the courts may decide that exclusionary zoning is invalid and at the same time provide a judicial remedy preventing the continuation of the circumstances upon which the determination of illegality is based. There is ample precedent for this choice in the school desegregation cases,[188] in the public housing dispersal cases,[189] and more recently in New Jersey in exclusionary zoning cases.[190] But, as Judge Gelman conceded in *Washington*, "[s]ince judges have not been known to possess any particular expertise in either zoning or planning, it is incumbent upon the Court to utilize the services of independent expert consultants to assist in formulating a remedy consistent with effectuating the judgment."[191] This independent expertise may be obtained either from a court-appointed master or consultant. Another avenue is to require both parties to submit proposals for a judgment consistent with principles contained in the decision in the hope that they will suggest "judicially discoverable and manageable standards" for resolving the controversy.

There is no question but that in many cases the services of expert planning consultants can be valuable in narrowing the range of remedies in accordance with established planning principles. Some land is unsuitable for development; some developments have an obviously harmful impact upon traffic or community facilities; and some locations have inadequate public transportation, job opportunities or other facilities for low income groups. Professional planners can assist by suggesting criteria and by providing data to which those criteria may be applied. Neither judges nor planners, however, have the special expertise or mandate to make the fundamental policy decisions underlying the controversy. What "judicially discoverable and manageable standard" can resolve the issue of whether a standard of four, nine, twelve, or more dwelling units per acre is appropriate for a given community? What objective criterion is available to determine at what point, if any, the modification of existing socioeconomic characteristics will have a sufficient impact to upset the delicate balance of community amenities that make the community a desirable place to live?

In the last analysis, it would appear that, if a court decides to fashion a judicial remedy for exclusionary zoning, it must be prepared to make the kind of policy decisions that the legislatures have been unable or unwilling to make. As the Commonwealth Court of Pennsylvania said in *Commonwealth v. Bucks County*,[192]

> The Court's involvement in this type of function would clearly be an intrusion into the legislative field and hence be [in] violation of the whole concept of separation of legislative and judicial branches of the government. The Court would thereby be injected into a political, and hence non-justiciable, controversy, a position in which the judiciary should never permit itself to be placed.[193]

VI. CONCLUSION

The judicial response to the question of whether municipalities may enact zoning ordinances regulating the rate of community growth and its social and economic composition has been generally to declare these ordinances to be proper exercises of authority under the typical state enabling legislation, but at the same time, to recognize that this validity is necessarily limited by various constitutional restrictions. Although some state court decisions indicate that the legitimate zoning purpose of avoiding undue concentration of population does *not* allow the exclusion of certain groups of people, the Supreme Court has seemed to indicate that this is a valid use of the zoning power for certain limited community objectives, *e.g.*, preservation of family values in a quiet residential neighborhood. On the issue of whether the validity of a zoning ordinance depends upon its ability to accommodate population growth of a size and socioeconomic composition required to meet regional needs, the courts that have responded are divided. The strongest statement in the affirmative has come from New Jersey. On the other hand, several federal courts have held that there is no such federal constitutional requirement. The leading federal cases, however, are currently on appeal.

Furthermore, if the validity of a municipal zoning ordinance is to depend upon the achievement of a prescribed goal of population growth and socioeconomic composition, there are many unresolved questions relating to the criteria by which the extent of municipal obligation to the region will be measured and to the standard by which the region is to be delineated. All of these issues involve some combination of professional expertise, policy judgments and administrative mechanisms. During the years that *Mount Laurel* was on appeal there was a fanciful hope that the New Jersey Supreme Court would provide answers to the unresolved issues in exclusionary zoning and municipal growth management. That decision has now been rendered, yet major questions remain. Perhaps the lesson of *Mount Laurel* is that courts alone cannot resolve these questions. Eventually there may emerge a democratic consensus through which the legislature may provide more definitive answers.

Addendum to "Exclusionary Zoning and Managed Growth: Some Unresolved Issues."

On January 11, 1977, the United States Supreme Court reversed a decision of the United States Court of Appeals which had held that the Village of Arlington Heights violated the equal protection clause when it refused to rezone a local site in a single-family residential zone to permit multi-family use by a non profit corporation which proposed to build a federally funded low-income housing project. The Court of Appeals decision directed attention to the pattern of racial segregation in the suburban area around Chicago but found no evidence of racially discriminatory intent on the part of the municipal officials. Nevertheless the appeals court held that the municipal zoning regulations are unconstitutional if they foster continued housing segregation, regardless of intent. *Village of Arlington Heights* v. *Metropolitan Housing and Development Corp.* 517 F.2d 409 (7th Cir., 197).

In a five to three decision, the Supreme Court reversed and held that the refusal of a municipality to rezone does not violate the equal protection clause just because it has a "racially disproportionate impact." The majority opinion written by Justice Powell said, "disproportionate impact is not irrelevant, but it is not the sole touchstone of invidious racial discrimination. Proof of racially discriminatory intent or purpose is required to show a violation of the equal protection clause." The court then found that there was no proof that a discriminatory effect had been a motivating factor in the decision of Arlington Heights not to rezone the property to permit multi-family housing.

The specific holding of the *Arlington Heights* case is that the refusal of a municipality to change its zoning laws to permit low-income housing does not violate the provisions of the United States Constitution even though the effect of the zoning decision is to exclude members of racial minorities from the community. The significance of *Arlington Heights* is that when added to the United States Supreme Court decisions in *Eastlake* and *Belle Terre* it tends to diminish the moral imperative from the position of those who have argued that *Mount Laurel* is based upon fundamental rights protected by the United States Constitution. It seems clear that as of 1977, the proponents of suburban housing for the poor are going to have to rely upon state court decisions like *Mount Laurel*, rather than the United States Supreme Court, to advance their cause.

NOTES

1. The most comprehensive compilation of this material is the Urban Land Institute's three volume series to be published in 1975, entitled Urban Land Institute, Management and Control of Growth: Issues-Techniques-Problems-Trends. *See also* National Comm. Against Discrimination in Housing & Urban Land Institute, Fair Housing & Exclusionary Land Use (1974).
2. For the most recent bibliography of judicial decisions on exclusionary zoning, see Fair Housing & Exclusionary Land Use, *supra* note 1, at 3.
3. No. A-11 (N.J. Sup. Ct., Mar. 24, 1975) [hereinafter cited as No. A-11].
4. *Id.* at 25-26, 52.
5. U.S. Dep't of Commerce, Advisory Comm. on Zoning, Standard State Zoning Enabling Act (1926).
6. *See, e.g.,* Conn. Gen. Stat. Ann. § 8-2 (1958); Del. Code Ann. tit. 22, § § 301, 303 (1953); Mass. Gen. Laws Ann. ch. 40A, § § 2, 3 (1968); N.J.S.A. 40:55-30 (1967); N.Y. Town Law § § 261, 263 (McKinney 1965); N.Y. Village Law § 177 (McKinney 1973); 53 P.S. § § 14752 14754 (1957).
7. Standard State Zoning Enabling Act, *supra* note 5, § 1.
8. Standard State Zoning Enabling Act, *supra* note 5, § 3.
9. *Kirsch Holding Co. v. Borough of Manasquan,* 59 N.J. 241, 251, 281 A.2d 513, 518 (1971).
10. *See, e.g., Congregation of Temple Israel v. City of Creve Coeur,* 320 S.W.2d 451, 454-55 (Mo. 1959) and cases cited therein.
11. *Ronda Realty Corp. v. Lawton,* 414 Ill. 313, 111 N.E.2d 310 (1953).
12. *Arverne Bay Constr. Co. v. Thatcher,* 278 N.Y. 222, 15 N.E.2d 587, 5 N.Y.S.2d 222 (1938).
13. 314 U.S. 160 (1941).
14. *Id.* at 171-74.
15. *Id.* at 174.
16. 394 U.S. 618 (1969).
17. *Id.* at 634.
18. *Id.*
19. 405 U.S. 330 (1972).
20. *Id.* at 338.

21. *Memorial Hosp. v. Maricopa County,* 415 U.S. 250, 269-70 (1974).
22. *Id.* at 254, *quoting Shapiro v. Thompson,* 394 U.S. 618, 627 (1969).
23. 415 U.S. at 261-62.
24. *Id.* at 263-69.
25. *Id.* at 269-70. Justice Douglas, in a separate opinion, stated that he would have preferred to base the decision on the grounds that the residency requirement imposed an invidious discrimination against the poor. *Id.* at 270-74.
26. 375 F. Supp. 574 (N.D. Cal.), *appeal docketed,* No. 74-2100 (9th Cir., June 12, 1974).
27. *Id.* at 585-86.
28. *Id.* at 576.
29. *Id.* (emphasis added). The city had also argued that inadequate water supply and sewage treatment facilities constituted a compelling state interest to justify its policy, but the court found on the facts that the city was capable of increasing these facilities to serve a growing population. *Id.* at 577-78.
30. *Id.* at 583.
31. *Id.*
32. *Id.* at 584-86. Among the Pennsylvania decisions cited by the court were the following: *In re* Kit-Mar Builders, Inc., 439 Pa. 466, 268 A.2d 765 (1970) (invalidating two to three acre minimum lot size requirements); *In re* Girsh, 437 Pa. 237, 263 A.2d 395 (1970) (invalidating a zoning ordinance that effectively excluded apartments); *National Land & Inv. Co. v. Easttown Twp. Bd. of Adjustment,* 419 Pa. 504, 215 A.2d 597 (1966) (invalidating a four acre minimum lot size requirement).
33. 419 Pa. 504, 215 A.2d 597 (1965).
34. *Id.* at 532, 215 A.2d at 612, *quoted in* 375 F. Supp. at 585-86.
35. 439 Pa. 466, 268 A.2d 765 (1970).
36. *Id.* at 476, 268 A.2d at 768, *quoted in* 375 F. Supp. at 586.
37. 375 F. Supp. at 588.
38. Oral argument was held on February 14, 1975, in the Ninth Circuit Court of Appeals.
39. *Fishcer v. Township of Bedminister,* 11 N.J. 194, 205, 93 A.2d 378, 384 (1952).
40. *Lionshead Lake, Inc. v. Township of Wayne,* 10 N.J. 165, 174-75, 89 A.2d 693, 697-98 (1952), *appeal dismissed,* 344 U.S. 919 (1953).
41. *Vickers v. Township Comm. of Gloucester,* 37 N.J. 232, 248, 181 A.2d 129, 137 (1962), *cert. denied,* 371 U.S. 233 (1963).
42. *James v. Valtierra,* 402 U.S. 137 (1971). *See* note 104 *infra.*
43. *National Land & Inv. Co. v. Easttown Twp. Bd. of Adjustment,* 419 Pa. 504, 533, 215 A.2d 597, 613 (1965).
44. *In re* Kit-Mar Builders, Inc., 439 Pa. 466, 478, 268 A.2d 765, 770 (1970).
45. *Id.* at 474, 268 A.2d at 768 (reaffirming the decision in *National Land*).
46. *In re* Girsh, 437 Pa. 237, 240, 263 A.2d 395, 396 (1970). For other similar decisions in the Pennsylvania lower courts, see East Pikeland Twp. v. Bush Bros., Inc., _____ Pa. Commonwealth _____, 319 A.2d 701 (1974) (invalidating a prohibition of mobile homes); *Willistown Twp. v. Chesterdale Farms, Inc.,* 7 Pa. Commonwealth 453, 300 A.2d 107 (1973) (invalidating a zoning ordinance that made no provisions for apartments); *Sjomo v. Derry Borough,* 5 Pa. Commonwealth 216, 289 A.2d 513 (1972) (invalidating a prohibition of mobile homes).

47. *Southern Burlington County NAACP v. Township of Mount Laurel,* 119 N.J. Super. 164, 290 A.2d 465 (L. Div. 1972), *modified,* No. A-11 (N.J. Sup. Ct., Mar. 24, 1975); *Oakwood at Madison, Inc. v. Township of Madison,* 117 N.J. Super.11, 283 A.2d 353 (L. Div. 1971), *on remand,* 128 N.J. Super. 438, 320 A.2d 223 (L. Div. 1974), *certification granted,* 62 N.J. 185, 299 A.2d 720 (1972); *Molino v. Borough of Glassboro,* 116 N.J. Super. 195, 281 A.2d 401 (L. Div. 1971).
48. *See: Schere v. Township of Freehold,* 119 N.J. Super. 433, 435, 292 A.2d 35, 36 (App. Div. 1972), *cert denied,* 410 U.S. 931 (1973).
49. No. A-11, *supra* note 3, at 52.
50. *See: Green v. Lima Twp.,* 40 Mich. App. 655, 658-59, 199 N.W.2d 243, 246 (1972); *Bristow v. City of Woodhaven,* 35 Mich. App. 205, 217, 192 N.W.2d 322, 327-28 (1971).
51. *Taxpayers Ass'n of Weymouth Twp., Inc. v. Township of Weymouth,* 125 N.J. Super. 376, 311 A.2d 187 (App. Div. 1973); *Bridge Park Co. v. Borough of Highland Park,* 113 N.J. Super. 219, 273 A.2d 397 (App. Div. 1971); *Shepard v. Woodland Twp. Comm.,* 128 N.J. Super. 379, 320 A.2d 191 (Ch. Div. 1974); *Board of Supervisors of Fairfax County v. DeGroff Enterprises, Inc.,* 214 Va. 235, 198 S.E.2d 600 (1973).
52. 416 U.S. 1 (1974).
53. *Id.* at 7-9.
54. 214 Va. 235, 198 S.E.2d 600 (1973).
55. *Id.* at 238, 198 S.E.2d at 602. For a discussion of the use of this technique to encourage the construction of low and moderate income housing without direct government subsidy, see Rose, *The Mandatory Perdentage of Moderately Priced Dwelling Ordinance (MPMPD) Is the Latest Technique of Inclusionary Zoning,* 3 REAL ESTATE L.J. 176 (1974).
56. 214 Va. 235-36, 198 S.E.2d at 601.
57. *Id.* at 238, 198 S.E.2d at 602. The other ground on which the ordinance was held invalid was that the requirement to sell or rent 15% of the units at prices not fixed by a free market constituted a taking of property without just compensation. *Id.*
58. 113 N.J. Super. 219, 273 A.2d 397 (App. Div. 1971).
59. *Id.* at 222, 273 A.2d at 398-99.
60. *Id.*
61. 125 N.J. Super. 376, 311 A.2d 187 (App. Div. 1973).
62. *Id.* at 381-82, 311 A.2d at 189-90.
63. *Shepard v. Woodland Twp. Comm.,* 128 N.J. Super. 379, 384, 320, A.2d 191, 194 (Ch. Div. 1974).
64. Id. at 382, 320 A.2d at 193.
65. *Id.* at 384, 320 A.2d at 194.
66. No. A-11, *supra* note 3, at 33-34.
67. 416 U.S. 1 (1974).
68. *Id.* at 2.
69. *Id.*
70. *Id.* at 2-3.
71. *Boraas v. Village of Belle Terre,* 476 F.2d 806, 815-18 (d Cir. 1973), *aff'd,* 416 U.S. 1 (1974).
72. 416 U.S. at 8, *quoting Reed v. Reed,* 404 U.S. 71,76 (1971) (brackets by the Court).

73. *Id.* at 9. The Court also rejected the argument that the ordinance violated the students' and other potential residents' right to travel, on the ground that the ordinance was "not aimed at transients. *Cf. Shapiro v. Thompson*, 394 U.S. 618." 416 U.S. at 7 (italics omitted).
74. *Southern Burlington County NAACP v. Township of Mount Laurel*, No. A-11 at 26-27 (N.J. Sup. Ct., Mar. 24 1975).
75. *Id.* at 27.
76. 117 N.J. Super. 11, 283 A.2d 353 (L. Div. 1971), *on remand*, 128 N.J. Super. 438, 320 A.2d 233 (L. Div. 1974), *certification granted*, 62 N.J. 185, 299 A.2d 72((1972).
77. No. A-11 *supra* note 3.
78. *See* cases cited in note 46 *supra*.
79. *See* cases discussed in text accompanying notes 105-31 *infra*.
80. 117 N.J. Super. at 21 283 A2d at 358. *See* Rose, *The Courts and the Balanced Community: Recent Trends in New Jersey Zoning Law*, 39 J. AM. IN-STITUTE OF PLANNERS 265 (1973).
81. 117 N.J. Super. at 20, 283 A.2d at 358.
82. 62 N.J. 185, 299 A.2d 720 (1972) (certification granted).
83. *See Oakwood at Madison Inc. v. Township of Madison*, 128 N.J. Super. 438, 442-46, 320 A.2d 323, 225-27 (L. Div. 1974), *certification granted*, 62 N.J. 185, 299 A.2d 720 (1972).
84. *See* 128 N.J. at 442-46, 320 A.2d at 225-27.
85. *Id.* at 447, 320 A.2d at 227.
86. *Id.* at 441, 320 A.2d at 224.
87. *Id.* at 447, 320 A.2d at 227.
88. *Id.*
89. *See* text accompanying note 86 *supra*.
90. *Id.* at 447, 320 A.2d at 227.
91. *Id.*
92. No. A-11, *supra* note 3.
93. 119 N.J. Super. 164, 177, 290 A.2d 465, 473 (L. Div. 1972).
94. *Id.* at 178-79, 290 A.2d at 473-74.
95. No. A-11, *supra* note 3, at 52.
96. *Id.*
97. *Id.* at 33-34.
98. *Id.* at 34.
99. *Id.* at 25-26 (emphasis added).
100. 419 Pa. 504, 215 A.2d 597 (1966) (invalidating a four acre minimum lot size requirement).
101. 439 Pa. 466, 268 A.2d 765 (1970) (invalidating a two and three acre minimum lot size requirement).
102. 437 Pa. 237, 263 A.2d 395 (1970) (invalidating a ban on apartment construction).
103. 419 Pa. at 527-28, 215 A.2d at 610 (footnote omitted). Likewise, the *Kit-Mar* decision noted,
    The implication of our decision in *National Land* is that communities must deal with the problems of population growth. They may not refuse to confront the future by adopting zoning regulations that effectively restrict population to near present levels. It is not for any given township to say who may or may not live within its confines, while disregarding the interests of the entire area.

439 Pa. at 474, 268 A.2d at 768-69 (footnote omitted). The *Girsh* decision quoted the first paragraph of the selection from *National Land* that appears in the text herein, 437 Pa. at 243, 263 A.2d at 398, and added:

> The simple fact that someone is anxious to build apartments is strong indication that the location of this township is such that people are desirous of moving in, and we do not believe Nether Providence can close its doors to those people.

Id. at 245, 263 A.2d at 399.

104. This line of cases grows out of the Supreme Court's decision in *James v. Valtierra*, 402 U.S. 137 (1971), which sustained artivle XXXIV of the California Constitution against constitutional attack. Article XXXIV provided that no low income housing could be developed, constructed or acquired by any state public body without the approval of a majority of those voting at a community election. The challengers alleged that the article violated the equal protection clause of the fourteenth amendment on the ground that it created a racial classification because low income housing projects were usually inhabited by members of a racial minority group. They also maintained that the article violated the supremacy clause because it was contrary to the Housing Act of 1937, 42 U.S.C.§ 1401 *et seq.* (1970).

The Court quickly dismissed both challenges. First, it observed that the Housing Act did "not purport to require that local governments accept [federally subsidized low rent public housing] or to outlaw local referendums on whether the federal aid should be accepted." 402 U.S. at 140. *See:* note 119 *infra* and accompanying text. Consequently, the article was not in conflict with any federal statute. Secondly, the Court noted that the article required referendum approval for *all* low rent public housing, not merely for projects to be occupied by racial minorities, and that the record supported no claim that the article was aimed at any racial minority. 402 U.S. at 141. In fact California had had a long history of repeated use of referendums to allow citizen participation in public policy decisions and that referendums were not used solely for approval of low income housing. From these factors the Court concluded that the referendum was not designed to create racial distinctions and consequently did not violate the equal protection clause. *Id.* at 141-42. This case sets that standards for inquiry into a challenge to state and municipal actions dealing with low income housing projects.

105. 372 F. Supp. 319 (E.D.Mo.), *rev'd*, Nos. 74-1345 & 74-1378 (8th Cir., Dec. 27, 1974).

106. 42 U.S.C.§ 3601 *et seq.* (1970). The government contended that the language of 42 U.S.C.A.§ 3604 (a) (Supp. 1975), making it unlawful

> (a) To refuse to sell or rent after the making of a bona fide offer, or to refuse to negotiate for the sale or rental of, or otherwise make unavailable or deny, a dwelling to any person because of race, color, religion, sex, or national origin...

applied to a municipality's attempts to exercise its zoning power in a racially discriminatory manner so as to exclude housing which provides rental opportunities for significant numbers of nonwhite persons. The argument was based upon § 3602(b) of the Act which defines "dwelling" to include "any vacant land which is offered for sale or lease for the construction or location thereon" of residential property. The *Black Jack* court ultimately agreed with this argument in principle. 372 F. Supp. at 327. The court rejected, however, the government's argument that discrimination had in fact taken place. *Id.* at 330.

107. 372 F. Supp. at 328.
108. *Id.*
109. *Id.*
110. *Id.* at 329.
111. *Id.*
112. *United States v. City of Black Jack,* Nos. 74-1345 & 74-1378 (8th Cir., Dec. 27, 1974).
113. *Id.* at 11-13. *See* note 106 *supra.*
114. No. 73-2590 (2d Cir., Dec. 5, 1974), *affirming* 362 F. Supp. 651 (S.D.N.Y. 1973).
115. No. 73-2590 at 593-94.
116. *Id.* at 590.
117. *Id.* at 591 The court relied upon the case of *Palmer v. Thompson,* 403 U.S. 217 (1971), in which the city of Jackson, Mississippi, fearing a desegregation order, decided to close the segregated municipal swimming pools it had been operating. The Supreme Court found no denial of equal protection in the city's action because the closing was a policy, neutral on its face, which happened to have a greater effect upon blacks than whites. *Id.* at 224-26.
118. 500 F.2d 1087 (6th Cir. 1974).
119. 42 U.S.C.§§ 1415 (7) (a) (i), (ii) & (b) (i) (1970). These sections provide (emphasis added):
    (7) In recognition that there should be local determination of the need for low-rent housing to meet needs not being adequately met by private enterprise—
    (a) The Authority shall not make any contract with a public housing agency for preliminary loans (all of which shall be repaid out of any moneys which become available to such agency for the development of the projects involved) for surveys and planning in respect to any low-rent housing projects initiated after March 1, 1949, (i) *unless the governing body of the locality involved has by resolution approved the application of the public housing agency for such preliminary loan;* and (ii) unless the public housing agency has demonstrated to the satisfaction of the Authority that there is a need for such low-rent housing which is not being met by private enterprise; and
    (b) The Authority shall not make any contract for loans (other than preliminary loans) or for annual contributions pursuant to this chapter with respect to any low-rent housing project initiated after March 1, 1949, (i) *unless the governing body of the locality involved has entered into an agreement with the public housing agency providing for the local cooperation required by the Authority pursuant to this chapter....*
120. 500 F.2d at 1093, *citing Citizens Comm. for Faraday Wood v. Lindsay,* 362 F. Supp. 651 (S.D.N.Y. 1973), *aff'd* No 73-2590 (2d Cir., Dec. 5 1974). *See also* 500 F.2d at 1094-96 (Edwards, J., dissenting).
121. 500 F.2d at 1091-92.
122. *Id.* at 1092-93. The court, like the *Faraday Wood* court, relied on the *Palmer v. Thompson* requirement of specific discriminatory effect upon racial minority groups. *See* note 117 *supra.*
123. *Id.* at 1093.

124. *Id*. (citation omitted). *Lindsey v. Normet*, 405 U.S. 56 (1972), involved an unsuccessful constitutional challenge by tenants of housing condemned as unfit for human habitation against the Oregon Forcible Entry and Wrongful Detainer Statute which provided summary eviction procedures upon non-payment of rent but which did not allow a defense of uninhabitability. In rejecting plaintiff's equal protection argument, the Supreme Court said:

> We do not denigrate the importance of decent, safe, and sanitary housing. But the Constitution does not provide judicial remedies for every social and economic ill. We are unable to perceive in that document any constitutional guarantee of access to dwellings of a particular quality...Absent constitutional mandate, the assurance of adequate housing and the definition of land-lord-tenant relationships are legislative, not judicial, functions.

  Id. at 74.
125. 373 F. Supp. 208 (N.D. Ill.), *appeal docketed*, No. 74-1326 (7th Cir., April 29, 1974).
126. *Id*. at 209-10.
127. *Id*.at 209.
128. *Id*. at 211. Compare the following dicta in *Mount Laurel:*"[c]ertainly when a municipality zones for industry and commerce for local tax benefit purposes, it without question must zone to permit adequate housing within the means of the employees involved in such uses." No. A-11, *supra* note 3, at 46.
129. 373 F. Supp. at 211.
130. *Id*.
131. *Metropolitan Housing Development Corp. v. Village of Arlington Heights*, No. 74-1326 (7th Cir., April 29, 1974) (appeal docketed).
132. *Citizens Comm. for Faraday Wood v. Lindsay*, No. 73-2590 at 598 (2d Cir. Dec. 5, 1974) (Oakes, J., dissenting).
133. *E.g.*, Dade County Metropolitan Planning Board; Metropolitan Washington Council of Governments; Sacramento Regional Area Planning Commission; Metropolitan Council of Governments; Sacramento Regional Area Planning Commission; Metropolitan Council of the Twin City Area; Middlesex County (New Jersey) Planning Board. For a listing of publications describing the programs of these and other governmental agencies, see Listokin, *Fair Share Housing Distribution: Will It Open the Suburbs to Apartment Development?*, 2 REAL ESTATE L.J. 739, 740-41 (1974).
134. The best analysis of this subject appears in M. BROOKS, LOWER INCOME HOUSING: THE PLANNERS RESPONSE (American Soc'y of Planning Officials Rep. No. 282, 1972). Much of the material in this section is derived from this report. *See also* Listokin, *supra* note 133.
135. MASS. GEN. LAWS ANN. ch. 40B, §§ 20-23 (Supp. 1975).
136. *See* notes 55 & 57 *supra* and accompanying text.
137. N.Y. UNCONSOL. LAW § 6251 *et seq*. (McKinney Supp. 1974). This Act created the New York State Urban Development Corporation which,

> through issuance of bonds and notes to the private, investing public, by encouraging maximum participation by the private sector of the economy, including the sale or lease of the corporation's interest in projects at the earliest time deemed feasible, and through participation in programs undertaken by the state, its agencies and subdivisions, and by municipalities and the federal goverment, may provide or obtain the capital resources necessary to acquire, construct, reconstruct, rehabilitate or

improve such industrial, manufacturing, commercial, educational, recreational and cultural facilities, and housing accommodations for persons and families of low income, and facilities incidental or appurtenant thereto, and to carry out the clearance, replanning, reconstruction and rehabilitation of such substandard and insanitary areas.

N.Y. UNCONSOL. LAWS § 6252 (McKinney Supp. 1974).

138. The Act defines "public housing agency" as "any State, county, municipality or other governmental entity or public body (or agency or instrumentality thereof) which is authorized to engage in or assist in the development or operation of low-income housing." 42 U.S.C.A. § 1437a(6) (Supp. 1974).

139. 42 U.S.C.A. § 1437 (Supp. 1974).

140. R. ALEXANDER & M. NENNO, A LOCAL HOUSING ASSISTANCE PLAN: A NAHRO GUIDEBOOK (National Ass'n of Housing and Redevelopment Officials 1974).

141. *See*: notes 149-54 *infra* and accompanying text.

142. ALEXANDER & NENNO, *supra* note 140, at 26.

143. *Id.*

144. *Id.* at ⌐7.

145. Id. This procedure was derived from D. SAMUELSON, HOUSING: A COMMUNITY HANDBOOK (Illinois Housing Development Authority and Northeastern Illinois Planning Comm'n 1973).

146. F. JAMES & J. HUGHES, MODELING STATE GROWTH: NEW JERSEY 1980 (Rutgers Univ., Center for Urban Policy Research 1973).

147. *Id.* at 6.

148. *Id.* at 8.

149. 88 Stat. 633 (codified in scattered sections of 5, 12, 15, 20, 40, 42 & 49 U.S.C.A. (Supp. 1974)).

150. 42 U.S.C.A. §§ 1439(a) (1), (5) and 5304 (a)(4) (Supp. 1974). Section 1439 (b) excepts from this requirement (1) applications for assistance which involve twelve or fewer units in a single project or development; (2) applications involvin housing in new community developments approved under other statutes; and (3) applications with respcet to housing financed by loans from a state or state agency.

151. 42 U.S.C.A. § 5304(a)(4) (Supp. 1974). The housing assistance plan is only one requirement for a grant of community development funds. The application must also contain a summary of a three year community development plan, a proposed program of activities designed to improve the community and assurances of citizen approval of the proposed program. 42 U.S.C.A. § 5304(a) (Supp. 1974).

152. A "housing assistance plan" is defined in 42 U.S.C.A. § 5304(a)(4) (Supp. 1974) as a plan which

(A) accurately surveys the condition of the housing stock in the community and assesses the housing assistance needs of lower-income persons (including elderly and handicapped persons, large families, and persons displaced or to be displaced) residing in or expected to reside in the community,

(B) specifies a realistic annual goal for the number of dwelling units or persons to be assisted, including (i) the relative proportion of new, rehabilitated, and existing dwelling units, and (ii) the sizes and types of housing projects and assistance best suited to the needs of lower-income persons in the community, and

(C) indicates the general locations of proposed housing for lower-
income persons, with the objective of (i) furthering the revitalization of
the community, including the restoration and rehabilitation of stable
neighborhoods to the maximum extent possible, (ii) promoting greater
choice of housing opportunities and avoiding undue concentrations of assisted persons in areas containing a high proportion of low-income persons, and (iii) assuring the availability of public facilities and service
adequate to serve proposed housing projects.

153. 40 U.S.C.A. § 461(c) (Supp. 1974).

154. The "housing element" of a comprehensive plan must
take into account all available evidence of the assumption and statistical
bases upon which the projection of zoning community facilities, and
population growth is based, so that the housing needs of both the region
and the local communities studied in the planning will be adequately
covered in terms of existing and prospective population growth.
40 U.S.C.A. § 461(c)(1) (Supp. 1974).

155. The analysis should include these components: (1) soil types, e.g., the per-
meability and rate of percolation; (2) surface waters, e.g., the distance of the
site from the nearest surface water, as well as the sources, rate and destina-
tion of runoff water; (3) ground cover, e.g., the extent of existing impervious
ground cover and vegetative cover on the site; (4) topography, e.g., the
maximum and minimum elevation of the site; (5) ground water, e.g., the
minimum, average and maximum depth of the water table; (6) water supply,
e.g., the source of the water supply and the expected water requirements for
development; (7) sewage system, e.g., the location and description of the
sewage disposal system, if it is on a development site, or the effect of development upon any existing sewage treatment plant's present and authorized capacity; (8) air quality, e.g., the present air quality and the effect of
development on it; (9) noise, e.g., present noise levels and the effect of development on them; (10) critical areas, e.g., the effect of the development
upon such environmentally sensitive areas as stream corridors, streams, wetlands, estuaries, slopes greater than 20%, highly acid or highly erodible soils,
areas of high water table, mature stands of native vegetation and aquifer
recharge and discharge areas.

156. The study should include the following components: (1) schools, e.g., the
existing capacity and enrollment, the evaluation of existing facilities, and the
distance from existing and potential developments with respect to elementary, junior high school and high schools; (2) sewer service, e.g., the existing
capacity, use and anticipated use by projected developments; (3) water service, e.g., the existing capacity and the availability of additional supply; (4)
fire service, e.g., the adequacy of existing equipment and personnel, and the
proximity of arterial, collector and local roads to proposed developable sites;
(5) recreational facilities, e.g., the adequacy of both indoor and outdoor
facilities and the distance to proposed developments; (6) social services, e.g.,
the adequacy of day care, nursery, health center or other services required
by low income residents; (7) neighborhood commercial facilities, e.g., the
location and adequacy of neighborhood commercial services such as laun-
dromat, drugstore, grocery, etc.; (8) public transit facilities, a particularly
important item to families of low income.

157. E.g., Southern Burlington County NAACP v. Township of Mount Laurel,
119 N.J. Super. 164, 290 A.2d 465 (L. Div. 1972), modified, No. A-11 (N.J.

Sup. Ct., Mar. 24, 1975); Oakwood at Madison, Inc. v. Township of Madison, 117 N.J. Super. 11, 283 A.2d 353 (L. Div. 1971), *on remand,* 128 N.J. Super. 438, 320 A.2d 223 (L. Div. 1974), *certification granted,* 62 N.J. 185, 299 A.2d 720 (1972); Molino v. Borough of Glassboro, 116 N.J. Super. 195, 281 A.2d 401 (L. Div. 1971).

158. *See:* G. STERNLIEB, HOUSING DEVELOPMENT AND MUNICIPAL COSTS (Rutgers Univ., Center for Urban Policy Research 1973).

159. N.J. COUNTY AND MUNICIPAL GOV'T STUDY COMM'N, HOUSING & SUBURBS: FISHER AND SOCIAL IMPACT OF MULTIFAMILY DEVELOPMENT 7 (1974). The Commission study also found that multi-family developments are usually more fiscally advantageous to a municipality and school district than all but the most expensive single family housing. However, moderate rent three bedroom apartments are deficit producing. *Id.* at 30-47.

160. Gibbons, *Senate Bill No. 803: Progress or Stagnation?*, LAND USE CONTROLS QUARTERLY 18-19 (Fall 1969).

161. *See:* Rose, *From the Legislatures: State Government Role in Land Use Planning and Control is Growing,* 2 REAL ESTATE L.J. 809 (1974).

162. HAWAII REV. STAT. § 205-1 *et seq.* (Supp. 1974). For and extensive discussion of the Hawaiian land use system, see F. BOSSELMAN & D. CALLIES, THE QUIET REVOLUTION IN LAND USE CONTROL (U.S. Council on Environmental Quality 1971). *See also* J. KUSLER, STATE LAND PLANNING AND REGULATORY FUNCTIONS: PROPOSALS AND PROGRAMS FROM THE SEVERAL STATES AND A DRAFT BILL FOR WISCONSIN (University of Wisconsin, Institute for Environmental Studies 1972).

163. *See, e.g.,*: Meckler, *Hawaii Had a Good Idea . . . But It Failed,* PLANNING, Vol. 39, Sept. 1973, at 20.

164. *See, e.g.:* M. LEVIN, J. ROSE & J. SLAVET, NEW APPROACHES TO STATE LAND-USE POLICIES 95-106 (1974).

165. ORE. REV. STAT. ch. 215 (1973).

166. WIS. STAT. ANN. § 59.971 (1974); WIS. STAT. ANN. § 144.26 (Supp. 1975). Section 59.971 deals with the ability of counties to zone shoreland on navigable waters in order to further the purposes of § 144.26, the Navigable Waters Protection Law.

167. *See:* N.J. COUNTY AND MUNICIPAL GOV'T STUDY COMM'N, COUNTY GOVERNMENT: CHALLENGE AND CHANGE (1969). *See also* U.S. ADVISORY COMM'N COMM,N ON INTERGOVERNMENTAL RELATIONS, FOR A MORE PERFECT UNION: COUNTY REFORM (1971).

168. *See, e.g.,*: Hackensack Meadowlands Reclamation & Development Act, N.J.S.A. 13:17-1 *et seq.* (Supp. 1974); Adirondack Park Agency Act, N.Y. EXEC. LAW § § 800-10 (McKinney Supp. 1974). For examples of comprehensive environmental impact regulations, see ME. REV. STAT. ANN. tit. 38, § § 481-88 (Supp. 1973); VT. STAT. ANN. tit. 10, § § 6001-91 (Supp. 1974).

169. 117 N.J. Super. 11, 283 A.2d 353 (L. Div. 1971), *on remand* 128 N.J. Super. 438, 320 A.2d 223 (L. Div. 1974), *certification granted,* 62 N.J. 185, 299 A.2d 720 (1972).

170. 117 N.J. Super. at 20-21, 283 A.2d at 358.

171. *See:* Burchell, Listokin & James, *Exclusionary Zoning: Pitfalls of the Regional Remedy,* in RUTGERS UNIV. CENTER FOR URBAN POLICY RESEARCH, NEW DIMENSIONS IN URBAN PLANNING: GROWTH CONTROLS 31 (J.

Hughes, ed. 1974). *See also* G. STERNLIEB, HOUSING DEVELOPMENT AND MUNICIPAL COSTS (Rutgers Univ., Center For Urban Policy Research 1973).

172. *See*: LEVIN ROSE & SLAVET, *supra* note 164, at 99.

173. No. A-11, *supra* note 3, at 49.

174. *Id.*

175. *Id.*

176. *See*: MANAGEMENT AND CONTROL OF GROWTH: ISSUES-TECHNIQUES-PROBLEMS-TRENDS, *supra* note 1.

177. For an excellent summary of each of these arguments, see M. BROOKS, EXCLUSIONARY ZONING (ASPO Planning Advisory Service Report No. 254, 1970). Most of the arguments are based upon the premise that exclusionary zoning laws result in de facto racial and economic discrimination. For a discussion of the kinds of evidence required to support this premise, see Davidoff, Davidoff & Gold, *Suburban Action: Advocate Planning for an Open Society*, 36 J. AM. INST. OF PLANNERS 12 (1970).

178. *See*: cases cited in notes 46 & 47 *supra*.

179. *See*: cases cited in notes 39-41, 114 & 125 *supra*.

180. *See, e.g., Boraas v. Village of Belle Terre*, 416 U.S. 1 (1974).

181. *See*: text accompanying notes 76-113 *supra*.

182. Davidoff, Davidoff & Gold, *supra* note 177, at 19.

183. *See*: the Supreme Court's rejection of plaintiff's equal protection argument in *Lindsey v. Normet*, 405 U.S. 56 (1972), *quoted in* note 124 *supra*.

184. *See*: text accompanying notes 100-03 *supra*.

185. 62 N.J. 473, 303 A.2d 273, *supplemented*, 63 N.J. 196, 306 A.2d 65 (1973).

186. 117 N.J. Super. 11, 283 A.2d 353 (L. Div. 1971), *on remand*, 128 N.J. Super. 438, 320 A.2d 223 (L. Div. 1974), *certification granted*, 62 N.J. 185, 299 A.2d 720 (1972).

187. 131 N.J. Super. 195, 329 A.2d 89 (L. Div. 1974).

188. *See, e.g.,: Swann v. Charlotte-Mecklenburg Bd. of Educ.*, 402 U.S. 1 (1971); *Brown v. Board of Educ.*, 347 U.S. 483 (1954), *supplemented*, 349 U.S. 294 (1955).

189. *See, e.g.,: Gautreaux v. Chicago Housing Authority*, 296 F. Supp. 907 (N.D. Ill. *enforced*, 304 F. Supp. 736 (N.D. Ill. 1969, *aff'd*, 436 F.2d 306 (7th Cir. 1970), *cert. denied*, 414 U.S. 1144 (1974).

190. *See, e.g.,: Pascack Ass'n, Inc. v. Township of Washington*, 131 N.J. Super. 195, 329 A.2d 89 (L. Div. 1974); *Southern Burlington County NAACP v. Township of Mount Laurel*, 119 N.J. Super. 164 178-80, 290 A.2d 465, 473-74 (L. Div. 1972), *modified*, No. A-11 (N.J. Sup. Ct., Mar. 24, 1974).

191. 131 N.J. Super. at 207, 329 A.2d at 96. For a discussion of this case from the perspective of the consultants, see Levin & Rose, *The Suburban Land Use War: Skirmish in Washington Township, New Jersey*, URBAN LAND, May 1974, at 14.

192. 8 Pa. Commonwealth 295, 302 A.2d 897 (1973).

193. *Id.* at 298, 302 A.2d at 902.